# TELEPHONE

1. "Electricity." This bronze statue, modeled by Evelyn Beatrice Longman, stands 434 feet above street level on the tower of the American Telephone and Telegraph Building at 195 Broadway.

# TELEPHONE

## THE FIRST HUNDRED YEARS

### John Brooks

HARPER & ROW, PUBLISHERS

NEW YORK
HAGERSTOWN
SAN FRANCISCO
LONDON

1817

Portions of this book originally appeared in *Forbes* magazine.

FIRST EDITION

*Designed by Sidney Feinberg*

Library of Congress Cataloging in Publication Data

Brooks, John, date
  Telephone.
  Includes bibliographical references and index.
  1. Telephone—United States—History.
2. American Telephone and Telegraph Company.
I. Title.
HE8815.B76    384.6'0973    75–23874
ISBN 0–06–010540–2

76 77 78 79 10 9 8 7 6 5 4 3 2 1

# Contents

# Illustrations

*All photographs courtesy AT&T with these exceptions: 32, 33, 34, 35 (Western Electric); 19, 27 (GTE Automatic Electric); 22 (Bell Family Collection, Library of Congress)*

# Foreword

Hoy, hoy! Thus Alexander Graham Bell always insisted that his invention, the telephone, should be answered, rather than with "Hello," to which, he said late in life, he had "always had great objection." And, in tribute, Bell's rejected form of greeting may appropriately open a history of the telephone's first century.

There is no comprehensive and objective history of the telephone, telephoning as a social act, or the American Telephone and Telegraph Company, which was originally based on Bell's patents of 1876 and 1877 and has dominated American telephony ever since. Therefore this book sets out, among other things, to fill a need.

I have long felt (and have insisted in print) that, because books about corporate affairs are commissioned or subsidized so often as to raise well-founded suspicions about the arrangements behind all such books, the author of a corporate history owes it to both his craft and his readers to set forth plainly at the outset the essential terms and conditions under which he has done his work. For one thing, such revelation eliminates the possibility of deceiving the reader by offering him an unlabeled product; for another, it gives future historians information necessary to them in evaluating the book as source material. Here, accordingly, is a brief account of how this book came to be written.

Several years ago, Harper & Row, publisher of seven of my previous books, asked me to undertake a centennial history of the Bell System (of which, of course, AT&T is the parent company), to be based on the promise of access to AT&T files. A meeting ensued between me, my publisher, and representatives of AT&T, at which those representatives agreed to turn me loose in their corporate files and executive offices, with no control over what I might write, provided only that they satisfy themselves initially that I would begin with no special prejudice either for or against their company. In due course, they did satisfy themselves of that. For my part, I suggested that the project be broadened to include material on the social history of the telephone itself. This suggestion was readily accepted. Following further negotiations, I signed a normal publishing contract with Harper & Row, dealing with royalties, rights, and the like, and a separate contract with AT&T, involving not money but only terms between myself and the company. In the latter document, AT&T, as promised, agreed to give me complete access to its files—something, incidentally, that it had given no outside writer previously in modern times— with the exception of material concerning pending litigation, economic forecasts, and undisclosed scientific data. The company further acknowledged that its sole consideration for entering into the agreement was its interest in having published an objective history of AT&T and of the telephone, and agreed that it would have no right of approval over the style, form, or content of the book, all of which would be within my sole discretion.

In the course of the project, AT&T—and in particular, James V. Ryan and Vi Graeper—offered unstinting and painstaking help, up to and in some cases beyond the letter of the contract. For this, I offer my thanks. For editorial and research help, my thanks to Nancy Hallinan and Barbara S. Mahoney, and to Ann Harris and Joseph Vergara of Harper & Row. For ideas and anecdotes about AT&T, I am particularly grateful to Robert K. Greenleaf.

J.B.

# TELEPHONE

# CHAPTER 1

# The Colossus of Talk

The American Telephone and Telegraph Company, along with being the richest corporation on the face of the earth, is one of the most widely experienced. In the hundred years that it or its forebear corporations have existed, it has been through just about every trial, triumph, and disaster that corporate flesh in America is heir to. In its earliest years it fought a mortal battle against a huge and formidable rival many times its size, Western Union Telegraph, which was bent on destroying it, and emerged from that jungle struggle intact. At the turn of the century it engaged in competition fair and foul with a multiplicity of smaller rivals, gave as good or better than it got, and destroyed or swallowed most of them. On the brink of financial disaster in 1907, it fell partly into the hands of bankers—only to escape their embrace and regain its regal independence. Engaged in a business unusually sensitive to the elements, it has been threatened by, and faced down, floods, blizzards, earthquakes, fires, and hurricanes. It has been through nationwide strikes; it has survived a great depression in the classic corporate style, by drastically cutting its payroll but not its dividend payments to stockholders; it has been praised justly for responsibility to its customers and to the public at large, and reviled justly for occasional scandals and for ruthless treatment of both rival companies and its own subscribers. It has endured bitter internal struggles for top positions in its hierarchy. Its relations with government—surely more extensive and complex than those of any other corporation anywhere—constitute in them-

selves a capsule history of the "mixed economy," the principal
economic invention of the United States in its two centuries. Its
activities have been regulated, with mixed results, by state governments since its early days and by the federal government since
early in this century. It has been, during World War I, through a
government seizure of its property and operation of its business—
that is, it has operated under nominal socialism. It has been sued
twice by United States governments seeking to dismantle it in
whole or in part, and has so far survived. It has known public
approbation and public hatred. It has become a case history in
the twentieth-century corporate trend toward separation of ownership and management. All in all, if we wish to know the corporation in the Age of the Corporation, we can hardly begin at a better
place than by studying AT&T.

At the heart of AT&T's story is a paradox—one that makes it
the frustration if not the despair of the ideologues of both free
enterprise and social organization. This is the paradox of a monopoly in a competitive economy. Broadly speaking, AT&T operates
as a monopoly and has done so with government consent since
1913. With certain specific exceptions, involving intercity radio
circuits, no one may erect and operate a telephone service—lines
and poles and switchboards—in competition with AT&T's. Congress, for what it considers good and sufficient reason having to do
with the particular nature of telephone service, has long since
decided that such competition would (and in fact, at one time
did) result in confusion and waste. As a monopoly, the company
represents outright heresy against the main tenet of the American
economic religion, stemming back to Adam Smith and his followers among the republic's founders—the belief that free competition serves the public interest while monopoly does not. As a
monopoly that operates more efficiently and arguably more democratically than most companies subject to the theoretical benefits
of intense competition—a monopoly that usually seems to work in
the public interest—AT&T confirms the heresy and threatens the
religion at its roots. For virtually no one disputes the statement
that, with certain marked exceptions, AT&T offers the best telephone service in the world. (To compound the paradox, while
serving as a living argument for the benefits of controlled monopoly over those of free competition, AT&T also serves as one for
private rather than government control or ownership of the tele-

phone business; it is the only major telephone company in the world that is not owned and run by a national government.) As to cost of that service, the comparative facts are clear. The cost of telephone service in the United States, local and long-distance, rose less than 20 percent between 1960 and 1974, while the consumer price index of all goods and services was rising almost 70 percent; the work time currently required to purchase basic telephone service in the United States is less than one-third that in West Germany, Italy, and Great Britain, and less than one-seventh that in France and Japan.

On those terms, AT&T is unmistakably a triumph of the mixed economy. But it is less than one in other terms. If it has strengths that are unique, it has weaknesses that are generic. At the practical level, it has had and has its quota of economic waste, clock-watching employees, corner-cutting careerist executives, managers without vision or public concern—all the familiar mediocrities of corporate and bureaucratic life. As an investment—even as a prudent capital-conserving one—it has been largely a failure over the long term. Since 1900, when the company in its present form was organized, the value of its common stock, leaving aside the benefits of an unbroken string of dividends and an irregular flow of valuable rights offerings to stockholders, has no more than doubled, over a period when the general cost of living has more than quintupled. An original investor who has spent his dividends, as most investors do, has far less buying-power capital than he had to start with. And this failure leads directly to a moral flaw, in terms of free-enterprise ideology. The flaw arises out of the fact that AT&T, like other regulated utilities and unlike unregulated companies subject to competition, is able to claim that its private profits are directly in the interest not only of its private investors but also of its customers, the public at large.

Briefly stated, the logic is as follows: If the company has adequate and rising profits, it will be able to raise new money in the capital markets on favorable terms by borrowing (selling bonds and debentures) and persuading investors to become part owners (selling new common stock). The money thus obtained can be used to invest in new plant, thus improving current telephone service and providing facilities to meet increased telephone demand in the future. Conversely, if the company has inadequate profits, it will find the raising of new money difficult or impossible and may not be able to afford to invest in enough new plant. Thus AT&T is able to treat its profits as a boon not only to its three million stockholders but to its hundred million-plus customers—as not only pleasant, but holy, too. Apparently it can do good only when doing well. The trouble is that the argument can be turned on its head; like all moral Valhallas, this one is an illusion. If AT&T decides to eschew the always unpopular course of seeking increased profits by asking regulators to allow it higher rates, it can achieve them another way—by economizing on current service and plans for future service. That is, instead of putting profits into service, it can take profits out of service. Profits thus obtained obviously lack sanctity. And, as will emerge in this narrative, there is evidence that in the middle 1960s AT&T obtained profits to a certain extent by just such policies and thereby contributed to the greatest single technical and public-relations setback in the company's modern history, the service failures of 1969–70.

The dilemma of profits and service is only the largest of many such dilemmas—both intellectually puzzling and nationally important—that face AT&T executives, whose problems are among the most complex and far-reaching in the business world. With some seventy-five billion dollars in assets, almost three million stockholders, and almost one million employees—well over 1 percent of the national labor force—their enterprise has no rival as to corporate bulk. (Its closest pursuer in 1974, General Motors, had at that time about twenty billion in assets, 1,300,000 stockholders, and 734,000 employees.) Parent company of the network called the Bell System, AT&T grew directly out of the patents obtained by the telephone's inventor, Alexander Graham Bell. It is both a corporate model and an antimodel, setting or following styles in some matters and going its own lordly way in others. For years it has been regulated at the national level by the Federal Communications Commission, at the state level by public-service commissions in all states except Texas, and there by municipalities. Yet no amount of public surveillance, and no amount of devotion to its ideal of supplying the best possible service to the greatest number of people, can, now or probably ever, prevent its being viewed by many as a colossal and potentially dangerous monolith. Its current president, Robert D. Lilley, believes that AT&T probably has more daily dealings with United States citizens than the United States government itself. Obviously, many of these dealings involve service difficulties and unpaid bills; and AT&T holds over its subscribers a sanction unique to utility companies, the power to withdraw for cause a service that is not available elsewhere. It uses that sanction necessarily or ruthlessly, according to one's viewpoint. It is not the most beloved of companies. Its leaders loudly and regularly trumpet the virtues of free-enterprise principles—except for the most important of these principles, competition, to which, at least on the terms currently proposed by federal authorities, they are vigorously and forthrightly opposed.

All this is not to say that AT&T is the only telephone company in the United States; to the contrary, there are about seventeen hundred others, serving something like one-half of the national land area, including cities as large as Rochester, New York, and Tampa, Florida. Independent companies—all of which are regulated like the Bell system, and all interconnected with it so that the user of any Bell phone can talk with the user of any independent phone, and vice versa—also serve the capital cities of Alaska, Florida, Hawaii, Missouri, and Nebraska. As a group, the independents have annual revenues of about five billion dollars, plant investment of about twenty billion dollars, and more than 150,000 employees. The largest of them, General Telephone and Electronics, serves almost 12 million telephones; more than 300 other independents have annual revenues of over one million dollars, and six are listed on the New York Stock Exchange. Of total telephones in use in the U.S. in 1974, the Bell companies had about 118 million and the independents 26 million.

But this is diversity, not competition, since AT&T and the independents have long since agreed, with government approval, to live with each other and not to poach on each other's geographical preserves. Such competition as AT&T faces in the 1970s involves not rival telephone-operating companies, but rather rival suppliers of terminal equipment for attachment to AT&T wires, and rival microwave radio systems for intercity private lines.

2

Let us pause to consider AT&T's product and purpose. Lifeline of the lonely and lifeblood of the busy, the telephone is taken for granted, and for good reason. It comes as near as any human invention to being an extension of the human body. For all the vast and miraculous technology that supports it—the banks of computers and relays that switch messages, the cables that carry them across ocean floors, the wires, radio beams, and satellite stations that carry them over and above the earth—what is the telephone? Only (to translate its name literally from its Greek roots) "far speaking"—only a way of increasing human earshot. With it, man, instead of being able to make himself heard a few hundred yards away with a shout, can make himself heard and understood around the world with a whisper.

What has the telephone done to us, or for us, in the hundred years of its existence? A few effects suggest themselves at once. It has saved lives by getting rapid word of illness, injury, or famine from remote places. By joining with the elevator to make possible the multistory residence or office building, it has made possible—for better or worse—the modern city. By bringing about a quantum leap in the speed and ease with which information moves from place to place, it has greatly accelerated the rate of scientific and technological change and growth in industry. Beyond doubt it has crippled if not killed the ancient art of letter writing. It has made living alone possible for persons with normal social impulses; by so doing, it has played a role in one of the greatest social changes of this century, the breakup of the multi-generational household. It has made the waging of war chillingly more efficient than formerly. Perhaps (though not provably) it has prevented wars that might have arisen out of international misunderstanding caused by written communication. Or perhaps— —again not provably—by magnifying and extending irrational personal conflicts based on voice contact, it has caused wars. Certainly it has extended the scope of human conflicts, since it impartially disseminates the useful knowledge of scientists and the babble of bores, the affection of the affectionate and the malice of the malicious.

But the question remains unanswered. The obvious effects just cited seem inadequate, mechanistic; they only scratch the surface. Perhaps the crucial effects are evanescent and unmeasurable. Use of the telephone involves personal risk because it involves exposure; for some, to be "hung up on" is among the worst of fears; others dream of a ringing telephone and wake up with a pounding heart. The telephone's actual ring—more, perhaps, than any other sound in our daily lives—evokes hope, relief, fear, anxiety, joy, according to our expectations. The telephone is our nerve-end to society.

In some ways it is in itself a thing of paradox. In one sense a metaphor for the times it helped create, in another sense the telephone is their polar opposite. It is small and gentle—relying on low voltages and miniature parts—in times of hugeness and violence. It is basically simple in times of complexity. It is so nearly human, recreating voices so faithfully that friends or lovers need not identify themselves by name even when talking across oceans, that to ask its effects on human life may seem hardly more fruitful than to ask the effect of the hand or the foot. The Canadian philosopher Marshall McLuhan—one of the few who have addressed themselves to these questions—was perhaps not far from the mark when he spoke of the telephone as creating "a kind of extra-sensory perception."

Statistics on the growth of telephone use, both nationwide and worldwide, have long puzzled and continue to puzzle sociologists and mathematicians who have applied themselves to the subject. One would expect rapid and continuous telephone growth as technology advances and affluence spreads—up to a saturation point. But one would also expect that in such a highly developed nation as the United States, where telephone use has for some time been not far from universal, the saturation point had long since been reached. Yet telephone use continues to grow at a rapid rate. The obvious explanation is population growth—but the figures show that telephone use is growing much faster than the population. Attempting to explain this phenomenon, social scientists have postulated that since two new telephone talkers may logically be expected to have four new telephone conversations for every conversation by a preexisting user, telephone use increases not directly with population growth but by the square of population growth. However, the social scientists found that the model does not apply; telephone use, it turns out, increases markedly faster than the square of population growth, with no leveling off in sight.[1] The model will not do; another one, perhaps more metaphysical, must be found. "Not to eat, not for love," Emerson said of some puzzling snakes gliding in a hollow for no discernible

---

* Notes begin on page 347.

purpose; similarly, the rate of telephone growth remains an enigma of human behavior.

How is it to be explained, and how dealt with? The latter question preoccupies research scientists in telephony, and may perhaps preoccupy a layman who wonders whether it will end in a creeping paralysis of the world's work brought about by worldwide, simultaneous, continuous telephone communication. Meanwhile, both AT&T and its state and federal watchdogs, ignoring such dangers, are dedicated to the idea that their job is to make such communication possible if the customers want it.

3

The largest component part of the Bell System is Western Electric Company, the manufacturing arm, a nationwide firm so vast that, if it were not wholly owned by AT&T, it would by itself be counted as the twelfth largest industrial company in the nation. Each year it solemnly issues an elaborately printed and illustrated annual report to its single stockholder, AT&T; its report for 1974 showed assets of $5.2 billion, sales of $7 billion ($6.6 billion to the Bell System and most of the rest to the United States government), and almost 200,000 employees—about one-fifth of all employees of the Bell System.

It is a curious fact, of which Western Electric people like to make much, that one of the firm's original partners was Elisha Gray, the Chicago inventor whose claim to have invented the telephone came closest of many such claims to overthrowing Alexander Graham Bell's. Furthermore, in the competitive struggle of 1878–79 when Western Union bent every effort to crush the newborn Bell Company, Western Electric Manufacturing Company was Western Union's ally and supplier. Found in Cleveland in 1869 as an electric-equipment shop then called Gray and Barton, it shortly thereafter moved its headquarters to Chicago, and in the 1870s became a mecca for inventors, manufacturing the world's first commercial typewriters as well as Thomas A. Edison's electric pen, predecessor of the mimeograph machine, and playing a role in his invention of the incandescent lamp. In 1881, two years after the competitive war had ended in victory for the Bell people, they bought a major interest in Western Electric, and the following year it formally became the manufacturer of Bell telephones and equipment. Such it has remained. Along the way, besides producing or procuring practically all Bell System telephone equipment, it has seen (in 1913) one of its scientists, Harold Arnold, improve on Lee De Forest's invention and develop the high-vacuum electronic amplifying tube that made possible coast-to-coast telephone calls and cleared the way for radio broadcasting, sound motion pictures, and television; it produced the first air-to-ground radio telephones; it made and installed one of the pioneer commercial radio broadcasting systems, WEAF in New York; it developed the first motion-picture sound system; in World War II, it built half of all the radar used by the U.S. armed forces; and in the space age, it built the Nike missile systems, the DEW line radar defense system, the Sentinel and Safeguard antiballistic missile systems, and much of the communications and control equipment for the U.S. space program.

Western Electric's supplier relationship with its owner, AT&T —a relationship usually described as one of "vertical integration"— has long been under challenge by various critics, including many in high federal office. If the Bell System has only one supplier and owns that one, the critics say, what is to prevent Western Electric from charging prices as high as it chooses, resulting in high telephone rates? Western Electric replies that its average prices rose only 7 percent between 1950 and 1974—far less than the government price indexes—and that in the latter year the average price of Western equipment was 28 percent below that of other telephone-equipment manufacturers; as for the matter of depriving other manufacturers of AT&T's vast supply business, Western retorts that they are actually not deprived, since Western itself buys over three billion dollars' worth of equipment annually from fifty thousand suppliers, the majority of them small. The challenge has been directly involved in the three historic confrontations between AT&T and the federal government: the Kingsbury Commitment of 1913, entered into under threat of federal antitrust action, whereby AT&T formally abandoned its dreams of monopolizing all forms of telecommunications in the United States; the government antitrust suit of 1949, which ended in 1956 with a consent decree, under which AT&T made important patent-licensing concessions but was not required, as the complaint had asked, to divest itself of Western Electric; and the new antitrust suit of 1974—pending as this is written—that goes much further, seeking divestiture not only of Western Electric but of either AT&T's long-distance business or some of its regional operating companies, and possibly even of its research-and-development arm, Bell Telephone Laboratories. As the Bell System and the telephone itself approached their centennial in 1976, the future of the Western Electric relationship, and of the system's integration in general, was the largest question hanging over it.

Western Electric today operates twenty-three major plants scattered around the country from Atlanta, Georgia to Phoenix, Arizona to North Andover, Massachusetts. They vary in structure from glassy modern to solid-brick elderly, in function from up-to-the-minute high technology to basic wire and cable making. At the Allentown (Pennsylvania) Works, for example, the principal products are semiconductors, thin-film circuits, integrated circuits, ferrite devices, electron tubes, and sealed contacts; at the Atlanta (Georgia) Works, cable and wire; at the Indianapolis (Indiana) Works, telephones; at the Hawthorne Works near Chicago, grandfather of Western Electric plants, cable, switching devices, and a wide variety of power equipment; and at the Merrimac Valley Works in North Andover, all sorts of advanced transmission systems, such as the irresistibly ingenious TASI system, which increases long-distance line capacity by contriving to fit one conversation into the blank spaces in another.

Sprawling from coast to coast and border to border, engaged in manufacturing everything from simple strands of copper wire to the most occult and futuristic of telecommunications equipment, Western Electric in recent years has proved to be a training ground for AT&T bosses; two recent chief executives, Frederick R. Kappel and H. I. Romnes, were former presidents of Western, and other top officers at AT&T headquarters have come from there. These men usually bring with them and retain a strong bias toward Western; one of them said recently—joking, but with an edge of seriousness—"I always like to think of AT&T as a manufacturing company that happens to have a few operating departments." The captive giant of which they were once part has their loyalty always.

Bell Telephone Laboratories, innovator of the equipment that Western Electric manufactures and the Bell System uses, has had formal existence—as a corporation owned half by AT&T and half by Western Electric—only since 1925, but a quite similar predecessor organization dates back to 1907, when the engineering departments of AT&T and Western Electric were centralized at 463 West Street, on the edge of Greenwich Village in New York City (now reincarnated as Westbeth, a moderate-cost housing project for artists). Originally a small organization, Bell Labs grew into a giant on World War II military hardware requirements, and has since become a supergiant. Today it is the most celebrated of all industrial labs and one of the most celebrated research labs of any kind. It maintains seventeen locations in nine states, and an eighteenth on Kwajalein atoll in the Pacific Ocean. It has about 16,500 employees, of whom 44 percent are professionals and 23 percent technical assistants; these include more than two thousand Ph.D. holders and almost four thousand with master's degrees. It prefers to hire scientists and engineers fresh out of school, and those who hold only bachelor's degrees are routinely sent back to school, at the Lab's expense, for further training. It pays its people as well as any other laboratories, industrial or academic, except for those of a few small specialized scientific companies. Bell Labs describes itself as a "misson-oriented" organization, the mission being the advance of telecommunications technology. Structurally, it is divided into departments of research, which is defined as work that is "possibly important" to telecommunications; development, defined either "very probably important" or "known to be important"; and "systems engineering"—a concept that itself originated at Bell Labs—which is responsible for deciding on a systematic basis what research and development projects are most worth undertaking. Between research and development, the total effort is divided about 64 percent development, 12 percent research, and the rest mostly military work. The total Bell Labs budget for a recent year (1974) was $625 million, of which about $200 million came from operating companies via AT&T, about $290 million from Western Electric, and most of the rest from the government for the fulfillment of military contracts.

These rather lavish outlays of talent and money have paid off more than handsomely; indeed, Bell Labs is constantly cited as the prize example of how profitable capital investment in research can be to industry. Bell Labs men like to tell how a single one of the Labs' developments, the use of plastic cable sheathing instead of

lead, alone paid for the entire research-and-development operation through most of the postwar period; since 1948 the use of
plastic sheathing has saved the Bell operating companies $1.9
billion, while over the same period the operating companies' contribution to Bell Labs has amounted to $1.25 billion. But certainly
the prize jewels in the Labs' crown are the accomplishments not
in cost-cutting but in basic innovation. By 1975, about eighteen
thousand patents had been issued to Bell Labs people over its
fifty-year history, adding up to more than one patent for each
working day. Bell Labs developments applicable chiefly to telephony include just about every such development of the past half
century, among them coaxial cable transmission and microwave
radio relay, which have brought about a spectacular rise in the
capacity and reduction of the cost of long-distance telephony; direct distance dialing, introduced commercially in 1951 and now in
all but universal use in the United States; electronic switching,
Bell Labs' biggest single project, which took four thousand man-
years of development work and resulted in techniques without
which the telephone traffic of the 1970s could not be accommodated; and the Picturephone, introduced to commercial exchange
service in 1970, a development of great technical elegance, which,
to Bell Labs' great disappointment, up to now has found only a
small amount of public acceptance.

But it is in the realm of inventions with wide application outside telephony that the Labs' accomplishments have been the
most dazzling, and have led to the greatest changes in the world.
To mention just a few of many: There was—in 1926, the year after
Bell Labs' formal birth—the first synchronous-sound motion-picture system, providing the basic technology for the modern art of
film. There was the negative-feedback amplifier, invented by Harold S. Black of Bell Labs, which, besides making possible transcontinental multichannel telephone transmission, paved the way
for high-fidelity recording and was basic to gun-control instruments in World War II and to computers and industrial-control
systems since then. There was the pioneer electrical-relay digital
computer itself, constructed in 1937 by G. R. Stibitz and S. B. Williams of Bell Labs. There was "information theory," the corner-
stone of current theoretical understanding of the communication
process, developed by Claude E. Shannon in the middle 1940s.
There was the laser, a coherent-light device the limits of the use of

which, in and out of telecommunications, are only now being explored; a paper on it, published in 1958 by Arthur L. Schawlow (then of Bell Labs) and Charles H. Townes, provided the stimulus for further work by others, and their patent is still considered perhaps the most basic in the field. Above all, in terms of social and economic effects, there is the transistor, invented at Bell Labs in 1947 by John Bardeen, William Shockley, and Walter H. Brattain, who were awarded the 1956 Nobel Prize for Physics for their achievement. By vastly improving on the speed and efficiency of vacuum tubes, the transistor has accomplished nothing less (apart from being probably the most important development in telephony since the invention of the telephone) than making possible communication with men on the moon and creating the modern computer industry.[2]

Bell Labs' standing in the academic scientific establishment is attested to, and confirmed by, the facts that some two thousand technical and scientific papers a year by Bell Labs men are published in scientific journals or read at scientific meetings, and that Bell Labs men are often elected to high office in scientific learned societies. (Bell Labs management, like that of some but not all other industrial research organizations, strongly encourages publication of new findings and participation in scientific organizations.) A count of the papers published in a typical recent year in a key scientific journal, *The Physical Review,* shows the University of California at Berkeley in first place with 150; Bell Labs tied for second with 101; and General Electric, the nearest competitor among industrial companies, trailing in twenty-sixth place with 33 papers. So convincing to foreigners is Bell Labs' image as an academic research facility that commentators in the Soviet Union, which in recent years has become intensely interested in the Labs and their work, insist on describing Bell scientists as "professors," and the Labs' true role as not that of an industrial facility but rather that of a national science laboratory.

Is Bell Labs, as a mission-oriented organization, a place where scientists and engineers are held captive to the task of producing telecommunications hardware? Its dynamic president, William O. Baker—like all Bell Labs presidents, a scientist himself—insists that the contrary is true, that "there just isn't a conflict between the freedom of a scientist to pursue the truth and our mission." He points to the fact that telecommunications as interpreted there is so broad as to embrace even research in human behavior and the workings of the human nervous system ("the most elegant of all communications systems," Baker calls it); and he likes to recall, wryly, an occasion when he got into all kinds of trouble by saying to a newspaper interviewer, "Science is not degraded by being used. Nobody ever ate a Rembrandt." An outside criticism that is received more seriously at Bell Labs is that it has a tendency to take what might be called a bulldozer approach to delicate problems—in the words of one commentator, "to plow on regardless, to save face."[3] Scientific elegance is sometimes a casualty of huge resources and a demanding parent organization.

Indeed, the Labs' relations with AT&T specifically resemble those of a brilliant and sometimes willful son or daughter with a proud but strict and demanding parent. Routinely, when the Labs wish to undertake a new project, they submit a "case" to AT&T for approval; the project is then approved or rejected by a "council" comprising representatives of AT&T, Western Electric, and Bell Labs itself. Baker says of the Labs' relations with AT&T, "Every once in a while there's a little rub." The rub is almost always the same one—that the proposed project is too impractical or too expensive—and the reason for the rub is obvious: research projects that do not quickly justify their cost in improved telephone service, present or future, raise the expenditures of AT&T and ultimately reduce the profits of AT&T, or raise the cost of telephone service, or both. At a seminar of Bell Labs people at Murray Hill, New Jersey, in 1974, J. A. Baird, AT&T vice-president for engineering, and a former Bell Labs man himself, remarked with a certain asperity, "I could hope that in the future Bell Labs would get out more and find out what the real telephone world is like." A couple of years earlier, the parent-child relationship had come to a point of strain when an article had appeared in *The New York Times* about a Bell Labs' researcher's project on synthesizing the sound of a violin. AT&T had expressed outrage at such fiddle-faddling, but had been placated on learning that the project was for the most part the researcher's hobby, pursued on his own time. Such incidents are rare. "They're generally very decent," Baker says.

Moving from scientific philosophy to wires and jacks, we come to the end product, the operating network. Long Lines, the only operating arm of the Bell System that is a department of AT&T rather than a separate company, is responsible for providing telephone circuits between states and across oceans and international boundaries; its interstate facilities are jointly owned, and the revenues from them shared, with the various regional Bell and non-Bell operating companies, and similar arrangements with foreign telephone companies pertain to international circuits. Long Lines has been a part of AT&T from the beginning of long-distance service (indeed, from 1885 until 1899, when AT&T first became the parent Bell company, Long Lines *was* AT&T); it remains so in the interests of efficiency and economy. The Department of Justice would like to see it separated by legal mandate from AT&T; the company argues—just as it argues in most of its differences with reformers and regulators—that such a move would result in duplication of facilities, lost efficiency, and higher rates, and up to now their argument has won the day. Over thirty-five thousand people work for Long Lines; they switch, route, and service some three and a half billion interstate calls per year, and another hundred thousand or so overseas calls per day. The resulting revenue, which constitutes almost one-third of Bell System gross income, goes about 30 percent to Long Lines and the rest to the various regional companies.

Originally, all domestic long-distance calls went over simple pairs of copper wire, either enclosed in multi-pair cables or not; but now the advance of technology has reduced the paired-wire share of such calls to about 1 percent. Today, coaxial cable—a far more efficient medium of transmission consisting essentially of a core conductor encased in a layer of insulation, another conductor in the form of a flexible pipe, and an outer layer of insulation—carries 30 percent of interstate business. As of 1974, more than twenty thousand miles of coaxial cable, buried four feet deep and made capable of carrying intelligible speech over unlimited distances by electronic repeater units installed one to every mile, crisscross the hills and dales and river bottoms of the nation; the latest Bell System coaxial cable system, the L-5, used cables 3.05 inches in diameter and is capable of carrying 108,000 simultaneous conversations. But the lion's share of interstate traffic—69 percent in 1974—is carried by microwave relay—ultra-shortwave radio transmitted by line of sight between the queer-looking towers, topped with antennas like great horns, that stand on high ground every few miles in every direction from coast to coast. Microwave relay was first used in commercial telephony in 1950; 95 percent of *all* Long Lines domestic plant and equipment now in use has been built and installed since 1945.

Overseas traffic was entirely by long-wave radio—noisier and less reliable than microwave, which because of its line-of-sight requirement is ill adapted to transoceanic service—until 1956, when, at long last, the first transatlantic telephone cable was laid, a century after the first such telegraph cable. Since 1965, another means of intercontinental transmission has been commercially available—by earth satellite. Equipment-laden communications satellites, ingeniously put into orbits that coincide with the earth's turning so that they remain permanently over the same spot, serve as relay stations that defeat the line-of-sight problem created by the earth's curvature, and thus make possible the transmission by microwave radio of telephone conversations or television programs from any point on earth to any other point. Signals are bounced off the satellites, and received back undisturbed at distant points by ground stations equipped with bowl-shaped antennae ninety-seven feet in diameter. At present about half of all international calls are by submarine cable, half by satellite.

Long Lines strikes one as a calm, controlled operation, almost a smug one. If it is smug, it has its reasons. Improved technology and generally efficient use of it have made long-distance tele-phoning one of the few services of any kind that have become steadily and markedly cheaper over the past half century, not just relative to inflation but in absolute dollars-and-cents costs. In 1915 the average peak-hour, three-minute, weekday coast-to-coast call cost $20.70; in 1930, $9; in 1950, $2.50; in 1974 (customer dialled), $1.45. Meanwhile, the cost of living as measured by wholesale commodity prices tripled, meaning that the real cost of the long-distance call had been reduced by a factor of over forty.

Then there are the "operating companies," twenty-two of them in all, each one charged with actually providing telephone service in its assigned area. Sixteen of them—ranging geograph-ically from New York Telephone in the Northeast to Southwest-ern Bell Telephone Company in the Southwest—are fully owned by AT&T; four of them, New England Tel. & Tel., Mountain States Tel. & Tel., Pacific Northwest Bell Tel., and Pacific Tel. & Tel., are more than half owned by AT&T; and in the other two,

Southern New England Tel. and Cincinnati & Suburban Bell Tel., AT&T holds only a minority interest. Whatever their ownership, all the operating companies pay sums amounting to 1.5 percent to 2.5 percent of their gross annual revenues to AT&T under what is called the "license contract," which obliges AT&T to manufacture and supply the operating companies' telephonic equipment, to operate long-distance lines for their subscribers' use, to supply central staff services, and to conduct research and development; moreover, all of them pay AT&T cash dividends, which constitute the bulk of AT&T's revenues and enable *it* to pay dividends on its stock; and all of them, when the chips are down, take their orders from AT&T headquarters, at 195 Broadway in downtown New York City. More commonly what they take from there is guidance; most AT&T chief executives pride themselves on seldom if ever giving a direct order to an operating company. An operating-company president said in 1974, "We are pretty much left to our own devices. . . . On the other hand, I have heard from some of my colleagues—other Bell operating company presidents—that when there is serious trouble they are apt to get a kind of supervision that I, personally, wouldn't care for. . . . In the end, a lot flows back to earnings: if your earnings are good, AT&T is very permissive; if not, it isn't." That standard sometimes leads to problems of intense interest to the telephone-using public that will be explored presently.

4

In the end, everything flows back to 195 Broadway, from which the system is run. Standing on the west side of Broadway between Fulton and Dey Streets, across Fulton from the historic St. Paul's Chapel and a short walk from Wall Street, 195 Broadway is an imposing twenty-nine-story building of neoclassical design, begun in 1913 and finished in 1924. Its huge, columned ground-floor portico—called by the architectural critic Henry Hope Reed "New York's link with Periclean Athens"—inspires awe, or seems to be intended to do so. The building's rather spare offices and ringing marble hallways—the latter uncarpeted except on the twenty-sixth floor, where the top executives hold court, and all featuring drinking fountains whose spouts are supported by turbaned Oriental maidens carved in bronze—suggest tradition and solidity rather than light-footedness, dash, or modernity. (The building was heated by coal until 1947, and air conditioning was not installed until 1959–61.) The epitome of stateliness is reached in the Board Room, at the east side of the top floor. Entered through an anteroom featuring a large portrait of Alexander Graham Bell, it is a rather simple chamber framed by four stately Doric columns and furnished with heavy draperies, portraits of former chief executives, a podium for speakers, and a large oblong table surrounded by chairs bearing bronze plaques on which the directors' names are inscribed. The directors meet here on the third Wednesday morning of every month. The board comprises nineteen members, three of them the company's top officers, and the other sixteen "outsiders"—almost all eminences of American business and finance, among them, only since 1972, one woman, Catherine B. Cleary, and one black man, Jerome H. Holland. At a typical directors' meeting, there are reports from officers or department heads on general business conditions, company financing plans, the current state of telephone service around the nation, Bell System growth, recent financial results, and other topics of current importance. Whatever matters require decision are discussed by the directors and then voted upon by them. If such a decision is of crucial importance to investors—say, a change in the rate of dividend—a ritual of public disclosure is followed that, curiously enough, conspicuously avoids use of the telephone. The company secretary (not a board member, but of course a regular attender of board meetings) conveys the news in code to a company public-relations man in an office several floors below, by pressing certain buttons hidden in a drawer under the oval table. The PR man (falling back on the telephone at this juncture) immediately informs the New York Stock Exchange, where AT&T shares are traded; he then waits three minutes to allow the Exchange time to prepare for whatever deluge of buying or selling of AT&T may be occasioned, whereupon he gives the news to the wire services. The purpose of this procedure is to minimize the possibility of anyone's making improper use of inside information, and to prevent any disturbance of the even tenor of the directors' meeting.

August as they are and solemn their counsels, charged though they are with formally making the ultimate decisions, the

AT&T directors cannot by any stretch be called the key decision-making body of the company. As with the directors of most large companies, most of them are not close enough to day-to-day company affairs to be in a position to refute the views of company management. With rare exceptions, they ratify management policies; they do not originate decisions, and high AT&T officers have said that the directors' chief usefulness is that their very existence forces top management to do its homework on all aspects of a vast and complex business. Two bodies that do originate decisions—that are, in fact, the places where AT&T policy evolves—are the Executive Policy Committee and the so-called Cabinet. The EPC, consisting of the chief executive and five other top officers, meets in the Chairman's office every other Monday, and has frequent additional sessions with the presidents of the operating companies, usually on the third Thursday of each month and almost always at an airport motel at the site of an operating-company headquarters. The meetings are informally conducted, but their agendas are disciplined; according to an EPC member, the most effective ones are confined to a single subject. They are exploratory rather than explicitly decision-making, but they often result in explicit decisions. It was an EPC meeting in 1970, following the service failures in New York City and elsewhere, that decided on the establishment of a program of regularly sending Bell Labs scientists out to work directly with the operating companies.

The most grandiloquently named and conceivably the most powerful of AT&T's top-management bodies is the one called the Cabinet. It consists of the members of the EPC, the presidents of Western Electric and Bell Laboratories, and seventeen AT&T vice-presidents with various responsibilities; together they make up the company's top-management cadre. Its meetings, attendance at which is not compulsory but is customarily very good indeed, take place in the board room on alternate Mondays. Its purpose is the exchange of information and opinions, and although, like the EPC, it has no formally granted decision-making power, its consensus on an important matter is inevitably taken seriously by the chief executive. Does its very name, "Cabinet," suggesting an advisory council to the chief of a national government (and indeed defined that way in dictionaries), indicate a certain presumptuousness on AT&T's part? "Occasionally there's a spasm of embarrassment within the company about the name," says Alvin von Auw, a current vice-president and assistant to the chairman, "but other names that are tried out just don't seem to take." In fact, AT&T is larger and, in terms of the number of people it affects, more powerful than all but a handful of the world's national governments. Say what one will, it is entitled to have a Cabinet.

At the apex of the pyramid is the chief executive officer, who was called president until 1961 and since then has been called chairman of the board. At present he is John D. deButts, a big, bluff man of about sixty with an avuncular air that tends to conceal an emergent vein of iron within. Like most recent AT&T chief executives, he grew up far from 195 Broadway. (The last five of them, their terms in office spanning more than a quarter century, have come from the Midwest or South, and the wife of one of these—Mrs. Cleo F. Craig, originally of Rich Hill, Missouri—cried when he first told her they had to move to New York.) DeButts was born in Greensboro, North Carolina, and educated at Virginia Military Institute. Again like most of them, and indeed most AT&T top-level executives, he has spent his entire working life in the Bell System; his first job was as a traffic student with the Chesapeake and Potomac Telephone Company of Virginia, in 1936. Finally, as is the case with all AT&T chief executives, his personal style greatly influences the corporate style of the whole Bell System, much as a president of the United States tends to set the national style during his time in office. DeButts' is a no-nonsense style. One of his key subordinates, an old hand at working with AT&T chief executives, said of him recently, "I have never seen anyone who handles paper work so crisply, whether in his office or traveling"; another, an expert in the mysteries of finance, says that deButts "seizes on the dimensions of a problem so quickly that you can't believe he really has it." DeButts operates out of a comfortable but dull suite of offices on the twenty-sixth floor at 195 Broadway, containing a fireplace that works but is never lighted and a set of bird prints of which he is proud; but he is often away from it, since he makes a particular point of regularly visiting all the operating companies and talking to their management groups. When conducting meetings of the Cabinet, the Executive Policy Committee, or some lesser management group, he concentrates on making sure everyone has an opportunity to speak, interrupting the discussion only occasionally to say something like, "Well, let me try to sum up and see if this is where we are." He answers his own telephone, except when a visitor is in his office; he reads every letter addressed to him either by name or by title. His basic management philosophy is as plain as an old shoe: he wants his people "to get their work done promptly and thoroughly." Sometimes he wonders at the end of a business day, "What the hell have I accomplished today?"—but not often. He lives in a Manhattan apartment, and in free time enjoys hunting, fishing, and golf, but most of all, it seems safe to say, he enjoys the time that is not free.[4]

Down the hallway from this cool paragon of executive efficiency is one of the hottest and most crucial seats of AT&T management, the office of the chief financial officer. From 1963 until the middle of 1974 it was occupied by John J. Scanlon, and since then by Charles L. Brown. Besides being so big, AT&T engages in a type of business that is "capital intensive," that is, one that requires a relatively high capital investment in relation to revenues; therefore its appetite for new cash from the money markets is voracious. As one AT&T financial man has described his work, "Oh, it's just the same old grind, raising another billion dollars every ninety days." *A billion dollars every ninety days?* The figure boggles the mind of a layman, yet for 1974 it was just about on target. To put the Bell System's financial needs into more manageable perspective, between 1945 and 1965 it raised enough money in the capital markets to buy up the total gold reserves of the United States, Great Britain, and several other European countries.[5] One may be grateful that it used the money instead to provide telephone service.

Scanlon—a keen-looking, precise man who started his Bell System career with Pennsylvania Bell at the age of sixteen, and got his formal education in the mysteries of finance by going to the University of Pennsylvania Evening School of Accounts and Finance while working during the day—explained the AT&T financial situation for 1974 to a visitor to his office early in that year. The company's budget for new construction expenditures for 1974, he said, was ten billion dollars—about three times more than the budget of any other American corporation, and something like one-tenth of the capital expenditures planned for the

year by *all* American corporations. AT&T's staggering capital
budget is built, Scanlon said, "from the ground up." To begin
with, the various operating companies submitted their requests
based on their needs. Next, Hubert L. Kertz, then AT&T vice-
president in charge of construction plans, and his staff got to
work applying various tests to the submitted figures. Is a certain
operating company's revenue growth commensurate with growth
in the number of telephones it has in service? What is its projected telephone growth rate? What will its equipment needs
probably be in five or ten years? The company economist, Kenneth H. Militzer, would then join in by applying various economic calipers and predicting money-market conditions based
on projections of the state of the national economy. Finally, the
budget would be submitted to and approved by the board of
directors. And then it was up to the chief financial officer to raise
the money.

Happily for him, he need not raise all of it; the company's
reserve resources and its prudent dividend-paying policies are
such that much new construction money can come from AT&T's
own treasury. In some recent years the company was compelled
to raise more than half of its new capital needs from outside, but
for 1974 it was in a position to put up six billion dollars, or 60
percent, leaving four billion dollars to be raised outside. The
question, then, was whether to raise the four billion dollars by
selling new stock, new bonds, or some combination of the two,
such as preferred stock or convertible debentures. And the answer, for 1974, was comparatively simple. In the palmy stock-
market days of the 1960s, AT&T had raised much money by selling common stock, through offerings of stock rights to existing
stockholders; but beginning late in the decade, a generally bad
stock market and increasing regulatory pressure on utility companies had forced AT&T's stock price down so low that new
shares could not be issued on terms favorable to existing stockholders. That meant that the answer for 1974 would be to issue
primarily bonds—debt securities. Scanlon would have to go to
the great Wall Street underwriting syndicates—the so-called Morgan Group, headed by Morgan Stanley & Company, once considered AT&T's "traditional" banker, and the rival combination,
informally called the "Fearsome Foursome," consisting of Merrill
Lynch, Salomon Brothers, Lehman Brothers, and Blyth Eastman

Dillon. (In 1974, Lehman Brothers announced that it would henceforth no longer bid on utility issues except those of firms with which it had a direct relationship, and thus broke up the "Fearsome Foursome.") These firms and others would bid competitively for the right to assume the privilege and responsibility of distributing AT&T's bonds to investors, institutional and private. And so they did; the necessary four billion dollars—one billion dollars every ninety days—was duly raised, but, under 1974 market conditions, on terms that meant AT&T had to pay upward of 9 percent annual interest on its new money.

There are disadvantages beyond high interest rates to debt financing. Too much debt in a company's capital structure makes it top-heavy and unstable, and eventually damages its credit rating, leading to still higher interest rates. Equity money has the advantage that it doesn't incur interest costs or have to be paid back; but on the other hand, too high a percentage of equity capital tends to make a firm financially sluggish and to keep profits too low.

To Scanlon, who had a talent for putting financial complexities into homey language, it was a matter of striking a balance between "eat well" (too much debt) and "sleep well" (too much equity). In AT&T's case, the recent trend toward more debt in the capital structure represented a correction of a historic imbalance. Traditionally ultraconservative in this as in other matters, AT&T once kept its debt down at about one-third of capital; the policy of increasing the ratio was begun out of choice—as a deliberately more liberal policy strongly encouraged by the Federal Communications Commission—and continued out of necessity imposed by the stock-market conditions. As of mid-1974, when Scanlon retired, the ratio stood at around 48%, putting AT&T's capital structure about where in Scanlon's view it belonged—barely within the limits of top rating in the bond market. Since then, however, the limits have been dangerously stretched.

Nothing can better dramatize the stakes for which the chief financial officer of AT&T plays than the case of the 1975 warrants. In 1970 the company resorted, for the first time in its history, to the comparatively flashy financial policy, more often associated with conglomerates, of issuing common-stock warrants. As part of a debenture issue that May, each stockholder got one warrant for each ten shares of stock he held and each warrant entitled the owner to purchase one more share of AT&T stock at any time through May 15, 1975, at fifty-two dollars per share. Over the subsequent years, the warrants themselves were traded actively in the New York Stock Exchange, at prices varying according to the hopes or fears of investors. To Scanlon and his colleagues, such trading meant only one thing. What mattered to them was, quite simply, whether or not AT&T stock would be above fifty-two dollars at the expiration date. If so, the warrants would be exercised by their holders and $1.6 billion would immediately flow into the AT&T treasury; if not, the warrants would expire quietly and nothing would flow in. So in 1974 John Scanlon, looking at the stock-market tables of a morning, found himself contemplating a straightforward, yes-or-no question. A billion and a half dollars, so to speak, on the turn of the card; such are the dreamlike situations that face the chief financial officer of AT&T.

In fact, the warrant issue ended in comparative failure under hair-raising circumstances. As May 15, 1975, approached, the stock price was hovering just below 52, and the fate of AT&T warrants was a question dominating the whole stock market. An investment-banking syndicate headed by Morgan Stanley & Company was engaged by AT&T to absorb or resell warrants that might be sold by their holders at the last minute. In the last days before the deadline, the syndicate—as such a syndicate is permitted to do under Securities and Exchange Commission rules— entered a general bid for AT&T at 51⅞, thereby effectively pegging it at that price or higher. Since AT&T charged no commission to deliver stock at 52 in exchange for warrants, this made the warrants marginally valuable to holders who wanted to buy the stock, and while nine-tenths of them were allowed to expire unused, the other one-tenth was exercised. This brought into the AT&T treasury $160 million—only one-tenth of the sum hoped for, and, moreover, a figure that was drastically reduced by fees the company owed to the syndicate. The failure of the warrants was a major cause of the company's decision later in 1975 to sell outright twelve million new common shares, in the first stock sale in AT&T history in which the existing stockholders were not granted preemptive rights to subscribe to the new shares ahead of anyone else.

But after May 15 the stock price dropped below 50 again

(making those who had exercised their warrants immediate losers). The ratio of debt in capital, which had risen to 49.8 percent at the end of 1974 and had passed the fifty percent mark early in 1975, was not significantly reduced; and the prospects for Scanlon's successor to "sleep well," while continuing to raise the same old billion dollars every ninety days, did not look bright.[6]

5

Wandering the corridors of 195 Broadway and dropping in on some of the executives who fulfill AT&T's various staff functions—engineering, personnel, marketing and rate plans, advertising and public relations, relations with state and federal regulators, and so on—one gets a sense, however fleeting, of the character of the company. There is a certain sameness about AT&T people. Their dress and manner is conservative, but not to the point of stuffiness; they keep their neckties on in their offices, but their shirts are not necessarily white nor their ties narrow and subdued. They seem far more vivid, dashing, and enterprising than a buildingful of government bureaucrats, but far less so than, say, the brainy and hungry young hotshots of some rising new high-technology company. Almost to a man, the top ones, like their boss, John deButts, are lifetime Bell System careerists. The company's habit of recruiting management—and its almost invariable rule to date of recruiting top management—not only from inside the company but from the ranks of people who have scarcely or never worked for any employer other than the Bell System, has a crucial effect on AT&T's corporate style. Indeed, it has little to do with other corporations in the matter of style, simply because other corporate styles do not filter in over the transom as they do in most other companies. Top AT&T people's tastes and interests tend to be similar, and for those who are going places, their primary interest is the Bell System; in times of company crisis they are sometimes called upon to work practically around the clock, and they do not seem to mind. (They are, of course, well paid, in line with the top corporate scale nationally; at the summit, for 1974 Chairman deButts was paid $381,000 and President Lilley and Vice-Chairman William L. Lindholm $309,000, plus retirement benefits.) The company-issued biographical data on eighteen officers who make up a good cross section of AT&T top management shows no blacks or women and, to judge by names, a strong preponderance of men of Anglo-Saxon lineage; nine from the Midwest or South, six from the East apart from New York City, two from the West or Far West, and one lone native New Yorker; a majority of small-college men, and only five graduates of Ivy League colleges; and—perhaps most surprisingly—only four, three of them lawyers, who ever worked full time for more than a year or two for any employer other than the national armed forces and the Bell System. Sixteen of them commute from suburbs, two live in New York City. Golf is their preferred hobby. They give off an aura of straight-arrow probity, and there is no reason to think that the air is a false one; AT&T, much as its policies have been attacked, has only recently been accused, for the first time since 1907, of anything resembling a major internal scandal.

Their relations with each other are surprisingly easy and informal for so large and traditionally stiff-backed an organization. Subordinates often address their bosses by first name, and bosses shy away from issuing direct orders. Life at 195, on the surface at least, is bland and civil; only very occasionally does one catch a whiff of the corporate jungle (although in the past, as will become clear, jungle struggles have gone on there at the company's top levels). Still, their life is not an easy one, if only because of AT&T's long-standing and continuing penchant for moving the men it values most and of whom it expects the most from place to place within the Bell System, at regular intervals of a few years. A typical vice-president at 195 Broadway has worked at one time or another in at least one operating company as well as in either Western Electric or Bell Laboratories, and in the course of his career has had to uproot and move his family upwards of four or five times. Critics of this shuffle-them-around policy, as practiced at AT&T and elsewhere, insist that its real purpose is to render the executives geographically rootless and ensure that their foremost loyalty is to the company rather than to a community. AT&T insists that the purpose is to ensure that its leaders will have a general grasp of the whole system; at all events, most AT&T executives accept their moving orders with outward good grace, for ample reason. As a former AT&T personnel chief has explained the matter, "You don't say no to a move without a good reason, or you commit advancement suicide." (There are exceptions: a few say no to moves and keep their reasons to themselves, and somehow emerge with both increased respect within the company and further promotions.) Occasionally a wife is the one who says no; the executive moves anyhow, at the risk of sacrificing his marriage to his career.

If this summary makes the AT&T executive cadre seem collectively a bit dull and tamed to a corporate yoke, the impression is not entirely wrong. But AT&T—while its executives are fiercely loyal to it, and quick to react to criticism with what seems to be genuine indignation—is big, self-assured, and forward-looking enough to allow them a good deal of mental flexibility, even, in the company's more rarefied precincts, a kind of academic freedom as regards the matters in which the company has the greatest stake. "If the telephone had not been invented, or telephony developed—if all the millions of billions of telephone conversations since 1876 had not taken place—how much poorer would the world be? Could this huge effort have been more usefully put into something else? I wonder." That rhetorical question was posed, and its equivocal answer given, not by an academic gadfly or radical critic of the telephone business; rather, it was posed to a casual visitor in 1974 by Warren A. Tyrrell, executive director for technical relations of Bell Telephone Laboratories. True enough, the point Tyrrell was making was hardly that AT&T ought to retire from business; he was raising the question of whether it ought ever to have been started, and of whether all the effort, talent, and money that go into the Bell System might better have been applied to something else. It is hardly the sort of philosophical question one is accustomed to hearing raised in the executive offices of an American corporation.

Some of the other easily discernible characteristics of AT&T are heartening, some less so. In the late 1960s and early 1970s the company, repeatedly made a test case of by the federal Equal Employment Opportunity Commission, suddenly became a leader in the matters of equal employment opportunity for racial minorities and equal pay for women—even though it had previously been something of a laggard in the matter of equal pay, and until the late 1930s did not employ a single black anywhere in its entire system in any capacity higher than that of building janitor. It is a company that, like most other companies, has its polite fictions.

For example, for a generation following the Second World War AT&T more or less continuously pretended that its various operating companies did their own negotiating with organized labor, when in reality, as everyone involved in the negotiations knew well enough, AT&T usually set the bargaining pattern for the whole system. (This polite fiction was abandoned in 1974, when for the first time negotiations were openly conducted on a System-wide basis.) Again, as we have seen, AT&T insists almost ad nauseam on the point that its profits are in the interest of better service and lower rates; one sometimes longs to hear an AT&T man say right out, just once, that AT&T likes profits because they support high executive salaries and good shareholder dividends. Further, there is much official AT&T rhetoric about the management independence of the operating companies, when actually their policies are rather closely controlled by the parent company, and their chief executives, although nominally elected by their individual boards of directors, are in simple fact appointed at 195 Broadway, and an AT&T officer occupies a strategic seat on the board of each one of them. Yet again, the company constantly and in stentorian tones proclaims itself in favor of regulation—and has fought the regulators tooth and nail whenever it disapproved of their edicts or policies. In defense of AT&T's institutional pieties, however, it should be said that to a marked extent they are enforced by regulation. If, for example, the company were to announce officially that its primary objective was to make profits, the statement would assuredly be used against it by the FCC and the state public service commissions. The discipline of regulation gives rise to unctuousness in the regulated, as that of organized religion gives rise to it in the congregation.


6


Looked upon as a "corporate state," AT&T has some three million "citizens"—its stockholders. Like any other corporation, once a year it complies with the law by issuing a written invitation to each stockholder to attend its annual meeting. It has been noted that the three million annual-meeting notices sent out each spring by AT&T probably constitute the largest number of individual invitations ever issued for any event of any sort anywhere in the world; and one might think that the AT&T man chiefly responsible for planning the event—Frank A. Hutson, Jr., the Yale-trained lawyer who serves as company secretary—while waiting for the answers to the invitations, might suffer in surrealistically extreme form from an overenthusiastic host's nightmare that all or nearly all of his invitees may accept. But he does not; with rare exceptions, attendance at AT&T annual meetings runs predictably in the general area of three to four thousand persons, or a little over one-tenth of one percent of the stockholder total. Attendance is limited by geography, stockholder indifference, and the fact that absent stockholders are permitted to vote at annual meetings by proxy. AT&T meetings were held each year in New York City until 1961 (on company premises until 1959); since then they have been rotated among various large cities around the country. The all-time record attendance was at the first one ever to be held outside New York—the 1961 meeting in Chicago, which drew over eighteen thousand. Of those stockholders who do attend annual meetings, some appear to seek information, some diversion, some a chance to put questions or express their views on company policy to company officers, and a few—those who customarily dress in bizarre costumes and address the chairman in bizarre or aggressive ways—publicity for either themselves or their opinions. The methods of AT&T chief executives in dealing with these few have varied widely over the years; for example, Kappel, who was chief executive from 1956 to 1967, was notoriously brusque with them, while his successor, Romnes, 1967–72, tended to rely on sweet reasonableness.

The annual meeting is AT&T's day in direct public view, its manifest of "corporate democracy." Wild-eyed eccentrics air their odd opinions, and are listened to more or less patiently by the company's top managers; afterward, the old lady from Dubuque totters up and mingles with the officers and directors. AT&T considers the annual meeting important enough to devote much management time and effort to its preparation; Hutson works on little else for a couple of months before its scheduled date, and is willing to say that he has private preliminary conversations with stockholders who are known to be planning to speak at it, such as Mrs. Wilma Soss and Lewis Gilbert. In 1951 President Leroy A. Wilson, suffering from leukemia, insisted on attending and conducting it against his doctor's orders, and probably shortened his life thereby; he died about three months later.

But is the corporate democracy real or illusory? In the case of AT&T, as in that of other corporations, the question is controversial. Each stockholder has one vote for each share he holds, and no attempt is made to restrain anyone from voting as he wishes. But as corporate procedures now exist, and are practiced at AT&T, the odds are heavily stacked against a stockholder, large or small, who wishes to oppose the appointments or policies of management. In the matter of the election of directors, which is formally the privilege of stockholders, management nominates a slate; the names, photographs, and brief biographical sketches of the nominees are printed in a proxy statement sent to stockholders in advance of the meeting; and the stockholders may mail in their votes on the accompanying proxy ballot—that is to say, they may mark a box indicating that they are "For" the management slate, or they may mark a box labeled "Withheld." No provision is made for write-in votes. Any stockholder wishing to put forward his own candidate or candidates for director may solicit proxies at his own expense, or may make his own nomination or nominations from the floor at the annual meeting. But the former course would be prohibitively expensive and is therefore never resorted to, while the latter has no chance of success, because an overwhelming majority of all outstanding stock has invariably been voted by proxy for the management slate weeks before the meeting is gaveled to order. Voting at the meeting is a formality. There is a movement afoot at AT&T and elsewhere to allow stockholder nominations for director to be included in the proxy material mailed out by the company, but this democratic reform belongs to the future.

Again, as regards stockholder attempts to influence company policies and procedures, the chances of success through exercise of voting rights is slim indeed. Management has often shown itself to be somewhat responsive to what it believes to be public and stockholder sentiment, as with the nomination of a woman and a black to the board in 1971—but always at its own initiative and discretion. A stockholder who can show a nominal amount of support for his point of view is entitled to have his "shareholder proposal," along with his reasons for making it, printed in the management proxy statement and included on the stockholder ballot, where stockholders may mark a box for or against it. But the law gives management a crucial edge by allowing it, in cases where a stockholder has signed his ballot but not marked himself either "For" or "Against" stockholder proposals, to count the shares as being voted "For." What is literally a noncommittal vote may legally be considered a commitment to management's side. Just how crucial management's edge can be is shown by the voting statistics for 1974, when the proxy statement contained two stockholder proposals, one regarding attendance of directors at annual meetings and the other regarding the very voting procedures that we discuss here. In each case, the result with unmarked ballots counted for management was a vote of about 92 percent for management, while with the unmarked ballots not counted either way, the vote for management would have been only about 62 percent, or victory by a rather narrow margin.

It is these procedures and results that give rise to the charges that AT&T's management (like that of other corporations) is self-perpetuating and its allegedly democratic voting procedures heavily weighted in management's favor. Hutson insists that there would be a larger margin for error if only marked ballots were counted, since, in his view, an unmarked stockholder ballot usually *means* a vote for management. He contends, moreover, that under existing rules a stockholder revolt might actually unseat management, although he concedes that it would be a difficult and expensive undertaking. But a fair-minded observer can hardly avoid the conclusion that by any reasonable standard, AT&T management is indeed virtually self-perpetuating and its procedures and policies scarcely subject to stockholder reversal.

Is this wrong, as it appears on its face to be? Or is it, perhaps, in the public interest that "corporate democracy" should be mostly form rather than substance—that AT&T's chief executives, for example, should choose their successors, as for practical purposes they do, on grounds that the retiring head of the business knows better than anyone else which of his subordinates can do the job best? As will emerge in the succeeding chapters, over the past century the AT&T chief executives thus chosen—less than a dozen, up to now—have shown themselves to be more or less farsighted, more or less tough, more or less diplomatic, more or less brilliant. The history of the company and the industry has been, in large part, a history of their differing personal styles. The common denominator is the fact that, to a striking extent, each seems to have been the appropriate man for his times. As to the overall, long-term character of their organization, that, too, has had its ups and downs. But the harshest of all critics of AT&T in book form—N. R. Danielian, whose *AT&T, the Story of Industrial Conquest* is still spoken of through gritted teeth at 195 Broadway a generation after its publication in 1939—had to concede that "AT&T is not a predatory organization; it has rendered good service at a profit to itself that is larger than necessary, perhaps, but not too excessive."[7] Autocratic and generally benign, cool-headed and sometimes emotional, directive and permissive within itself, the colossus of talk is a modern sphinx, an industrial enigma.

CHAPTER 2

# Beginnings

It is suggestive of the power of the idea of telephony—one step from telepathy—to stir the imagination that the telephone had a myth before it existed. In New York City, beginning at least a decade before the telephone's invention in 1876, a story went the rounds that one Joshua Coppersmith had been convicted of fraud for exhibiting a device called a telephone, which he said was capable of transmitting a human voice over metal wires. Few sane persons doubted that such transmission was impossible, and that Coppersmith was a charlatan; that was the accepted wisdom of the time. But the significant thing is that there is no official record or evidence of any kind that Coppersmith ever existed.[1] If he was indeed imaginary, we may speculate that some secret social need, some threatening prescience of the group mind that had to be canceled by a myth, made it necessary to invent him.

To be sure, the idea of the telephone and the word "telephone" itself had been in currency for a long time. For many centuries—perhaps back to the time of Alexander the Great, in the fourth century B.C.—men had been shouting to each other between distant towers and hilltops through various kinds of megaphones, but they had not called them telephones. The word (as "telephon," from Greek roots meaning "far speaking") seems to have been used first in Germany in 1796 to describe a system of directive megaphones not involving electricity. Sir Charles Wheatstone used the word "telephonic" in connection with his

35

"enchanted lyre," invented in 1821, which transmitted music acoustically by means of rods of wood, glass, or metal. Later Wheatstone applied the term "rhythmical telephone" to an electric bell—actually a telegraphic device—that he invented in 1839. In 1845 another Englishman invented a nonelectrical instrument that he flatly called "the telephone"; it was "for conveying signals during foggy weather by sounds produced by means of compressed air forced through trumpets." Meanwhile the telegraph—indubitably capable of transmitting words by electricity over wires for great distances, by the use of Morse-code signals rather than speech—had arrived, to universal acclaim. In 1854, three years after the first successful telegraph cables had been laid across the English Channel, English and French newspapers were seriously discussing a wholly fanciful report that the cables would be used to convey speech in the following way: "A plate of silver and one of zinc are taken into the mouth, the one above, the other below the tongue. They are then placed in contact with the wire, and words issuing from the mouth so prepared are conveyed by the wire." Of course, no such gagging and probably shocking apparatus worked or could possibly have worked. But the reports show how much the idea of telephony was in the air. In 1860 Philipp Reis, of Germany, made what just missed being a telephone—missed, it was said later, by the turn of a screw. It used a membrane, electrodes, and intermittent electric current, and could transmit the pitch but not the quality of a sound—that is to say, musical notes but not words. In 1881, when the Reis telephone was under consideration as a threat to the Bell patents, Judge Lowell of the U.S. Circuit Court of Massachusetts decided that "The deficiency was inherent in the principle of the machine . . . a century of Reis would never have produced a speaking telephone." But a present-day scientist—Bernard S. Finn, curator of the division of electricity of the Smithsonian Museum of History and Technology—has come to a strikingly different conclusion. After making his own experiments with models of the Reis telephone, he concluded that it could have been made to transmit speech, with small changes, and that if Reis had described it correctly, which he did not, he would have had a prior claim on the Bell patent. Yet Reis never knew how close he came, and never claimed that he had invented the telephone. Thus the first of the several great ironies of early telephony.[2]

The telephone was technically near—but philosophically far. Human speech, as opposed to dot-and-dash code, was considered sacred, a gift of God beyond man's contrivance through science. Public reactions to the very idea of telephony in the 1860s and 1870s wavered between fear of the supernatural and ridicule of the impractical. People were made uneasy by the very notion. Hearing voices when there was no one there was looked upon as a manifestation of either mystical communion or insanity. Perhaps reacting to this climate, most physicists and electricians took it as an axiom that electricity could not carry the human voice. To have the freedom of mind to take the last step, there was needed a man whose thought was centered not on electricity but on the human voice, and the man was Alexander Graham Bell.

2

By family tradition and personal predilection, Bell was as steeped in the physiology of human speech as a man could be. From an early age, his thought and will centered on the technique of elocution (speech transmission) and the problem of deafness (speech reception); on the other hand, he had no knowledge of or association with electricity until he began the long series of experiments that culminated in the invention of the telephone. The story of that invention is more a study of human anatomy than of electrical laws, more of man than of a machine. Bell's grandfather, Alexander Bell, was a Scottish shoemaker who became first a Shakespearean actor, then a public reader of Shakespeare, and eventually the proprietor of a celebrated elocution school in London that specialized in curing stammering, and is alleged by many scholars to have been the basis for George Bernard Shaw's play *Pygmalion*. His father, Melville Bell, was a distinguished teacher of elocution at the University of Edinburgh, who came to enjoy a worldwide reputation as a teacher, as author of textbooks on correct speech, and above all, as the inventor of "Visible Speech"—a written code, indicating the exact positions and actions of the throat, tongue, and lips during speech, that was originally intended to help people pronounce foreign languages but that finally proved most useful in training deaf people to speak intelligibly.

Alexander Graham Bell, born in Edinburgh on March 3, 1847, the second of three sons of Melville, seems never to have wavered for a moment from determination to follow the profession of his grandfather and father. At school in Edinburgh, he was a shy, alert, musical boy whose slightly aquiline nose and unassertive chin suggested intensity and introspection. When he was twelve, his mother, Eliza, a portrait painter and accomplished musician, began to lose her hearing, and thus began her son's lifelong intimacy with and sympathy for the deaf, which was to be the leitmotif of his life. Beginning when he was fifteen, Graham (as he then preferred to be called) joined his brothers in assisting their father in public lectures, pronouncing odd sounds and symbols that Melville Bell had written down, in Visible Speech code, while they were out of the room. At sixteen, Graham with his older brother, Melly—responding to their father's offer of a prize for the construction of a successful speaking machine—made an artificial skull of gutta-percha, furnished it with vocal parts made of tin, India rubber, and a lamb's larynx, and at last, by blowing through it, made it cry out "Ma-ma!" At about the same time Graham managed, by manipulating his Skye terrier's mouth and vocal cords, to make the dog utter something approximating the equally filial sentiment "How are you, Grandmama?"[3]

Meanwhile the learning years of this precocious elocutionist were also a time of teaching. At seventeen or eighteen he enrolled as a student teacher at Weston House, a boys' school near Edinburgh, where he taught music and elocution in exchange for instruction in other subjects. While there he carried out a series of experiments to identify how the position of the mouth and tongue determine the resonances of vowel sounds, and these led to his first contact, fleeting but fateful, with the association of acoustics and electricity. His father showed Graham's work to a learned scientist in London, who told Graham about the work of the contemporary German scientist Hermann von Helmholtz. Helmholtz had published a book called *On the Sensations of Tone*, in which he described how he had produced vowel sounds with electrically driven tuning forks. Young Bell got a copy of the book and tried to read it. But it was in German and concerned electricity, and Bell knew little of either; he emerged with the notion that Helmholtz had telegraphed the vowel sounds over a wire. The notion was entirely mistaken, but the mistake was an accident of destiny. It turned Bell's thoughts for the first time to electric telephony.[4]

After a year of teaching and studying at Somersetshire College, in Bath, Bell, at twenty-one, settled in London, where he divided his time between serving as his father's partner in the teaching of Visible Speech and studying the anatomy of the vocal apparatus at University College, London. He seemed well launched on a career in which he could scarcely fail, and in which he showed every indication of being headed for a brilliant success. But personal events contrived to change abruptly his direction, and perhaps that of the life of his time. In 1867, while Graham was living at Bath, his younger brother, Edward, had died of tuberculosis; now, in May 1870, his older brother, Melly, succumbed to the same disease, and the event affected him so deeply that he wrote to his father, "The dream you know I have cherished for so long has perished with poor Melly. It is gone for *ever*." Exactly what the dream may have been is not clear; what is clear is that the year 1870 was a low point in Graham Bell's life. Besides suffering from the recurrent headaches that would plague him through most of his life, he was undergoing the pain of a hopeless love for Marie Eccleston, a woman several years older than he, whose rejection of him he would later describe as "the one sore subject of my life." In all these circumstances, it does not seem surprising that Graham Bell raised no objection when, the same summer, Melville Bell—disillusioned by waning attendance at his lectures, disheartened by the loss of two of his sons, and obsessed with the idea that his one remaining son would also fall victim to tuberculosis—decided to move with his wife, his son Alexander Graham, and his son Melly's widow to the physically and spiritually more bracing air of Canada.[5]

The place where the Bells settled in August 1870 was Brantford, a small industrial town some thirty miles north of the shore of Lake Erie and sixty miles west of Niagara Falls. Whatever had ailed Graham in London, ills of the body or of the soul, he recovered quickly. When Melville Bell, whose fame as a teacher of the deaf had preceded him to the New World, was invited to teach Visible Speech to the instructors of a school for the deaf in Boston, he sent his regenerated son as a substitute. Through

1871 and most of 1872, Alexander Graham Bell demonstrated and taught his father's system at schools for the deaf in Boston, Northampton, Massachusetts, and Hartford, Connecticut. He quickly made a considerable name for himself. Deafness, in those days before antibiotics and modern surgical techniques, was a far larger social problem than it is in the second half of the twentieth century, and the Bell method—with its commitment to teaching the deaf to talk normally and thus join human society, rather than to use sign language and therefore live in a world of their own—represented a revolutionary advance in America. By October 1872, Bell was ready to open up his own school of "Vocal Physiology and Mechanics of Speech" in Boston, and the following year he was made a professor of vocal physiology at Boston University. But meanwhile a related interest, long present but dormant, was gaining place in his life. He had not forgotten Helmholtz; he had the itch to create; and unquestionably, he was ambitious to make a fortune more impressive than was available to a teacher of the deaf. By the autumn of 1872, he was producing the first crude drawings and experiments aimed at the invention of a "harmonic telegraph" that would distinguish between musical notes and thus make possible the transmission of several messages simultaneously on a single wire. Such an invention would, of course, have immediate commercial application in telegraphy; and Bell, even at this early stage, showed his acute awareness of that fact by locking up his work in his desk after each session to keep it away from prying eyes.

And he was beginning to meet people who could give him the financial backing necessary to continuing his enterprise. One of his first private pupils was George Sanders, the five-year-old son, born deaf, of Thomas Sanders, a prominent leather merchant from Salem, north of Boston. Under Bell's tutelage the boy showed progress in learning to talk, and the father was grateful—so grateful that in October 1873, Bell went to live in the Sanders home in Salem and remained there for over two years. Another substantial citizen whom Bell met in the course of his work was Gardiner Greene Hubbard, a prominent lawyer and public-spirited citizen of Boston, who was president of the Clarke School for the Deaf in Northampton, where Bell taught for a time—and whose daughter, Mabel, had been struck deaf by scarlet fever at the age of four. Hubbard and Bell became friends, and the deaf Mabel, now in her middle teens, his informal pupil. ("I did not like him," Mabel later recalled of their first meeting. "He was tall and dark, with jet black hair and eyes, but dressed badly and carelessly in an old-fashioned suit of black broadcloth, making his hair look shiny, and altogether, to one accustomed to the dainty neatness of Harvard students, he seemed hardly a gentleman."[6])

Through the winter and spring of 1873–74, Bell pressed on with his harmonic telegraph experiments, and gradually some force—his training and tradition, or the sudden gleam of a new and far more alluring objective—pressed the direction of the experiments away from musical sounds and toward human speech and hearing. Tuned steel reeds were used in his equipment; his instinctive way of tuning them was by pressing them against his own ear while the transmitting instrument was in operation. That summer, while visiting his parents at Brantford, he worked—at the suggestion of his friend Dr. Clarence J. Blake of Boston—on a "phonautograph," a somewhat macabre device to translate sounds into visible markings with equipment using the actual ear of a dead man. When words were spoken, the ear's membrane vibrated and moved a lever that made a wave pattern on a piece of smoked glass. Theoretically, the phonautograph would be helpful in teaching the deaf. But the real achievement of the experiment was the vistas that it opened up. It set Bell to marveling over the way the tiny membrane of the ear could move relatively heavy bones. By analogy, he speculated, could not a single such membrane, rather than a system of tuned reeds, cause an electric current to vary in intensity in precise, mathematical conformity with the air waves made by sound—including the sound of speech? Thus in Brantford in July 1874, Bell came upon the principle of the telephone.[7]

Meanwhile Hubbard and Sanders, men of substance and fathers of deaf children, had become interested in the commercial possibilities of Bell's telegraphy experiments. In October 1874, Hubbard, after carefully searching the Patent Office in Washington for any possible anticipation of the harmonic telegraph idea, offered Bell funds for further experiments in exchange for a share of patent rights. Sanders, too, was eager to be a backer. On February 27, 1875, Bell, Hubbard, and Sanders formally signed a Bell Patent Association agreement under which Hubbard and Sanders were to furnish the money and Bell the experimental work, all three to share equally in any patents obtained. Bell thus had financial backing and the services of a skilled patent lawyer familiar with telegraphy; the only catch was that his backers wanted him to invent a harmonic telegraph rather than a telephone, the very idea of which his partners viewed with suspicion bordering on hostility.

3

Bell—still wavering between the two objectives—was now in the grip of the inventing frenzy. It was a frenzy that was in the air in 1875, when the century of invention was at zenith. Robert Fulton's first commercially successful steamboat dated from 1807, Michael Faraday's dynamo from 1831, Samuel F. B. Morse's telegraph from 1835, the steam-driven electric generator from 1858; in 1875 Thomas A. Edison's phonograph was three years ahead, his incandescent lamp four years, the skyscraper about a decade, the automobile and the airplane a generation or less. Behind them all was a persuasive idea; as Alfred North Whitehead would write, "The greatest invention of the nineteenth century was the method of invention." Moreover, the economic rewards of invention under the U.S. patent system were great and well advertised; Bell and others like him knew well enough that the inventor and original backers of the telegraph had become millionaires, and his passion for secrecy about his experiments, along with his early and intimate association with the Patent Office through Hubbard, suggest how well he realized he might be onto something commercially big. And he was urged on by both his philosophical background and the current social climate in America. The Scottish Calvinism of the nineteenth century made a primary virtue of material success achieved through hard work, and as an example Bell had his countryman Andrew Carnegie, twelve years his senior, who had come to the United States from Scotland in 1848 and by 1875 was already a millionaire in the process of consolidating the largest steel company in the world. As to the social climate, 1875 was the heyday in America of laissez-faire venture capitalism, when men had a kind of savage fury for fame and fortune that the more jaded twentieth century can scarcely conceive of. Bell, teaching his deaf classes by day and bending over his experiments at night, was desperately poor; and he was soon to have the most urgent of all reasons for wanting money quickly— that of being in love.

Beginning in January 1875, Bell did his experimenting at the electrical shop of Charles Williams, Jr., at 109 Court Street, Boston. There he had as his assistant a remarkable young machinist named Thomas A. Watson. The son of a stable foreman in Salem, Watson (no relation to Thomas J. Watson of IBM) had for a time been interested in table tipping and "spirit sessions," and at another time had imagined that he saw a halo around his own head; this mystical strain was balanced by a marked competence in mechanical matters, and Watson also had what was to be a crucial asset in his work with Bell, an unusually sensitive ear. On their first meeting, Watson was deeply impressed by Bell, who, interestingly enough, seemed to him the exact opposite of what he first appeared to be to Mabel Hubbard. Watson wrote later, "He was the first educated man I had ever known intimately. . . . He was a master of expressive speech. . . . His clear, crisp articulation delighted me and made other men's speech seem uncouth . . . and his table manners were most interesting. Up to that time, the knife had been the principal implement for eating in my family. . . . I was much embarrassed the first time I had supper with Bell at his house, in trying to imitate his exclusive use of a fork in the conveyance of food."[8]

The polished Bell and the rough-hewn Watson bent to their experiments. Bell was always saying optimistically, "Watson, we are on the verge of a great discovery," and when an experiment was even partially successful, the two would characteristically celebrate by doing a little victory dance. But as the spring of 1875 passed, the harmonic telegraph still did not work, and Bell's courage began to flag. He knew by this time that he was involved in a race with Elisha Gray of Chicago, co-founder of the Western Electric Company, an expert electrician who was also at work on a harmonic telegraph. As early as November 1874, Bell had written to Hubbard and Sanders, "It is a neck and neck race between Mr. Gray and myself who shall complete an apparatus first." Bell began to feel he was losing the race. In February 1875, he went to Washington to demonstrate his apparatus to William Orton, president of the powerful Western Union Telegraph Company;

his reception there was encouraging, but at a subsequent meeting with Orton in New York, Bell got a polite brushoff. On March 1, 1875, Bell was granted an audience in Washington by Joseph Henry, the world-famous scientist and inventor of the electromagnetic telegraph, then approaching eighty, who was secretary of the Smithsonian Institution. Henry's interest focused on Bell's half-developed notions on the electrical transmission of speech. They constituted, Henry said, "the germ of a great invention"; he urged Bell to drop all else and press on with the telephone. When Bell protested that he feared he lacked the necessary electrical knowledge, the old man snapped, "Get it!"[9]

The meeting with Henry served crucially to turn Bell's thoughts away from the race with Gray on the harmonic telegraph, and toward the telephone. Later that month—March 1875 —he decided to cancel all his private classes except those with George Sanders, his partner's son. That meant less income, and by early June he was borrowing small sums from his assistant, Watson. Early in May, he wrote Hubbard—who was still urging him to concentrate on improvements in telegraphy, and scoffing at the idea of the telephone—"I have read somewhere that the resistance of a wire . . . is affected by the *tension of the wire.* If this is so, a *continuous current of electricity* passed through a vibrating wire should meet with a varying resistance. . . . The *timbre* of a sound could be transmitted." For all the unscientific casualness of "I have read somewhere," Bell would later insist that this letter established his priority in conceiving the final concept in the theoretical evolution of the modern telephone, variable resistance.

A great breakthrough was inexorably near; it came on June 2, 1875—and came, as so many scientific breakthroughs do, as the by-product of an accident. Bell and Watson were testing the harmonic telegraph apparatus between two rooms on the top floor of 109 Court Street, Watson operating the transmitting equipment in one room and Bell the receiving in another. As usual, the thing would not work right; when Watson pressed the keys that set his transmitting reeds to vibrating at their carefully tuned pitches, one of the corresponding receiving reeds stubbornly did not respond. At Bell's instruction, Watson began plucking the recalcitrant transmitting reed with his fingers. Suddenly he heard a shout from the other room, and then Bell burst in on him, demanding excitedly, "What did you do then? Don't change anything!"

Faintly, but distinctly, Bell had heard the sound of the reed, plucked at a moment when a too-tightly-adjusted contact screw had accidentally made the supposedly intermittent transmitter current into a steady current—and one modulated into a sound carrier by the air waves caused by Watson's plucking.

Bell and Watson were now in hot pursuit of the telephone. After repetitions and variations of the experiment, Bell sketched the first electric speaking telephone, gave Watson the sketch, and urged him to build it for testing the very next day. It was to consist of a wooden frame on which was mounted a harmonic receiver with one end of its steel-reed armature touching a tightly stretched membrane of parchment. That night from Salem, Bell wrote excitedly to Hubbard, "I have accidentally made a discovery of the very greatest importance. . . ." Next morning Watson set to work constructing the new device, which, because of the shape of the wooden frame, is known in telephone history as the "gallows" telephone. He had it finished and ready for testing by the same evening. Watson shouted into the telephone, and Bell heard nothing. They changed places, thus getting the advantage of Bell's precise and sonorous speech and Watson's razor-sharp hearing; this time, as Watson wrote later, "I could unmistakably hear the tones of his voice and almost catch a word now and then." But to "almost catch a word" was not telephony; it was merely a repetition of what Reis had achieved. The first telephone was a disheartening and anticlimactic failure.[10]

Some modern historians of technology, like the Smithsonian's Bernard S. Finn, believe that Bell's 1875 gallows transmitter would have worked with another receiver, and that the failure was principally due to some casual factor like background noise. But a failure it was. "I am like a man in a fog who is sure of his latitude and longitude," Bell wrote his parents late in June. "I know that I am close to the land for which I am bound and when the fog lifts I shall see it right before me." Hubbard was not encouraging; on July 2 he wrote Bell, "I am very much afraid that Mr. Gray has anticipated you in your membrane attachment." Meanwhile Bell's relations with the Hubbards had become complicated by his relations with Hubbard's charming deaf daughter, Mabel, now approaching eighteen and an accomplished lip-reader able to speak normally. During June he wrote Mrs. Hubbard, "I have discovered that my interest in my dear pupil . . . has ripened

into a far deeper feeling. . . . I have learned to love her." Mrs.
Hubbard asked him to hide his feelings for a year in consideration
of Mabel's age. But even in 1875 such austere sentences of silence
were seldom served. In July—ill again and despairing, as he had
been during the last months in London—he burst out in a letter to
Mabel, "I have loved you with a passionate attachment that you
cannot understand, and that is to myself new and uncomprehen-
sible." For a time thereafter, the Victorian maiden shrank from a
face-to-face encounter.[11]

To judge from dates and events, Bell's invention of the telephone was inextricably bound up with his love for Mabel Hubbard,
which welled up just at the time of the big technical breakthrough and would come to fruition just two days after the formation of the Bell Telephone Company. Surely it is not too romantic
to call her both the inspiration and the prize for the invention;
apart from a crucial generic figure—the operator—she is the only
woman to loom large in the history of telephony. But now, in the
second half of 1875, comes a trough, a slowing of pace—or perhaps, the eye of a hurricane of human events. Bell was acutely
poor and in such depressed health and spirits that he could
scarcely carry on either classes or experiments. " 'Blood ill-tem-
pered vexeth you,' " his father wrote him, and in September he
went home to Brantford; there he revived and began writing telephone patent specifications, anticipating the final triumph. Back
in Salem and Boston later that fall, and taking a renewed interest
in lecturing on Visible Speech, he found himself locked in a classic
conflict with his partner, the father of his beloved. "I have been
sorry to see how little interest you seem to take in telegraph matters," Gardiner Hubbard wrote him testily. "Your whole course
since you returned has been a very great disappointment to me,
and a sore trial." At Thanksgiving time, Hubbard—an impatient,
commanding man used to the exercise of power—went too far, like
a father in Italian opera: he tried to force Bell back to telegraphy
with promises and threats involving Mabel. Bell predictably ex-
ploded, and a bitter quarrel ensued, which ended with Bell apolo-
gizing and pleading, "Please bear with me a little longer." But a
day later—love and invention trembling in unison like tuned reeds
in Bell's mind—he and Mabel defiantly became engaged.

Bell moved his residence in January 1876 from the Sanders
house in Salem to two rooms in the attic of a boardinghouse at

5 Exeter Place, Boston, and one of the rooms became his principal workshop; there, throughout January, he worked feverishly on his patent specifications, meanwhile trying to perfect the gallows-type electromagnetic telephone transmitter that had failed so discouragingly the previous June. Early in February the patent application was finished, and on the morning of February 14, 1876, Hubbard on Bell's behalf had it filed at the Patent Office in Washington. A few hours later the same day—the precise times are not recorded, but the order of events is unquestioned—Elisha Gray came to the same Patent Office and filed a "caveat," or warning to other inventors, for a speaking telephone. On those lucky few hours' priority rests Bell's legal claim to the telephone patent—and on them, ultimately, rests the foundation of the Bell System.[12]

This is not the place for a full discussion of U.S. Patent No. 174,465, which was allowed on March 3, 1876 and issued on March 7; which would be the subject of thousands of pages of testimony in hundreds of suits to annul it, all unsuccessful; and which would be called, with few challengers, the most valuable patent ever issued. Only a few facts and speculations about it need be included here. To begin with, it was titled "Improvements in Telegraphy," it did not so much as mention the word "telephone," and it did not promise the electrical transmission of speech—only of "vocal or other sounds," which might mean no more than musical sounds. It described two general methods of transmission: one by induction caused by placing a membrane near an electromagnet, the so-called magneto-induction principle used in Bell's unsuccessful 1875 transmitter, a method to flourish briefly and then vanish from the annals of telephony; the other by causing speech to bring about varying resistance in a circuit— the method, vastly superior because it makes possible amplification, that became and remains the basis of all telephone transmission. The crucial point, and the bone of contention in later litigation, was the manner of Bell's inclusion of the crucial variable-resistance principle in his patent application.

The rough draft of Bell's application shows the single paragraph on the variable-resistance principle written into the margin of a page, apparently as an afterthought. Bell later maintained, alluding to his letter to Hubbard of May 1875, that he had known of the principle for a long time, and moreover, in December 1875 or January 1876 he had given George Brown, a Canadian friend of his who was planning to apply on his behalf for a British patent, a crude sketch of a variable-resistance transmitter. But the fact is that prior to his patent application Bell had not made any experiments with variable-resistance transmission. Why not—and why was the clause in his application a marginal addition? And how did it come about that Gray's caveat described a variable-resistance transmitter using acidulated water—the very method that Bell himself would begin using a month later? In a subsequent patent challenge, the People's and Overland Telephone Companies would maintain that Bell's attorneys had been allowed to see Gray's caveat and that as a result, Bell had altered his application to include variable resistance *after* his original filing. This would have been grossly illegal, and the court, after weighing all the evidence, rejected the allegation.

Bell's own explanation was that "almost at the last moment . . . I discovered that I had neglected to include . . . variable resistance," and that he immediately wrote it in; then, in the days immediately after his filing, he went to the Patent Office, asked to see Gray's caveat, and was properly refused, but was told in general terms that it involved variable resistance caused by a wire in liquid.[13]

Thus, a century later, certain mysteries remain about Patent No. 174,465. The coincidence of filings, Bell's last-minute remembering of variable resistance, the marginal addition of the key passage—circumstantial evidence against Bell, or nothing but red herrings? But this should be clear: underneath the legal intricacies and the suspicions of foul play, it appears that by any rational standard Bell actually invented the telephone; Gray had not transmitted speech at the time of the filings and would not do so for many months afterward. Indeed, the final irony of the drama is that as of February 14, 1876, no one had transmitted a single intelligible human word. But it would not be long before someone did.

Back in Boston, Bell and Watson, with the patent in hand, went furiously to work to make it come true—Bell experimenting in his Exeter Place attic, Watson making equipment to Bell's specifications at the Williams shop on Court Street. From February 18 to 24, Bell struggled with the harmonic telegraph, which was still what Hubbard wanted him to concentrate on. On March 8, back from his trip to Washington, he was trying to transmit

the sound of a tuning fork by magneto-induction when he suddenly, and without explanation, took a new tack. He replaced the
electromagnet with a dish of water containing sulfuric acid,
thereby introducing the variable-resistance principle. The tuning
fork was plucked, and Bell, his ear pressed to his now-familiar
reed receiver, reported in his notes, "A faint sound audible." He
added more acid, and the sound became louder. He then directed
Watson to build a new transmitter in which a wire, attached to a
diaphragm, touched acidulated water in a metal cup; one would
speak downward into the diaphragm, whose vibration would
cause the wire's depth of immersion into the water to vary and
thus presumably set up varying resistance in the battery-powered
circuit. Working with his customary dispatch, Watson had the
new transmitter ready on March 10, and that historic evening, he
brought it to 5 Exeter Place for testing. The transmitter was set
up in Bell's workroom, its cup filled with acid water and the
booming-voiced Bell, perhaps now trembling with anticipation,
bending over its diaphragm. Watson went into Bell's bedroom
and stood by the bureau with his sensitive ear pressed to the
receiving telephone. Watson wrote later, "Almost at once I was
astonished to hear Bell's voice . . . distinctly saying, 'Mr. Watson, come here, I want you!' . . . I rushed down the hall into
his room and found he had upset the acid of a battery over his
clothes. He forgot the accident in his joy over the success of the
new transmitter." Bell's laboratory notes, written two days later,
read in part, "I shouted into M [the mouthpiece] the following
sentence: 'Mr. Watson—come here—I want to see you.' To my
delight he came and declared that he had heard and understood
what I said."[14] It will be noted that in Bell's version the wording
of the famous first telephone utterance is slightly different, and
that he does not mention the acid accident. No matter; the telephone was born at last.

## 4

But Bell's and the telephone's troubles were not over; in several
senses they were only beginning. News of the first transmission
of intelligible speech failed to impress the one man Bell most
needed to impress—Gardiner Hubbard. On March 13, 1876, Hub-

bard and a friend climbed the stairs of 5 Exeter Place to listen for themselves. Something went wrong with the equipment, and when Bell spoke into the transmitter, Hubbard could at first hear nothing, then only sounds too indistinct to understand. In April Hubbard wrote Bell, "If you could make one good invention in the telegraph, you would secure an annual income . . . and then you could settle that on your wife and teach Visible Speech and experiment in telegraphy with an easy and undisturbed conscience." In May Hubbard provided a sort of second-act-curtain climax when he persuaded Mabel to tell Bell that she would not marry him until he completed the *telegraph* device.

Thus sorely tried by philistine obtuseness in the moment when he should have been crowned with bay leaves, the inventor of the telephone—a hotheaded man of twenty-nine—kept his head like a hero. Coolly and simultaneously, he continued his experiments with both telegraphy and telephony. He began varying the conditions of the successful March 10 experiment, to improve the device's reliability. Instead of water and acid in the little metal cup, he tried plain water (no sound), cod liver oil (no sound), salt water (loud sound), mercury (no sound because complete electrical contact), soapy water (no sound), and liquor (loud sound). And now comes a new irony: on or about April 1, he apparently concluded that the variable-resistance transmitter could not be made reliable, and abandoned it to return to the magneto-induction transmitter that he had worked on so long in vain. On that date, using a transmitter in which a piece of steel spring was glued to the transmitter membrane, Bell achieved the first successful transmission of words by magneto-induction. Now he had an instrument that, in a limited way, was practical, and was to be, for a brief moment, in commercial use. Its advantage, apart from its reliability, was that with the magneto system the same piece of equipment could be used as both transmitter and receiver; its disadvantage was that the signal was maddeningly weak and shouting tended to be necessary to achieve audibility. The irony is that Bell, in achieving a degree of practicality, had moved from the potentially superior kind of transmitter to the inferior kind.[15]

Now came a burst of publicity, perfectly timed and at least half fortuitous, that put the existence of the telephone in the public consciousness in the United States and, shortly thereafter, in Europe. During May Bell gave two telephone lectures and one demonstration before scientific groups in Boston; although both were well received, word of them scarcely reached beyond local and scientific circles. It was—it just happened to be—the centennial year of the United States, and the event was celebrated that summer by a huge Centennial Exposition in Philadelphia, beginning in mid-May. The exposition included scientific exhibitions, and Hubbard—impressed now by Bell's telephone work, but still urging him to concentrate on multiple telegraphy—pressed Bell to go. But Bell, with examination papers at Boston University to correct and a speech course to complete, protested that he had "not the remotest intention of leaving Boston." It was Mabel Hubbard who, with tears and pleadings, persuaded him at the last minute to go, taking with him both magneto and variable-resistance telephone equipment.

On Sunday, June 25—a stifling midsummer day in Philadelphia and, by the Little Big Horn River more than two thousand miles to the west, the day of the famous death of General George Armstrong Custer and his men—Bell demonstrated his telephone to a panel of learned judges at the Centennial Exposition, using a magneto transmitter like the one tested on April 1. It not only worked, but worked under the most favorable of circumstances. Dom Pedro II, the spirited, convivial, English-speaking emperor of Brazil, who was touring the United States, attracting royalty-loving American crowds wherever he went, happened to be at the exposition that day, and by further chance he happened to have met and taken a liking to Bell at the Boston School for the Deaf several weeks earlier. The perspiring judges were apparently on the way to ignoring Bell's exhibit when Dom Pedro attracted their attention to it by coming up and greeting Bell as an old friend. After first explaining the principles of his still-impractical harmonic telegraph, Bell began declaiming Hamlet's "To be, or not to be" soliloquy into his telephone. Dom Pedro, his ear pressed to the receiver at the far end of a gallery, started from his chair and cried out, "I hear, I hear!" (In another version, he exclaimed in Portuguese, "My God! It talks!") The most distinguished member of the panel of judges—the British physicist Sir William Thomson, later Lord Kelvin—took his turn at the receiver, and later wrote in his formal report, "I need hardly say I was astonished and delighted. . . . This, perhaps the greatest marvel hitherto achieved by the electric telegraph, has been obtained by appliances of quite a homespun and rudimentary character." "I have never quite forgiven Sir William for that last sentence," commented Watson, maker of the appliances.[16]

The telephone was launched; it was almost ready for commercial use. The second half of 1876 was devoted to its first tests under operating conditions, and to the establishment of a business organization. On August 10 Bell, at Paris, Ontario, succeeded in hearing a few words spoken by his father and uncle at Brantford, several miles away. It was a one-way call, using borrowed telegraph wires; nevertheless, it was the world's first telephone call over outdoor wires. Early in September Watson became the forefather of Bell Laboratories, agreeing to give up his job at Williams' shop and devote himself to development of telephony and telegraphy in exchange for a one-tenth interest in any and all Bell patents. On October 9, using magneto telephones designed to both transmit and receive, Bell and Watson carried out the first two-way conversation over outdoor wires between Boston and Cambridge, on opposite sides of the Charles River. "Hoy! hoy! Are you there?" Bell shouted. Watson hoyed back, and Bell said testily, "Where have you been all this time?"—just like someone whose call has not been returned. On December 3, over the telegraph wires of the Eastern Railroad, Bell and Watson tried to converse between Boston and North Conway, New Hampshire, 143 miles apart. "We could hear each other over the wire," Watson reported, "but the telegraph line was in such bad shape with its high resistance and rusty joints that the talking was unsatisfactory to both of us." The demonstration that seems most to have astonished the people of Boston occurred in January 1877, when a Japanese student of Bell's and two of his countrymen who were Harvard students tried Bell's equipment at Exeter Place and found that it worked. Yankee Boston was thereby convinced that the telephone was no trick—it could speak Japanese.

However, this procession of encouraging tests was paralleled by a period of despondency about the telephone's commercial promise, and by a resulting near-disaster for the Bell commercial interests. In November Watson felt that technical development had come to a dead end; the telephone "would talk moderately well over a short line, but the apparatus was delicate and complicated and it didn't talk distinctly enough for practical use." In despair, he consulted a spirit medium "to see if there was any help to be got from that source"; apparently there was none. Meanwhile Hubbard's old skepticism about telephony was increased when he caught the new contagion of pessimism; and sometime during the fall or winter of 1876–77—the date is unrecorded and the exact facts unknown—he seems to have offered all rights in the telephone to President Orton of Western Union for one hundred thousand dollars. Orton flatly rejected the offer, for reasons that are unrecorded. He had had previous conflicts with Hubbard over matters of telegraphy, and frankly distrusted and disliked the man. Was it for this reason that this leading businessman turned down the core and basis of the future greatest corporation on earth? Of such frail human stuff, at any rate, have been made many other pivotal business decisions, good and bad.[17]

With the issuance to Bell in January 1877 of his second basic patent—No. 186,787, covering the combined receiver-transmitter instrument and various of its mechanical features—the telephone was protected by a patent fortress that would prove to be impregnable to hundreds of urgent assaults. On February 12 of that year, the telephone was first used in news reporting, when word of a lecture by Bell in Salem was telephoned to Watson and a Boston *Globe* reporter at 5 Exeter Place; on April 3, Watson and Bell managed to talk, with difficulty, between Boston and New York over telegraph wires; on April 4, the first permanent outdoor telephone wire was strung between the Williams shop at 109 Court Street and Williams' home in Somerville, three miles away; on May 1, the first telephones were rented for business use—a private line between the Boston office of two young bankers and the home of one of them in Somerville; and later that month, the first experimental central exchange was opened in Boston by E. T. Holmes, as an adjunct to his electric burglar-alarm system. By this time Bell and Watson had for the most part abandoned the laboratory to devote themselves to publicizing the telephone through public lecture-demonstrations in Boston and other northeastern cities. They seem to have taken to this new show-business aspect of their work like ducks to water. Bell would sit on the stage of the lecture hall with a telephone beside him, and there would be three or four other receiving instruments placed strategically around the hall. Watson, along with various musicians, would be at a remote point five to twenty-five miles away, with a telephone connected to the lecture hall by a hired telegraph wire. A cornet player or a brass band would broadcast lustily over the wire, to the audience's astonishment; but the star of the show was usually Watson—in whom, as he put it, "two years of strenuous shouting into mouthpieces of various sizes and shapes had developed a voice with the carrying capacity of a steam calliope." "How do you do? Good evening! What do you think of the telephone?" Watson would bellow to Bell and the audience. Then he would sing songs, including "Hold the Fort," "Yankee Doodle," "Oh! 'Twas My Last Cigar," "Auld Lang Syne," and everybody's favorite, "Do not Trust Him, Gentle Lady." According to Watson, "This repertoire always brought down the house." Nevertheless, the almost superstitious public suspicion of telephony was not dispelled, as contemporary press reaction to the lectures shows. The Providence *Press* said, "It is indeed difficult, hearing the sounds out of the mysterious box, to wholly resist the notion that the powers of darkness are somehow in league with it." The Boston *Advertiser* commented that "the weirdness and novelty were something never before felt in Boston," and even in New York, which was accustomed to weirdness, the *Herald* found the telephone "almost supernatural."

The lecture-demonstrations that probably did the cause of telephony the most good were three held in Boston early in May, at the signed invitation of a galaxy of Boston-area worthies including Charles W. Eliot, president of Harvard; Benjamin Peirce, Joseph Lovering, E. N. Horsford, Wolcott Gibbs, and Edward Pickering, Harvard professors eminent in the natural sciences; the governor of Massachusetts; the mayor of Boston; the celebrated author and physician Oliver Wendell Holmes; the prominent diplomat and Brahmin Charles Francis Adams; and the poet Henry Wadsworth Longfellow.[18] At least in Boston, as this list amply attests, the telephone had passed out of the realm of suspected witchcraft and become something of intense interest to the innermost circle of the Establishment.

Not all the lectures were successful; at one of them, in Lawrence, Massachusetts, on May 28, the equipment somehow failed and not a sound could be heard, making the event a total fiasco; and the strain of them gave Bell headaches and a nervous rash. But the successful ones had their effect on Hubbard, and by summer 1877 he was ready to accept both the telephone as the basis for a business and its inventor as a son-in-law. Somewhere along the way Hubbard had made what would prove to be one of the key decisions in telephony's corporate history—the decision to rent telephone service rather than to sell telephones, apparently based on a previous successful experience of Hubbard's in leasing shoemaking machines. On July 9, 1877, the Bell Telephone Company, superseding the Bell-Hubbard-Sanders patent partnership, was formed as a voluntary, unincorporated association with Hubbard as trustee; on August 1, the first 5,000 shares of Bell stock were issued, as follows: Thomas Sanders and Mabel Hubbard, 1,497 shares each; Gardiner Hubbard, 1,387 shares; Thomas A. Watson, 499 shares; Gertrude McC. Hubbard, 100 shares; Charles Eustis Hubbard (Gardiner's brother), 10 shares; and Alexander Graham Bell—who, with characteristic impulsiveness, had turned over all but a token holding to Mabel—10 shares. Bell was to be the company's "electrician" at a salary of $3,000 a year, and Watson, besides being "superintendent" in charge of research and manufacturing, was for a brief time its bookkeeper. At last—to complete the almost implausibly story-book plot of the beginnings of AT&T and of American telephony—on July 11, 1877, Bell and Mabel Hubbard were married with the bride's parents' blessing in their home on Brattle Street, Cambridge. At the wedding, Tom Watson wore white gloves for the first time in his life. Early in August, after a stay in Brantford with Bell's parents, the couple sailed for England to begin what would be a forty-five-year marriage and, by all accounts, an unusually happy one.[19]

## 5

Within five years after the invention of the telephone, the four men most closely associated with that event—Bell, Watson, Hubbard, and Sanders—would be effectively out of both technical work in telephony and the administration of the business it created. Let them not pass from this account without due summary of their lives and due tribute to their accomplishments.

In England in 1877, Bell demonstrated the telephone for Queen Victoria (who found it "most extraordinary"), and tried, with only partial success, to get British patents. Back in Boston in November, he nominally took up his duties as the Bell Telephone Company's electrician. But he was an inventor, not a corporate officer; he had a sense of a mission accomplished. Already his mind was straying to other matters. He wrote Hubbard, in deep chagrin about Edison's new phonograph, "It is a most astonishing thing to me that I could possibly have let this invention slip through my fingers." Still, he held his job and sat on the Bell Telephone board until 1879, when Gardiner Hubbard, accused, by the Boston financiers who were coming to hold the purse strings, of "fiscal irresponsibility," was replaced as president by William H. Forbes; then Bell left the board at his own request. The following year, after differences with Forbes on various matters, he resigned from the company. Between 1879 and 1883, he and Mabel sold enough of their shares, wildly rising in the markets, to put them modestly in the millionaire class. But only modestly. Because of the voracious demands of the expanding business for new capital, and the fact that all the founders sold off most of their original shares too soon, no mighty self-perpetuating fortunes came out of telephony in America; no counterpart to a Ford, Rockefeller, or Duke now survives as a "telephone heir." Sanders lost most of his money in the 1890s; Hubbard died in 1897, well-to-do but not extremely rich; Watson used his stake from the telephone to support a vivid and varied later life; and Bell used his to live as he pleased and do what he liked.

He spent his winters mostly in Washington, his summers on Cape Breton Island, Nova Scotia; he and Mabel had two daughters; and—keeping no telephone in his study because he resented interruptions—he worked on a wide variety of inventions, none destined to rival the telephone in importance. He invented what he called a Photophone, which could actually transmit sound for a short distance over a beam of light, and thus anticipated current work in fiber optics—but it had no practical application in its time. He conceived an early artificial-respiration device, an apparatus (before x-ray) to locate metal objects within the human body, and a hydrofoil boat that could go seventy miles per hour. With the aviation pioneer Samuel P. Langley, he conducted extensive experiments with man-lifting kites. Meanwhile he pursued what he always regarded as his lifework, teaching the deaf to speak; he founded the American Association to

Promote the Teaching of Speech to the Deaf, and endowed it with three hundred thousand dollars. Meanwhile, too, he became a living public monument—portly and impressive, with a white Santa Claus beard but without Santa Claus geniality; his eyes remained analytical and shrewd, his brow furrowed and his disposition darkened by recurring headaches. In their old age, the Bells became pioneer movie buffs, perhaps in part because the early silent films accommodated the deafness of Mrs. Bell. Bell died of diabetes in August 1922, full of years and honors; Mabel Bell's death followed five months later.[20]

Watson spent four years with the fledgling company and made several significant technical contributions, including a crank-activated magneto ringer that gave the telephone its ring; previously, call signaling had been clumsily and inefficiently accomplished by rapping the transmitter with any sort of small hammer. In 1881—by which time he was all of twenty-five years old—this remarkable man's inherent restlessness overtook him, and he resigned from the Bell company to seek "a larger life and new experiences." He found both. He married a Cohasset girl and bought a farm in East Braintree, Massachusetts; he read and speculated about reincarnation; he studied speech and geology; he started an adult-education center, a kindergarten, and a political association based on the utopian socialist ideas of Edward Bellamy. In 1897 he embarked on a naval shipbuilding venture, the Fore River Engine Company, and lost a bundle. Undaunted, he plunged in gold mining and lost some more. In 1910—middle-aged in body but not in spirit—he studied acting in London, and then spent a season as a touring Shakespeare player, appearing in rural British theaters and suffering insect bites in village boardinghouses. In 1914, after he had delivered a speech in Chicago on the beginnings of telephony, Bell telephoned him to congratulate him. "Hoy, hoy, Watson, are you there?" the old man asked. Honors were piled on him in his later years, but they did not comfort him. On the night of Bell's death he wrote in his diary, "I have often wondered whether Bell or I would be the last surviving member of the four original associates. The fates have assigned to me that pathetic honor, but I feel a strange loneliness." He died in 1934, at the age of eighty, with a tidy fortune of about half a million dollars.

Mabel Hubbard, achieving an almost Shakespearean cadence under the stress of her feelings, wrote what might well stand as Bell's epitaph in a letter to her son-in-law soon after Bell's death: "He is big enough to stand as he is, very imperfect, lacking in things that are lovely in other men, but a good big man all the same. . . ."[21]

CHAPTER 3

# Through the Valley

The year that commercial telephone service began in the United States—1877—was a politically, socially, and economically troubled time that bears comparison with the early 1970s. The previous year had seen impeachment by the House of Representatives of the Secretary of War, William W. Belknap, on charges that he had accepted bribes while in office, and his subsequent resignation to avoid trial in the Senate. In 1877 the nation had a new president, Rutherford B. Hayes, who had apparently not been elected by the people; Samuel J. Tilden had won a popular majority of 250,000 in the previous November's election, but not an electoral majority, whereupon a specially appointed Electoral Commission—under heavy pressure from the Republicans, who had been firmly entrenched in power since the Civil War—narrowly voted to award the office to the Republican Hayes, in clear defiance of the popular will. The price of this victory had been a political deal with southern Democrats to remove federal troops from the South, thus effectively ending radical reconstruction there under black leadership, and ushering in the era of racial segregation. The country was still overwhelmingly rural, largely undeveloped, and lacking in confidence. There were railway lines from ocean to ocean, the national population was increasing by a million a year, the Brooklyn Bridge was under construction, and Colorado had just been admitted as the thirty-eighth state; but the whole West was still raw and lawless, there were as yet no electric lights, trolley cars, or skyscrapers anywhere, and there were people alive who had been born before the Declaration of Independence.

It was a lonely, far-separated, underpopulated nation, crying out for the telephone to bind its people closer together; but the economic conditions to make possible the change were far from propitious. The financial panic of 1873, brought about by general overexpansion and uncontrolled speculation in railroads, had plunged the country into a depression from which it had not yet recovered. In 1875 the Erie, greatest railway of the Northeast—sucked dry financially by the depredations of three unscrupulous financiers, Daniel Drew, Jay Gould, and James Fisk—had gone bankrupt. Capital was wary, particularly in conservative, tradition-oriented Boston, and that wariness was to play a determining role in the organization of a telephone system in the United States.

In brief, Hubbard and Sanders had no more money, or no more that they were willing to risk on telephony; Sanders had invested over one hundred thousand dollars without getting anything in return. Still, they pushed ahead with what they had. In May 1877—two months before the creation of the Bell Telephone Company—Hubbard issued the first telephone advertisement in the form of a handbill. Its promises and claims were modest to the point of defensiveness. "The proprietors of the Telephone . . . are now prepared to furnish Telephones for the transmission of articulate speech through instruments not more than twenty miles apart," it began. "Conversation can easily be carried on after slight practice and with occasional repetition of a word or sentence. On first listening to the Telephone, though the sound is perfectly audible, the articulation seems to be indistinct; but after a few trials the ear becomes accustomed to the peculiar sound. . . ." The advertisement went on to offer the use of two telephones, and a line connecting them, for twenty dollars a year for social or forty dollars a year for business purposes, with free maintenance guaranteed by the lessors.[1]

By all accounts, the modesty was well justified. By fall there were more than six hundred telephone subscribers (all of them using private lines, since the central exchange had not yet come into use); but they were not necessarily satisfied subscribers. The standard equipment consisted of a single piece made of wood—black walnut or mahogany—in size and shape very much like the receiver of the old desk telephone sets in use in the United States until the coming of the "French" phone in the 1920s. The difference was that in the case of the 1877 instrument, the same piece of equipment served as both transmitter and receiver. No battery was used, power being supplied by a permanent magnet inside the device. The user spoke into it as loudly and distinctly as possible; when finished, he removed it from his mouth and with as much dispatch as possible pressed it tightly to his ear, to listen to the "peculiar sound." The necessity for this feat of neuromuscular coordination, combined with the poor transmission capability of the magneto transmitter and the fact that static was generally equivalent to that on a modern AM radio during a thunderstorm, made for frustratingly poor communications. As an early ad pleaded, with a kind of desperate patience, "After speaking, transfer the telephone from the mouth to the ear very promptly. When replying to communication from another, do not speak too promptly . . . much trouble is caused from both parties speaking at the same time. When you are not speaking, you should be listening." But even those who scrupulously followed these instructions had their troubles; among other things, the first telephone users sometimes found themselves afflicted with a kind of stage fright that made them tongue-tied. All in all, it was tough going conducting even the simplest conversation, and as early as October 1877, the purveyors of a rival product were plausibly offering "proof" to potential customers that the Bell telephone simply didn't work.

The rival that emerged that fall, and that over the next two years was to come within an ace of putting the Bell interests out of business, was none other than Western Union Telegraph Company, the same company that less than two years earlier had turned down a chance to buy out all Bell patents for one hundred thousand dollars. In the interim, Western Union had undergone a change of heart as to the prospects of telephony, and had decided to spend millions of dollars challenging the Bell patents. Apart from straight business policy—the survival-of-the-fittest law of the jungle that largely ruled American business at the time—the challenge was based on Western Union's ownership of rights to the work of Elisha Gray and of Professor Amos E. Dolbear of Tufts College, who in September 1876 had made a sketch of what he considered to be an improvement on the Bell telephone and who since then had become convinced that he deserved a share of the Bell profits. Refused, he had entered into an agreement with Western Union—as had Gray, whose 1876 telephone caveat application had come so close to being simultaneous with Bell's first patent application. Western Union now argued that Gray's caveat, buttressed by Dolbear's work, constituted a valid challenge to the Bell patents, and proceeded to enter the telephone business in a big way. In December 1877, it set up a subsidiary, the American Speaking Telephone Company, to conduct its telephone business; further-more, since early 1876 it had had the commissioned services of a promising inventor from Menlo Park, New Jersey, Thomas Alva Edison. Edison in 1877 was thirty years old; the principal in-ventions that he had to his credit were a vote-recording telegraph system and an electric pen; and he was on the brink of the great creative outburst that would produce the incandescent lamp and the phonograph, and would make him the most celebrated in-ventor of that time or perhaps of any time.[2]

Western Union was, to say the least, a formidable rival. In the business hierarchy of its time it occupied a position somewhat analogous to that of AT&T today. Founded in 1856 to exploit the then-new invention of telegraphy, it had had a meteoric rise; a decade later it had increased its capital by 11,000 percent, all its original investors were millionaires, and one of them, Ezra Cornell, would soon achieve a kind of immortality by founding a famous university. By 1877 it had capital of $41 mil-lion; through an agreement with another monopoly, the Associ-ated Press, it had a monopoly on the transmission of news to all newspapers in the country; it was the only American corporation of truly nationwide scope. Equally to the point, it had offices, connected by its own network of wires, in every town and village of any size from coast to coast, and it had the equipment and facilities to augment those wires for telephone use. Structurally and financially, it was ideally situated to take over the telephone business by main force; and when its new inventor, Edison, promptly came through with a carbon-button variable-resistance telephone transmitter that did away with messy cups of acid water and was also far superior in performance to Bell's magneto transmitter, it was—apart from its highly dubious patent status— equally well situated technically.

Happily for the Bell interests, though, Western Union had its own corporate troubles; the financial predator Jay Gould was seeking to devour it as he had devoured the Erie a decade earlier. Beginning in the middle 1870s, Gould had launched a characteristically intricate scheme to conquer Western Union by first bringing it to its knees. While attacking Western Union's stock price in a series of bear raids in which, according to a contemporary observer, he used "every trick and art of Stock Exchange manipulation," he quietly established a rival telegraph network of his own, the Atlantic and Pacific Company. As a result, Western Union's business declined by two million dollars in one year. When the combination of stock manipulation and competition had forced Western Union's price down to rock bottom, Gould secretly bought up its stock, and at last, in 1881, emerged in control of Western Union and of the national telegraph business. During 1877–79, when Western Union was striving to take over the telephone business from Bell, Gould's Byzantine maneuver was in full cry. Western Union, at that time, was controlled by another notorious financier not noted for gentleness or sensitivity, William H. Vanderbilt. In sum, Western Union was in the thick of battle between jungle titans. If Vanderbilt had been victorious over Bell as Gould eventually was over Vanderbilt, the telephone business would have fallen into the hands of the most sinister and devious of all the beasts in the post–Civil War financial jungle, and one hesitates to think what its subsequent development might have been.[3]

That it did not happen that way was, as we shall see, due principally to the patent situation; and the patent situation in late 1877 boiled down to the question of whether Bell or Gray had invented the telephone—a question that at the time was still very much unsettled. An exchange of correspondence between the two men that had occurred early in the year threw more heat than light on the matter. An item in the Chicago *Tribune* of February 16 referred to the local man, Gray, as "the real inventor of the telephone" and spoke of "the spurious claims of Professor Bell." Five days later Gray wrote Bell asking for permission to demonstrate Bell's telephone in a public lecture, and commenting ruefully that he had been "unfortunate" in filing his caveat a few hours after Bell's patent application. Bell hotly replied by telegram that the permission was granted on condition that Gray refute the *Tribune*'s "libel." Gray answered placatingly, disclaiming the newspaper's view, whereupon Bell, mollified, wrote back thanking Gray for acting honorably. And then—the rivalry having softened into something approaching craftsmen's solidarity—Gray on March 5 wrote Bell, "I do not . . . claim even the credit for inventing [the telephone], as I do not believe a mere description of an idea that has never been *reduced to practice* . . . should be dignified with the name invention."[4] Gray would regret that burst of candor and magnanimity the rest of his life, and more bitterly as his life went on. But meanwhile Western Union with its great power took the position that Gray *had* invented the telephone; and in September 1878—after almost a year of temporizing while they hoped that Western Union could be persuaded to desist without litigation—the Bell interests formally commenced suit to protect the Bell patents against infringement by Western Union.

2

The telephone began to catch the public imagination. True enough, there were still many who regarded it with suspicion as a fake, with fear as an agent of the supernatural, or with contempt as something vulgarly new. In Chicopee, Massachusetts, a petition was presented to the village selectmen to have the newly erected telephone poles taken down. (It was rejected.) The telephone was received coldly in patrician Philadelphia, where, according to an early telephone salesman, the courtly gentlemen of Walnut Street "would carefully wipe their glasses, look up and down the street . . . and exclaim, 'Bless my soul! What's this, what's this? Telephone, do you say? We don't want it. Take it away!'" And in even more conservative and stand-offish London, on its first appearance it was dismissed as a "scientific toy," of no practical importance. Nevertheless, as early as October 1877, the London *Telegraphic Journal* could comment, "The telephone seems to have established a literature of its own"—a literature that was to expand vastly, and that will engage our attention presently. The *Journal* went on to explain what it meant by "literature": "The comic papers have employed it as a vehicle for their wit . . . Poets have eagerly welcomed it as a new image, and there have not been wanting preachers who have hailed it as a new symbol." In the New World, in 1878, among those who had telephones installed in their homes were James A. Garfield, then a congressman and later to be president, and the famous humorist Mark Twain, then living in Hartford, Connecticut, who used the installation as an occasion to exercise his wit. "If Bell had invented a muffler or gag, he would have done a real service," said Twain to the installers. "Here we have been hollering 'Shut up' to our neighbors for centuries, and now you fellows come along and seek to complicate matters."[5]

Early in 1878, the usefulness of the telephone was greatly increased by the development of a workable exchange, making possible switched calls among any number of subscribers rather than merely direct connections between two or three. In 1877 a rudimentary exchange—really an extended party line—had connected the Capitol Avenue Drug Store in Hartford with various local doctors; but the first real exchange, devised by George W. Coy of New Haven, went into service at 219 Chapel Street in that city on January 28, 1878. It connected twenty-one subscribers, who were called by name rather than number; its operators, like those of all the earliest exchanges, were boys, many of them with experience as telegraph clerks and messengers; and it was valued on the books of the New Haven District Telephone Company at $39.50. A second exchange was opened at Meriden, Connecticut, three days later, and then the floodgates were open. The first exchange in California was opened at San Francisco in February; the first in New York, at Albany in March; the first in Massachusetts, at Lowell in April; the first in Missouri, at St. Louis in May; the first in Illinois, at Chicago in June; the first in Oregon, at Portland in August; the first in Iowa, at Keokuk in September; the first in Wisconsin and Pennsylvania, Neenah and Philadelphia, respectively, in November. Most of these pioneer exchanges were Western Union rather than Bell installations particularly in places distant from Boston, where Western Union had existing telegraph facilities while the Bell company had to start from scratch. Often a Bell exchange would follow quickly on the establishment of a Western Union one, giving American towns their first taste of the curious problem of having two telephone systems, not interconnected. There were other regional problems—that of gophers chewing through the insulation on telephone wires in the Midwest, that of cowboys using insulators for target practice in the Southwest. And adding to the ubiquitous difficulty of transmission with primitive equipment, there were local language problems. In Wisconsin, there were people who spoke primarily Finnish, German, French, or Swedish. "By yimminy, she talks Swedish!" one Wisconsin lumberman after another exclaimed to the Bell pioneer Angus Hibbard; but of course she spoke Swedish no better than she spoke English, which was not very well.

The year 1878 was the year of male operators, who seem to have been an instant and memorable disaster. The lads, most of them in their late teens, who manned the first telephone exchanges were simply too impatient and high-spirited for the job, which, in view of the imperfections of the equipment and the inexperience of the subscribers, was one demanding above all patience and calm. According to the later reminiscences of some of them, they were given to lightening the tedium of their work by roughhousing, shouting constantly at each other, and swearing frequently at the customers. An early visitor to the Chicago exchange said of it, "The racket is almost deafening. Boys are rushing madly hither and thither, while others are putting in or taking out pegs from a central framework as if they were lunatics engaged in a game of fox and geese." A visitor to the Buffalo exchange called it "a perfect Bedlam." Within a few months, as Hibbard said, "a cry for help arose throughout the land." Help was at hand. In the 1870s, girls were raised to have manners different from those of boys; they were expected to be, and usually were, all the things that were described by the vanished word "ladylike"—calm, gracious, diffident, never profane. As early as September 1878, Emma M. Nutt was hired by the New England Bell company in Boston as the first woman operator. Miss Nutt worked for the Bell System until her retirement in 1911, and within a few years of her hiring the male telephone operator was extinct—only to make a reappearance, in very different guise, in the late 1960s.[6]

The telephone was launched, but the Bell company was all but foundering. The years 1878 and 1879 were its time of greatest trial, its Valley Forge. Early in 1878, the Bell Telephone Company, desperate for funds to finance expansion, reorganized itself by dividing into two entities—the New England Telephone

Company, charged with issuing licenses for the establishment of telephone-operating companies in New England, and a new Bell Telephone Company, with headquarters at first in New York City, to grant licenses elsewhere. What the reorganization meant was that the founders, in the cause of bringing in new capital, had relinquished control to a group of aristocratic yet venturesome Boston capitalists, among them Charles S. Bradley, Alexander Cochrane, William F. Saltonstall, and Richard S. Fay. By the end of July, the stockholders had passed a bylaw giving the men who had paid cash for their stock two votes per share to one vote per share for the patentees. Thus control passed out of the hands of the Bell and Hubbard families only a year after the company had been formed. The well-born Bostonians were to make the decisions and set the tone of the company for years to come. But Hubbard, in the last months before he bowed out, made his final and perhaps greatest contribution, that of bringing in the man who was to be the key figure in the formation and growth of AT&T as it is today, Theodore N. Vail.

3

Vail's early life gave little indication that he would become a genius at the corporate organization of telephony. To be sure, he had telegraphy in his blood, and had heard tales of its heroic first days from his earliest chidhood: his first cousin once removed, Alfred Vail, had been Samuel F. B. Morse's closest technical collaborator and was the man to whom, in 1844, Morse had sent from Washington to Baltimore the grandiloquent and unforgotten message "What hath God wrought." The son of the not very prosperous head of an ironworks plant in Morristown, New Jersey, Theodore Vail attended grade and high school there, worked for a time as a drugstore clerk and for a time as a medical student with his physician uncle, thought of entering the ministry, and in 1864, at the age of nineteen, took a job with Western Union as an apprentice telegrapher in New York City. His diary entries during his two years at that occupation show a young man in whom a strongly religious sense of duty was at war with a sensual and self-indulgent nature. "We must discourage all wastefull slothfull untidy Base Wicked thoughts and actions in ourselves," he reminded himself in September 1864. The following March, apparently discouraged with the progress of his self-discouragement, he carried on for four pages in the following vein: "Staying up late of nights playing Billiards and drinking lager is not what young men should be doing and for one I am determined to stop it. But what am I saying 'Determined to stop it.' But how many times have you said the same before and are you stoping it now." The diary was then silent for nearly a year, details of which are lacking except that at some point his boss said to him, "Vail, I think you'd better look for another job," and dispatched him to the Western Union office at White Plains. His next diary entry sums up the year: "I have been thrown around quite considerably—got into difficulties and out again, only to get into some fresh ones. When will I become so sober and settled that I shall not continuously involve myself."

In later years Vail would develop a taste for good food and wine and other expensive things, and would maintain that he had never saved a dollar in his life; at Western Union in New York and White Plains he seems to have had no ambitions except, as he said later, to own a sable coat and a ruby ring. In 1866, when his family moved to Waterloo, Iowa, he went with them and became a telegraph operator for the Union Pacific; in 1869 he married his cousin, Emma Louise Righter, and settled in Omaha as a postal clerk, reading law on the side. Now his executive ability began to assert itself, and he rose rapidly, moving to the Washington headquarters of the Railway Mail Service in 1873, quickly revolutionizing its service, and becoming its assistant general superintendent in 1874 and in 1876 its superintendent. One of the many responsibilities of Gardiner Hubbard, that man of the Establishment, was to serve as a member of the Congressional Postal Committee, and in that capacity he came to know Vail well and to value his ability. Vail, for his part, became convinced as a result of his association with Hubbard that the telephone would eventually revolutionize world communication, and he became a vigorous, though generally unsuccessful, promoter of Bell stock. But Hubbard had other ideas for the young postal executive. Early in 1878, he offered Vail the job of general manager of the new Bell Telephone Company at a first-year salary of thirty-five hundred dollars—more than one thousand dollars less than he was currently earning—with a promised increase to five thousand dollars the second year if the business should develop and his work prove satisfactory. After consideration—but not much, for he found his dealings with Congress increasingly frustrating—Vail accepted.

His friends and mentors in Washington were appalled. Joseph Gurney Cannon, a young congressman from Illinois later to become the powerful "Uncle Joe" of the House, exclaimed, "Vail resigned his place? What for? I always liked Vail. Hubbard tried to sell *me* some of that [Bell] stock. I'm sorry he got hold of a nice fellow like Vail." His boss, the assistant postmaster general, wrote Vail warmly:

My only wish is that you may have—before the acceptance of your resignation by the P. M. Gen'l—a telephone tube fastened to your ear and another connecting at the top of your head with a wire running perpendicular and horizontal, and while in this condition be compelled to listen to the sweet bye-and-byes of every yelping canine and the solos of all the tom cats in the State of N.Y. Telephone! . . . Listen to the prophesy of an old fool to a friend. One or two years hence there will be more Telephone companies in existence than there are sewing machine companies today. . . . I can scarcely believe that a man of your sound judgment, one who holds an honorable and far more respectable position than any man under the P. M. Genl., with honor and respect attached to the same, should throw it up for a d——d old Yankee notion . . . called a telephone![7]

But Vail's mind was made up, and in June 1878—by which time there were 10,755 Bell telephones in service—he went to New York to take up his new duties.

Established in July at the Bell company's new headquarters on Reade Street, Vail showed his mettle in his first action. He sent a copy of Bell's 1876 patent to every Bell agent in the country, along with a letter exhorting them to keep up the fight against Western Union's infringements. "We have the original telephone patents," he wrote. "We have organized and introduced the business and do not propose to have it taken from us by any other corporation." In September the infringement suit—technically against Peter A. Dowd, agent for Western Union's telephone subsidiary—was filed in the U.S. Circuit Court for the District of Massachusetts. Meanwhile Vail moved forcefully on the legal and technical front. The Bell company's problem, as previously noted, was that its transmitter did not work as well as the one Edison had devised for Western Union (and which the Bell company maintained was an infringement of Bell's 1876 patent). The solution was to counter with a new transmitter based on a separate new patent—and quickly, before Western Union could get a nationwide strangle hold on the telephone business. Back in May, on Watson's recommendation the company had acquired rights to a variable-resistance transmitter, based on a loose electrical contact rather than a carbon button like Edison's, that had been invented by Emile Berliner, a recent immigrant from Germany who worked in Washington as a dry-goods clerk. Berliner's principle was sound—indeed, it is the principle used in modern telephone transmitters—and it provided for the convenience of separate transmitting and receiving instruments; a patent had been applied for in 1877, and it was protected while the patent was pending. But it had not been developed to the point of practicality—an omission soon to be repaired. The acquisition of rights to Berliner's work cleared the way for the Bell company in September to file an "interference" against Edison's not-yet-patented transmitter—and then to use a carbon transmitter itself without being immediately enjoined by the courts. This deft bit of legal infighting under Vail's direction made it possible for the Bell company to acquire rights to—and in December 1878 to begin using—a carbon transmitter newly invented by Francis Black, Jr., of Weston, Massachusetts. The Blake transmitter was very similar to Edison's, but better; it transmitted the voice more clearly over short distances, and was more durable. Thus, within six months of Vail's arrival, the Bell interests were back in the lead technically.[8]

They had shown that they could hold their own in the laboratories and the law courts, but not yet in the financial markets. At the beginning of 1879, the Bell company's position was precarious in the extreme. Its stock was generally regarded with scornful amusement by investors, and brought only a few dollars a share; the corporate treasury was nearly bare; and the sole Bell factory, the little Charles Williams shop in Boston, could not turn out Blake transmitters fast enough to have much immediate effect on competitive operations in the field. As a result, Western Union's strangle hold began to tighten into a death grip; it augmented its field operations with purchases of Bell stock, seeking to devour and destroy its rival simultaneously.

In desperation, the Bell interests in March recombined Bell Telephone and New England Telephone into a single entity, National Bell Telephone Company, and in March—hanging on gamely, and with a certain style—they installed as president Colonel William H. Forbes, a swashbuckling and aristocratic young Boston financier fully in the tradition of Raleigh and Lord Nelson.

But the enemy had his own troubles, and on the brink of victory, he hesitated. Jay Gould's relentless attacks on Western Union were having their effect; Vanderbilt was beginning to feel that he needed an ally rather than a beaten competitor. In May negotiations to settle their differences began between Western Union and National Bell. They dragged through a painful summer during which Western Union continued to increase its competitive lead by opening more new exchanges than National Bell did. But in truth Western Union, beleaguered as it was, was losing stomach for the fight. The Bell evidence in the Dowd suit, begun in May 1879 and not completed until September, contained over six hundred pages of pleadings and a mountain of documentation. It was convincing evidence. After all, when all was said and done, Bell *had* filed his 1876 patent application before Gray had filed his caveat, and the application *had* set forth all the basic principles of the telephone. Unless fraud could be proved—and it could not—the case was clear. Among those who found it convincing was George Gifford, a leading patent lawyer, who had been engaged by Western Union as its chief counsel in the case. Even before the Bell evidence was complete, Gifford informed his clients that their cause was hopeless and that they should make a settlement. It was done; on November 10, 1879, before the Dowd case could be decided by the court, an agreement was reached under which Western Union gave up all its patents, claims, and facilities in the telephone business—the Edison transmitter, various other technical improvements, and a network of 56,000 telephones in fifty-five cities—in return for 20 percent of telephone rental receipts over the seventeen-year life of the Bell patents.

Whether or not Vanderbilt, in surrendering when he seemed to have the upper hand, was influenced more by the force of law or the threat of Jay Gould is not known. In any case, it was a famous victory for the Bell interests—probably the greatest victory in the whole history of the world's largest corporation, formally giving National Bell a legal monopoly of the telephone business in the United States that would last until the Bell patents' expiration in 1893 and 1894. After all, there had been considerable reason for Bell to make a fifty-fifty compromise; since the Blake transmitter was only an elaboration of Edison's, Bell had been in effect pirating the Edison transmitter while Western Union pirated the Bell receiver. Thomas Watson—who, of course, had been one of the key witnesses in the case—was among the first to recognize the victory as such, and to celebrate in his characteristic way. "If Bell had been in Boston I should have invited him to join in one of our old war dances," Watson wrote later. "But, as he was unavailable, I had to have my dance all by myself, celebrating this great event in my life with a whole day alone in my old haunts—the woods and shores of Swampscott and Marblehead, declaiming to the skies all the poetry I remembered. It was an undignified thing for the Chief Engineer of the Telephone Company to do . . . but I certainly felt better for it next day."[9]

## 4

National Bell's financial worries were over, at least for the present; so, too, were those of the people fortunate enough to hold some of its 8,500 shares of stock. Back in March the stock had been valued at $50 a share, with few takers. By mid-September, with the Bell case looking stronger by the day and rumors of an impending settlement in the air, it touched $370 before falling back to around $300; and on November 11—the day after the settlement—it reached $1,000, completing an appreciation of 2,000 percent in eight months. Never again, not even in the wild speculative boom of 1929, would the company's stock increase in price even 100 percent in so short a period. Stock prices reflect not current facts but hopes for the future, and Telephone's time as a go-go stock reached its climax the first day in its history that the company's continued existence was assured.

Institutionalized, the telephone was on its way to becoming part of American life, and thus was bound soon to find its way into literature, the criticism of life. And who but the prescient Mark Twain produced the first piece of telephone fiction? Published in 1880, it was a casual essay entitled "A Telephonic Conversation," describing the author's reactions to the then-novel experience of listening to one end only of a telephone conversation being conducted by someone else. In Mark Twain's case the conversation was between two women, and the end he overheard included more or less cryptic references to cooking, the Bible, beauty care, children, church, and a husband—all followed by protracted goodbyes. It is a slight piece, but it shows how quickly the telephone assumed one of its immemorial functions, and it serves to introduce, gracefully and authoritatively, the American literature of the telephone, and its persistent hero, the woman user.

Early in 1881, the American Bell Telephone Company—as it came to be called beginning in March 1880—issued its first annual report to stockholders. President Forbes was able to report that "the business of the company . . . has been in every respect satisfactory," and that the year's net earnings had been over $200,000, of which $178,500 had been paid in dividends. Since there were then 540 stockholders, the average payout per stockholder was about $330. Forbes also reported that there were now 132,692 telephones in the hands of American Bell licensees, and that, five years after Bell had beaten Gray to the patent office, there were only nine cities in the United States with populations over 10,000 that did not yet have a telephone exchange.[10]

CHAPTER 4

# God's Electric Clerk

Late in 1879, telephone subscribers began for the first time to be designated and called by numbers rather than by their names. It happened in Lowell, Massachusetts, and it seems to have happened as a result of an epidemic of measles. When the epidemic struck that fall, it occurred to a local physician, Dr. Moses Greeley Parker, that if the ailment should simultaneously attack all of Lowell's four telephone operators, inexperienced substitutes would have so much trouble learning which name went with each of the two hundred jacks on the switchboard that service would be paralyzed. Accordingly, he recommended that numbers be used instead. The local Bell company management at first protested that its customers would consider their designation by numbers to be beneath their dignity; nevertheless, it saw the logic of the doctor's suggestion, and followed it. The subscribers were not outraged; the epidemic quickly passed, but telephone numbers did not.[1]

2

William H. Forbes, the man who as president would guide the affairs of National Bell Telephone Company over most of the next decade (in tandem with his chief operating man, Theodore Vail), was a well-born Civil War hero with a head for figures and a taste for making money. Like many men who are rash and daring

74

in war action, he tended to be cautious and conservative in civil affairs. The son of John Murray Forbes, who had grown prosperous in the China trade and railroads, and Sarah Hathaway, a New Bedford Quaker, he grew up in and around Boston in a family that was on close terms with the Boston sage Ralph Waldo Emerson. In 1856 he entered Harvard as a handsome freshman with a cool eye, the beginnings of a neat mustache, and an aristocratic bearing. His most favored young lady was Emerson's daughter, Edith. A smooth passage into Boston's power elite seemed to be ahead, but his impulsiveness proved an obstacle. In January of his junior year, he took part in a prankish attempt to place a Bible stolen from Harvard's rival institution, Yale, in the Harvard chapel, smashing two windows in the process. A watchman caught him, there was a struggle, and the watchman fired, apparently to kill, whereupon Forbes injured the watchman seriously with a blow on the head with a billy club. Forbes was sent briefly to jail, then fined fifty dollars and expelled from Harvard—for a rich young Bostonian in those days, the ultimate fall from grace. A little later, when the Civil War broke out, Forbes was commissioned in the First Massachusetts Cavalry, and over the next few years he went under fire at Antietam; found himself compelled to order an execution in the trial of a Union deserter over which he presided; had an affair with a southern girl in a captured southern town; had his horse shot from under him by the legendary rebel raider John S. Mosby (who in later days became Forbes' fast friend); was captured and imprisoned, escaped and was recaptured, then was exchanged for a Confederate prisoner and returned to battle; and was in action as a lieutenant colonel near Appomattox when the war ended with Lee's surrender there. Back home, he married Edith Emerson, who was to bear him six boys, and became a partner in his father's enterprises. On a visit to London he was introduced to Thomas Carlyle, and for a time he served as an aggressive literary agent for his celebrated father-in-law. In 1871 the president and fellows of Harvard relented and gave him his degree, after all. Thus, through a brilliant war record and a brilliant marriage, was he reinstated to his proper place in Boston society. In 1879, at the age of thirty-eight, he joined the group of local capitalists who were taking over the Bell interests. Bell himself gave an accurate picture of Forbes at the time when he described him as "a wealthy man of great influence who has a reputation of thorough integrity."[2]

The first task facing Forbes as National Bell president was to beat off a series of legal challenges to and infringements of the Bell patents, the basis of the now-established Bell monopoly. The first of these actions was an infringement suit by the Bell company and its New York City operating licensee against an upstart called the Eaton Telephone Company. Like Western Union in the Dowd suit, Eaton based its case against Bell largely on the work of Philipp Reis, the German who in 1860 had *almost* invented the telephone; since the Dowd case had been settled out of court, this one provided a court test of the main issues in it. The outcome—Judge Lowell's famous opinion of June 27, 1881, in which he declared that "a century of Reis would never have produced a speaking telephone by mere improvement in construction"—was a resounding victory for Bell. But the courts had not heard the last of Reis. Shortly thereafter came the case of Amos E. Dolbear, the Tufts physics professor who had assigned his telephone claims to Western Union. Western Union, as we have seen, had abandoned Dolbear's claims, but Dolbear himself had not. Maintaining that the Bell patents covered only the magneto transmitter and receiver, Dolbear, in October 1880, applied for a patent on his own carbon transmitter and condenser receiver—instruments that were technically, but not substantively, different from Bell's; in April 1881, the patent was granted, whereupon Dolbear proceeded to incorporate the Dolbear Electric Telephone Company and to begin operations. American Bell (as it was called by then) brought suit for infringement, and in the course of the suit Dolbear's lawyers made the fatal mistake of bringing into court a model of the 1860 Reis machine, hoping to demonstrate once and for all that it could "talk" and that Bell's patents were therefore invalid. To the courtroom's amusement, experts and professors wrestled with the Reis telephone in vain. It would squeak, but not speak. "It *can* speak, but it won't," one of Dolbear's lawyers explained desperately. In January 1883, the judge decided that Bell's first patent was valid and covered all forms of speaking telephones, and issued an injunction against Dolbear, effectively putting him out of the telephone business. He was beaten, but unconvinced; in his later years, a popular lecturer known to his Tufts students as "Dolly," he used to display a box to his freshman physics class and say, defiantly, "That is the first telephone. I invented it."[3]

In truth, Dolbear's claim was sounder than many that were to follow it. The Eaton and Dolbear decisions were legal victories for American Bell, but public-relations setbacks; they created in the public mind a picture of the young company as a ruthless monopoly run by cold-eyed Boston capitalists with invincibly shrewd and well-placed lawyers. The Bell company thus had its first taste of public disapproval, creating a favorable climate for every scientific charlatan and every fast-buck stock promoter in the nation—and it was a nation that contained many of both—to claim priority in invention of the telephone, set up a company, and sell stock to the unwary. Over the next decade, the Bell company would be involved in more than six hundred lawsuits for patent infringement, all of which it would win. There was, for example, Antonio Meucci, an old Italian-born candlemaker and brewer from Staten Island, New York, who claimed to have invented a telephone as early as 1857. Close examination by the courts failed to show that he had achieved any practical results except with an acoustical, or nonelectric, "telephone" consisting of a taut wire stretched between two cans; but for generations thereafter, some loyal Italian-Americans claimed him as the telephone's true inventor. There was another claimant who told of having heard a bullfrog creak over a telegraph wire in Racine, Wisconsin, back in 1851.[4]

And there was Elisha Gray, the man who but for an accident of timing might have beaten Bell to the patent office, and who, in all justice, deserves a share of the credit for inventing the telephone. After Western Union had abandoned its claims in the Dowd settlement of 1879, Gray remained quiet for several years, apparently satisfied that he was fairly beaten. But then in 1885 and 1886, Zenas F. Wilbur, the patent examiner who had handled the Bell and Gray filings in 1876, testified to a congressional inquiry that he had illegally notified Bell's attorneys when he had discovered the conflict between the two filings. Gray reopened the case, enlarging on Wilbur's statement by maintaining that "Mr. Bell's attorneys had an underground railroad in operation between their office and examiner Wilbur's room in the Patent Office, by which they were enabled to have unlawful and guilty knowledge of Gray's papers." In sum, Gray was implying that the crucial variable-resistance part of Bell's application had been fraudulently added *after* its original submission—and after Bell had seen Gray's caveat. This grave charge of private and public misconduct—not fully substantiated by Wilbur's confession, and of course denied by Bell—many have been a reflection of the understandable bitterness of one who had come so close and lost so much; at any rate, the congressional inquiry refused to take sides, and when the matter went to the Supreme Court in 1888, it found for Bell, declaring that the evidence was "not sufficient to brand Mr. Bell, and his attorneys, and the officers of the Patent Office, with the infamy which the charge made against them implies." But Gray was not comforted; on a scrap of paper found after his death in 1901 he had written, "The history of the telephone will never be fully written. It is partly hidden away in 20 or 30 thousand pages of [court] testimony and partly lying in the hearts and consciences of a few whose lips are sealed—some in death and others by a golden clasp whose grip is even tighter."[5]

So Elisha Gray, who perhaps with an earlier rising hour or a faster horse cab to the Patent Office on February 14, 1876, might now be considered the inventor of the telephone—and who, by a stranger irony, was a founder of the future largest single arm of the Bell System, Western Electric—passes from our drama as a spear-carrier when he might have been a king. One of the great themes in the history of invention is simultaneity; almost every invention has its forgotten Elisha Gray, and in almost every case, history's decision was dictated in part by luck. Luck, too, may have played a role in the fact that the challenge to the Bell patents that came closest to success was not that of a serious inventor but that of a comic-opera character, Daniel Drawbaugh.

Born in 1827, Drawbaugh, flowing-bearded and rustic of manner, was a village mechanic and tinkerer with a shop at Eberly's Mills, on the edge of Yellow Breeches Creek, in the hills west of Harrisburg, Pennsylvania. His taxes were always in arrears and his bills unpaid; according to a neighbor, his wife once became so disgusted with his bootless tinkering that she smashed much of his equipment. As for his other neighbors, those who knew of his experiments considered him a harmless lunatic. Nevertheless, between 1851 and 1867 he was granted eight patents —a faucet for dispensing molasses among them—rights to all of which he sold for small sums. According to his later testimony, about 1863 he began experimenting with telephony; in 1867 he made a telephone with a teacup for a transmitter that (he said later) worked fairly well; and by 1870, he insisted, he had an electrical instrument that would transmit any speech above a whisper from one room of his house to another. Somewhere along the way he boasted to a neighbor that he could talk across the Atlantic Ocean, and got the skeptical reply, "Try it first across Yellow Breeches Creek."

So life went on in Eberly's Mills until 1880, when the telephone was big news and suddenly a group of investors and their lawyers heard of Drawbaugh and saw their chance for a coup. They applied for a patent on his behalf, organized the Peoples Telephone Company, and began producing telephones. American Bell sued for infringement in the Southern District Court of New York, and there ensued the most celebrated and hard-fought of all telephone infringement cases, with testimony that finally came to over 6,000 pages. Lysander Hill, the eminent lawyer retained by the Drawbaugh interests, called hundreds of witnesses, almost all of them rustics like Drawbaugh from Eberly's Mills and vicinity, of whom no fewer than forty-nine—Drawbaugh's neighbors, friends, and even bill collectors—testified that they had talked or heard speech on Drawbaugh's telephone before the first Bell patent. The Bell lawyers, led by James J. Storrow, a cool-headed, tart-tongued Yankee, were able to show that Drawbaugh had a long history of studying the inventions of others and then cleverly imitating them, and also the curious fact that Drawbaugh had no memory of *how* he had invented the telephone. "I don't remember how I came to it," Drawbaugh said in court. "I had been experimenting in that direction. I don't remember of getting at it by accident either. I don't remember of anyone talking to me of it."

Above all, the Bell lawyers wanted to know, why hadn't Drawbaugh applied for a patent until 1880? His reply was that "utter and abject poverty" had prevented him from doing so. This argument had little standing in law, but much in public opinion, and perhaps it provides a key to the Drawbaugh case. Politically and socially, the nation in the 1880s was largely polarized between the rich, urban slickers east of the Charles and Hudson Rivers and the poor, rural hicks west of them. Bell, with his Scottish background, his beautiful elocution, and his wealthy

Boston backers, was the perfect slicker; the man of Yellow Breeches Creek was in all respects the perfect hick. And they lived in a democratic country in which hicks vastly outdistanced slickers in numbers, if not in financial power. Like all the best-remembered trials, the Drawbaugh case recapitulated and heightened the social drama of its time.

Public opinion veered back and forth as the two sides presented their cases; at the height of the trial, in August 1883, the strength of the evidence for Drawbaugh apparently caused Bell stock to drop fifty points. But in December 1884, Judge William C. Wallace affirmed the validity of the Bell patents and adjudged them infringed by the defendants; the following year, after further arguments, he stood by his decision. Drawbaugh's lawyers appealed to the Supreme Court, which rendered its decision on March 19, 1888. It was a close call such as the Bell System had never had before and would never have again. Since there was one vacancy on the Court at the time and one justice was ill, only seven heard the case. The opinion of the majority was expressed by Chief Justice Morrison R. Waite: "We do not doubt that Drawbaugh may have conceived the idea that speech could be transmitted to a distance by means of electricity and that he was experimenting upon that subject, but to hold that he had discovered the art of doing it before Bell did would be to construe testimony without regard to 'the ordinary laws that govern human conduct.'" The minority opinion, written by Justice Joseph P. Bradley and concurred in by Justices John M. Harlan and Stephen J. Field, said in part, "We think that Drawbaugh anticipated the invention of Mr. Bell . . . we think that the evidence on this point is . . . overwhelming . . . we think that Bell's patent is void by the anticipations of Drawbaugh." The Court's vote to sustain the lower court, and thus save the Bell System, was four to three.[6]

Two points are worth making about this hairbreadth escape from disaster. The first is that two of the dissenting justices, Field and Harlan, were celebrated mavericks, known to believe in the value of dissenting opinions as a curb on the power of the majority. Given these beliefs, it is possible to imagine that Field and Harlan might not have dissented in the Drawbaugh case if they had not known they were outvoted. The other is the reaction of American Bell. In its annual report on the year 1887, issued just after the Supreme Court decision, the company commented, "Mr. Justice Bradley, in behalf of himself and Justices Field and Harlan, expressed an oral dissent on the question of fact concerning Drawbaugh's priority of invention. Otherwise the opinion of the Court expresses the unanimous opinion of all members of it." The use of the word "unanimous" to describe a decision that was, precisely, as far from unanimity as possible seems to reflect a confusion that may have arisen out of hysteria. Well may it have; an enterprise worth many millions, conducting a major national industry, had by one vote escaped falling to a clown.

3

Meanwhile, business not only went on, it flourished. In 1881 American Bell's net earnings were over $500,000; in 1882, almost twice as much; in 1883, almost three times; and by the end of the decade, five times. These gains were made in the face of generally adverse business conditions. In the 1880s—a decade marked by the formation of huge industrial trusts, agrarian discontent, rapid westward expansion, and the assassination of a president, James Garfield—the American economic system, unregulated by any formal monetary authority, seemed to be caught in a perpetual cycle of overexpansion followed by panic and then depression. There were money panics and succeeding depressions in 1884, 1890, and 1893. Deflation was the rule; it is hard in these days of seemingly permanent inflation to realize that between 1880 and 1896 the wholesale price of commodities actually declined by nearly one-third, not to reach the 1880 level again until 1909. The problem of business was to keep prices up, and of course, the best way to keep prices up is to have a monopoly. Bell Telephone prices did not noticeably decline during this period. Typical charges in the 1880s were $150 for 1,000 messages or $240 for 2,500; use of pay stations usually cost fifteen cents. The policy of the company under Forbes' leadership was to pay out most of the resulting profits to stockholders as dividends, rather than to plow them back into the company for maintenance and expansion, as would be done later on. In 1882, for instance, American Bell earned about $1 million and paid out $600,000 in dividends; in 1883, $1.5 million and paid out $1 million;

while in 1884, a bad business year, it actually paid out slightly more than it earned. By the 1890s, the company had paid $25 million in dividends, and early owners' stock was worth ten times what they had paid for it.

The Yankee capitalists were making the most of their monopoly while it lasted. The idea of the telephone business as a public service did not move them. "The complaints as to rates are often made thoughtlessly, and in ignorance of the expenses and risks which attend the business," President Forbes remarked in his 1883 annual report. Nevertheless, the complaints continued, and in 1885 in Indiana they gave rise to passage of a state law limiting the basic charge of telephone service to three dollars a month. This first attempt at government regulation of telephone charges was too rigid and Draconian to work, and would be repealed in 1888; but it was not the specific measure, but the principle of regulation itself, that Forbes attacked in his report on that year. "Why should the telephone business be regulated as to price more than other industries?" he asked. "No State in fairness ought to destroy that which [the] patent system has created. . . . Sound public policy is surely against the regulation of the price of any class of commodities by law." The question Forbes posed has, of course, an obvious answer, to which all concerned, including the Bell System, would later agree: the telephone business should be regulated as to price more than other industries because when operated as a monopoly as it was in Forbes' time and for the most part is now, it is not subject to regulation by the law of supply and demand through competition. But Forbes, we must remember, was working in America's time of innocence, when unrestricted free enterprise was generally accepted as an article of national faith—and when there was not yet an antitrust law to prevent *any* industry from circumventing competition through combinations. In his view, American Bell was merely doing in the telephone business through patent law what the oil and steel industries were doing through the formation of giant trusts. In places where government meddling, or unfavorable technical or economic conditions, made the prospects for profitable telephone service poor, American Bell's recourse was simply to refuse to extend service, or even to discontinue existing service. "The attack upon rates is one of the most direct methods of removing all inducement to extend telephone facili-

2. Alexander Graham Bell in 1876, the year he invented the telephone.

3. Dr. and Mrs. Alexander Graham Bell with their daughters, Elsie May (left) and Marian ("Daisy"), December 1885.

4. Gardiner Greene Hubbard, Bell's father-in-law and sponsor, helped finance Bell's experiment for a share in his patents.

5. Thomas Sanders, another sponsor, borrowed until he risked bankruptcy to launch the telephone service.

6. Alexander Graham Bell's garret laboratory at 109 Court Street. This reconstruction was made from material saved from the original building. Old photographs were used to re-create the 1875 view from the windows.

7. Thomas A. Watson in 1874, the year he met Alexander Graham Bell.

8. Watson at transcontinental telephone line opening, San Francisco end, January 25, 1915.

9. Bell in later life.

10. Bell in 1867, at age twenty.

11. The 1876 liquid telephone: "Mr. Watson, come here, I want you!" These historic words, the first ever transmitted over the electric telephone, were uttered by Alexander Graham Bell on the night of March 10, 1876.

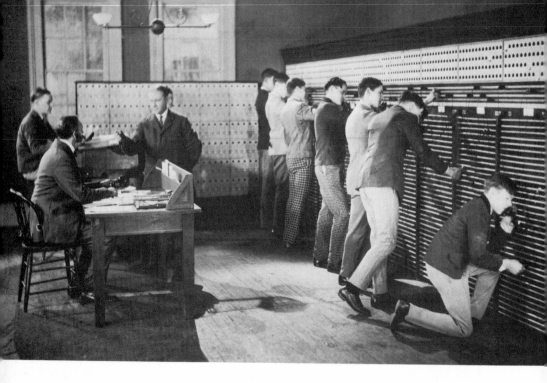

12. Boy operators in an 1879 central office. Boys were employed in the first telephone exchanges until they proved to be unruly and somewhat unreliable.

13. They were soon replaced by bustle-clad ladies, shown here in this 1885 New York City central office.

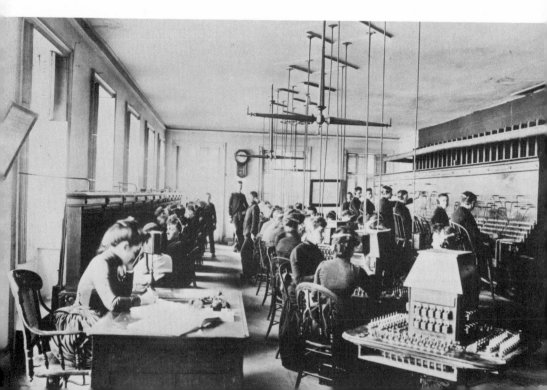

14.  New Street, New York City, during the blizzard of 1888. Huge snowdrifts paralyzed telephone service from March to May, when overall restoration of telephone lines was finally completed.

15.  The telephone soon captured popular fancy, and became the subject for songs, greeting cards, and music hall skits.

16.  An advertisement for an exhibition of Professor Bell's "Speaking and Singing Telephone," 1877.

**EVERY**
MAN, WOMAN and CHILD
SHOULD CAREFULLY EXAMINE THE WORKINGS O
**PROF. BELL'S**
**Speaking and Singing Telephone**
In its practical work of conveying
**INSTANTANEOUS COMMUNICATION BY DIRECT SOUN**
Giving the tones of the voice so that the person speaking can
recognized by the sound at the other end of the line.
**The Sunday School of the**
**Old John Street M. E. Church**
Having secured a large number of Prof. A. G. Bell's TELEPHONES, will give
**EXHIBITION** at the **CHURCH, 44 & 46 JOHN ST. N.**
where all visitors desiring can make for themselves a practical investigation of
**Telephone,** by asking questions, hearing the answers to their question
and listening to the singing conveyed through the Telephones from the oth
end of the line.
**On Tuesday and Wednesday Afternoon**
**November 20th & 21st, 1877.**
From 11½ A. M. until 7 P. M.
Admission to either Afternoon Exhibition 15 Cents.

**AN ENTERTAINMENT**
OF THE
Sunday School of Old John St. M.E.Churc
WILL BE HELD
**IN THE CHURCH,**
TUESDAY EVENING, Nov. 20th, 1877, at 7.30 P. M
CONSISTING OF
**RECITATIONS** by PROF'S SHANNON and McMULLEN,
**SINGING** by LITTLE NELLIE TERRY and othe
Concluding with the **TELEPHONE EXHIBITIO**
ADMISSION TO EVENING ENTERTAINMENT 25 Cen
**COME AND SEE THE TELEPHON**

ties," Forbes warned in the 1885 report; and indeed, in that year there was an actual decrease from the previous year in the number of Bell exchanges in operation, coast to coast.[7]

By the standards of his time, Forbes was an upright man, conceiving his responsibility as being primarily to take care of the interests of his firm's stockholders, and fulfilling it by paying out nearly ten million dollars in dividends during his eight years in office. Happily for the future of the Bell System, his operating chief, Vail, was a man with a larger view. It was primarily Vail who thought ahead to what would happen after the Bell patents' expiration in 1893 and 1894, and set about establishing an organization strong enough to survive without a monopoly. "What we wanted to do was get possession of the field in such a way that, patent or no patent, we could control it," Vail said later. The first big step was to arrange for a manufacturing operation to supply the equipment for a fast-expanding industry. Until the spring of 1879, all Bell equipment was made in the little Charles Williams, Jr., plant in Boston, where Bell and Watson had conducted their pioneer experiments; then other small shops, principally that of Ezra T. Gilliland of Indianapolis, were licensed to manufacture telephones and related equipment to Watson's specifications. But the capacity still fell far short of being adequate to meet the demand. There existed, however, another experienced and competent manufacturer of telephone equipment. It was the Western Electric Manufacturing Company, of Chicago, formerly Gray and Barton—the very company that had supplied Western Union's telephone equipment in 1878–79 when it was seeking to destroy the Bell company, and in 1880 survived as the largest electrical manufacturing company in the United States. Now the leader of Western Electric, Enos N. Barton—the co-founder with Elisha Gray of Gray and Barton, an early telephone skeptic who would later say, "I well remember my disgust when some one told me it was possible to send conversation along a wire"—convinced Vail and his Bell colleagues that Western Electric, with its built-in telephone capability, was the logical choice as the Bell System manufacturing unit. In 1880 the Massachusetts legislature had granted American Bell the power to own stock in its own licensees and in other companies. Taking advantage of this dispensation, in November 1881 American Bell bought the controlling interest in Western Electric from Western Union and General Anson

Stager; at the same time, the Williams and Gilliland licenses were transferred to Western Electric, and in February 1882, Western Electric formally became the sole supplier of Bell equipment and a part of the Bell System. As for Enos Barton, having overcome his disgust, he was to direct that sole supplier for forty years.

Meanwhile Vail aggressively set about the task of getting "possession of the field" in other ways. His approach to virgin territory, where no telephone service had yet been established, was so businesslike as to verge on the predatory. His salesman would approach local promoters with the suggestion that they organize a local telephone company and sell stock. The promoters needed little capital for their own; their asset was their license from American Bell, in exchange for which they customarily gave American Bell a 30 percent to 50 percent stock interest in their newly formed companies, as well as an annual rental fee for instruments of around $10 per telephone. The monopoly enabled American Bell to dictate the terms; if a local promoter didn't like them, he simply could not start a telephone company—or if he tried, he was promptly hit with a patent-infringement suit. By this method, combined with a vigorous policy of buying up new patents on each development and refinement of telephony as it came along, Vail had by 1885 established the basic framework of the Bell System as it exists today—vertically integrated supply; a network of licensees substantially owned by the parent company; emphasis on research and development; and strong supervision of the whole system by the parent. But for all his hard-headedness, Vail stood philosophically far from Forbes and the State Street capitalists Forbes represented. When the question arose as to whether to form a company or to open a new exchange in some doubtfully profitable farm area, the Bostonians tended to say: "Why bother, if it probably won't make money?" Vail—a man with a western background, with no inherited sense of capital, and with a mind set toward public service stemming from his days with the Post Office—would reply, in effect, "Let's take a chance. That area needs telephones as much as any other—and moreover, if we move in there now, it will be one more area where we will be established and operating when our patents run out."

It was this philosophical difference, reducible, perhaps, to immediate versus long-term self-interest, that brought Vail and Forbes increasingly into conflict. In September 1887, Vail resigned all connection with American Bell. His rather bland biographer explains that he was "carrying too heavy a burden." But Vail himself said, at the time, "my present position in the company . . . is in some ways embarrassing and unpleasant," and a certain bitterness on the other side is strongly implied by the fact that American Bell's annual report for 1887 contained no word of Vail's resignation, no tribute to his service—indeed, no mention of his name. Thus a leader of unusual vision, ahead of his time like all such leaders, passed out of telephony, a prophet virtually without honor, while telephony was still in its infancy; but he would be back.[8]

4

Apart from policy differences within the company, there were technical problems. In sum, the telephones didn't work very well. Hardly had the Blake transmitter and other improvements come along than a new, extrinsic source of trouble appeared. The first Edison central electric-lighting station was opened in New York City in 1882, and the first experimental electric-powered street-railway system in Chicago the same year; by the end of the decade, there were electric-light and electric-trolley systems in all principal cities. The instant effect of these new inventions on telephones was to cause, through electrical induction, so much static as to make communication next to impossible. The switching of a trolley car or the sputtering of an electric street lamp would cause all telephone lines in the vicinity to give off a racket that was all but deafening. And when man-made electrical inductions did not assault telephone users' eardrums, natural electricity did. The approach of a thunderstorm in those days could be detected by rising telephone static long before a cloud had appeared in the sky, and at the height of such a storm, telephones in the area were unusable. As Herbert N. Casson summed up the whole situation:

Such a jangle of meaningless noises had never been heard by human ears. There were spluttering and bubbling, jerking and rasping, whistling and screaming. There were the rustling of leaves, the croaking of frogs, the hissing of steam, the flapping of birds' wings. There were clicks from telegraph wires, scraps of talk from other telephones and curious little squeals that were unlike any known sound. The lines running east and west were noisier than the lines running north and south. The night was noisier than the day, and at the ghostly hour of midnight the babel was at its height.

But it was not caused by ghosts; the trouble lay chiefly in the fact that all the original telephone connections were by one-wire circuits, consisting of a single overhead line between the communicating telephones, with both telephones also connected to "ground," using the earth itself as a conductor to complete the circuit. And the earth in the 1880s was fairly pulsating with strange electrical currents, crudely new and ill-controlled; in a sense, the strange noises heard on telephones were the Delphic speech of the earth itself. The solution to them—first proposed in 1881 by John J. Carty, a young American Bell electrician, previously among the original boy operators, who would go on to become one of the key figures in the technical development of telephony—was to replace the one-wire circuits with two-wire, or metallic, circuits, insulated from the earth, thus eliminating the ground and its strange emanations. But that meant stringing twice as many wires to serve the same number of telephones, and reconstituting every circuit in the system; and that, of course, meant time and expense.

Another problem of the 1880s was the proliferation of telephone poles and of the wires sustained by them. The first underground telephone cables were laid in 1882, but their use did not become widespread until a decade later. As telephone use increased, poles in urban areas where there were the most subscribers became taller and taller, with more and more crossarms to carry more and more wires; eventually, on West Street in New York City, there stood the tallest and thickest telephone-pole forest of all—each pole ninety feet high, with thirty crossarms carrying three hundred wires. One effect was to blight the urban landscape by darkening the sky. But the mischief done by the proliferation of overhead wires was not only aesthetic or what is now called environmental; it also meant that telephone service was predictably interrupted for days or weeks in every northern city every winter, by sleet storms that brought down the tightly bunched wires, coating them with up to three pounds of ice per foot of wire.

On the matters of both metallic circuits and underground wires, Vail was considerably more progressive than the Yankee capitalists who employed him, and these differences contributed to the eventual break between them. So long as subscribers were willing to tolerate interference on their lines—and their only recourse was to give up something for nothing—the owners of American Bell preferred not to make the huge capital outlays necessary for conversion to two-wire circuits; as a result, only 12 percent of subscribers enjoyed use of them in 1892. As for the dark and ever-darkening forests of poles and overhead wires, public objections to them were so strident and insistent that in 1884 the New York State Legislature passed a law requiring that by November 1, 1885, all telephone wires be underground in cities with more than five hundred thousand population. This was about as effective as a law against sin; as American Bell promptly and inarguably pointed out, it could not comply because it did not yet know how to make underground wires work over distances of more than a few miles. The law was repealed in 1885, providing one more victory for American Bell; but that same year Vail set in motion a research project that led in 1890 to the development of the first practical underground telephone cable: a "dry-core" cable, sheathed in lead and having the wires in it insulated with crumpled paper and—instead of wax, resin, or oil, as had been used previously—plain air. Thereafter, the burying of telephone wires went on apace; but if Forbes and his fellow directors had shared Vail's enthusiasm for research and development despite their high price, it seems likely that most urban lines might have been underground in time to head off one of the greatest of all disasters for telephone service and for American Bell—the one caused by the great blizzard of 1888.[9]

Forbes was a man of action, simple and direct. As a Union officer in the Civil War, his job was simply to defeat the enemy with honor. As president of American Bell, he saw his task as equally straightforward: to defend the Bell patents against infringement, and to make as much money as possible out of them while they lasted, with little thought for the public interest or even the future of his own company. He treated employees paternally. He was at his best at fighting battles that posed no ambiguities or questions of ideology, such as the Pan Electric matter, a blatant case of infringement that, unlike all the others, involved the suspicion of misconduct at the highest level of federal government.

In 1883 the Pan Electric Company of Memphis, Tennessee, was organized with a nominal capital of five million dollars, to offer telephone service based on patents held by one James W. Rogers. The Rogers claims were insubstantial, consisting, as Alexander Graham Bell's biographer Robert V. Bruce has put it, of "about one per cent inspiration and ninety-nine per cent tracing paper." Pan Electric's purpose, it appears, was to circumvent the patent system by setting up telephone service over a wide area of the South and then, with the help of political influence, delaying the conclusion of American Bell's inevitable legal challenge until the expiration of the Bell patents would leave Pan Electric in the clear. To strengthen its political muscle, Pan Electric issued stock, in exchange for the use of their names for promotion, to various Confederate war heroes and southern political figures; among the latter was Augustus H. Garland, former governor of Arkansas and later a U.S. senator from that state, who received five hundred thousand shares of Pan Electric for no payment and was made the company's counsel. Predictably, American Bell sought injunctions against Pan Electric and various subsidiaries that it had formed in Maryland, Texas, and elsewhere. Pan Electric did not even defend itself in some of these suits; instead it fought back on the political front, attempting in 1884 to get a bill through Congress authorizing the federal government to vacate any patent at will. (The bill actually passed in the House, but was defeated in the Senate.) What Pan Electric was seeking to do, of course, was to take the control of telephony in America out of the realm of scientific priority and make it a political matter between North and South. The prospects for success of that undertaking were considerably increased that November when Grover Cleveland, a Democrat, was elected president; and they were apparently increased even more in March 1885, when the newly inaugurated Cleveland appointed Augustus H. Garland as his attorney general.

Garland lost no time in using his office to further the interests of Pan Electric and of himself by ordering, or at least allowing, his solicitor general to file suit in the name of the United States for annulment of the Bell patents, on the familiar ground that they had been obtained by fraud. Pan Electric's delaying tactic now had the best possible sponsor—the federal government itself—and

Forbes, who had previously regarded the Pan Electric case as just one more nuisance, saw that American Bell's survival was clearly threatened by a coalition of southern chauvinism and government dishonesty. In January 1886, Forbes went to Washington and obtained an interview with President Cleveland. Forbes said afterward, "He impressed me as not much *up* on the matter, quite ready to listen in a friendly way." Evidently Cleveland was up on it after listening to Forbes, because thereafter the tide turned. The government case against Bell was allowed to fall of its own weight, and Pan Electric, enjoined not to engage in the telephone business, passed out of existence. As for Garland—whitewashed by a friendly Congressional committee, and not thrown out of office as he probably should have been—he, like the other Pan Electric backers, was left holding an empty bag. But the sordid case had done something important for American Bell—it had inaugurated the company's relations with the federal government (other than the Patent Office) with a matter in which the company was clearly and unmistakably in the right.[10]

The greatest technological advance in telephony in the 1880s was the establishment and rapid growth of long-distance service. Here was a matter on which Vail and Forbes could agree: long-distance service was obviously in the public interest, and moreover, it proved to be almost immediately profitable. The first long-distance line for public use was opened between Boston and Providence, Rhode Island—a distance of forty-five miles—on January 12, 1881. The circuits consisted of several single lengths of galvanized-iron wire, with ground used as the return conductor, and the resulting interference, caused chiefly by telegraph traffic, was so bad that the line had to be considered for practical purposes a failure; but before it could be abandoned, the young engineer Carty, more or less by accident, saved it by discovering the advantage of a metallic circuit. Carty related later:

One day, upon my own initiative, I connected wires 1 and 2 together at Boston and looped my telephone and transmitter into the circuit. I gave directions to the girl at the Providence end, showing her how to connect the two wires at that end. This she did, and I shall never forget the remarkable change which it made. . . . The operator asked me what caused the change and I told her I put the line on a metallic circuit. . . . She said, "I wish I had one of those things down here."

Ten months later, the Inter-State Telephone Company, a Bell licensee, put a metallic circuit between Boston and Providence into commercial service and proudly, if overenthusiastically, advertised it as "the only perfect system of telephony yet devised."

Even with interference greatly reduced, the span of long-distance service was sharply limited by the fact that telephone voices—unaided by amplification along the line, the principle of which had not been discovered—grew weaker with every mile and soon faded out entirely. Not until three years later, in 1884, could commercial service be inaugurated over the 292 miles of wire between Boston and New York; this accomplishment was made possible by the discovery that hard-drawn copper wire, although weaker than galvanized iron, caused far less attenuation of telephone voices. A call between the two great cities of the Northeast cost two dollars in daytime and one dollar at night.

Also in 1884, successful toll lines were opened between Colorado Springs and Pueblo, Colorado (forty mountainous miles) and between San Francisco and Sacramento, California (eighty miles). Vail, above all, felt that rapid development of a large and efficient long-distance network was of the highest importance. Empire-builder that he was by instinct, he saw that the existence of such a network at the time of the Bell patents' expiration would be the surest guarantee of American Bell's survival. Subscribers would want to talk from city to city as well as locally, and it would take a newly formed telephone company years to establish its own long-distance network; the Bell System, Vail shrewdly reasoned, would keep the edge through its head start on facilities. But meanwhile there was an administrative problem in connection with building the facilities. Long-distance lines crossed the territories of local telephone companies that held Bell licenses, and used poles belonging to those companies, causing confusion and disputes as to who got the resulting revenue. Moreover, the capitalization of American Bell, set by the Massachusetts Legislature at ten million dollars, was inadequate to finance the expansion of long-distance lines. The solution was to form a new subsidiary of American Bell, the sole task of which would be to build and operate long-distance lines. The new company—thus strictly limited in its scope, and with a modest initial capitalization of one hundred thousand dollars—was chartered under the laws of New York State on February 28, 1885. Its president was Vail, who was also serving at the time as general manager of American Bell and as president of the Metropolitan Telephone and Telegraph Company, American Bell's New York City licensee—and who, as we have seen, would two and a half years later resign rather unhappily from all connections with American Bell. Its name was the American Telephone and Telegraph Company, and it was to remain limited in its mission, and generally referred to within American Bell as the Long-Distance Company, until 1900. (The new company's certificate of incorporation declared its purpose to be "constructing, buying, owning, leasing, or otherwise obtaining, lines of electric *telegraph* [italics added] partly within and partly beyond the limits of the State of New York, and of equipping, using, operating, or otherwise maintaining the same." The word "telephone" appears nowhere in the certificate other than the company's name—an undeniable oddity, like the absence of the word from Bell's first patent. But only an oddity. The word "telegraph" was often used, as it was here, as a generic term to cover all wire communication by electricity. Moreover, the ambiguity of the charter reflected a degree of craftiness; it left AT&T free to enter telegraphy if it should ever want to.)

Forbes, feeling that he had done his stint, retired as president of American Bell in 1887, at the age of forty-six, to devote himself to such pursuits of a gentleman of leisure as sailing, riding, writing little poems, and dabbling in stock speculation. He was succeeded on an interim basis by Howard Stockton, another Civil War veteran of conservative leanings, and Stockton was succeeded less than two years later by John E. Hudson, a Boston lawyer who had followed Vail as general manager of American Bell. Essentially something of a dilettante, Forbes, for all his lack of vision, had set a tone for the Bell management that it would keep for many years, perhaps too many—a tone of aristocracy, ultraconservatism, and imperial calm.[11]

5

Telephony had been making a shaky and erratic debut in other countries around the world. Almost everywhere, its early development contrasted sharply with that in the United States in two respects: that the telephones were owned or controlled to some extent by government rather than by private interests, and that telephone service was received with a marked lack of enthusiasm by the public.

In Great Britain, the establishment of service was delayed partly by the widespread public conviction that the new device was merely a "scientific toy," and partly by a confused patent situation. Bell's British patent grant was far more limited than his American one, covering the receiver but not the transmitter; Edison held the British transmitter patent for his carbon transmitter. Sensing a chance to take complete command of British telephony by fast action, Edison called upon his preternatural agility and versatility as an inventor by coming up with and patenting a receiver using an entirely new principle—all in a matter of weeks. The new receiver, called an electro-motograph, could "speak" much louder than any receiver produced up to then; the trouble—a crucial one—was that it could be operated only when a crank was being turned continuously by hand. Let a telephone user stop cranking, and he or she could not hear; a telephonic monologue of, say, fifteen minutes would surely have left the cranking listener gasping with exhaustion as well as boredom. Moreover, its talk was *too* loud, certainly for the discreet British. George Bernard Shaw—who, astonishingly enough, was in 1879 an employee of the Edison Telephone Company of London in a capacity mysteriously described as "wayleave manager"—called the electro-motograph "a telephone of such stentorian efficiency that it bellowed your most private communications all over the house instead of whispering them with some sort of discretion." Eventually, in 1880, the Bell and Edison interests compromised, the United Telephone Company was formed with the two factions sharing its stock, and exchanges using the Bell magneto receiver and the Edison carbon transmitter began to be opened throughout the country.

But the telephone in Britain was scarcely an instantaneous hit with the public. Britishers just didn't seem to get the idea—or if they did, they pretended not to. "Are you there?" a caller would inquire, after a connection had been made. If the reply was affirmative—and after all, a negative reply would have verged on the bizarre—the caller might say, "I will come right over. I want to talk to you." Newspaper editors would not use the telephone, considering it useful only for divers and coal miners. There was no telephone in the Bank of England until after 1900. Additionally, there was the problem that the British Post Office from the first considered itself a rival of the United or any other privately owned telephone company. It had taken over the United Kingdom's telegraphic system in 1869, and now it wanted the new scientific toy. It soon began demanding 10 percent of gross telephone revenues, and otherwise harassing the industry. By the early 1890s, when the patents were expiring, British telephone companies were being organized right and left by ambitious entrepreneurs, one of them no lesser eminence than the Duke of Marlborough. In 1895 a parliamentary inquiry concluded that the Post Office should take over the telephone business entirely; the following year it did take over trunk, or long-distance, lines—setting rates for their use too low to maintain good equipment or service—and finally, in 1912, it assumed full control of the entire system. But even by that time there were only six hundred thousand telephones in use in all Great Britain, a density per population less than one fourth that in the United States at the time.

In France, Gallic temperament seems from the outset to have had a catastrophic effect on the quality of telephone service. Originally conducted by private interests, French telephony was virtually confiscated in 1889 by the government, which proceeded to inflict upon it the worst evils of bureaucracy. Rates were inequitable; there was no national plan or research effort; subscribers were required to buy their telephones; and operators were subjected to baroque bureaucratic rules, such as being forbidden to marry policemen, cashiers, foreigners, or mayors of towns, lest they betray the secrets of the switchboard. Frenchmen considered the resulting service to be a national disgrace. By 1898 there were 31,681 telephones in use in France—one for every 1,216 citizens.

So it went in other countries. In Germany, where the government had a monopoly from the beginning, it made many technical mistakes and maintained a low standard of service. The Italians put up fancy wall brackets to hold telephone wires that were a delight to the eye, but the telephones seldom worked. In Switzerland, the government monopoly set up a highly efficient telephone system very early, but had trouble getting people to use it; as late as 1910, despite moderate rates, the traffic averaged only two calls per subscriber per day, either because of Swiss frugality or because the Swiss had nothing to say to each other. Throughout Europe only the Scandinavian countries had the combination of efficient early telephone facilities and a population eager to use them. For the rest of the world—even though exchanges were opened in Australia in 1880, in Brazil in 1881, and in India in 1882 —large-scale telephony was to await the coming of the new century.

To sum up, at the turn of the century Sweden had one telephone for every 115 persons of all ages, Switzerland one for every 129, Germany one for every 397, France one for every 1,216, Italy one for every 2,629, and Russia one for every 6,988, while the United States at the same time had slightly more than one for every sixty, and several individual states had more telephones in use than any European nation, while the State of New York had nearly as many as the whole of Europe. Besides, service was generally better in the United States than almost anywhere in Europe. Clearly, telephony in its early days was a peculiarly American institution. One reason seems to be that the European habit of entrusting telephone service to government resulted again and again in rates so low that, while politically popular, they did not provide the funds necessary for good equipment or service. But another and perhaps more important reason is the vast, and at that time unique, American appetite for making telephone calls, morning, noon, and night, long-distance and short-duration—an appetite natural as rain to a lonely, far-spread people addicted with equal fervor to new gadgets and to the art and pastime of talking.[12]

And the invention Americans took to so enthusiastically was meanwhile having its effects on them. By the end of the 1880s, telephones were beginning to save the sanity of remote farm wives by lessening their sense of isolation; they were beginning to bring women in cities "out of the kitchen" by reducing the time required for shopping; they were drastically simplifying the conduct of love affairs; and to the dismay of moralists, they were bringing into being the American institution of the "call girl." Along with landscape-blighting high poles, the telephone had created objects pleasanter to look upon (and just as soon to disappear): the first telephone booths, which were sometimes made of golden oak, ornately carved, with glass doors and silk draperies, and which were sometimes unfortunately mistaken by the uninitiated for privies. It had introduced the world to broadcasting, through music and sports programs conveyed by telephone to such public halls as Madison Square Garden in New York.

It had introduced a new social amenity to be mastered, telephone manners. "There seems to be a popular misconception about conversing through a telephone," the New York *World* explained in 1880. "It is not necessary to roar into the instrument so that you can be heard eight blocks away. The telephone don't [*sic*] work on that principle. . . . Stand back two or three feet [*sic!*] from the mouthpiece of the transmitter and speak slowly and distinctly in your ordinary voice. The telephone is not deaf." That year in Council Bluffs, Iowa, a man walked into the office of the Council Bluffs *Nonpareil,* said, "Oh, good, I see you have a telephone in use here," and began talking earnestly into a hole in the wall.

Telephone literature, so gracefully inaugurated by Mark Twain in 1880, proceeded in a few years to a stage of epic celebration. In 1886 Benjamin Franklin Taylor produced a poem entitled "The Wonders of Forty Years," which included these lines:

> The far is near. Our feeblest whispers fly
> Where cannon falter, thunders faint and die.
> Your little song the telephone can float
> As free of fetters as a bluebird's note,
> Quick as a prayer ascending into Heaven,
> Quick as the answer, "all thy sins forgiven" . . .
> The Lightning writes it, God's electric clerk;
> The engine bears it, buckling to the work
> Till miles are minutes and the minutes breaths. . . .

But this epic strain in telephone literature was to fade quickly. Literary men, with their love of privacy and their anti-scientific bias, began to strike a querulous note on the subject. Robert Louis Stevenson, coming upon an American-made telephone in Honolulu in 1889, wrote to a local newspaper about the problem of admitting "this interesting instrument . . . into our bed and board, into our business and bosoms . . . bleating like a deserted infant." And in 1890, Mark Twain was back on his old topic, using a harsher tone now in a Christmas piece for the New York *World:*

It is my heart-warm and world-embracing Christmas hope and aspiration that all of us—the high, the low, the rich, the poor, the admired, the despised, the loved, the hated, the civilized, the savage—may eventually be gathered together in a heaven of everlasting rest and peace and bliss—except the inventor of the telephone.[13]

6

Suddenly bereft of both Forbes and Vail, American Bell in late 1887 was in danger of losing its momentum. Stockton, who briefly replaced Forbes, was a man of much the same stripe, but there was no replacing Vail, who was one of a kind.

The shadow of Vail loomed over the Switchboard Conference of 1887, held in New York City that December. The conference—participated in by the fifteen top American Bell technical and scientific men, among them Barton of Western Electric; Edward J. Hall, chief of long-distance traffic; and Charles E. Scribner, who through some six hundred inventions would eventually contribute more to the development of the switchboard than anyone else—had, indeed, been largely organized by Vail as one of his last acts in office, earlier that year. It represents the first attempt to put the art of telephone-exchange engineering and management on a scientific basis. The first problem regarding switchboards to be dealt with by the conferees was the need to move them out of the stuffy attics and lofts that had been used previously, with their cupolas full of tangled masses of wires, into more spacious and agreeable quarters. Then there was the question of the education of telephone users; one participant estimated that two-thirds of all service troubles were directly traceable to abuses by the customers. More obviously, operators needed more and better training, too; there were schools for operators in some areas at the time, but in others new operators went to work with little more than a few friendly hints from the next girl on the board. One of the conferees, Wiley W. Smith, complained that many operators were in the habit of saying, when a call could not be completed, "They won't answer," rather than "They don't answer." The word "won't," Smith pointed out, implied willful, possibly perverse refusal to pick up the telephone on the part of the party being called, when in fact it could be assumed that he or she simply wasn't there. This implication of public refusal to answer was giving telephony a bad name, the participants all agreed, and operators thereafter were instructed to say "don't" rather than "won't." Another interesting conclusion arrived at was that business subscribers should be encouraged not to print their telephone numbers on their business stationery—only the word "Telephone" to indicate that they had one. "A man pays no attention to the number of the telephone printed on a card," one conferee said. "He goes directly to the book." As to ringing, it was decided that operators (who in those days rang manually) should be instructed to give only short rings, on the theory that "a short ring excites the curiosity of the subscriber."

In spite of much attention to such details of psychology rather than technology, the Switchboard Conference was an important step toward the attainment of two of Vail's key principles—uniformity of equipment and methods throughout the system, and management by generalists rather than specialists. As one participant put it, "Mr. Vail thought it would be a good thing if we could find somebody somewhere who was a first-class man in every other respect but who had not devoted his attention to switchboards." Vail was gone, but hardly forgotten.

Less than three months after the conference, disaster struck the heart of the system, the area between New York and Boston, in a form not susceptible to correction by short rings or saying "don't" instead of "won't." As Angus Hibbard, the young general superintendent of the newly formed AT&T Company, put it later, the great blizzard of March 12–13, 1888, "almost, but not quite, knocked out the long distance lines" in the Northeast. Striking before dawn on the twelfth, the storm had by noon created the greatest paralysis of daily and business life of the whole nineteenth century in America. In Connecticut, almost all telegraph wires except those in the immediate vicinity of New Haven were out of service, and the New Haven telephone exchange could reach only twelve of the thirty-two other exchanges in the state. New York City by that time had no telegraph or train service, but still retained one telephone circuit each to Philadelphia, Boston, New Haven, and Albany. By the following afternoon, when the storm was subsiding, even local telephone service in New Haven had to be suspended entirely, not to be restored until two days later, but in New York, minimal service, including long-distance, was maintained continuously. For several days thereafter, telephones remained New York's only means of communication with the rest of the world.

Hibbard in his autobiography has given a vivid picture of his life as the man in charge of Long Lines during the first day of the blizzard. After awakening that morning at his home on Fifty-ninth Street, he caught a Sixth Avenue elevated train, which took him downtown as far as Fourteenth Street, where the passengers were told that further progress was impossible. Having struggled across town on foot to Third Avenue in hopes of catching another southbound train, he found that line not running, and eventually reached Park Row via a horse-drawn sleigh and a ten-dollar payment to its driver. From there he walked to the AT&T office on Cortlandt Street, in the process once being blown down a stairway buried in snow. After checking out the state of service, Hibbard took a turn as an operator at the switchboard on Fulton Street, which was both underattended and jammed with the greatest volume of attempted calls on record up to that time. Next he turned his attention to the ominous problem of the huge forest of high poles and wires that crisscrossed Manhattan. All poles along Morningside Heights were down for miles; the greatest pole row of all, the ninety-foot, thirty-crossarm, three-hundred-wire row along West Street, was reported to be standing but "the poles waving around like feathers." At midafternoon, Hibbard and an assistant decided to make an inspection of this row. "I never heard a sound quite like the shriek of the wind as it tore through the wires above us," Hibbard wrote.

There was something grand about the sight and the sound of it. . . . At last we reached Twelfth Street, where the line turned east for several blocks; no breaks as yet, not even a broken wire. . . . Halfway along the block, however, and for two or three blocks beyond, there was very real trouble. About twenty poles had broken, and with their three hundred wires had fallen in various kinds of a mass. It was amazing to see how deliberately, almost gracefully, this mass of wires had been draped along and over the streets and buildings. . . . One situation in the second block was rather disturbing. A pole had been snapped off at the top, carrying the thirty crossarms, and had crashed through the roof of a two-and-a-half-story building . . . cutting into it like a knife.

By the following afternoon, most of the wires of downtown Manhattan were draped more or less gracefully over the streets and buildings, and the city's telephone system was a shambles.

The blizzard came close to ruining the Southern New England Telephone Company, which suffered the greatest damage. Reconstruction costs were so great that the company's earnings were cut in half, two quarterly dividends were skipped, and the company's management was reshuffled. It also served to end any foot-dragging by American Bell about getting wires underground. If a single storm could not only disrupt service but wipe out a large part of a company's plant, then a different kind of plant was needed. Not just the New York Legislature had spoken against high poles; God had added His voice. By the end of 1889 there were more than a thousand miles of underground wire installed in New York City alone, and the following year, when dry-core cable made underground wires effective over longer distances, the conversion process began in earnest. Once again, the hand of the vanished Vail seemed to be on the tiller.[14]

John Elbridge Hudson, who assumed the presidency of American Bell in April 1889 and would hold it until 1900, was a man to inspire awe rather than affection. He may hardly be said to have had the common touch. A Harvard graduate, class of 1862, a solid Boston Unitarian, he had tutored in Greek, Latin, and ancient history while studying for his Harvard law degree, then become general counsel of American Bell in 1878, general manager in 1885, and vice president in 1887; now, as president of American Bell, he remained remote and scholarly, famous within the company for making Greek memoranda in his office and for being difficult if not impossible to get an appointment with. Hibbard wrote, "To me Mr. Hudson was a rather formidable gentleman. He was large in stature, had a bushy beard and mustachios, a lot of hair brushed back from a high forehead, and what might be called a 'commanding presence' . . . Mr. Hudson was certainly hard to get at." There was a company story that a man who wanted to see Hudson once sat patiently in his anteroom day after day for several weeks, leaving only for lunch; Hudson would pass coolly through the anteroom, neither smiling encouragement nor advising the petitioner to give up the vigil. According to the story, the interview never did take place. Another time, an American Bell official, seeing Hudson in a vaudeville theater laughing heartily at a performance, exclaimed, "Great Scott! I can't believe my eyes!"

Under the command of this rather icy paladin, progress was slow at American Bell during the last years of the patent monopoly. Nevertheless, there were several important technical advances during those years, one of them the first such advance to originate outside the Bell company since Edison's carbon transmitter. For one thing, there was the common-battery system, originally patented in 1888 by Hammond V. Hayes, later chief engineer of AT&T, and gradually introduced into service over the succeeding years. This made it possible for a central switchboard battery to supply current to virtually all telephones connected with it, and made it no longer necessary for each telephone to have its own troublesome battery. In 1889 the first public coin telephone was installed in the Hartford Bank in Hartford, Connecticut. During 1891, two-party and four-party service—to be a familiar and fascinating feature of rural telephone use for more than half a century —were introduced in, of all places, New York City, as a way of making telephones available at bargain rates. Those years also saw the further extension of long-distance service. A New York–Chicago line was opened in 1892, with Bell himself participating in the opening ceremony, and lines between New York and Cincinnati and between Boston and Chicago the following year.

And also in 1891, the first automatic dial system was patented by a Kansas City undertaker, Almon B. Strowger. Strowger—at least according to the engaging legend—had been having trouble with malicious or corrupt Kansas City telephone operators who, he was convinced, deliberately gave busy signals or wrong numbers when potential customers called him, thus depriving him of business. Accordingly, he resolved to invent a switchboard system that would eliminate the operator. Building on a couple of earlier Bell System inventions—the so-called Connolly-McTighe patent of 1879, a dial switchboard that unfortunately did not work, and a primitive automatic switching system devised by Ezra Gilliland in 1884, which had worked for a maximum of fifteen telephones— Strowger came up with a system that could serve ninety-nine telephones, based on a sort of windshield wiper in the central office that automatically moved around to touch the contacts of the number being called when the caller pressed the correct number of times on two buttons attached to his telephone. To get number 99, the caller had to punch each button nine times. This remarkable contrivance of a man who might be expected to have been handier with embalming fluid than with mechanical devices was, beyond question, the first successful automatic switchboard, and the lineal forebear of the "step-by-step" system, the original dial-telephone switchboard. On the strength of his patent, Strowger in 1891 set up the Automatic Electric Company. Later American

Bell, starting with licenses from Strowger, would refine out the crudities of his system and make dial telephony commercially acceptable; but the fact that in 1891 someone outside the Bell System had made this important breakthrough was a harbinger of competition to come.[15]

And to come soon. The American Bell annual report for 1893, issued the following March, gave stockholders the good news that in a year of national financial panic, the company had achieved a 38 per cent improvement in its earnings. It also gave the following news that was less than good: "The second Bell patent, that numbered 186,787, dated January 30, 1877, expired on the 30th of January last, and magneto receiving telephones are no longer covered by patent." Telephony was up for grabs, and the strangest era in its history was begun.

# CHAPTER 5

# "Both Phones"

In the early 1890s, American Bell's hopes of continuing its monopoly were pinned on the Berliner patent, which had originally been applied for in 1877 and to which the Bell company had acquired all rights the following year. Although Berliner's transmitter (specifically, microphone) had been clearly the best one developed up to that time, the Patent Office had mysteriously failed to act on the application until November 1891, when, equally inscrutably, it granted the patent.

The delay was the crux of the matter. Since the term of patents was seventeen years, American Bell was now able to claim that it held a new patent broadly covering all telephone transmitters and running until 1908, and that therefore any competition before that date would be infringement. To emphasize the point, in 1894, shortly after the expiration of the second Bell patent, American Bell sent every officer of each of the newly emerging independent telephone companies a notice of infringement of the Berliner patent, along with a warning that American Bell had won every one of the hundreds of infringement suits it had brought in the past.

On the face of the matter, though, it was obviously unfair that the Bell monopoly should be preserved for fourteen years more solely because of foot-dragging in the Patent Office. James Storrow, American Bell's lawyer, realized this. Late in 1891 he wrote to President Hudson, "The Bell Company has had a monopoly more profitable and more controlling—and more generally hated—

than any ever given by any patent. The attempt to prolong it . . .
by the Berliner patent will bring a great strain on that patent and
a great pressure on the courts." This advice was ignored by Hudson. In 1893 the pressure on the courts of which Storrow had
written took the form of a suit brought by the Department of
Justice in Massachusetts to annul the Berliner patent on the
ground that its issuance had been wrongfully delayed by the
Patent Office—with the connivance of American Bell. In 1894 the
Federal Court of Massachusetts declared the patent void; the
Circuit Court of Appeals subsequently reversed this judgment,
and finally, in 1897, the Supreme Court sustained the patent; but
in a subsequent Bell suit against the National Telephone Manufacturing Company, the court construed the patent in such a narrow way as to destroy its effectiveness in prolonging the Bell
monopoly. The Berliner patent was thus put effectively out of
business.

All through this welter of litigation, and right up to the turn
of the century, American Bell chose to compete with the rising
independents chiefly in the courts rather than by trying to provide
better and cheaper telephone service. But there were now thousands of telephone patents in force other than Berliner's, and in
1897 American Bell for the first time began to lose cases when
within a few weeks two other important Bell-held patents—on the
switch hook and the automatic switch—were struck down in Chicago. The tide was turning. As late as 1901, two suits by the Bell
company against major independents were defeated in Massachusetts; the suits had been based on the battered Berliner patent.[1]

In truth, by 1894 the public was tired of the Bell monopoly
and strongly favored telephone competition. Dubious and prolonged litigation could no longer preserve the monopoly against a
public outcry for lower rates and better service. As a Bell System
financial historian has put it, "where the Bell company enjoyed
monopoly privileges, officials of the company were discourteous
and dictatorial, and the service was not satisfactory." Whether or
not competition could correct these faults was another matter. The
same historian goes on, "The independent companies, for the most
part, were concerned not to improve service for the public good,
but rather to make money by corporate manipulations." American
Bell had been such a tidily profitable operation throughout the
1880s as to make independent entrepreneurs' mouths water for a

share of the boodle, and when the Bell patents expired they were quick to leap into the fray with stock promotions based on rosy promises—many of which never resulted in the installation of a single telephone.

On the other hand, many did. Since Western Electric would not sell telephone equipment to independents, they needed their own manufacturers, and in 1894 they had several all ready to accommodate them, such as the Monarch Telephone Manufacturing Company of Chicago and the American Electric Telephone Company of Kokomo, Indiana. Naturally enough, the first independent operating companies set up operations in rural areas where American Bell provided no service. Suddenly a new life was opened up for the isolated farmer or the bored villager—a wider, brighter world with more people in it, a whole new existence. Noblesville, Indiana, claimed the distinction of having the first independent telephone exchange in the United States. Others followed quickly, among them Wichita Falls, Texas; Salina, Kansas; Canton, Ohio; Rock Falls, Illinois; and many, many others. Iowa, heart of the farm country, became the natural nexus of independent telephony, with local exchanges springing up so exuberantly that by the turn of the century the state held more than one thousand of them, out of some six thousand coast to coast.

As the decade wore on, the independents gained confidence, and for good reason. In 1898 the Michigan Independent Telephone Association could claim that independents operated sixteen thousand telephones in that state against fourteen thousand for American Bell. In most instances the independents operated in places where there was no Bell service, but in a few, in Michigan and elsewhere, competition was coming to be direct. In some towns there were two telephone systems, not interconnected. A citizen who wished to be in touch with all other telephone users needed to have two phones and two directories; before making a call, he had to know which system the person being called was a subscriber to. In 1897 the independent companies—now some five thousand strong—formed themselves into the National Independent Telephone Association to "plan joint resistance to any aggressions of the American Bell Telephone Company."

What were these aggressions? Although they were later to be many and vigorous, American Bell's reaction to competition in its early years was, as we have seen, chiefly to sue and hope for the best. Indeed, hopes seem not to have been very high, since the American Bell directors reacted to the very threat of competition by selling much of their stock; in 1895 the directors as a group owned six thousand shares, less than half the number they had held in 1881. Apprehension, tempered by a certain defiance, seems to have been the mood at the company's Boston headquarters. Meanwhile business remained good. American Bell continued in most instances to charge high rates—in general, about $125 to $150 per year for a business phone, $100 for a residence one—and its business continued to grow in a steady, orderly way. After a setback in 1894, net profits and dividends increased each year for the rest of the decade, until, for the year 1899, earnings went over the $5 million mark for the first time and $3.88 million was paid out in dividends. Technical advance was also proceeding in a steady, if leisurely, way. During the 1890s virtually the entire Bell plant was made over from single-wire to two-wire circuits, vastly reducing the problem of static. Many additional long-distance lines were put into service, among them New York–Chicago in 1892, Chicago–Nashville in 1895, New York–Omaha and New York–Minneapolis in 1897. The first complete common-battery switchboard, eliminating the need for a battery at each telephone, was put into service in Worcester, Massachusetts, in 1896, and New York City got its first in Harlem the following year.

The lofty disdain with which American Bell looked upon the independents in their early years is indicated by the fact that apart from periodic reports on the Berliner patent litigation, it never so much as mentioned competition in its annual reports to stockholders until 1901.

But in the latter half of the decade there came an omnious change in the independents' tactics. Flushed with their success in the Midwest and West, they began to make frontal assaults on the Bell heartland—the urban Northeast, from which it derived its important revenues. As early as 1895, a small independent system competing with Bell's was operating in Washington, D.C., although somewhat nervously; as a trade publication in the nation's capital reported, "The manufacturer of the transmitters is evidently dubious about the decision rendered by the Boston Circuit Court of Appeals sustaining the Berliner patent." (There was a single telephone in the White House at the time—a Bell phone.) By 1897 American Bell had already taken steps to defend its richly profitable New York City territory by setting up the Hudson River Telephone Company, in New Jersey, as a sort of kept "independent" to serve as a buffer against competition infiltrating from the West. Nevertheless, by 1899 the Bell interests were fighting it out in the streets of New York—or rather, in the conduits under the streets. The New York Telephone Company had its underground wires in the conduits of the Empire City Subway Company, and when the promoters of would-be telephone competition asked permission to install wires of their own there, the Empire City Subway Company refused—logically enough, since New York Telephone controlled Empire City Subway through stock ownership. The courts refused the independents permission to build their own underground conduits, and that was the end of the threat of telephone competition in New York City.

In New England—heartland of the Bell heartland—competition never really got off the ground, partly because American Bell was so well entrenched both technically and politically in that area, partly because its licensees there responded promptly with better service and lower rates. In Connecticut, for example, competition developed for the first time in 1899 in the form of an independent company that planned to established service in New London using the Strowger automatic system. After extended court hearings—at which the president and superintendent of the local Bell licensee, the Southern New England Telephone Company, testified at length—the petition for a charter was denied, and so the competitive project died. Nevertheless, as the historian of the Southern New England Company points out, the supporters of independent telephony in Connecticut "formed a powerful opposition and presented the company with a public relations problem of considerable magnitude. Their agitation also forced a hastening of the program of expansion." In addition, it hastened the process of conversion to a common-battery system, and surely played a role in bringing about a reduction in the average basic annual rental per telephone in Connecticut by about 34 percent between 1891 and 1901.[2]

Not just in Connecticut, but in many other places, competition—along with accelerating public demand—stimulated American Bell to much more rapid expansion than it had previously experienced or even wanted; whereas there had been 240,000 Bell phones in service in 1892, at the end of 1899 there were over 800,000. Such expansion created a need for huge quantities of new capital, thereby confronting the company with a problem. American Bell was still a Massachusetts corporation, subject to the exceptionally restrictive Massachusetts corporation laws, which required, among other things, that any increase in capitalization be approved by the state legislature; that stockholdings by the parent company in subsidiaries be limited; and that new stock could not be offered to existing stockholders below the market price. American Bell's authorized capitalization was still only ten million dollars, and the other restrictions now severely cramped its financial style. However, an elegant solution was at hand. American Bell already had a fully-owned subsidiary corporation in New York, a state with a much more permissive attitude toward corporate expansion. That subsidiary was the American Telephone and Telegraph Corporation, the "long-distance company," which since its founding had progressively increased its capitalization from one hundred thousand to twenty million dollars. The solution was to transfer the assets of American Bell to AT&T, which would then take over American Bell's function as well as continuing to provide long-distance service. Accordingly, the American Bell management bade farewell to Boston and gradually moved its offices to downtown Manhattan, and on December 30, 1899—the next-to-last day of the old century—AT&T, with a new capitalization of over seventy million dollars, became the parent company of the Bell System, which, of course, it has remained ever since.

2

As the reconstituted company, and indeed the nation, moved into the new century, American imperialism had reached its high-water mark with the recent conquest of the Philippines and the recent annexation of Hawaii and part of Samoa; conservative national monetary policy was enshrined with the passage of the Gold Standard Act, dashing the hopes of debtors for cheap money through free coinage of silver; public hatred of monopolies was building up and would soon explode in the era of muckraking and trust busting; and Scott Joplin had just introduced a good part of white America to the glories of ragtime with his "Maple Leaf Rag."

As the year 1900 began, the Bell System had 800,000 telephones in service to some 600,000 for the independents, and assets of over $120 million to the independents' $55 million. But Bell was losing ground. Its financial policies still leaned heavily to the side of conservatism; the original Yankee capitalists were still in firm control, as evidenced by the fact that the majority of the 1877 board of directors was still the majority in 1900. The need for large amounts of new capital to meet competition implied financial weakness, present or future; and in the meantime, service was bad or inadequate, or both. As Theodore Vail wrote in 1901—from the knowledgeable but detached point of view of a former general manager now engaged in other matters: "The worst of the opposition has come from the lack of facilities afforded by our companies—that is, either no service, or poor service." Quick to sense weakness, a group of alert and hungry outside financiers mounted in 1899 the first organized challenge to Bell's domination of the telephone industry since Western Union's in 1878–79. The Philadelphia traction magnates Peter A. B. Widener and W. J. Elkins, with support from the Rockefeller oil interests, organized the Telephone, Telegraph and Cable Company with the announced intention of setting up independent telephone companies in Boston and New York. What they did first, rather, was to buy stock control of the Erie Telephone & Telegraph Company, a holding company of Bell licensees, in which American Bell had only minority holdings, that controlled the telephone business in seven states—North and South Dakota, Minnesota, Wisconsin, Texas, Arkansas, and Michigan. The move, had it succeeded, might well have proved to be an entering wedge to getting control of AT&T itself. It failed because the insurgents were unable to raise the money to pay for their purchase; Bell representatives took over a large bad debt of the Erie company that its new owners had incurred, the Erie company thereby fell back into Bell hands, and so the whole venture failed. The significant thing about it is that the reason for its failure appears to have been the disapproval of the banking suzerain of the time, J. P. Morgan, who persuaded his banking allies not to support the Philadelphia group. Later events, to be recounted, suggest that his motive for doing this was that he had designs of his own on the Bell System.[3]

It was immediately after the turn of the century that independent telephony came to be a national institution, and a serious matter for the Bell System. Virgin territory—places where there was no telephone service and enough potential customers to make it profitable—was getting to be in short supply; as a result, head-on competition, in the form of two or even three telephone systems operating simultaneously in a single town or city, became increasingly common. There were three main results: competitive rate-cutting, wasteful duplication, and public inconvenience. In Indianapolis, for example, there was a Bell licensee operating that in 1898 had 2,000 telephones in service, at rates of $72 per year for a business place and $48 for a residence. Then the independent New Telephone Company was organized with local capital. Charging about half the Bell rates, it immediately attracted 2,500 subscribers, and by 1906 the situation was a standoff —10,000 Bell phones, 10,000 independent, and several thousand duplications. Businesses, in particular, had to maintain and advertise "Both phones" or be unavailable by telephone to one set of subscribers or the other. In Toledo, the independent Home Telephone Company obtained a franchise in 1901, again cutting Bell rates almost in half; by 1906 Toledo had 10,000 independent phones to 6,700 for Bell, with 3,400 duplications. Cleveland, Pittsburgh, and Detroit had rather similar experiences. In Nebraska and Iowa, there came at one time to be 260,000 independent phones to 80,000 for Bell, and in Iowa in 1905, there were 147 towns with two telephone exchanges and a few with three. In some cases, though, the independents came a cropper by cutting rates at the expense of their own profitability. In Pittsburgh in 1906, the Bell company had about 45,000 subscribers and the independent about 12,000; Bell charged $125 for business and $100 for residence, the independent $72 and $36; the Bell company was prosperous and the independent was losing money.

Lower rates, combined with the appeal of their underdog status, made the independents popular and usually able to win the referendums that were often resorted to as a means of deciding whether or not an independent franchise should be granted. In Portland, Oregon, in 1906, after an initial independent competitor had failed and been forced to sell out to Bell, a new one won a franchise by an overwhelming vote of 12,213 to 560. It was closer in Omaha: Bell 3,625, the independent 7,653. The same year, a national survey of 1,400 businessmen, conducted by the organization that now grandly called itself the International Independent Telephone Association of America, showed that 1,245 believed that competition had resulted in better telephone service in the respondents' cities, while 982 believed that it had forced Bell to improve its own service there.[4]

A curious and intriguing feature of the era of telephone competition is that in the older cities where it occurred, there was a tendency for the sides to be drawn along class lines. The two competing systems not being interconnected, it was possible to talk only to those on the same system; naturally, one wanted to be able to talk to one's friends, and perhaps those one would like to be able to claim as friends. In Minneapolis, for example—according to the recollection of a survivor of the competitive era there—the Bell exchange, being the longer-established, was the exchange of the socially elite, while the competing Tri-State Telephone Company was for just about everybody else. To become a Bell subscriber showed either social acceptance or pretensions to it. This was, of course, a club that anyone could join who could pay the tariff—but if a new joiner wasn't really "in," would the other members talk to *him?* Thus the telephone became a sort of electric embodiment of the sentiment contained in the old Boston jingle about

> The land of the bean and the cod,
> When the Lowells speak only to Cabots
> And the Cabots speak only to God.

A striking parallel development to the rise of the independent companies was the springing up of independent farmer or rural lines—do-it-yourself, not-for-profit telephone systems in remote areas served by neither Bell nor the independents, constructed, maintained, and cooperatively financed by the users, who might number a few dozen, a half dozen, or only two. A Census Bureau report of the time explained the process:

A group of farmers who lived within a reasonable distance of one another, having come to the conclusion that telephone service was an essential comfort of life . . . would meet together and arrange to establish a telephone system which should connect them with one another. The work involved . . . would be so divided that each member of the association would contribute an equivalent part of the material and labor. If the country was wooded, the farmers making up the association agreed to cut and supply the poles and haul them to the places where they were needed. . . . The farmers' boys and the farmhands did the work of setting the poles and putting on the crossarms. . . . The wire and the insulators, the switchboard and the instruments, would have to be bought. . . . The work of stringing the wires and installing the instruments was taken up by the mechanically-minded farmers and their boys, and in a very short time a complete telephone system was in operation. The switchboard was placed in the house of one of the members of the association situated at some convenient point, and the operation of the lines was attended to by the wife and dauhgters of the farmer in whose home the board was located.

Sooner or later the members would feel the need for connection with the "outside world," and arrangements would be made for the cooperative to be taken over either by Bell or by the nearest independent company; but in 1907, at the height of the do-it-yourself movement, the Census Bureau counted 17,702 separate private rural circuits with 565,000 telephones and 486,000 miles of wire in service. How many lives were saved by calls for medical help or warnings of approaching tornadoes over such lines, and how many times did those straggling wires, strung and hooked up by barely literate amateurs puzzling over electrical manuals, rescue an isolated farm wife from winter stir-craziness? The Census Bureau could not count such things.

In 1903 Bell claimed 1,514 main telephone exchanges with 1,278,000 subscribers, and the independent companies, excluding the nonprofit rural cooperatives, 6,150 exchanges with something like two million subscribers. By both standards, Bell was decisively outnumbered. In 1905 a well-known electrical engineer could entitle a book on telephone development *How the Bell Lost Its Grip*. Perhaps that was an exaggeration, but if the Bell had not lost its grip, it had its work cut out for it.[5]

3

The Bell company's abandonment of its attempt to maintain monopoly through patent suits, and its entry into all-out direct competition with the independents, coincided approximately with its headquarters move to New York and assumption of the new corporate name of AT&T. In that competition, it used every fair method available to it, and some that were not fair. In its annual report for 1901, the company finally admitted formally to its stockholders that there was a problem: "Competition from telephone companies not associated with this Company has existed for several years and is likely to continue in some places for some time to come. While it has in some localities affected the Licensees of this Company disadvantageously, by reducing, for a time at least, the number of their subscribers and forcing them to meet competitive rates . . . the consequences of the competition to the business as a whole have not been of serious moment." (Indeed they had not: AT&T's net earnings that year were $7.4 million as against $5.48 million the previous year.)

Of AT&T's competitive tactics, rate cutting to meet the independents' rates was the most orthodox and, in the short run, the most beneficial to telephone users. In Cleveland, for example, competition forced the local Bell licensee to reduce annual rates from $120 to $72 for a business phone and from $72 to $48 for a home phone. By many accounts, the generally rude and arrogant attitude of Bell officials that had prevailed during monopoly days tended to disappear and be replaced by a far more attractive blandness, or even an active desire to please.

Among the more devious competitive methods used, there was the establishment of spurious competition, like the buffer company that was set up to protect the rich New York City area's vulnerable western flank. Then there was the use of business muscle to persuade local banks to deny lines of credit to independents—a process that the Federal Communications Commission later called "slow financial strangulation"—and the use of political muscle, in places where it was available, to bring about the denial of franchises to independents or to make the conditions for the granting of franchises as onerous as possible. In Buffalo, for example, a franchise was granted to the Frontier Telephone Company on condition that it pay the city fifty thousand dollars in cash and a 3 percent gross receipts tax, and give the city the free use of one hundred telephones, while none of these impositions were put upon the local Bell licensee. Frontier soon went broke. In one case, that of San Francisco, representatives of the Bell licensee were accused of outright bribery to bring about the defeat of a competing franchise—in response, it is true, to an attempt by the city's political boss to extort an improper payment from the franchise seeker. At the subsequent trial of Louis Glass, vice-president of Pacific States Telephone & Telegraph Company, who was accused of authorizing payments out of the company treasury to the city supervisors, the special prosecutor sarcastically denounced the Bell executives as "these respectable broad-cloth wearers, these highest members of society," and exclaimed, rather floridly, "Oh, if it were not that I love my country, these conditions would fill me with disgust, and I would vomit in reply." Glass was sentenced to a five-year prison term, but his conviction was later set aside on technical grounds.

The San Francisco case was apparently an isolated one, in which the briber, if such he was, could be defended on the grounds that he was fighting fire with fire in the climate of a city that was an ethical shambles politically and, indeed, a physical shambles after the earthquake of 1906. The same cannot be said about the secret buy-ups of independents that AT&T went in for beginning soon after 1900. In June of 1903, the telephone industry was startled to learn that the Kellogg Switchboard & Supply Company, an important independent manufacturer, was not only controlled by agents of AT&T, but had been so controlled, under a pledge of secrecy by the sellers, for the previous eighteen months. During that period, Kellogg had been continuing to supply the unsuspecting independents, including some of the largest of them, while agents of the independents' great rival, AT&T, had been reaping most of the profits. But the potential plot was thicker than that. At that time, some of the most vital parts of Kellogg apparatus were in suit under Bell claims of patent infringement. Whether or not these claims had merit, the Bell company was for eighteen months in a position, if it chose, to strike at the independents not one at a time but en masse. With its secret control of Kellogg, it could order Kellogg not to defend the patent suits, or to put up only a mock defense; if the infringement claims were then affirmed, every independent operating company using Kellogg apparatus would find itself with a plant that it could not legally use, and would probably be forced to shut down operations. The scheme (if it was one; there is no affirmative evidence that AT&T contemplated such a Balkan course of action) failed—first because the Bell control of Kellogg was dragged into the open through a suit by minority stockholders of Kellogg, and, second, because in 1909 the stockholder suit was sustained by the Illinois Supreme Court, and the Kellogg sale to Bell was set aside.[6]

There was also a string of direct purchases by Bell of independent operating companies, most of which were kept secret at least for a time for no reason more devious than to postpone public and government disapproval. In 1905, according to Harry B. MacMeal, the historian of independent telephony, "a storm of indignation swept independent circles" with the news that the United Telephone Company of Bluffton, Indiana, had been sold to a Bell licensee. That was only one of many such buy-ups. In 1906 the corporation council of Chicago described the Bell System as a "ruthless, grinding, oppressive monopoly"—a view clearly in reflection of the popular opinion of the day. AT&T about that time took to buying up independents through nominees who presumably could not be identified as Bell agents. Thus in 1909, after James E. Brailey, Jr. bought the majority holdings in two fairly large independents, he first denied but later admitted that it had been actually a Bell deal.

But AT&T's real ace in the hole in its battle with the independents was its steadfast refusal to interconnect. Bell, of course, had all the long-distance lines except for comparatively few over intermediate distances that had latterly been put up by the independents, which usually lacked the capital to undertake anything more than local service. So a user who wanted to talk other than locally needed to be a Bell subscriber. AT&T's strict policy against interconnection was legal; it was obviously logical from a business point of view; and it could be ethically justified under free-enterprise ideology, since Bell, under patent protection, had got there first. But independent subscribers wanted to make long-distance calls, and independent companies were noisy in their demands that they be allowed to do so. Beginning in 1904, various state legislatures passed laws mandating interconnection between telephone companies. AT&T always attacked the laws, and, at first, always won. Indeed, the Bell policy against interconnection could reasonably be attacked only under a public-utility concept of the telephone business that would put service equal to or ahead of private profit. And such a concept had not yet gained the ascendancy at AT&T, or in the courts, or in the federal government in 1907.[7]

4

By this time the telephone was settling into the national consciousness as a fixed and permanent part of American life. In the process, it was bringing about great changes in ways of working, living, and thinking.

The most easily visible and economically significant such change was in the operation of the financial markets. Timing, along with intrinsic value, is and always has been one of the two key factors in the trading of securities; elaborate devices to gain time, like Nathan Rothschild's signal-and-carrier system, which brought him advance news of Wellington's victory at Waterloo in 1815, had been the basis of many a fortune. In pre-telephone days, securities trading in America, although it had often had disastrous national consequences, had essentially been a matter between a few men in the downtown areas of the big eastern cities. Now it was, at least potentially, nationwide; a person in a distant city—if he was lucky enough to get a call through to New York and to make himself heard over it—could buy a stock on favorable news almost as fast as his counterpart in Wall Street. A foreshortening of time and space, amounting almost to a new dimension, came into stock and bond trading; Wall Street went national. The economic effect was to increase the liquidity of securities and to increase vastly the fund-raising capability of businesses, paving the way for economic expansion. Most dramatically, telephone communication between bankers in different cities made possible the rapid raising of huge pools of capital in times of crisis. J. P. Morgan boasted that his partner, George W. Perkins, by means of a series of telephone calls, could "raise twenty million in twenty minutes." Morgan is generally, and properly, credited with heading off the financial panic of 1907 by extending a $25 million credit to other banks in the nick of time; in view of the role in the crisis of rapidly arranged cooperation between New York banks and those in Chicago and St. Louis, the telephone deserves some of the credit, too.

If Perkins of the Morgan firm was the first banker to appreciate the possibilities of the telephone, the stock trader and railroad man E. H. Harriman was the first industrialist to do so. Indeed, Harriman may be said to have been the first of a long line of telephone fanatics of the executive life. Long before his death in 1909, he had installed in his country mansion at Arden, New York, a hundred telephones, including one in his bathroom; he also had one in his private car (requiring connection to a stationary plug, since radio telephony was not yet practicable) and one at his camp in the Oregon wilderness. Accused of being a slave to the telephone, Harriman retorted—as many an executive faced with the same charge would later repeat—"Nonsense. It is a slave to me."

The telephone's effect on rural America was as extensive as its effect on financial life was intensive. The increase in the number of rural telephones between 1902 and 1907 was truly phenomenal—from 267,000 to 1,465,000, or 449 percent. In fact, by the latter date the states with the densest concentrations of telephones per population were not the eastern states where telephony had begun, but Iowa, Nebraska, Washington, California, and Nevada, each of which had less than ten persons to a telephone, while each of the northeastern states had between ten and thirty per telephone. (The national laggards were four southern states— the Carolinas, Alabama, and Mississippi—which had less than one telephone per fifty people.) The rise in the morale of farmers and their families brought about by this quasi revolution was quickly reflected in an increase in farm productivity. In addition to conversation with neighbors, in those pre-radio days the telephone sometimes brought the farmer news; the magazine *Scientific American* reported in 1906 that in Minnesota, Iowa, and South Dakota news reports were being broadcast once and sometimes twice daily. (The newspapers at first feared injury to their circulation, but in a curious preview of events to come later, the reverse proved to be true: thus was discovered the McLuhanite principle that the appetite for communication grows by what it feeds on.) All in all, at the end of the decade President Theodore Roosevelt's Country Life Commission was able to designate the telephone as one of the foremost influences making for "the solution of the rural problem."

The effects were not all unequivocally beneficial; some were merely human. Party lines were the rule rather than the exception in rural telephony, and often a farmer cooperative circuit was just one big party line. Eavesdropping on the neighbors came to be a standard country entertainment, sometimes productive of quarrels. A new temptation had been introduced into life. The magazine *The World's Work* reported in 1905 that a farm wife who had had telephone service just a few months was asked how her family liked it and replied, "Well, we liked it a lot at first, and do yet, only spring work is coming on so heavy that we don't hardly have time to listen now." A short story about early-in-the-century rural telephony, Harriet Prescott Spofford's "A Rural Telephone," turns on the community's discovery of a tyrannical old woman's eavesdropping through the fact that her grandfather clock's ticking can be heard on the line, and the old woman's subsequent realization, resulting from further listening in, that she is mistreating her daughter. Tampering with the instrument itself occasionally led to trouble. MacMeal assures us that in Gratiot, Wisconsin, in 1907, "a rural subscriber took the transmitter of his telephone apart to see what made it work. In doing so, he spilled the granular carbon. Being unable to retrieve the carbon, he decided that as they looked pretty much alike, gunpowder probably would do as a substitute. He put the instrument together and manipulated the switchhook. Bang!"[8]

"My heart, what a blessin' the telephone is!" is the last line of "A Rural Telephone." All over the Great Plains and the Great West, the telephone brought surcease from a kind of desperation not amenable to change by the most benevolent government policy. It also brought into being a new American figure, always necessary and sometimes heroic, the rural operator. In the natural course of things, she became an involuntary message center. According to a 1905 magazine article, among typical requests of the operator were the following: "Oh, Central! Ring me up in fifteen minutes, so I won't forget to take the bread out of the oven." "Say, Central, I have put the receiver of the phone in the baby's cradle, and if she wakes up and cries, call me up." "Central, ring me up half an hour before the 2:17 train in the morning. See if it's late before you call, please." It can be presumed that "Central"—probably more often addressed by her first name—reacted to such demands for service beyond the call of duty according to her nature, long-suffering or otherwise. In popular literature, though, she became a heroine, intelligent, level-headed, and self-sacrificing, solving crimes and domestic crises and, most particularly, giving warning of floods and fires.

In city and country alike, the telephone was creating a new

habit of mind—a habit of tenseness and alertness, of demanding and expecting immediate results, whether in business, love, or other forms of social intercourse. The twentieth-century decline in the art of letter writing, which can legitimately be laid at the telephone's door, is only one symptom of the change of mood. The fact seems to be that the United States is the telephone's natural home and the twentieth its natural century, and that the instruments and the people found each other when the century was hardly begun. The cause and effect of the matter remain problematical. It is certain, though, that the familiar modern complaint of "telephonitis" existed already by 1909, and that women were already being accused of being most susceptible to it. An article in *Lippincott's Monthly* in 1909 declared that "telephoning from habit finally becomes a vice, and a nuisance to the courtesies," and that "for the exchange of twaddle between foolish women . . . it has become an unmitigated domestic curse."[9]

Before the coming of the new century, the telephone had found its way into American public art with its prominent inclusion, along with the telegraph, in a mural in the Boston Public Library by the celebrated French artist Puvis de Chavannes, which showed the telephone allegorically as a flying figure over the orotund inscription: "By the wondrous agency of electricity, speech flashes through space and swift as lightning bears tidings of good and evil." The infiltration of the telephone and its uses into the public consciousness of Europe, as of the United States, in the early years of the twentieth century is beautifully reflected in two of the major novels of modern literature. James Joyce's *Ulysses* was first published in 1922, but the events it describes take place in Dublin on June 16, 1904, and to judge from the prominence of the telephone in its action and in the ruminations of its characters—even allowing for possible anachronism—Irish acceptance of the innovation at that time was more on the American pattern than the British. The telephone appears eight times in *Ulysses*, and appears, surprisingly, not as something new and strange but as an accepted part of life; indeed, it seems to have graduated from the status of an object to something alive and with a personality of its own. Twice its ring is described as an irritating "whir"; once it rings "rudely" in a woman's ear; once it becomes a sort of pander in the flirtation of a young rogue, Blazes Boylan, with a flower girl. It figures twice in the famous Nighttown scene, first when a drunk uses it for a ribald joke, then, more interestingly, in a fantasy of the guilt-ridden hero Leopold Bloom, who imagines a "medley of voices" cataloguing the sins of his past: "He went through a form of clandestine marriage with at least one woman in the shadow of the Black Church. Unspeakable messages he telephoned mentally to Miss Dunn at an address in d'Olier Street while he presented himself indecently to the instrument in the callbox. . . ." The word "indecently" gives the clue to why the telephone has a personality in *Ulysses:* in Bloom's imagination, and Joyce's, the instrument *becomes* the person on the other end of the line. And the fact that Bloom reproaches himself for unspeakable messages that were telephoned only mentally is dramatic proof of how the telephone was, so soon, finding its way into the deep places of human psychology.

Marcel Proust's *The Captive*—the fifth volume of his masterwork, *Remembrance of Things Past*—contains a passage that relates the telephone to early-in-the-century society rather than psychology. It is perhaps the most famous telephone passage in great, as opposed to popular, literature. The hero, Marcel, possessor of a telephone that apparently works better than most telephones in France did at the time of the action (about 1905), has an aged housemaid, Françoise, who epitomizes French resistance to using the instrument, an act that she finds "as unpleasant as vaccination or as dangerous as the aeroplane." She simply refuses to learn to use it. Marcel uses it enthusiastically, but of course has trouble with the notorious French operators. Calling Andrée, a friend of his flirtatious mistress, Albertine, to get information about Albertine's comings and goings, Marcel reports:

. . . I took hold of the receiver, invoked the implacable deities, but succeeded only in arousing their fury which expressed itself in the single word "Engaged!" Andrée was indeed engaged in talking to some one else. As I waited for her to finish her conversation, I asked myself how it was—now that so many of our painters are seeking to revive the feminine portraits of the eighteenth century, in which the cleverly devised setting is a pretext for portraying expressions of expectation, spleen, interest, distraction—how it was that none of our modern Bouchers or Fragonards had yet painted, instead of "The Letter" or "The Harpischord," this scene which might be entitled "At the Telephone," in which there would come spontaneously to the lips of the listener a smile all the more genuine in that it is conscious of being unobserved.

At last Marcel gets Andrée on the line, but his telephonic troubles have only begun. As soon as he falls silent for a moment, the operator—now called an "irascible" deity—comes on the line and says, "Come along, I've been holding the line for you all this time; I shall cut you off." He hastily resumes the conversation, and continues it without further pauses, placating the irascible deity who might cut him off by thinking of her as a "great poet" able not only to evoke "Andrée's presence" but to envelop it "in the atmosphere peculiar to the home, the district, the very life itself of Albertine's friend." With all its charm and high spirits, this passage shows eloquently how early the emotional force of the telephone and the operator in human lives was understood by the people who used telephones, as interpreted by their artists.

5

AT&T actually flourished through the peak years of competition; the rapid forced expansion and the telephone's growing popularity brought about increased revenues and profits at the expense of financial weakness caused by vastly increased demands for capital. President Hudson, having died in 1900, was temporarily replaced by Alexander Cochrane, a long-time member of the Yankee board, and then, in 1901, formally succeeded by Frederick Perry Fish, a Boston corporation and patent lawyer who, his conservative background notwithstanding, tried earnestly to repair the faults of the Hudson administration, traveling the country to become acquainted with the officers and problems of the regional Bell companies and trying to improve the public view of the Bell System. In 1902—the year AT&T abandoned the old system of leasing instruments to the operating companies, and adopted the so-called license contract, under which the companies pay AT&T a percentage of gross revenue in return for services—profits were up sharply; in 1903 they were up again by more than one-third, and in that year's annual report President Fish felt confident enough to crow that "the competing companies, in almost every city of any size . . . have found, sometimes as the result of a bitter experience, that the cost of doing the business was far greater than they anticipated." By the end of 1904, the number of Bell subscribers was about double what it had been three years earlier, and 1905 saw the company's greatest one-year growth up to that time.

And meanwhile technical progress was continuing. The greatest such advance in the early years of the century was the development of the loading coil, a device for turning inductance, that old enemy of one-wire telephony, to advantage by harnessing it to reduce attenuation, the tendency of a telephonic signal to grow weaker the longer the line over which it is transmitted. The loading coil's inventor was Dr. Michael Idvorsky Pupin, a professor of mathematics at Columbia University, who had arrived in the United States in 1874 as a Serbian immigrant with neither a penny to his name nor a word of English on his tongue; Pupin applied for a patent on the loading coil in December 1899 and was granted it in June 1900. A Bell System scientist, George A. Campbell, had been working on the same device concurrently with Pupin and made his unsuccessful patent application only a month after Pupin's; thus, through a non-Bell man's narrow victory of priority, Elisha Gray was avenged. At all events, AT&T promptly bought patent rights from Dr. Pupin—who would never again be penniless, or anything like it; he lived his later years like a grand duke of his native land—and soon began putting his invention into service.

The loading coil was a huge advance in long-distance telephony, though not the definitive advance that the electronic repeater would later prove to be. Before loading coils, transmission over great distances above ground required copper wires of considerable thickness and resulting expense, while underground cables would work for distances of no more than a few miles. The advantage of loading coils was that, installed at intervals of a mile or so along open wire, they made possible the use of thin wire instead of thick, effecting a saving of as much as forty dollars per mile; while similarly deployed along underground cables, they made possible for the first time the use of cables over substantial distances. The first such cable, between New York and Philadelphia, equipped with inductance coils every mile and a quarter, was begun in 1905 and put into service in 1906. But the weakness of the inductance coil was that it could not amplify sound—only reduce attenuation. Long-distance telephone service was still unreliable and the signals often maddeningly weak. In effect, the loading coil was the first half of the invention that would ultimately solve the problem; the other half, the repeater, would not come for several more years.[10]

Apparently, then, competition was just the thing the Bell System had needed to force it to expand and grow. But the pressure for growth had taken its toll: it had caused a financial drain that was leeching away the company's strength and making it a potential prize for whoever could finance it. Between 1902 and 1907, debt grew from around $60 million to over $200 million. Earnings were no longer sufficient to finance expansion, so new Bell securities in quantity came to be available to the public, which, by and large, showed little interest in them. The financial battle over AT&T, which had been previewed with the abortive Widener-Elkins foray in 1899, began in earnest in 1902. It was a three-way battle involving the doughty Yankee capitalists who had been in control since 1880; the telegraph man Clarence Mackay; and a syndicate of bankers headed by J. P. Morgan & Company. When the dust would finally settle five years later, the Yankee capitalists would be unhorsed at last.

They were very much in the saddle in 1902; the key decision-making body, the executive committee, was still unanimously and impeccably Bostonian, consisting of Fish, Cochrane, C. W. Amory, and H. S. Howe. Early that year, however, a block of fifty thousand shares of AT&T stock was sold to a group that included the leading outside bankers George F. Baker, T. Jefferson Coolidge, Jr., and John I. Waterbury, on condition that Baker and Waterbury be elected directors of AT&T. The company's need for money thus led the Bostonians to loosen their grip on its control. And the challenger was the most powerful financier not just of that time but of any time in the United States; for the man behind the buying group was the man behind almost everything in early-century high finance, J. P. Morgan.

Morgan's plans, it soon became clear, involved not only control of AT&T but consolidation of the telephone and telegraph systems of the nation. He wanted to do with the communications industry what he had done with steel through United States Steel and was doing with electrical manufacturing through General Electric. In 1903 his allies Coolidge and Waterbury became trustees of The Mackay Companies, the holding company that controlled Postal Telegraph, the chief rival of Western Union in telegraphy—a company that had been founded in 1886 by the old silver miner John W. Mackay, greatest of the bonanza kings of Virginia City, and now, following his death in 1902, was in the hands of his equally adventurous son Clarence. But Clarence Mackay had his own ambitions to seize control of AT&T, and they now conflicted with those of the Morgan group. Mackay later maintained that Coolidge and Waterbury had first led him to believe that the Bell System was to be handed to him virtually on a platter, and had later gone back on their promise; at all events, the Morgan emissaries, temporarily abandoning the dream of consolidation, went forward with a plan to gain domination of AT&T without Mackay's help. In 1904, fighting a rearguard action to stave off the advancing opposition, the Bell Bostonians sold a twenty-million-dollar bond issue to an anti-Morgan banking syndicate; it was the last time for more than a generation that AT&T bonds would be sold other than under the auspices of the Morgan interests. By that time the AT&T board was divided within its own councils. Early in 1905, Waterbury, now an AT&T director, proposed the sale of eighty-five million dollars of convertible bonds, with an option on fifty million dollars more, directly to the Morgan bank and its associates, without competitive bidding. Seeing the handwriting on the wall, the Bostonians balked; Fish, after consultations with them, flatly rejected the plan. But the need for money pressed ever more fiercely. That December the issue came dramatically to a head at a special meeting of AT&T stockholders. Which was it to be—corporate austerity that might mean inability to compete with the independents, or a sellout to Morgan? The Bostonians appointed a proxy committee heavily stacked in their favor, giving the stockholders no place on the form to vote for substitutes; many stockholders protested by refusing to send in their proxies, and one, Francis Goodwin, wrote to AT&T complaining of "the exceeding insignificance of the individual stockholder." Nevertheless, the directors and officers won the vote, and thereby won the right to sell one hundred million dollars in convertible bonds—by far the largest bundle of corporate securities ever offered up to that time —to anyone they chose, along with an option on fifty million dollars more. The AT&T board, then, had a mandate to do what it wanted. But what did it want? The Bostonian and the Morgan forces now held approximately equal power on it. After an intricate internal struggle, in February 1906 the die was cast when the bonds were sold to J. P. Morgan & Company and its associates, including Kuhn, Loeb & Company, Kidder, Peabody & Company, and Baring Brothers, of London.

The bankers did not yet control AT&T, and indeed, they found themselves with a struggle on their hands for its control. In 1905 Clarence Mackay, having been abandoned by the Morgan faction, decided to go it alone in the most direct possible fashion: he began buying AT&T stock in the open market. By February 1907 he has amassed seventy thousand shares—by far the largest single holding, representing over 5 percent of all stock outstanding. But the Morgan banking syndicate, meanwhile, had resold to the public only ten million dollars of the convertible bonds, keeping the remaining ninety million dollars, which gave *them* potential control through control of the company's financing. Mackay chose that month to demand representation on the AT&T board on the basis of his large holdings, and was roughly rebuffed by Morgan's ally Coolidge, who wrote to President Fish, "The Mackay Companies have nerve. Their interests are opposed to ours and of course at this time cannot secure representation." There followed a final round of infighting between the Bostonians and the Morganians on the AT&T board. In April the Bostonians surrendered. On the seventh, Cochrane and Amory resigned from the executive committee, and on the twenty-third, Fish resigned the presidency and his directorship. Mackay, with the board room door firmly closed to him despite the fact that his AT&T holding eventually reached 82,906 shares, finally gave up his aspirations to have a voice in management. (At last, in 1910, he would sell the entire holding to an AT&T subsidiary for approximately what it had cost him.) So the bankers, led by J. P. Morgan, were in effective control. And the man they installed as the new president of AT&T on May 1, 1907, was Theodore N. Vail.[11]

# 6

Vail's life since his departure from American Bell in 1887 had been that of a gentleman farmer, investor, and adventurer. He had invested in an unsuccessful steam-heating system; he had traveled extensively in Europe, and engaged in various ventures there; he had unexpectedly hit a bonanza in Colorado mining shares; he had developed a hydroelectric power plant in Argentina; he had sailed his yacht, the *Norna,* in the waters off Boston and driven his Kentucky grays on the roads around Speedwell Farms, his country seat in Vermont. It was clearly an interesting life, and evidently a satisfying one. But sometime just after the turn of the century, fortunetellers in both Paris and London had told him that he was destined to do his greatest work after sixty— and more to the point, he remembered the predictions and repeated them to his family and friends. In 1905—the year he turned sixty—his wife, Emma, died, and less than two years later his only son, Davis, followed her. Saddened, and deprived of immediate family (although thereafter he lived much of the time with his sister, Louise Brainard, and his niece Katherine Vail), he was ready in 1907 for the distraction of new challenges.

Indeed, over most of the previous twenty years he had been watching the development of telephony, and of his former company, from afar but with intense interest. In London during the 1890s, his affairs brought him into close contact with the partners of Baring Brothers & Company, the London merchant bankers who were later to become part of the international syndicate headed by J. P. Morgan & Company that would take over financial control of AT&T. In 1901, after Hudson's death, he was asked by the board to assume the company's presidency, but declined. Nevertheless, his continuing personal feeling about AT&T is eloquently suggested in the 1901 memorandum, quoted earlier, in which he criticized it sharply while using the personal pronoun: "The worst of the opposition has come from the lack of facilities afforded by our companies." Not "your" companies, but "our." In 1902—with the approval of the Morgan banking group, which was then making its preparatory moves—he was elected a director of AT&T. He had good reason for allying himself with the Morgan group. It was, after all, his differences with the conservative Bostonians, with their rather narrow and caste-bound concept of the business, that had led to Vail's departure in 1887; now came the insurgent New York and London bankers, with larger visions of a comprehensive system of nationwide communications —the very visions Vail had nourished from the first. And so when

Vail came at last to power in 1907 it was unmistakable—and it was natural—that he came as a representative of the banking group that now held the company in financial thrall.

Early in 1907, not long before Vail, at the age of sixty-two, assumed the presidency of AT&T for the second time (he had, of course, been its president in the middle 1880s—but at that time AT&T had been only the "long-distance company," not the parent of the system), he attended a dinner in Boston with leading officials of AT&T, including President Fish. No announcement was made of the occasion for his presence. To the younger telephone men present, most of whom had never seen him before, a myth and a monument had come to life. Here in their presence, with an avuncular countenance and a Foxy Grandpa full white mustache, was Theodore Vail himself—Theodore Vail, who had managed the affairs of the company when subscribers had been counted in the hundreds rather than the millions, when the very patent on the telephone had been in question, when calls had been made by names rather than numbers, and when a long-distance call had been one across the Charles River. But Vail was not a myth or a monument; rather, he was a man at the apex of his powers who—after sixty—would, for better or worse, do far more than anyone else to build the modern Bell System.[12]

CHAPTER **6**

# A Big Man

But had Vail fallen heir to a prize or to a moribund invalid? In 1907, according to the Census Bureau report, the Bell System had 3,132,000 telephones in service, to about 2,987,000 for the independents exclusive of farmer mutual systems. More competitive Bell policies, the failure of many independents, and the purchase of others by AT&T had served to turn around the situation of a few years earlier, and restored Bell's numerical lead. But the battle was far from over, and the interim winner was a company *in extremis*. Financially, the battle had left it hanging on the ropes. Frequently poor service and heavy-handed competitive tactics had resulted in a terrible public image. Internal struggles for power had left its management largely devoid of aggressive and creative leadership. A concomitant of this lack was a demoralized employee force; as a result of poor supervision and planning, plant work in the Bell System was notoriously dangerous—in some years there were fifty or more fatalities, mostly resulting from falls from high poles—and jobs as operators were shunned by many respectable women because of the company's not wholly undeserved reputation for laxity in controlling the conduct of its male office employees. Finally, in the technical area the business had simply outrun technology; in particular, most of the long-distance circuits were plagued with such noise and delays as to deter all but the most determined callers, and coast-to-coast service was still technologically impossible. All in all, a company that, for all its monetary power and profitability, appeared in imminent danger of a plunge into oblivion—a fact not unnoticed by investors, who saw its stock, which had sold as high as 186 in 1902, sink in 1907 to a low of 88.

As the new president, Vail apparently had an unrestricted hand except in financial policy. The man he was practically, though not nominally, accountable to in that matter was J. P. Morgan, holder of the purse strings. Through the early part of Vail's presidency, Morgan was effectively serving as chairman of AT&T's board of directors, even though in fact he did not sit on the board at all, preferring, as he so often did, to exercise his influence from behind the scenes while delegating formal power to nominees he could count upon. Such a nominee was Vail. The amount of Morgan's influence on Vail's policies as president of AT&T is a matter for debate, since it is little recorded in company documents; some astute students of the company believe that it was greater than has been generally recognized. What is certain, however, is that Vail, with a sure touch so rare in corporate management as to amount to a kind of genius, identified the problems facing AT&T and dealt with them so successfully that within little more than a decade, he transformed a battle-scarred and none too public-spirited company not far from collapse into the modern Bell System.

Almost his first move was to test the financial climate prevailing in the new regime. A representative of Baring Brothers of London, concerned about his firm's inability to sell any part of its huge inventory of AT&T bonds, visited Vail on one of his first days in office. "Don't worry," Vail told him. "You will get rid of those bonds and want more of our bonds before the year is out." The Baring man left still skeptical, and told his associates that he was sorry to have to report that the new president of AT&T didn't realize the financial situation. A couple of weeks later, in late May, when depressed conditions in the stock market had helped drive AT&T stock down to around 115, Vail suddenly announced a new stock issue of about 220,000 shares, to be offered to existing AT&T stockholders on a basis of one new share at $100 for each six old shares held. The issue was an astonishing success, bringing in more than $20 million in cash and setting the pattern for a long series of subsequent new stock offerings to old stockholders on a rights basis. More crucially, the success of the offering restored the financial markets' confidence in telephone securities and enabled the company to weather the terrible national panic later the same year with its credit unshaken.

Another early Vail move—and one with far-reaching effects for the future not just of the Bell System but of American industry—was consolidation of research and development. Previously those functions had been fragmented between the AT&T Engineering Department in Boston, which established standards for plant design, prepared central-office specifications, and outlined service requirements, and the Western Electric engineers in New York and Chicago, who carried out development work. Now Vail concentrated virtually all these operations at the Western Electric plant at 463 West Street, New York, thereby creating the lineal ancestor of Bell Laboratories and laying the foundation for his own later reputation as the inventor of basic industrial research. (He was not its inventor, but he was the first to see its possibilities and to act vigorously to realize them.) To head this new establishment, Vail made the first of the brilliant staff appointments that were to become the chief evidence and flower of his genius. The man he chose was John J. Carty, the pioneer boy telephone operator whom we have already encountered as the resourceful young discoverer in 1881 of the advantage of two-wire telephone circuits. Since those early days, Carty had come a long way. Now, at forty-six, he was a dapper, charming man with a beautiful actress wife and one of the most ingenious minds in telephony—a former head of the cable department of Western Electric and former chief engineer of the old Long Distance Company, with two dozen separate telephone patents to his credit. But until 1907, his exceptional qualities had never been fully recognized at AT&T. Vail's swift appointment of the self-educated son of a Cambridge bellmaker showed at the outset that the company's old aristocratic habit of weighing breeding heavily in the matter of top staff appointments was at an end, and that AT&T under his command would be a meritocracy.

It is a curious footnote to the Carty appointment, and a measure of Carty's influence, that his very first action as chief engineer was to affect the shape and structure of telephones in America—by no means beneficially to the user—for two decades to come. For three years prior to 1907, the so-called "French" phone, with the transmitter and receiver combined in a single handset, had been used by the Bell System in a few experimental installations. Carty now stopped all that. On July 3, 1907—the day after his appointment as chief engineer—Carty wrote to the associated companies, "There are grave reasons . . . why we should avoid taking the slightest step which might precipitate a general demand for [French handsets]. . . . I am about to call in all which we have placed experimentally on desks of telephone officials." The grave reasons seem to have been that French handsets cost somewhat more than desk sets, and that Carty was under strict orders from Morgan, via Vail, to cut expenses to the bone. It would not be until the 1927 Annual Report that the company would announce that "a new type of telephone having the receiver and transmitter on a single handle was made available during the year." Carty's astonishingly effective and lasting suppression of the French handset in 1907 was dictated partly by the order to cut expenses, but perhaps just as much by the fact that Carty just didn't like French phones, and was a man who usually got what he wanted.

Indeed, most of Vail's early moves, including the research-and-development consolidation, resulted from Morgan's urgent warnings about the need for retrenchment, as embodied in a letter from Morgan to Vail written the week after Vail's appointment: "We consider it of vital consequence to the financial welfare of the Company that no expenditures should be entered upon in the near future, except such as are absolutely necessary, no matter what the prospective profits on other expenditures may be."[1] But in the principal activity of his first year—that of building up a strong staff to guide the activities of the whole system—he acted entirely without direction, and began to reveal his philosophy of management. That philosophy, it would later become clear, involved leaving telephone network operations to practical men and concentrating conceptual talent in a central staff consisting, to the extent possible, of men capable of the vision to look beyond the immediate problems of installing telephones and making them work, to the larger questions, such as the relations of the company with the communities it served, the relations between people within the company, and the relations of the company with government—men with a touch of the thinker in them, whose thought and instinct would cause them to avoid decisions that might seem right today but prove to be disastrously wrong tomorrow. Eventually most of Vail's key staff men—Carty and Bancroft Gherardi in engineering, Charles G. DuBois in accounting, Carl W. Waterson in personnel, Reginald H. Burcher in plant, to name just a few—came to have national reputations transcending the boundaries of their company or industry, and it was in large part the work of such men that would give Vail's administration a quality of statesmanship rather than of mere business shrewdness.

In the summer of 1907, feeling his way into the job, Vail chartered a yacht, the *Mohican,* and began inviting Bell System officials from all over the country to cruise with him, in small groups, up the Hudson and along Long Island Sound. According to his biographer, he "listened to their problems, entertained them in regal fashion, and made their acquaintance in a way that insured close cooperation and friendship." By autumn, his efforts to revitalize the staff were beginning to bear fruit in improved service and better employee morale. By early the following year, when the Annual Report for 1907 was issued, Vail was ready to begin committing his business philosophy to paper.

Vail's presidential essays in AT&T annual reports are like nothing else in American business literature, before or since. They are personal, revealing, discursive, sometimes pontifical. "If we don't tell the truth about ourselves, some one else will," Vail said in 1911—reversing the secretive attitude of management that was the traditional and accepted one of the time—and in telling his version of the truth to stockholders in the annual reports, Vail thought nothing of running on for twenty or thirty pages. However, close perusal of those pages was usually rewarding. In his first and perhaps most famous annual essay, that for 1907, he led off with a section entitled "Public Relations"—by which, as the context made clear, he meant not advertising and promotion, but the whole scope of relations between the corporation and the public. For two decades, it is fair to say, the corporation had in a pinch put the welfare of its stockholders first and that of its customers, the telephone users, second. "Public relations" in the Vail sense had therefore been defensive, designed to keep customer dissatisfaction within manageable bounds and to forestall drastic government action. Now Vail introduced the concept—all but new to American industry, and indeed outright heresy to its leading thinkers then—that maximum private profit was not necessarily the *primary* objective of private enterprise. Profit was necessary to ensure the financial health that made possible renovation and innovation of facilities; but it was only one element in an equation. The problem was to achieve a proper balance. It was a new concept of the corporation.

The rest of Vail's philosophy as originally stated flowed from that basic tenet. On the subject of regulation, he said in the 1907 report that he saw "no serious objection" to public control over telephone rates, "provided it is independent, intelligent, considerate, thorough, and just." He pointed out what few telephone officials had ever before thought it proper to point out—that given the profit system, cheap rates depended on high use, which made possible lower unit costs. As to telephone competition, Vail had no good word for it. Practically, he insisted that the independent promoters' promises of high dividends to investors and low rates for telephone users had proved to be pie in the sky; most independents were unprofitable, most offered erratic service, and many were now asking for increased rates to increase their revenues. Philosophically, Vail argued that competition simply did not fit the telephone business: "Two exchange systems in the same community, each serving the same members, cannot be conceived of as a permanency." Summing up, Vail wrote:

Each year has seen some progress in annihilating distance and bringing people closer to each other. Thirty years more may bring about results which will be almost as astonishing as those of the past thirty years. To the public, this "Bell System" furnishes facilities, in its "universality" of service and connection, of infinite value to the business world, a service which could not be furnished by dissociated companies. The strength of the Bell System lies in this "universality."[2]

2

The monopolist tendency so evident in those words was a view wholeheartedly shared by Morgan and Vail. Morgan, who devoted most of his career to bringing about consolidations in many industries, was a free-enterprise monopolist who, from whatever logic or motive, simply did not believe in the traditional free-enterprise view that competition serves the public welfare; probably he was the greatest monopolist in American business history. Vail, whose early training was in government rather than in private business, had come to the telephone business uninfluenced by that tradition and steeped, rather, in the government tradition that public services are best supplied by a single source. Apparently Morgan and Vail, from their contrasting points of view, were in complete agreement in wishing to make AT&T the sole supplier of telecommunications services in the United States. What they did was to continue with increased vigor the policy of buying up independent telephone companies and adding them to the Bell System. As time went on, this process became increasingly easy and less productive of public outcry. The independents, underfinanced and underequipped to maintain their plants, came more and more to annoy their stockholders with bad financial results and their subscribers with bad service. When the word leaked out that an independent telephone company was in trouble, Bell's ally, Morgan, who effectively controlled commercial credit, needed only to cut off that company's money supply to force it to the wall. Then AT&T would make an offer for the company's stock; thus the company would fall easily into Bell control to everyone's benefit—the stockholders of the failing independent company happy to be bailed out of their investment, its telephone subscribers benefiting from improved service and connection with Bell's long-distance lines. (It is in the methods used in such consolidations that Vail has most often been accused, with some justice, of ruthlessness.) By 1911 the Bell System had collected so many local companies that their diversity presented a management problem, and in that year Vail announced a consolidation of them into a much smaller number of state and regional companies, thus laying out the geographical lines of the Bell associated companies much as they are today.

But a far more grandiose push toward a telecommunications monopoly was simultaneously under way. It was nothing less than consolidation into AT&T of the Western Union Telegraph Company, the pioneer and giant of American telegraphy that had, back in 1878–79, bent every effort to wrest the telephone business away from the Bell interests. Before assuming office in 1907, Vail had expressed himself as favoring the acquisition by AT&T of Western Union's great rival in telegraphy, Postal Telegraph. (As we have seen, quite another notion was held by Postal's head, Clarence Mackay, who wanted it to be the other way around.) However, by 1908 Vail had changed his mind and decided that AT&T's foray into telegraphy should be accomplished by gaining control not of Postal but of Western Union. "There are a great many statistics and reasons," Vail wrote to an AT&T director in that year, "why it would be advantageous to the company to acquire the Western Union Telegraph Company." Apparently the board concurred in Vail's view, because during 1909, 300,000 shares of Western Union stock were bought privately by AT&T, through a subsidiary, at prices somewhat above the public market price. This block of stock—much of it acquired from the heirs of Jay Gould, who, it will be remembered, had taken over Western Union shortly after its battle with the Bell interests —constituted 30 percent of Western Union, and was enough to give AT&T working control. In 1910 Vail became president of Western Union, and the boards of the two companies were rearranged in such a way that they had seven directors in common, including Vail, a partner in J. P. Morgan & Company, and three other bankers generally considered to be Morgan allies. Beginning in 1911, Western Union financial results were included in AT&T annual reports.

For practical purposes, the two companies were merged into one, and the implications were enormous. Telephone subscribers were automatically put on the credit books of Western Union, and it became possible for the first time for telegrams to be sent and delivered by telephone. Long-distance telephone wires became available for emergency telegraph use, and vice versa. Economies in staff and plant of the two companies were made possible. Western Union gained a crucial advantage over its rival, Postal Telegraph, in that telegraph messages received by telephone could be routinely turned over to Western Union even when the sender did not specify which telegraph company he chose to use.[3]

The monopoly-bound bandwagon was rolling along, then: independent telephone companies were falling into the Bell basket by the dozens, and now the largest and oldest of telegraph companies had come into Bell control. And then, three years later, came one of the astonishing concessions, amounting in this case to a reversal of policy, that showed Vail's flexibility and marked him as a business statesman.

Like his predecessors, Vail until 1912 was adamant against physical connection of Bell facilities with the wires of independents, seeing it simply as giving a huge advantage to a competitor. In his 1910 Annual Report he explained in more detail: interconnection, he said, "would force the Bell System to place at the disposal of and under the control of any opposition company . . . one of [our] circuits . . . and disconnect it, for the time being, from the circuits of the Bell System. . . . The fact that the opposition exchange could get such facilities would enhance its importance at the expense of the Bell System." It was sound business sense, but it was also Vail's least public-spirited policy. Perhaps there is a note of defensiveness in the argument; Vail knew well enough that the subscribers to independent telephones, still numbered in the millions and many living in areas not served by Bell, wanted to have available to them the Bell long-distance network—and according to his public-service concept of telephony they were entitled to have it. Moreover, public pressure for interconnection continued to mount, and it was reflected in political pressure. In 1912 Clarence Mackay and a group of independent companies protested to the Department of Justice that AT&T was operating in violation of the antitrust laws. In January 1913, Attorney General George W. Wickersham responded by advising AT&T that, in his opinion, certain of its currently planned acquisitions of independent companies in the Middle West were indeed in violation of the Sherman Antitrust Act, and that same month the Interstate Commerce Commission, which had assumed jurisdiction over the telephone business in 1910, began an investigation to determine whether or not AT&T was attempting to monopolize communications in the United States. The pressure was mounting, and with the accession that spring of the new Democratic administration under Woodrow Wilson, it mounted still more.

Times were changing; clearly, the people and their representatives had decided that the Bell System was becoming too large and powerful. And something else changed: with the death in March 1913 of J. P. Morgan, the strongest single pressure on Vail and AT&T in the direction of monopoly-seeking was lifted. Two courses were now open—to push on toward monopoly at the expense of certain public hatred and a probable huge government antitrust suit to dismantle the company, or to compromise.

Vail, in what is regarded, with justice, as one of his most states-manlike acts, chose the latter course.

The compromise took the form of a letter dated December 19, 1913, from an AT&T vice-president, Nathan C. Kingsbury, to James McReynolds, Wickersham's successor as attorney general. AT&T and its associated companies, Kingsbury wrote, "wishing to put their affairs beyond criticism and in compliance with your suggestions formulated as a result of a number of interviews be-tween us during the last sixty days," agreed to three separate ac-tions: first, to dispose of its holding of Western Union stock "in such a way that the control and management of [Western Union] will be entirely independent"; second, to purchase no more inde-pendent telephone companies except with the approval of the Interstate Commerce Commission; third—and perhaps most mo-mentous—to make "arrangements . . . promptly under which all other telephone companies may secure for their subscribers toll service over the lines of the companies in the Bell System."

The "Kingsbury Commitment," which was immediately hailed by the leaders of the independent telephone business as a great victory, and by President Wilson as an act of business statesmanship, cost AT&T directly about $10 million—$7.5 million lost in the sale of the Western Union stock, and another $2.5 mil-lion paid to J. P. Morgan & Company to restore losses sustained by the bankers in connection with pending contracts to buy up independent companies. It proved a boon to telephone users, first, because now all the millions of subscribers of independent companies gained access to Bell long-distance lines, and second, because people in two-company towns no longer needed to have two telephones to reach any of their fellow citizens. In corporate and economic terms, its significance went far beyond that. Selling the Western Union stock signaled the end of AT&T's dream of a national telecommunications monopoly; agreement to stop buy-ing up independents meant abandoning the dream of a national telephone monopoly; and agreement to interconnection meant giving up AT&T's chief means of bringing independents to their knees. Taken all in all, the Kingsbury Commitment was a flat reversal of several of AT&T's key policies of the time, and consti-tutes one of the three or four most important turning points in the history of both the company and the telephone industry in Amer-ica. In addition, it provides a striking example of the resolution of government-corporation conflicts by compromise, and sets the stage for the modern era of the telephone.[4]

3

The modern era was approaching fast; the last important technical element in long-distance telephony was finally coming into place.

The beginning of this process came in 1906, when Dr. Lee De Forest, a young inventor out of Council Bluffs, Iowa, and Sheffield Scientific School at Yale, read a paper at a scientific meeting on a new invention of his that he called the audion—a three-element vacuum tube, an improvement on Sir Ambrose Fleming's earlier two-element tube, which had not only the capacity to send or generate radio waves more effectively than any previous device, but also the capacity to amplify them. Vail and Carty, learning of De Forest's work, were quick to sense its potentialities for telephony. If a series of audions—"repeaters"— installed along a telephone line could be used to amplify the sound waves traveling along it, could not they, combined with Pupin loading coils, make possible what was not possible with loading coils alone—that is, coast-to-coast telephone conversations, which in turn would make possible a national network enabling anyone anywhere in the United States to talk to anyone anywhere else?

The electronic age had dawned; but unfortunately, De Forest's audion was too crude to serve the purpose envisaged. In 1907, following Carty's appointment as chief engineer and the consolidation of AT&T research staffs, the combined research facility in New York City began experiments toward making a telephone repeater of the audion; meanwhile De Forest continued his own independent work. By 1909 Vail was optimistic enough about progress to make a crucial promise. That March, on the day of the inauguration of President Taft, a sleet storm in the vicinity of Washington, D.C., brought down so many wires that for hours the city was isolated, telephonically and tele-graphically, from the rest of the country, and news of the inauguration was therefore delayed. The untimely mischance served to dramatize the urgent need for improvements in long-distance telephony. A month later, Carty sent a memorandum to Vail's right-hand man, Vice-President Harry B. Thayer, asking for an increased engineering staff and proposing to extend long-distance service from New York to Denver with the help of loading coils; that span would represent just about the outer limit of telephone range using loading alone. But if that step could first be accomplished, Carty went on, "the development of a successful repeater would enable us to accomplish speech between San Francisco and New York." Later the same year, on a visit to the West Coast, Vail, Carty, and Plant Engineer Gherardi all but flatly promised the management of the Panama-Pacific Exposition, scheduled to open there in 1914, that telephone service between the two coasts would be available by that date.

Obviously, it was a bold gamble. A workable telephone repeater did not yet exist; in making the promise, Vail was anticipating invention. Company legend declares that Vail said to his engineers in effect, "We've promised it; now you find a way to do it." At all events, the fact is that they did it. In 1911 service between New York and Denver was successfully established, using overhead copper wires nearly as thick as a lead pencil and equipped with loading coils every eight miles. Carty's precondition for coast-to-coast service was thus met. Early in 1912, De Forest achieved a breakthrough. His new, improved audion, now called a triode, would amplify telephone conversations—too weakly for practical use, but unmistakably. Sensing victory, and racing the 1914 deadline, the Bell System put its engineers to work to develop the triode from an impractical invention to a usable product. The one who succeeded in this undertaking, and did so within a remarkably short time, was Harold D. Arnold, a young physicist hired in 1911 by Western Electric on the recommendation of the celebrated Professor Robert A. Millikan of the University of Chicago. Analyzing the De Forest triode, Arnold concluded that its weakness was caused by an insufficiently complete vacuum within it. He put to work evacuation methods that had only recently been developed, and produced a very-high-vacuum tube in 1912.

Eureka! The high-vacuum tube proved to be the basis for a highly efficient telephone repeater, and the problem was solved. It remained for the Bell System to buy rights to De Forest's audion and triode patents, which it did in 1913, and to construct a

New York–San Francisco circuit using loading coils and repeaters. The first vacuum-tube repeater in commercial service was installed at Philadelphia, in the New York–Baltimore line, in October 1913. All through that fall and winter, and the following spring, work went forward on the stringing of the transcontinental line and the installation of loading coils and repeaters along it. Wires were attached to the last pole, on the Utah-Nevada border, on June 17, 1914, and the circuit was successfully tested on July 29. Almost miraculously, Vail and his engineers had met the deadline they had promised five years earlier—more than the sponsors of the Panama-Pacific Exposition could say, since the opening had meanwhile been postponed until 1915. With that pressure off, AT&T set back the formal opening of the New York–San Francisco line until January 25, 1915. On that occasion, a telephone ceremony was arranged involving connections between Jekyll Island, Georgia, where Vail was recovering from an illness; the AT&T offices in New York, where those present included Carty, the chief architect of the triumph, and the old, white-bearded author of telephony itself, Alexander Graham Bell; and San Francisco, where sat Bell's old collaborator Thomas Watson. (Strangely, and some thought unfairly, De Forest was not invited to participate in the ceremony.) When all was ready, the first coast-to-coast telephone conversation, only thirty-nine years after the first telephone conversation of all and involving the same participants, must have tingled the scalps of those listening in:

DR. BELL: "Hoy! Hoy! Mr. Watson? Are you there? Do you hear me?

MR. WATSON (in San Francisco): Yes, Dr. Bell, I hear you perfectly. Do you hear me well?

DR. BELL: Yes, your voice is perfectly distinct. It is as clear as if you were here in New York. . . .

A little later, Bell said, "I have been asked to say to you the words that you understood over the telephone and through the old instrument, 'Mr. Watson, come here, I want you.'" With his old quick high spirits Watson replied from San Francisco, "It would take me a week to get there now!" When the ceremony ended, one of the greatest technical triumphs of telephony was complete.[5]

Completion of the transcontinental circuit was by no means the only major technical advance of the Vail years. Substantial progress was made, for example, toward the development of mechanical switching devices that would be able, unlike Strowger's, to accomplish automatic switching of large numbers of calls—although, as it happened, the first such Bell System switching office would not be installed until 1921, the year after Vail's death. The "phantom circuit"—an imaginative form of electrical hookup, dating back to 1883, that permits three telephone conversations to be conducted on two pairs of wires—had initially not been adapted to use in cables, but this difficulty was overcome by Bell engineers, and in 1910 the first cable-borne phantom circuits began operating between Boston and Neponset, Massachusetts. (Within a short time after that, every important intercity cable had been so arranged as to make possible phantom operation.) By late 1914, vacuum-tube technology had advanced to the point where carrier systems—an application of radio techniques to wire lines, which would eventually prove to be a far more effective way of increasing their call-carrying capacity than phantom circuits—were under development at 463 West Street. And meanwhile, the development of radio telephony was under way.

Vail was uncharacteristically slow in seeing the revolutionary potential of the application of radio to telephony. As early as 1901, Guglielmo Marconi had succeeded in transmitting wireless telegraph signals from Cornwall, England, to Newfoundland, and by the summer of 1907 De Forest had shown the possibilities of radio telephony by transmitting voice without wires between two buildings in New York City. Nevertheless, that same summer Vail wrote to one of AT&T's London bankers, "The difficulties of the wireless telegraph are as nothing compared with the difficulties in the way of the wireless telephone." It was Carty who had the vision to press Vail to authorize an all-out company effort in radio research. His 1909 memorandum asking for additional staff emphasized the need to develop a telephone repeater, but also made the point that "a successful telephone repeater . . . would not only react most favorably upon our service where wires are used, but might put us in a position of control with respect to the art of wireless telephony, should it turn out to be a factor of importance." Thereafter, no effort or expense was spared by AT&T in pursuing radio research. The efforts were quite soon crowned with success. In 1915—the year after the success of the amplified transcontinental telephone line—the vacuum tube made possible a whole group of successful tests of long-distance radiotelephony by Bell engineers. On April 4 they achieved one-way wireless voice transmission over the two hundred and fifty miles of water between Montauk Point, Long Island, and Wilmington, Delaware. Encouraged, they decided to try a more ambitious test, and on May 18, Carty's words, spoken in New York, transmitted by wire to Montauk Point and on from there by radio, were weakly heard at a Bell radio receiving station near Brunswick, Georgia, one thousand miles down the coast. It was time to try the big one—talking by radio across the Atlantic. Tests began late in August, and at first they were discouraging. A successful radio transmission from Vail in New York to Carty in California was made in September, but the Atlantic remained unconquered. Not for long; on October 21, the first transatlantic raido transmission of voice was accomplished when H. R. Shreeve, a Bell engineer listening at the Eiffel Tower, Paris, with French equipment graciously lent by a government already at war, caught a few words addressed to him by B. B. Webb in Arlington, Virginia. The words heard were few and weak, consisting essentially of "Hello, Shreeve! Hello, Shreeve!" and "And now, Shreeve, good night." Hardly a useful conversation, and transatlantic telephone service by radio was more than a decade away; but as Carty said later, "the record was nailed to the mast for America."[6]

For all these concrete accomplishments, probably Vail's greatest achievement in the field of research and development was abstract: the consolidation of staff, the free hand with funds, and the strong emphasis on creativity that would bear fruit not in his time, but later.

4

The perfection of techniques making possible unlimited long-distance telephone conversations instantly and radically changed the place of the telephone in American life—socially, economically, and politically. Suddenly it was a national rather than a local phenomenon—one that almost immediately came to be regarded as a national rather than a local necessity. People assimilated national telephony into their minds as if into their bodies—as if it were the result of a new step in human evolution that increased the range of their voices to the limits of the national map. "I am a copper wire slung in the air," Carl Sandburg wrote in a 1916 poem entitled "Under a Telephone Pole":

Night and day I keep singing—humming and thrumming:
It is love and war and money; it is the fighting and the tears, the
    work and want,
Death and laughter of men and women passing through me . . .

Passing through, of course, at a cost to the caller. Economically and politically, national calling facilities, combined with the interconnection of Bell long-distance facilities with local independent companies pursuant to the Kingsbury Commitment, made the telephone as much a matter of federal interest as the railroads were. Gone were the pre-repeater days when long-distance facilities had been so limited and inefficient that the thousands of independents, and in many respects the Bell-associated companies too, had been essentially local concerns. The new national interest in good service at fair rates naturally raised the question of federal as well as local regulation. In dealing with that question, Vail was at his most statesmanlike.

The attitude he found prevalent at AT&T on coming to the presidency in 1907 was not one of statesmanship. Having been forced at the turn of the century to abandon its original stance as a monopoly proprietorship based on patents, the company had since then pressed with almost unswerving stubbornness for a restoration of de facto monopoly through competitive success, and against regulation in any form. It did not expect to win all the battles, but it was inclined to fight rather than to recognize changed conditions by negotiating. The secretiveness, and defensiveness toward public and government, characteristic of AT&T in this period is eloquently suggested in a famous memorandum sent in 1906 by President Fish of AT&T to President Enos Barton of Western Electric (who obviously did not comply with its final instruction): "The Western Electric Company is making too much money, and at the present time it would be enormously harmful . . . if it were known what its profits are. I trust that there will be no information given until matters are in better shape. I think it well for you to destroy this letter."

Right from the start, Vail reversed this attitude. We have already heard him on secretiveness: "If we don't tell the truth about ourselves, some one else will." We have already seen how, in his first annual report as president, he astounded stockholders and colleagues alike by saying that he had "no serious objection" to public control over telephone rates. Over the following years, he gradually evolved—far ahead of other industrialists, and ahead of most government officials and legislators, too—a philosophy of the proper relations between the telephone industry and the government, which was to become, and remain for many years, the accepted view of both the industry and the government. Baldly stated, the philosophy went as follows: Telephony is by its technical nature a form of service that is most efficiently provided without local competition—a "natural" monopoly. Therefore, in the public interest, the telephone business should be operated as a monopoly insofar as possible. (Ideally, it appears, Vail would have chosen to have it an absolute monopoly, but he permanently abandoned that ideal with the Kingsbury Commitment.) However, the privilege of being allowed to operate as a monopoly imposed, in Vail's view, a corresponding obligation. That obligation was to submit to, and cooperate with, regulation by state and federal authorities, to serve as a check—in the absence of the traditional check of competition—on abuse of power by the monopoly-holder. Rejecting the old AT&T policy of opposing regulation, Vail not only accepted regulation, but went further and—so long as it met his standards and specifications—welcomed it.

It is interesting to watch how Vail's philosophy on regulation evolved. By the 1910 Annual Report, three years after he had seen "no serious objection" to regulation, he was describing what the character of the regulation should be: "such . . . as to encourage the highest possible standard in plant, the utmost extension of facilities, the highest efficiency in service, and to that end should allow rates that will warrant the highest wages for the best service, some reward for high efficiency in administration, and such certainty of return on investment as will induce investors . . . to supply all the capital needed to meet the demands of the public." If that statement, which stood then and still stands today as an able summary of the corporate side of the regulation question, nevertheless sounds a bit self-serving, by 1915 Vail had transcended the parochialism of his corporate chair and was ready to articulate a detached and rounded philosophy of telephone regulation. He did so in a speech given in San Francisco that year to the National Association of Railway Commissioners, demurely entitled "Some Observations on Western Tendencies." Vail began by putting the problem in the new social context in which the telephone was considered a necessity: "Society has never allowed that which is necessary to existence to be controlled by private interest." Nor should it now allow the telephone to be so controlled. He went on to argue for the monopolistic aspect of the Bell System—"If there were no Bell System, only dissociated individual companies or groups of companies, no line over a few hundred miles long would have been built, or if built it could not be operated . . . satisfactorily"—and then pitched into his specific ideas on regulation. Regulatory bodies, state and federal, should be thought of and should think of themselves as juries charged with "protecting the individual member of the public against corporate aggression or extortion, and the corporate member of the community against public extortion and aggression." They should see it as their duty "to restrain and suppress . . . certain evils that have been ingrained in our commercial practices," and also "to restrain an indignant and excited public." To those ends, Vail concluded, regulators should be men of the highest standard, appointed for life; there should be careful provisions safeguarding their independence from political or corporate pressures; and "their decisions, even if not entirely satisfactory, should not be subjected to captious criticism or objection."

With this "jury concept," Vail described an ideal model of the regulated-monopoly situation that, over the years since 1915, has all too seldom been attained—in part because government has never been able to confer on the regulatory function the mantle of prestige and high purpose that Vail called for. It is possible to deprecate Vail's wisdom and high-mindedness by saying that he was merely yielding to mounting public pressure, or by maintaining that he could well afford such grand talk because actual regulation in his time was weak and disorganized. Certainly the latter was true. State commissions proliferated after 1907; by 1915 most states had commissions more or less active in regulation of telephone rates, and by 1922 forty of the forty-eight had them. But their regulation was seldom very stringent. Federally, the Mann-Elkins Act of 1910 made the Interstate Commerce Commission applicable to telephone companies, thereby introducing federal telephone regulation for the first time, and in 1913 the ICC promulgated a uniform system of accounts for telephone companies that thereafter made their financial reports more intelligible and reliable. As to telephone rates, though, the ICC was understaffed and preoccupied with other matters—chiefly the regulation of railroads—and as a result, interstate telephone rates would go virtually unregulated until the 1930s. Even allowing for these conditions, Vail's San Francisco speech—with its talk about "corporate aggression or extortion" and "evils . . . ingrained in our commercial practices," which would be unusual enough from a corporate president in our time, but was nothing less than astounding in 1915—marks him clearly enough as deserving of what Thomas Edison called him in 1912: "Until his day the telephone was in the hands of men of little business capacity. Mr. Vail is a big man."[7]

## 5

Let us pause for a more rounded look, however brief, at the life and character of Vail—surely the biggest man in the first century of the telephone industry, and one of the biggest in the whole history of all American industry.

His life apart from business was a vivid and varied one, centered at Speedwell Farms up in Lyndonville, Vermont; he was in this sense the antithesis of his latter-day counterpart, the business executive so immersed in the demanding and beguiling task of managing a great enterprise that he has neither the time nor the heart for much of a separate life. He remarried in July 1907, almost immediately after assuming the AT&T presidency. His new bride was Mabel Sanderson, a Boston woman with a predilection for literature and French culture; he celebrated that summer with characteristic exuberance by buying four more farms to add to his Lyndonville property, and building a new tower there. Doubly reborn at sixty-two, Vail immediately adopted a style of work that involved evenings kept scrupulously free of after-hours business commitments, and frequent extended stays at Speedwell Farms. In New York, he lived at the Navarre apartments on Fifty-ninth

Street, and devoted his free time to theater, opera, and dinner parties at which the hostess was either his wife or his favorite niece—eventually his adopted daughter—Katherine Vail. He also adopted as a rule of life "No business talk after six o'clock"—a rule adhered to whether his companions were Bell System people, men of affairs in other fields, or J. P. Morgan himself, who was in the habit, when he had just acquired a new treasure for his celebrated library, of calling up Vail and saying, "I've got something new; come over and see it."

None of this, however, is to say or imply that Vail belonged to the category of dilettante executives who accomplish their work competently in the shortest time possible and find their deeper satisfactions in the rest of their lives. To the contrary, he was obsessed with his work, as all geniuses of management (and many nongeniuses) are; it was, rather, that he found that jealously guarded times of rest and relaxation set his mind free to attain the larger vision that was his hallmark as an industrial leader. Indeed, Vail in his sixties seems to have achieved such a synthesis in his life as Plato imagined, in which the usually conflicting forces of will, intellect, and emotion are pulling together in harmony like a team of horses. He was in the habit of attributing his long stays at Speedwell Farms to ill health, but his AT&T colleagues noticed that he always returned from these absences with a new charge of creativity, and some of them came to feel that Vail, consciously or not, was using illness as an excuse for a process, necessary to his work as much as to himself, not of rehabilitation but of the unfettered exercise of creative imagination.

At all events, Vail at Speedwell Farms appeared as very much the country gentleman and not at all the harassed executive. According to Katherine Vail—who spent every summer at Speedwell Farms and may eventually have come to be as close to him as anyone—Vail in Vermont appeared as a man at ease with himself and his world. A little shy, and quick to blush, he was at home with the country farmers of Lyndonville, and sometimes insisted that a ten-cow farm is the perfect place for any human being. Breakfast at Speedwell Farms—served at noon, after morning coffee in one's room—was hearty, consisting of corned beef hash, poached eggs, and waffles with both syrup and cream. Dinner, for which Vail always dressed formally whether in New York or Vermont, was preceded by alcoholic drinks; Vail liked Scotch whisky,

17. Blake transmitter (1880).

18. Desk set (1897).

19. Strowger automatic (1905).

20. Elisha Gray, the Chicago inventor. His claim to having invented the telephone came closest of many such claims to overthrowing Alexander Graham Bell's.

21. Francis Blake, Jr. The Blake transmitter, invented in 1878, employed carbon and greatly improved telephone service.

neighborhood of another wire — an undulatory current of electricity is induced in the latter.

When a cylinder upon which are arranged bar-magnets... is made to rotate in front of the pole of an electro-magnet an undulatory current of electricity is induced in the ~~latter~~ coils of the electro-magnet

Undulations ~~may also be~~ are ~~also~~ caused in a continuous voltaic current by the vibration or motion of bodies capable of inductive action; — or by the vibration of the conducting wire itself in the neighborhood of such bodies. *

In illustration of the method of creating electrical ~~currents~~ undulations, I shall show and describe one form of apparatus for producing the effect. I prefer to employ for this purpose an electro-magnet A fig. 5. having a coil upon only one of its legs (b). A steel spring armature c is firmly clamped by one extremity to the uncovered leg (d) of the magnet, and its free end is allowed to project above the pole of the covered leg. The armature c can be set in vibration in a variety of ways — one of which is by ~~wind~~ and in vibrating it produces a musical note of a certain definite pitch.

When the instrument A is placed in a voltaic circuit g b c f g the armature c becomes magnetic and the polarity of its free end is opposed to that of the magnet underneath.

So long as the armature c remains at rest, no effect is produced upon the voltaic current

*Electrical undulations may also be caused by alternately increasing and diminishing the resistance of a battery — For instance, by alternately increasing and diminishing the resistance of the circuit — the voltaic element N may be therefore occasionally put in or out of connection with the circuit. But an increase and diminution of the resistance of the circuit may also be caused by bringing the voltaic element N into contact with the rest of the circuit — thus alternately increasing and diminishing the resistance of the internal resistance of a battery — The reciprocal vibration of the elements of a battery therefore occasions undulatory action. Electrical undulations may also be caused in many other ways...

22. Bell's description of the variable-resistance mode of sound transmission in his patent application of February 14, 1876. The marginal insert, later described by Bell, represents a "last minute detail" he had "neglected to include" because his time was "so fully occupied...."

23. Theodore N. Vail in 1885, president of AT&T from 1885 to 1887, and again from 1907 to 1919. Vail's wisdom and farsightedness changed the Bell organization from a struggling Boston-based firm to a huge nationwide system.

24. Telephone operators trained for foreign service, France, 1918.

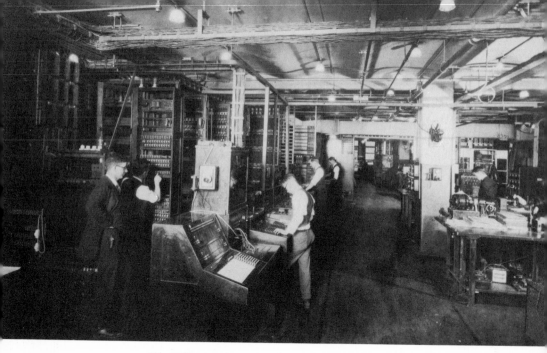

25.  Bell scientists at work in a 1920s laboratory.

26.  Lee De Forest, inventor of the three-element vacuum tube. This device, after considerable adapting, solved the telephone repeater problem, and became a reliable tool for amplifying speech.

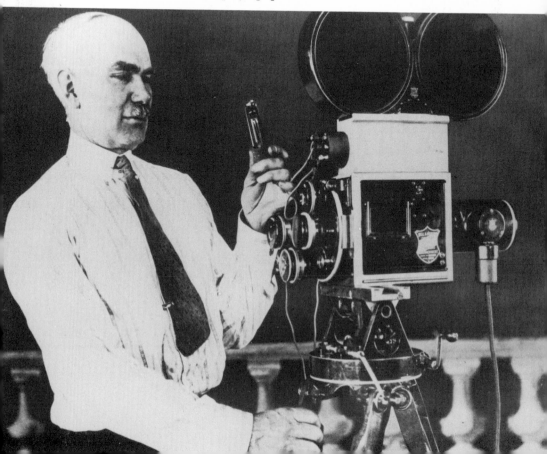

27. Strowger wall set (1907).

28. A 1919 dial telephone.

29. A 1928 "French phone."

30. Long-distance advertisements, 1890s.

31. Cathedral 8000 "Time of Day" service began in October 1927. As many as a hundred callers at a time could hear the operator's live announcement.

32. Southern California telephone crewmen repairing cables across flooded channel, 1938.

33. A mass of radar antennas crown the top of this Essex-class Navy carrier, which swept the Pacific waters during World War II.

34. The Army's first radar, located on a rugged Italian mountainside, searched the skies for Nazi bombers.

35. Draped with camouflage netting, this "Mickey Mouse" radar stood guard against the Luftwaffe near San Pietro, Italy.

and often proudly dispensed to his guests a "Speedwell cocktail" of his own invention, the ingredients of which he wouldn't reveal. Once a summer, J. P. Morgan would arrive with his entourage at Speedwell Farms for a visit, invariably bringing gifts for all members of the household. Vail's attitude toward women—characteristic of his time rather than ahead of it—was one of chivalry and condescension; he hated to see a woman drive an automobile or operate any kind of machinery beyond a telephone, and he always rather patronizingly admonished women driving his teams of horses to be sure to bring them back fresh. He liked to play solitaire, whistling softly all the while, and preferably with others watching him and conversing in the room. He doodled constantly while listening to someone else talk, and liked to carry on conversation and written correspondence at the same time; and he was distractable enough at times to call to mind that classic figure of fun the absent-minded professor.

In 1913 Katherine Vail married Arthur Marsters, secretary of AT&T and a protégé of Vail's. Vail gave the couple the old Vail family house in Morristown, New Jersey, and thereafter fell into the habit of visiting them there on weekends during periods when he was working in his New York office. As he approached old age, he became more avuncular than ever—a rather portly man with a full white mustache and eyes that were both kindly and commanding, with a predilection for silk waistcoats and wide cravats, the latter often made for him by Kate. His many trips around the country to visit Bell System installations and see Bell System people were always the occasion for a series of parties. His private railway car, on arriving at a destination, would immediately be plugged in to local telephone and electric services, and after six the local telephone officials would be piped aboard—for whiskey and, of course, conversation about anything but business.

There is a too-good-to-be-true quality about Vail; and a skeptical observer finds himself searching for the man's mortal mistakes. He reversed himself under the pressure of political and social change on telecommunications and telephone monopoly, and we will shortly see him reverse himself on another large matter of policy. Independent telephone men, during his monopoly-seeking period, looked upon him as nothing better than an early-twentieth-century robber baron. What separated him from other leading industrialists of his time—that hard-shelled and rather narrow breed—was the openness of heart and broadness of mind that enabled him to see both sides of the great questions, and the courage, or aristocratic detachment, to state both sides openly. Perhaps his special qualities as an industrial leader—his need for tranquil thought, his refusal to be hurried, his love of his work and pride in it—are most succinctly suggested in what he once said about himself and Harry Thayer, his closest professional associate (whom he always addressed as "Thayer") and eventually his successor as president. "Sometimes," Vail told his biographer, "old Thayer comes in to my office and we just sit and look at each other."[8]

## 6

On January 1, 1912, the British government finally assumed full ownership and control of the British telephone system. The United States now stood alone among major nations in having privately supplied telephone service. In a time of trust-busting and monopoly-hating in America, pressure began to mount for a government takeover here. Vail took note of this movement in his 1911 Annual Report, issued early in 1912, but his tone was unworried and offhand: "The discussion of the government ownership of the wire [telephone and telegraph] companies is not likely to become anything more than academic, at least for the present."

It became a good deal more than academic in 1913. With the coming of the new Wilson administration early that spring, the U.S. postmaster generalship was assumed by Albert Sidney Burleson, who would shortly make clear that he believed the telephone and telegraph systems of the nation should be "postalized"—that is, taken over lock, stock, and barrel by the Post Office Department. Burleson was an old-fashioned southwestern populist if there ever was one. His grandfather Edward Burleson served under Andrew Jackson in the war against the Creek Indians in the Southeast in 1813–14, moved to Texas as a pioneer settler, distinguished himself in the Texas Revolution, and became vice-president of the short-lived Texas Republic before its annexation as a state in 1845. Albert Burleson, a lawyer born at San Marcos in 1863 and graduated from the University of Texas law school in 1884, had served as a U.S. congressman from 1899 until the time he took office as postmaster general. Later he told a House committee that right from the start of his term in office he had favored incorporation of the telephone and telegraph into the postal service on the basis of "the provision of the Constitution which reposes in Congress the power to establish post offices and post roads." "I have never been able to understand," Burleson went on, "why the use of wires should be denied for the transmission of communications, any more than the use of a man on foot, or a boy on a horse, or the stage coach. . . ." He immediately got strong support from several representatives, led by David J. Lewis of Maryland, who collaborated with him in the preparation of a bill for government ownership. That December, Congressman Lewis made two important speeches, one in New York City and one in Congress, flatly calling for "postalization of the telephones and telegraphs." Newspaper editorial writers, and the government Commercial Engineer's Office, came to the defense of AT&T; nevertheless, Burleson shortly submitted to Congress a report, prepared by three members of his staff, advocating government acquisition.

Vail in his 1913 report reacted to these developments with a discourse on the rights of property owners, an admonition to stockholders to "rest quietly and not be scared or frightened into sacrifice of their securities" (the price of which was being seriously depressed by the official statements), and the memorable homily, "all monopolies should be regulated. Government ownership would be an unregulated monopoly." However, although government pressure for "postalization" abated in 1914 in the excitement over the outbreak of war in Europe, the worries of AT&T stockholders did not, and in that year's Annual Report—his longest so far, with seventy-two sonorous pages—Vail permitted himself to tell them, "It is perfectly within the bounds of conservatism to say the American Telephone and Telegraph Company and associated companies were never, as a whole, in a more satisfactory, if as satisfactory, a position." In the following two years—while the government advocates of nationalization seemed to hang back awaiting their opening—Vail harped implacably on the subject. In his 1915 report he for the first time defended AT&T's system of "vertical integration" with its supplier Western Electric, which had been reorganized during that year in a way that, in the private words of Vice-President Thayer, would "capitalize on surplus but . . . avoid the publicity of a 'melon cutting.'" Vail told the stockholders that the association was under government attack "from the questionable standpoint of self-interest"—questionable, he said, because Western Electric supplied topnotch equipment, and "high-class service and low-class equipment do not coordinate." He went on to pronounce that "the Bell System was something good, and always something better than any other. . . . It was never resting. . . . The Bell idea did not contemplate a monopoly; it contemplated a system and went about the building of it in the only possible way. . . ." If the tone of grandiosity and the stretching of facts can be excused at all, it can be excused on the grounds of overdedication to a good end, that of the best possible telephone service.

The year 1917 brought United States entry into the war in Europe, and with it a whole new situation in the U.S. telephone business. Even before the United States declaration of war that April, a test mobilization of national telephone facilities was conducted during which, for three days, the Navy Department successfully used nothing but Bell System facilities for all communications between headquarters in Washington and all naval yards and stations and ships. After the declaration, demands on the domestic telephone network soared, huge quantities of equipment were shipped to France for the establishment of a complete American telephone network there, and in a year or so fourteen thousand Bell System employees left to form fourteen Signal Corps battalions of the American Expeditionary Force.

With the coming of war, agitation for government ownership greatly increased, and many who had formerly opposed it became converted. Government takeover of the railroads that December fanned the flames; thereafter, advocates of a telephone takeover argued that government-run railroads and privately run wire communications constituted a logical inconsistency. Newspaper editorials urged a wire takeover, and Post Office officials spoke about eliminating all telegraph offices and substituting post offices for them. For more than a year, Vail and AT&T sat tight and conducted business as usual, or as nearly as usual as was possible under the circumstances. Facilities were taxed to the utmost, and the Bell construction budget for 1917 reached a record $118 million.

The next year, 1918—the year when Bell System telephones in

service reached the ten million mark—would later be characterized by Vail as "from every standpoint the most strenuous and difficult year in the whole history of the telephone." The matter of nationalization came to a head in the first week of July, when Congress began holding hearings on a joint resolution designed to give the president authority to assume control of all telephone and telegraph systems in the United States. Besides Burleson and his congressional supporters, the Secretaries of War and of the Navy pronounced themselves in favor of the resolution, the latter making the telling argument that government control of communications was "the only absolutely safe way in which the government may insure the dispatch of its messages and the secrecy of its business"; indeed, he went further and expressed the hope that the government would continue to own and operate the wires permanently.

No representative of the Bell System appeared before either the House or the Senate committee looking into the joint resolution (Nathan Kingsbury, the AT&T vice-president, said later that he had tried to gain admission to both but had been denied it), and AT&T took no public stand for or against it. Exactly where Vail stood on the question is not known. A company legend has it that sometime early in 1918 he went to President Wilson and said, reversing his previous stand, "As long as you've taken over the railroads, you might as well take us over, too." Since there is no written record of any such statement or even meeting, it cannot be confirmed. At all events—according to the subsequent testimony of AT&T Vice-President Kingsbury before a House committee—Vail never met Burleson until July 29, 1918, thirteen days after the joint resolution was approved by Congress, and a week after President Wilson, acting on the powers granted him in it, had issued a proclamation whereby he took possession of and assumed control and supervision of "each and every telegraph and telephone system, and every part thereof, within the jurisdiction of the United States, including all equipment thereof and appurtenances thereto." Thus the nation's first and only experiment in government-run telephones was begun.

Vail's business on July 29 in Burleson's office—where he went accompanied by his colleagues Kingsbury and Union N. Bethell —was to begin the process of negotiating the terms of the take-over. Certainly Vail had reason to be apprehensive, since the postmaster had previously been rumored to have said that his "first move would be to get rid of that man Vail." By his biographer's account, Vail said to his colleagues as they approached the Post Office Building, "Well, I never in my life felt so helpless. . . . These people . . . have taken over our property and probably intend to keep it. They can do what they please with us, and we cannot help ourselves. For once in my life I am completely at sea." But the atmosphere of the meeting proved to be the opposite of what all participants expected. Burleson said later, "I had never seen Mr. Vail up to that time, and I began to get a new impression of him, which grew as I proceeded. I thought he had a fine, generous face. . . . Every word that Mr. Vail said showed an entirely unselfish point of view, a desire to serve the government and the public at whatever cost. . . . When he came to discuss the compensation to be allowed his company, he said, 'You fix it, and I'll be satisfied.' We all parted the best of friends. I had thought of him as a man with the 'public be damned' idea. I found him to be a great, unselfish patriot. . . ." As for Vail, he said to his colleagues after the meeting, "Well, I feel a good deal improved. I was never better treated in my life. . . . I went in there helpless; I have come out feeling that everything is all right."[9]

This unexpected détente set the stage for a contract that was certainly "all right" for AT&T, and in the view of some critics, heavily in AT&T's favor. Worked out in a series of conferences between AT&T officials and the Post Office Department, the contract was accepted by both parties on October 5—ironically, only about a month before the Armistice ending the war that had brought about the government takeover. A Wire Control Board was established by the Post Office Department, and it in turn appointed a telephone and telegraph Operating Board, which consisted of the incumbent officers of the various telephone and telegraph companies; thus, in practice, AT&T continued to be managed by its regular officers at their regular salaries, and as far as both telephone employees and telephone users were concerned, things were as usual. The government got rate-setting powers, but would consult the judgment of AT&T in exercising them; it agreed to maintain the property and eventually to return it in as good condition as received. Financially, appropriation from revenue for depreciation and obsolescence was set at 5.72 percent of fixed capital, and for the duration of government control, the government agreed to pay all taxes on the property it had seized and to pay the 4½ percent annual license contract fees that the operating companies had previously paid to AT&T. The government also pledged to maintain the current eight-dollar-a-year dividend to AT&T stockholders, and to allow AT&T to inspect the books and accounts on telephone operations kept by the Post Office.

Although government operation later cost the Bell System dearly in terms of lost revenue needed for new construction, by almost any standard the contract was a satisfactory one for AT&T. "Very naturally the change to Government control was disturbing," Vail told stockholders in his 1918 Annual Report; but he was also able to say that net profit for the year was fifty-four million dollars, an increase of five million dollars over the previous year, and of course, that the dividend was being maintained. The only difference to the stockholders was that technically, their dividend was now "compensation" for the government takeover rather than their share in the profits of a corporation they jointly owned. In essence, the government had won its point—government ownership—in exchange for a contract that made the ownership largely nominal.

If this outcome was—as is suggested by the comments of Burleson himself—largely a diplomatic triumph for Vail in his dealings with the postmaster general, it was to be his last triumph. His apparently inexhaustible energy and resourcefulness were at last giving way to age.

Frequent trips to Washington during the broiling summer of 1918, in connection with the government contract negotiations, were exhausting for Vail, who had for some time been plagued with heart and kidney trouble. That October and November, on the urgent advice of his doctors, he went on vacation to Key West and Havana, and was in Havana when the Armistice was signed. Back in New York, with his health unimproved, he found his work increasingly burdensome, and in June 1919 he resigned as president, assuming the less demanding job of chairman of the board and turning over the presidency to his old friend and colleague Harry B. Thayer. He spent that summer at Speedwell Farms, playing solitaire, quietly celebrating his seventy-fourth birthday, and talking by telephone almost daily to AT&T headquarters in New York. He managed a stay at his New York apartment that fall and early winter, but the deterioration of his condition continued, and in April 1920, ten months after his retirement as president, he died at Johns Hopkins Hospital in Baltimore.[10]

As an industrialist, Vail was a man for all seasons, combining something of the iron spine and icy nerve of the nineteenth-century empire builders (and only a trace of their deviousness) with a mastery of the managerial art comparable to that of later masters such as Alfred P. Sloan and Owen D. Young; and combining the practicality of a day-to-day decision-maker with some of the detachment of an academic student of economic polity. It is particularly interesting to note that he conspicuously lacked the single-minded emphasis on company profits—the tunnel vision trained on the bottom line—so characteristic of many of the most celebrated of modern corporate leaders, who see their first duty as that of causing the price of their companies' stocks to rise. Indeed, as a stock promoter and dividend-raiser Vail was a decided failure; in 1907, the year he assumed office as president, AT&T's stock price range was about 190–135 and the dividend was eight dollars a share, while in 1919, the year he retired, the price range was 108⅜–95 and the dividend was still eight dollars. Net earnings per share were $10.67 for 1907, $10.05 for 1919. Throughout his tenure, they were relatively constant. But that failure was really Vail's triumph, the measure of his stature as a builder rather than a moneymaker. While the AT&T stock price and dividend remained no better than constant, the number of telephones in service more than doubled from less than six million to over twelve million, nationwide service was begun, and local service was vastly improved. What Vail accomplished financially was the conversion of the Bell System from a company on the brink of disaster to the safest and soundest of blue chips; what he accomplished structurally and politically was the end of the chaos of direct telephone competition, and the acceptance by government and most of the people of the telephone business as a regulated monopoly, or group of monopolies; what he accomplished technically—by creating a research-and-development facility that would lead directly to Bell Laboratories—was the perfection of long-distance service and the conversion of the telephone business from a local to a national affair.

To sum up, AT&T under Vail was almost certainly the first

large private corporation to adopt a conscious, clearly articulated policy of subordinating the maximization of profit to the provision of services to its customers. It was a policy not always followed, in Vail's time or later; but as a concept, the policy marked a milestone in industrial history.

# CHAPTER 7

# Happy Days and Happiness Boys

Bell System and independent telephone people, in a remarkable mobilization, carried the brunt of U.S. Army communications work in France in 1917–18. In 1916 the entire Army Signal Corps cadre consisted of 42 officers and 1,212 enlisted men; by the time of the Armistice, some 15,000 Bell System people had entered the service, of whom 7,500 had been sent overseas, 361 decorated, 550 wounded, and 235 killed in action. At the time of U.S. entry into the war, a call for volunteers was posted in Bell offices nationwide. Chief Engineer Carty was commissioned a major (and was eventually to become a general) in the Signal Corps Reserve and given the assignment of organizing Bell volunteers into military communications units; by mid-1918, when Carty left his Washington administrative post and went to France to take personal command of Bell units, he had put together twelve Signal Corps battalions consisting entirely of Bell employees. (Eventually there would be fourteen.) They were organized according to their old telephone operating units—for example, the 406th (Pennsylvania Bell) Telegraph Battalion, and the 411th (Pacific Bell) Telegraph Battalion, both of which played a prominent part in the celebrated and bloody American assault on St.-Mihiel in September 1918, and the latter of which included the first Americans to enter St.-Mihiel.

All in all, the Signal Corps established in France a complete and entirely new telephone network comprising some 100,000 miles of wire, about 100 switchboards, and over 3,600 stations. The French Marshal Foch used the American telephone facilities when he could because (true to form) they generally worked better than the French facilities; in fact, plans were laid, which never needed to be carried out due to the Armistice, for extending the system into Germany and to Berlin itself. In addition, Bell engineers developed usable, if primitive, two-way air-to-ground radio equipment in 1917, and in 1918 it was used extensively by American pilots in combat in France. A high-powered radio station was erected in Bordeaux to keep open transatlantic communications in support of the submarine telegraph cables, many of which were frequently out of service because of damage caused by German submarines.

A feature of telephone workers' involvement in the war effort was the role of women. In November 1917, General Pershing, the American commander in chief, called for the creation of a Women's Telephone Operating Unit. A wave of excitement swept telephone switchboards from Maine to California, and immediately there were 7,600 applications. Most of the applicants were disappointed, however, as only 100 were accepted, in part because of the requirement that they speak French fluently so as to be able to deal with French operators on interconnected lines. Eventually 233 American women telephone operators got overseas, some of whom worked under combat conditions close behind the lines, replacing male operators and thereby restoring order and efficiency just as the first women operators had done in 1879.

The Bell Battalions, which somehow sucessfully combined the experience and skill of a peacetime business organization with the imagination, esprit, and courage necessary to military operations, remain a striking—and stirring—example of the application of corporate resources, almost unchanged except for the wearing of uniforms and the assumption of military ranks, to national purposes.

On the home front, meanwhile, government control of the telephone system was proving to be considerably less than a complete success. In fact, it was proving to be in some respects just what Vail, before his change of heart (if he ever had a change of heart), had said that it would be—an "unregulated monopoly," able without obstruction to take actions from which the Bell System under private control had previously been restrained by the government. For example, for a number of years prior to 1918 the Bell System had been seeking to initiate a "service connection charge," payable by new subscribers as compensation for the physical installation and connection of telephones in their homes or offices; the move had been blocked by the opposition of state public-service commissions and the lack of cooperation of independent telephone companies. Now, within four weeks after the government takeover, the postmaster general instituted service connection charges ranging from five to fifteen dollars, depending on the type of service being installed. The rates were subsequently reduced, but the charge itself was never thereafter eliminated, and of course it remains in effect today, in both the Bell System and the independent companies—an odd legacy to the free-enterprise telephone business from "socialistic" government operation.

The government, too, found itself unable to operate the telephones without sharply raising rates. Wartime rate raises would probably have been inevitable no matter who was in charge, since the nation in 1918 and early 1919 was experiencing the most rapid rate of inflation since the Civil War; the fact remains, though, that reduced rates had been promised categorically as one of the benefits of government as opposed to private operation, and the breaking of the promise was bound to cause public disillusionment. In December 1918, Burleson—under pressure from Vail, who explained in detail that sharply increased costs made higher rates necessary—issued an order raising long-distance rates by about 20 percent, effective January 21, 1919. Two months later, in March, Burleson supplemented this action by authorizing a general increase in local Bell exchange rates that would augment the cost of such service to subscribers by almost twenty million dollars a year. There were protests from subscribers and from state commissions, and the matter went to the Supreme Court, which on June 2 confirmed all the increases ordered by the postmaster general. Later that month, a resolution was introduced in Congress proposing the immediate return of the telephone and telegraph systems to their original owners. It was passed on July 11, to be effective August 1; and on the latter date the wires went back to private ownership.

The one-year experiment was over, and by any statistical standard it had been a failure. The government, pledged to end the private owners' alleged practice of maintaining high rates in order to ensure high dividends for their stockholders, had itself been forced to make rate increases that for the Bell System alone amounted to forty-two million dollars a year. Nor had the financial results under government control been good. To the contrary, Bell operations for the year showed a deficit of over thirteen million dollars, of which four million was made up from AT&T's surplus and more than nine million from the United States Treasury. Government operation, then, appeared to have benefited no one but, of all people, the representatives of capitalism, the AT&T stockholders, whose eight-dollar dividend had been guaranteed and duly paid under the government contract.

Understandably, the return of the telephone and telegraph systems was popular with the public and its legislators. Republicans and Democrats alike denounced the inefficiency of the Post Office and Burleson's "grasping" and "domineering" administrative tactics, and Representative James B. Atwell of Louisiana, the man who had introduced the congressional resolution to take over the wire systems in 1918, felt called upon to apologize "to my people and to Congress" for what he had done. Whether such breast-beating was called for is doubtful; there is no real evidence that the extraordinary problems of wartime could have been met better by the telephone and telegraph companies under private ownership and control. What is certain, though, is that AT&T— even though it had to make exceptional plant and maintenance expenditures in the early postwar years, to regain lost ground— derived an adventitious political and psychological advantage from the experience. The ghost of government ownership was laid; agitation for it disappeared in popular and orthodox political circles, and for a decade to come, the view that the private communications companies could best serve the public interest with little or no government interference would prevail in all but the wilder of radical circles. On this friendly wave of laissez faire, AT&T was wafted into the 1920s—a decade of ample profits, of lavish growth, of wide public acceptance, and of heavy temptations to expand outside the realm of telephony.[1]

2

Harry Bates Thayer, the man who assumed the AT&T presidency in mid-1919, was a Vermonter who had graduated from Dartmouth in 1879, joined Western Electric as a shipping clerk two years later, and never left the Bell System thereafter, serving successively as New York manager, vice-president, and president of Western Electric and in 1909 becoming a vice-president of AT&T while continuing to run Western. A man, that is, in the traditional AT&T mold. He was a neat, formal, shrewd-eyed man with a cool glance from behind pince-nez spectacles; in the view of Katherine Vail Marsters, he was "shy, but possibly ruthless." At all events, as Vail's closest associate and friend in the company —and the man so attuned to Vail that they had liked to sit together in Vail's office in perfect silence—he was the precise man to carry on Vail's policies. It was fortuitous, but appropriate, that Thayer's second year in office, 1921, saw the passage by Congress of the Graham Act, which put the legislative seal on the Vail-sponsored Kingsbury Commitment of eight years earlier. The Graham Act formally exempted telephony from the Sherman Antitrust Act as far as consolidation of competing companies was concerned. Direct telephone competition—two separate systems in the same town—increasingly unpopular with subscribers, and all but meaningless since the Kingsbury Commitment had mandated interconnection with Bell facilities, was withering away by attrition anyway; now AT&T was legally free to clean up the pockets where it remained by buying up the last competing independents. There remained, of course, the many noncompeting, Bell-connected independent companies—some 8,500 of them in the late 1920s—and as a matter of policy, AT&T did not exercise its newly acquired right to absorb duplicating companies except in special cases, so that the last of the two-system cities, Philadelphia, would not become a one-system city until 1945, when Bell acquired the Keystone Telephone Company there. But the Graham Act was formal government recognition that competing telephone systems were mere survivals of a past time and that telephony was a "natural monopoly" subject to regulation. When the question of competition would come up again, in the 1960s, it would be in an entirely different context.[2]

A great new challenge faced AT&T as it entered the 1920s —the challenge of radio. Development work was going forward leading toward the establishment of regular transatlantic telephone service by radio. But radio, of course, had another and equally exciting dimension, that of broadcasting. By November

1920, when the first radio broadcasting station—the Westinghouse station KDKA, in Pittsburgh—inaugurated service by sending out returns of the Harding-Cox presidential election, Western Electric already had three experimental stations, ZXB at West Street, New York City, ZXF at Cliffwood, New Jersey, and ZXJ at Deal Beach, New Jersey, sending out test messages to each other and to the few radio operators and ships and ambitious amateur radio buffs who happened to be listening. That same year—at the urging of the federal government, which sought to forestall the monopolization of radio equipment by any single patent holder—AT&T entered into a cross-licensing patent agreement with General Electric Company; the agreement was later extended to include the other two corporate leaders in radio research, Radio Corporation of America and Westinghouse Electric Company.

AT&T's attitude toward radio in early 1921 was later summed up by Walter S. Gifford, then controller and later president: "Nobody knew . . . where radio was really headed. Everything about broadcasting was uncertain. For my own part I expected that since it was a form of telephony . . . we were sure to be involved in broadcasting somehow. Our first vague idea, as broadcasting appeared, was that perhaps people would expect to be able to pick up a telephone and call some radio station, so that they could give radio talks." But by the end of that year, the situation had clarified somewhat: hundreds wanted to broadcast, millions wanted to listen, and no one was sure how broadcasting was to be supported. AT&T decided to get into broadcasting on an experimental basis, as Thayer explained in the 1921 Annual Report: "A field in which the radio telephone has possibilities is the furnishing of . . . one-way service . . . news, music, speeches, and the like. . . . We are preparing to furnish this broadcasting service to such an extent as may meet the commercial demands of the public."

This promise began to be fulfilled on July 25, 1922, when station WBAY—the call letters were changed a month later to WEAF—began broadcasting from the Long Lines building on Walker Street, New York City. The transmitter, built by Western Electric, had a power output of 500 watts, and the plan was to derive revenues from renting program time to anyone who wanted to use the facilities, at $40 or $50 per fifteen minutes. Unrented time was to be filled by musical programs and the like.

It soon became evident that any dreams of a flood of people eager to air their messages were in vain; the station had to wait a month for its first paying customer, and its gross revenues for its first two months of operation was $550. Meanwhile it filled up time by calling on local talent; one evening's program featured vocal selections by Miss Helen Graves and Miss Anna Hermann accompanied by Mrs. M. W. Swayze, piano solos by Mr. F. R. Marion, a recitation of James Whitcomb Riley's poem "An Old Sweetheart of Mine" by Miss Edna Cunningham, and violin selections by Mr. Joseph Koznick. All of these performers were employees of the AT&T Long Lines Department except Mr. Koznick, who was from the AT&T Drafting Department. Audience reaction to the program is not recorded. At last, on August 28, the Queensborough Corporation, a real estate promotion of Jackson Heights, New York City, bought fifteen minutes to announce a development called Hawthorne Court, and thus WEAF gained the perhaps dubious distinction of carrying the first radio commercial.

There were thirteen commercial customers in December 1922 and a total of about two hundred and fifty during 1923, by the end of which there were nearly half a million receiving sets within the station's range. But WEAF officials quickly learned what all radio officials would later know—that listeners will accept commercials only when leavened by information and professional entertainment. In 1922 and 1923, WEAF broadcast sports, opera from the Metropolitan, lighter music from the Capitol Theatre, theatrical performances from the stages of Broadway, and radio's first comedy team, a pair of vaudeville performers called the Happiness Boys. Also Graham McNamee, soon to become the best-known of early radio announcers, made the first of his many appearances on WEAF. The station's audience grew rapidly, and by the end of 1923, letters and cards from listeners were coming in at the rate of eight hundred per day. Meanwhile the concept of sponsorship of entertainment programs by commercial interests gradually replaced the original one of simply leaving the use of time to advertisers. Moreover, in the interest of gaining public goodwill, the station imposed on its sponsors a set of rules that by the standards of later radio seem downright quaint: no "direct" sales pitches; no mention of such hard-sell details as the color of a can; no ad-libbing of advertising material; and no advertising that the station officials considered possibly offensive to good taste. On this ground, the first commercial for toothpaste was held up for several weeks because the WEAF station manager felt that toothpaste, regardless of how treated, might be too personal a matter to mention on the air.

In April 1923, the studios of WEAF were moved to the fourth floor of AT&T headquarters at 195 Broadway. While people on the upper floors went about the workaday business of maintaining the national telephone network and advancing the telephone art, a glamorous show-business atmosphere flourished down below, with stars like John McCormack and Ethel Barrymore regularly passing in and out. As radio expanded, AT&T sought to expand its radio operation—a task for which it was uniquely equipped because it had telephone wires to use in the establishment of the first radio network. In July 1923, the Bell System opened its second radio station, WCAP at Washington, D.C.; that June, an address by President Harding in St. Louis was broadcast to every state in the union by the first "nationwide hookup," made possible by Bell System telephone lines; and by the end of 1925, there was a national network of seventeen Bell-owned or Bell-licensed stations serving over 60 percent of all receiving sets in the United States, and bringing in gross annual revenues of about $750,000.[3]

It was all heady stuff for a sober telephone company, now suddenly deep in the tensions and delights of show business. All the while, a furious struggle was going on for position in the new and fast-growing radio business, between AT&T and competing companies. Was AT&T, through its radio patents and its telephone network, attempting to monopolize radio broadcasting? Almost immediately after the signing of the cross-licensing agreement of July 1920, it became the subject of conflicting interpretations and disputes among the rival communications companies. Up to early 1922, it was AT&T's policy to refuse the use of Bell telephone wires—necessary for remote pickups or for linking up distant stations—to radio stations not owned by Bell. There was a relaxation of this hard-line policy in April, 1922, when AT&T informed its operating telephone companies that it now seemed desirable, until further notice, to be liberal in the matter of leasing private lines to broadcasters. However, the stations owned by AT&T's chief competitors in broadcasting—Radio Corporation, General Electric, and Westinghouse—were specifically excluded from the new liberal policy, under AT&T's interpretation of the 1920 agreement. Those stations were forced to resort to the use of telegraph wires. AT&T's interpretation was challenged in 1923 by Radio Corporation, which contended that the right to broadcast *implied* the right to use telephone wires as an adjunct; the matter went to arbitration, but the arbitrator's decision was so equivocal as to leave both parties dissatisfied. Another aspect of the same matter came to a head in February 1924, when AT&T was accused of offering telephone wires to non-Bell stations at a prohibitive cost. That month, the Rotary Club of Chicago planned a nationwide broadcast of an address to be made from Washington by President Coolidge, using a hookup of eighteen well-scattered stations to be connected by wires. AT&T agreed to broadcast the address from Washington, New York, and Providence via its own facilities, and announced that it would charge $2,500 to connect the Washington station by wire with station WJAZ in Chicago, which the Rotarians wanted to use to reach western listeners. Station WJAZ protested that the charge was extortionate, and pointed out that ordinary long-distance service between Washington and Chicago for the ten minutes of the president's speech would cost only $14.40. AT&T retorted that a radio hookup installation was in no way comparable technically to a long-distance telephone call; that the installation and operation of the hookup for the president's speech would require more than twenty-five man-days of work; and that radio hookup charges could *never* be comparable to regular toll charges. WJAZ refused to pay the charge, and Coolidge's address was not broadcast in the Chicago area.

Whatever the proper charge for such a connection or the correct interpretation of the 1920 license agreement, there is no doubt that AT&T's balkiness about leasing wires to rival broadcasters in 1923 was motivated in part by a desire to gain a commanding position in radio broadcasting. In February 1923, A. H. Griswold, the company's assistant vice-president in charge of radio matters, said to a Bell System radio conference, "We have been very careful, up to the present time, not to state to the public in any way . . . the idea that the Bell System desires to monopolize broadcasting; but the fact remains that it's a telephone job, that we are telephone people, and that we can do it better than anybody else. . . . In one form or another, we have got to do the job." Griswold went on to assure his listeners that his view was shared by the company's top officers, including President Thayer. A year later, however, the company view—at least, as publicly expressed—had changed sharply. A statement to the press by Thayer in March 1924—by which time AT&T was in the thick of patent-infringement suits against rival radio stations and arbitration of the dispute with Radio Corporation over the availability of telephone lines—declared that AT&T "has not attempted and does not desire a monopoly of broadcasting"; that "any broadcasting station now infringing [AT&T's] patents can acquire a license . . . upon reasonable terms" and that "a monopoly, either of broadcasting for entertainment of the public or for hire, is not desirable from any point of view." The statement also strongly expressed approval of federal regulation of broadcasting. Evidently, there was taking place within AT&T a change of heart as to broadcasting monopoly and regulation closely analogous to the one that had taken place as to telephone monopoly and regulation in the Vail regime, and had culminated in the Kingsbury Commitment. But meanwhile, as the suits and the arbitration dragged on, AT&T was vigorously pursuing the enlargement of its radio network, and was continuing to make it difficult or impossible for rival broadcasting companies to use AT&T telephone wires.[4]

3

The telephone business, in the early 1920s, was booming along with most of the rest of American business. The count of Bell telephones in service was rising rapidly. In 1921, the directors established the nine-dollar-per-share dividend rate that was to endure through thick and thin for more than a generation, and to become the hallmark of the company's status as the bluest of blue-chip investments. Wide public holding of securities was a new American phenomenon, arising to a great extent out of the popularity of Liberty bonds during the First World War. AT&T, then as now, was by far the most widely held of all stocks, and its stockholders count was rising wildly; from 140,000 in 1920, it jumped in 1921 to 186,000 and in 1922 to 250,000, of whom 236,-000 held fewer than one hundred shares. This extraordinary proliferation of small stockholders was actively promoted by the company, which in 1921 began offering stock to its employees on the installment plan, and established a new entity, the Bell Telephone Securities Company, to acquire new capital and expand ownership by promoting the sale of the securities of AT&T and of the various Bell operating companies. The salesmen used were employees of the Bell companies, and so successful were they that in 1925, more than 43 percent of all new AT&T stockholders added to the ledgers for that year had been corralled through the efforts of the Securities Company. (Such a systematic promotion by a company of its own stock might now be considered illegal under the Securities Exchange Act of 1934. However, it was unquestionably legal in the 1920s, and—in those days of almost constantly rising prices of AT&T stock—was little criticized. Nor is there any question that it had the salutary effect of helping to break up the earlier concentration of AT&T stock ownership in the Northeast, and distribute it widely through the South, Midwest, and Far West.)

Meanwhile, in a time when the financial success of corporations and changing national mores were leading to the growth of labor unions that would greatly accelerate in the 1930s, labor relations in the Bell System continued to be—as they had always been previously—remarkably placid. The first formal agreement between a Bell company and any union had been one signed in 1900 in Buffalo with the International Brotherhood of Electrical Workers, then less than a decade old, but that agreement had fallen apart quickly, the telephone companies had opposed unionization effectively, and by 1910 the only union-organized situations in the telephone business, Bell or independent, were in Illinois, Montana, and parts of the West Coast. Operators as well as mechanical workers began to form unions, and in 1918 the locals of female telephone operators—which had previously been opposed by male employees on what were apparently sexist lines —were permitted to form an autonomous department within the IBEW. During the war, the telephone companies, with a certain amount of encouragement from Postmaster General Burleson, effectively opposed the IBEW by resorting to the then-common practice of promoting "company unions" friendly to management. The conservative political climate of postwar America encouraged these efforts. In 1920 the West Coast IBEW telephone locals were virtually destroyed by a strike against what they took to be a company ultimatum that all workers join the company union. Through the rest of the decade, there was hardly any new organizing of telephone workers by the IBEW, and in 1927 the national union virtually threw in the towel when its president said, "Our experience of the last few years convinces us that were we to attempt to organize the comparatively few [telephone workers] in each company who desired organization, it would only result in their being discharged."

The record is quite clear, then, that Bell System companies—in keeping with the prevailing business attitude of the time—opposed the incursion of a national union, and did so very effectively. There were, to be sure, structural conditions peculiar to the telephone industry that tended to discourage workers from joining a national union. Plant and maintenance workers were "industry conscious," proud of the uniqueness of their product and perhaps scornful of other electrical workers; as for telephone operators, their exceptionally high turnover rate, attributable in large part to their tendency to get married and bear children, made campaigns to organize them a kind of treadmill operation. And it is only fair to point out another reason for the IBEW's failure. AT&T in the 1920s was a paternalistic organization in the old tradition, that is, it treated its workers fairly according to its lights. Wages were generally competitive; working conditions had been vastly improved under Vail's management from the calamitous situation of 1907; a System-wide pension plan, one of the pioneers of such plans, had been inaugurated under Vail in 1913. In 1924 Western Electric became a pioneer in industrial relations research when it agreed to cooperate with the National Research Council, the National Academy of Sciences, and the Harvard Business School on a major study of working conditions at the huge Western Electric plant at Hawthorne, Illinois. The "Hawthorne Studies," as they came to be called—pursued over almost a decade, and mostly directed by the Australian psychologist Elton Mayo—resulted in a landmark book, *Management and the Worker*, published in 1939, which introduced students of industry to the now-famous "Hawthorne effect": that workers under study increase their production whether such factors as plant illumination are raised or lowered, suggesting that the increase is caused not by the nature of the change but by the change itself.

The Hawthorne studies, if they did not exactly benefit the worker, at least showed him that the company was thinking about him.[5]

As to technical progress, in 1921 the Bell System—well behind the independent telephone companies in this respect—began offering its subscribers dial service using its own equipment when its first "step-by-step" mechanical switching office was put into service in Dallas. Short-distance telephony by submarine cable began in 1923 when such a cable superseded radio as the carrier of commercial telephone service between Los Angeles and Santa Catalina island, twenty-five miles to the southwest. The radio engineers were edging, one step at a time, toward the establishment of commercial transatlantic radio service. And on January 1, 1925, in a logical extension of Vail's consolidation of research and development of 1907, the entire Bell System research-and-development effort (with the exception of the AT&T Development and Research Department, which would join up in 1934) became a separate company, Bell Telephone Laboratories, Inc., jointly owned and supplied with funds by AT&T and Western Electric, and with the grand old man of AT&T engineering, John J. Carty, as its first board chairman. Thus, in what was essentially an administrative reshuffle, was created a name that would become one to conjure with in the world of research.[6]

4

Thayer retired as president of AT&T in January 1925, and was succeeded as president by Walter S. Gifford, who would occupy the office for almost a quarter of a century—far longer than anyone else before or after—and would leave a personal stamp on the modern American telephone industry deeper than anyone's except Vail's.

Gifford was a man of paradox—a loner with social skill, an accountant with a philosopher's grasp of large issues. He was born in Salem, Massachusetts, in 1885—near where Bell had lived while conducting some of his earliest telephone researches—the son of a taciturn Yankee who owned a small lumber mill. As a high school boy, he was physically frail, specialized in dramatics, and disliked responsibilities. At Harvard he was bright enough to finish the undergraduate course in three years, graduating in 1904 just inside the top third of his class. His modest Yankee ambition at the time was to earn five thousand dollars a year. After graduation, he became a clerk in the Chicago office of Western Electric at ten dollars a week, taking the job over the objections of his father, who had a Yankee suspicion of all corporations. When, after two years, he was given a raise to twenty-four dollars a week, his father commented, deflatingly, "Any damn fool can make a success in a corporation." Soon afterward, when reprimanded for slouching in a Western Electric executive's office, Gifford replied, "It seems to me I was hired to do a certain job, not to sit in a certain way." The executive apologized. Gifford became a Vail protégé, and gradually replaced his reticent manner with one of self-confidence—some said conceit. In 1911 he resigned from Western Electric to reorganize a copper mining company in Arizona at a far higher salary, but the experience proved to be unsatisfactory, and six months later he was rehired by Vail as chief statistician of AT&T at seven thousand dollars a year. Visiting London in 1912, he tried wearing a monocle, but soon gave it up. One hesitates to think what a picnic the formidably antielitist government investigators of the 1930s would have had with an AT&T president who wore a monocle.

Married in 1916 to Florence Pitman, of Brooklyn, the daughter of a prominent industrialist, Gifford took civilian military training at Plattsburgh, New York, but ended up sitting out the war in Washington as an organizer and executive of the Council of National Defense. After the war he returned to AT&T as controller, a position Vail had always regarded as one of the four or five key staff positions. In 1922 he was made a director, then executive vice-president, and on Thayer's retirement, president. In the fat years of the late 1920s, the man whose ambition had once been to earn $5,000 a year would be earning $250,000.

Gifford's office style was laconic and precise; his sartorial trademark was a neat bow tie. One of his long-time close colleagues, Cleo Craig, much later described him as "the perfect executive," with the single flaw—one shared by many executives—that he hated to fire people and often avoided doing so when he knew he should. At home, he showed an intense dislike of social functions of all kinds. He habitually took telephone calls at all hours of the night, often using a carefully practiced accent to prevent callers from knowing, unless he wanted them to know, that they were talking to the president of AT&T. Among the telephone users with service problems who once called him after midnight—and succeeded in breaking through the disguise—was the humorist James Thurber. Thurber's phone was fixed immediately after the conversation.

There is another point about Gifford's executive style to be noted at once. Shortly after assuming office, he brought in Charles Proctor Cooper as his financial vice-president and, to all intents and purposes, right-hand man. Cooper was a man cast in quite a different mold from Gifford. Born in Caldwell, Ohio, educated in mechanical engineering at Ohio State University, Cooper had spent his whole career from 1908 on as a hard-boiled telephone operating man: as a plant manager and engineer with the New York Telephone Company for eight years, and later as general manager, vice-president, and finally president of the Ohio Bell Telephone Company. Where Gifford was a long-range thinker and ideal front man, Cooper—who will reappear in these pages as an increasingly potent influence in Gifford's administration— was a nuts-and-bolts manager of a telephone network, and as such, in the opinion of some of the closest students of AT&T history, he represented the leading edge of a new style of top management at AT&T. Gifford was to be the last Vail-trained, Vail-style philosopher-president.

Gifford's first important moves as president were in the direction of taking AT&T out of its proliferating ancillary ventures and inducing it to stick to its original task—providing the best possible telephone service in the United States. In 1925 the company sold all the various plants that it owned in places outside the United States to International Telephone & Telegraph Company, a new firm headed by a young man of Danish-French parentage named Sosthenes Behn, which would later become a power in international telephony and eventually the most controversial of United States conglomerate corporations, and had chosen its name (according to an IT&T historian, Anthony Sampson) deliberately to cause confusion in the public mind with AT&T, with which it had and has no connection. The sale was dictated in part by threatened antitrust action against Western Electric, owner of the foreign plants, but it also suited Gifford's conviction about where the limits of AT&T's activities should be set. The same conviction was behind the company's sale in 1928 of Graybar Electric Company, originally a subsidiary of Western Electric to sell various kinds of nontelephone equipment manufactured by Western Electric, but one that had come to be chiefly a supplier of electrical supplies not made by Western.

And—although it is arguable that the same thing would have happened without his intercession—Gifford got AT&T out of radio broadcasting. By a series of three contracts entered into on July 1, 1926, AT&T agreed to supply wire services to the Radio Corporation for broadcasting purposes, and gave the Radio Corporation an option to buy station WEAF outright, along with the licenses to operate the rest of what had been the AT&T radio network. The sale was consummated on November 1 for one million dollars, and was accompanied by a pledge not to return to the field of radio. As Gifford explained in the Annual Report for that year, "The Company undertook to develop radio broadcasting in order to ascertain how it could be made most useful in the business. . . . The further the experiment was carried, the more evident it became that the objective of a broadcasting station was quite different from that of a telephone system."[7]

The sale and agreement to provide wires constituted another, if lesser, Kingsbury Commitment, and evidence that Gifford was indeed Vail's spiritual successor. It meant that AT&T—under pressure, to be sure—had given up another dream of monopoly, and that entertainment stars would no longer enliven the scene at 195 Broadway. (They would, in fact, continue to enliven it until August 1927, when the Radio Corporation moved the station uptown.)

Gifford's process of putting the AT&T house in order, as he perceived it, included radical changes in the so-called license contract between AT&T and the Bell System operating companies. In 1925, under the license contract as it had existed since 1902, each operating company annually paid 4.5 percent of its gross revenue to AT&T in exchange for various services, and the sum thus paid also included rental of telephone instruments, all of which were owned by AT&T. For 1925, the license contract brought AT&T $30,197,214, while the cost of the services rendered in exchange was calculated to be $26,556,167. Up to that time, whenever the provisions of the contract had come up for review in the courts, they had been affirmed on grounds that the parent company actually delivered its services and the use of its instruments at below cost. But now, with AT&T making a profit of $3.5 million a year on the contract, it came to be a primary target for critics. Public and regulatory voices were raised to say that AT&T was fattening its treasury, and indirectly its stockholders, at the expense of the operating companies that supplied local telephone service and therefore the subscribers who used it. To a degree, the charge was true; the answer was that AT&T needed profit to attract investors and thereby to finance expansion of service. But Gifford had inherited Vail's consciousness of public relations; to him, the point was that the 4.5 percent license fee *looked* too high. The company's first step was to unilaterally reduce the license fee for 1926 to 4 percent, thereby bringing the fees paid about into line with the cost of services. The second step, taken the following year, consisted of knocking down the fee all the way to 2 percent, and simultaneously substituting outright sale of telephones to the operating companies for the rentals that had previously constituted a good part of the higher license fee. Financially, the effect of this seemingly radical change was comparatively minor; AT&T's annual profit on the license fee changed to a loss, though not a great one. Cosmetically, the dramatic reduction in the percentage fee was intended to silence the critics once and for all. It scarcely did that, even after 1928, when the charge was reduced to 1.5 percent; the fee at that level would be a bone of contention in the 1930s. But the change, made so abruptly after so many years of doing things the old way, gave the clue to how Gifford's mind worked.

The clue was followed by a full exposure of the new president's thought when, in October 1927, he addressed the National Association of Railroad and Utilities Commissioners in Dallas with a policy statement equal in importance to Vail's San Francisco speech in 1915. Gifford laid the company's social objectives on the line in a way that, in a national climate of rampant individualism and general greed to get in on the business and stock-market boom, was clearly business heresy. To begin with, stockholders were advised to forget about " 'melons' or extra dividends—it would be contrary to sound policy for the management to earn speculative or large profits." So much, then, for profit maximization as a company objective; rather:

the fact that the responsibility for such a large part of the entire telephone service of the country rests solely upon this Company and its Associated Companies . . . imposes on the management an unusual obligation to the public to see to it that the service shall at all times be adequate, dependable, and satisfactory to the user. Obviously, the only sound policy that will meet these obligations is . . . to furnish *the best possible telephone service at the lowest cost consistent with financial safety.*

Since the "Dallas speech"—literally and definitively putting service first and profit second among Bell System objectives—defined for the first time for many people the concept of the public service corporation, was widely hailed as signaling a change in Bell System direction, and has repeatedly been called the most important act of Gifford's whole twenty-three-year administration, we may well look into its origins. One of Gifford's most brilliant early staff appointments was that of Arthur W. Page to the job of vice-president for public relations. Coming to the job at the age of forty-four, Page, a Harvard classmate and old friend of Gifford's, was the son of Walter Hines Page, partner in the publishing firm of Doubleday, Page & Company and later Woodrow Wilson's ambassador to Great Britain. Arthur Page had devoted his entire career to his father's company, and in particular to serving as editor of the magazine *The World's Work*, until Gifford persuaded him to join AT&T early in 1927. Page later told an AT&T colleague, Robert K. Greenleaf, that he had written Gifford's Dallas speech and that he had derived all of the ideas in it from the writings and speeches of Theodore Vail. Far from being a break with the past, then, it was a restatement of earlier ideas with a fresh ring—and in a time when their restatement was badly needed. This revelation is not made in denigration of Gifford, who, after all, took responsibility for what he said, and committed AT&T to living up to it. The speech, indeed, sets him apart as one 1920s big businessman who stood against the prevailing mood of Babbitry and stock-market profiteering.[8]

5

It was in the 1920s that the telephone, reflecting its new place in real life, became almost all-pervasive in popular literature and, in particular, drama. Its literary role had changed sharply over the years. No longer did it appear as a fascinating and yet troublesome, new invention, the latest wonder in the march of scientific progress, as in the writings of Mark Twain; and no longer did it often appear as a quasi-human presence, to be loved or hated or feared or even wooed, as in Joyce and Proust. Now it had reached a third stage; it had come to be treated as a necessary and ever-present artifact in human intercourse, and as the most useful of all mechanical devices in the construction of drama—the ultimate stage prop. Vaudeville skits like "Cohen on the Telephone" drew comedy from the comically self-revealing ways people used it. Popular songs were built around it, by far the most celebrated of them Irving Berlin's "All Alone," written in 1924:

> All alone—I'm so all alone,
> There is no one else but you.
> All alone by the telephone
> Waiting for a ring . . .

The telephone onstage became the leading cliché of Broadway. The curtain would go up on an empty set—a well-furnished living room with a single telephone so placed as to claim the audience's attention immediately. The telephone would ring. The lady of the house would rush on and answer it; and the ensuing conversation, of which the audience would hear only one end, would announce the beginning of the plot. Thus, through the device of the telephone, the playwright had been able to create a sense of reality, start the action, accomplish some useful exposition, and arrange a dramatic entrance for a star actor, all at a single stroke. Noël Coward's 1923 sketch, *Sorry You've Been Troubled,* introduced in saucy fashion what was to become a staple of stage and later screen—the telephone monologue, or one-ended dialogue, by a woman. Poppy Baker, a young Londoner of fashion, is lying in bed of a morning when a call from the police informs her that her husband has committed suicide by jumping off Waterloo Bridge. In the course of several subsequent gossipy conversations of Poppy's with her friends, the audience learns that she regrets her husband's death scarcely at all; and the final twist comes when she learns, to her open disgust, that a mistake has been made and the man who jumped was not her husband but that of the woman who lives upstairs.

That kind of thing went on quite often in those days in the theaters of London, New York, and other cities. The play in which the telephone, as a prop rather than a character, became so important as to dominate the action was the Broadway hit of 1928, *The Front Page*, by Ben Hecht and Charles MacArthur. The action of *The Front Page* takes place in the press room of the Criminal Courts Building in Chicago. There are seven telephones, communicating with the city's seven newspapers. Throughout the play they are constantly ringing and being talked into; most of the action takes place offstage, and the audience learns about it by listening to one end of telephone conversations; and the memorably cynical final scene—in which a tough editor prevents his star reporter from quitting by first giving him a watch as a farewell present, and then notifying the police that the watch has been stolen—is depicted through a telephone call. Structurally the play is the ultimate telephone drama—without the telephone it simply wouldn't exist.

The year 1930—a time when the telephone was all but ubiquitous in most of American and European society, but had not yet been so long enough to be taken entirely for granted—may plausibly mark the all-time high-water mark of telephone literature; most subsequent writings on or around the subject would be variations on three works—a poem, a short story, and a play—produced in that year. The telephone in Robert Frost's poem "The Telephone" is not a real instrument at all, but an imagined one:

> There was an hour
> And still
> When leaning my head against a flower
> I heard you talk.
> Don't say I didn't, for I heard you . . .
> Someone said "Come"—I heard it as I bowed . . .

With Frost's poem, in which a flower serves as a telepathic telephone, a stage is reached in human apprehension of the instrument and its role that is new and yet old; with the telephone everywhere in everyday life, we are back to a perception of it similar to the one that had prevailed immediately after its invention, as magic and a part of nature or the supernatural. The telephone has found its way into the deeper reaches of the human psyche; thinking of the flower as a telephone, and hearing a lover's voice over it, seems as natural as holding a shell to one's ear to hear the sea.

Two other 1930 works carry the "alone by the telephone"

theme to somewhere near its ultimate point. Dorothy Parker's famous story "A Telephone Call" is a monologue addressed to God by a woman waiting in vain for a call from her lover. The telephone she waits besides is a palpable presence, and a hostile one because of its refusal to ring; the woman finally longs even for a call in which the lover would reject her, because it would release her from her torment. In a few pages, the author creates a spinning pattern around the telephone, an object that keeps the heroine sane with hope while it drives her insane with frustration. This minor classic ends with the telephone still not having rung, and the woman left counting to five hundred by fives.

A darker and more florid version of the same theme is the subject of Jean Cocteau's one-act play *The Human Voice,* in which "a woman in a long night-dress lies as if murdered" on the floor of her bedroom waiting for a promised call from her ex-lover. This time the telephone does ring, repeatedly. First there are two wrong numbers; then the ex-lover calls, and there follows a long conversation, interrupted several times by broken connections or by one or the other of the callers hanging up, in which we learn from what the woman says that her hopes of resuming the affair are in vain, and that she has recently attempted suicide. In her hysteria, she makes the telephone instrument an explicit symbol of her feelings; she takes it to bed with her as if it were the lover himself, she imagines it as a diver's air tube, without which she would drown, and finally she winds the cord around her neck in a symbolic suicide. Then, mastering her courage, she says to the ex-lover over the telephone, "I'm brave. Be quick. Break off. Quick. Break." The curiously crucial role of the telephone in modern love, and the way it makes the breaking off of love relationships both easier and harder than it would be with no telephone, has never been more painfully exposed than in *The Human Voice,* nor has the telephone's ability to both relieve and intensify the tensions and disappointments of life.[9]

# 6

The growth in the number of stockholders of AT&T during the 1920s was one of the important national economic and social phenomena of the time. The efforts of the Bell Telephone Securities Company and the Bell System's installment stock-buying plan for employees undoubtedly contributed to this phenomenon, but perhaps it would have occurred without them. With increasing general affluence, a widespread middle-class habit of owning corporate stock was developing—for the first time ever, in any country—and AT&T, with its steady earnings and dividends and its universally known product, was the perfect company to attract the first-time investor or the trustee investing for an heir. AT&T stock was leading the way toward the later situation that the New York Stock Exchange would proudly, and of course self-servingly, describe as "people's capitalism," which would reach a high point in 1970, when thirty million American stockholders could be counted.

From 250,000 in 1922, the Bell stockholder count went to 281,000 in 1923, 345,000 in 1924, and on upward to almost half a million in 1929, a banner year in which a record 857,000 new telephones were added to the Bell network, AT&T net profit per share reached a record $12.67, and it became the first corporation in history to have gross revenues of over one billion dollars. This astonishing new trend had several economic effects, of which the most important was a diffusion of power. The old "banker control" of the Bell System eroded during the 1920s almost to the vanishing point. It had, to be sure, been very real in 1907, when the company had had virtually no sources of new capital other than the Morgan banking group. The bankers' grip was progressively loosened during the Vail years as AT&T grew in technical and financial strength. During the 1920s, J. P. Morgan & Company continued to be the chief underwriters of all Bell System debt securities, as it and its successor firm, Morgan Stanley & Company would continue to be until two decades later, when competitive bidding for such securities would begin; moreover, the bankers did very well for themselves, collecting commissions from the sale of Bell securities, over the years between 1907 and the end of World War II, amounting to nearly forty million dollars. But while this money continued to flow to them, the control of the bankers over the conduct of AT&T gradually ebbed away. The passage in 1933 of the Glass-Steagall Act, separating by law the functions of investment banking and commercial banking, would mark, for American industry generally, a watershed between bank domination of industry and industrial domination of banks.

But in the case of AT&T, the watershed came earlier because of the company's new-found ability to finance itself by selling new common stock to its stockholders and the public. This it did, without banker help and therefore without paying commissions, by two devices that were perfected during the 1920s: straight stock offerings to existing stockholders, and the issue to stockholders of rights to buy stock below the market price—rights that the stockholders could exercise on their own behalf, or else sell to others who would then exercise them. In either case, new money would flow into the AT&T treasury without an increase in company debt. Late in the decade, as the price of AT&T stock soared to record highs in reflection of the general stock-market boom, the company varied the routine by offering convertible debentures—debt that could be changed into equity. All the while, J. P. Morgan & Company continued to lead the syndicates that sold AT&T bonds, just as it had done in 1907. But now, as everyone knew, the locus of power had shifted. *Any* banking firm or combination of firms, provided it had sufficient resources, could now easily sell AT&T bonds and would be delighted to have the chance to do so. The fact that the Morgan firm continued to be given the privilege was a function not of financial control but of tradition and sentiment; AT&T was giving Morgan its banking business as a favor, for the sake of the old school tie.

Who, then—in the absence of banker domination based on financial need—now had "control" of AT&T, that is to say, who could decide what it would do and not do? Theoretically, such control rested with its owners, those half-million stockholders; but since no single stockholder held as much as 1 percent of the total, and since half a million people or even a tiny fraction of that number cannot practically combine themselves into a decision-making unit, the decision-making power fell—as it does now —to the company's appointed managers. For better or for worse, Gifford, Cooper, and their aides—selected by their peers, and subject to review only by a board of directors seldom in close touch with the fine points of company affairs—could run AT&T as they chose. The largest and most widely held of all corporations was thus a pioneer example, perhaps *the* pioneer example, of the new phenomenon to be memorably described by Adolf A. Berle, Jr., and Gardiner C. Means in 1933, in their book *The Modern Corporation and Private Property:* the corporation run not by its owners but by professional managers.

Those managers were subjected, in the late 1920s to tremendous pressure to "split" the stock—simply issue all existing stockholders two or perhaps three new shares in exchange for each old share held. Such a move, common in times of stock-market booms, would, on the basis of experience, have tended to inflate the value of AT&T holdings and indirectly to fatten the company's treasury still further. But Gifford—in line with the policy of "no melons" announced in his Dallas speech—resisted the pressure; the stock remained unsplit, and the dividend held steady at nine dollars a share. Even so, none but the greediest of stockholders had reason to complain. By the end of 1928, when AT&T stock was selling at 193, a holder who had bought in 1925 had a profit of about 50 percent, and one who had bought in 1920 of about 100 percent. As for one who had invested five hundred dollars back in 1878, when Bell stock had first been offered to the public, the value of his holding at the end of 1928, counting all dividends and stock-rights offerings over the years, would have been $129,895.

So beneficent were economic conditions in those years—years of rapid expansion without inflation, which leading economists in and out of government were beginning to speak of as a "new era" of permanent prosperity—that the Bell System was able to make some rate reductions while improving service and increasing employees' wages. In October 1926, certain long-distance rates were reduced, and lower evening rates were introduced for the first time; fourteen months later, there was a further reduction amounting to an estimated customer saving of $1.5 million per year, and in February 1929, a third reduction amounting to $5 million more. Between 1925 and 1929 the average weekly earnings of Bell employees (of whom 65 percent were women) rose modestly from about twenty-six dollars a week to about twenty-nine dollars. Service, spurred by technical innovation and ample resources for new investment, leaped forward. Between 1925 and 1929, the average time elapsed between when a new customer asked for a telephone and when he got it was reduced from five days to two days; the average number of minutes required to establish a long-distance connection was reduced from seven to three; installation of dial phones, which constituted only nine percent of Bell instruments in 1925, got going in earnest; and, as previously noted, so-called "French" handsets finally became available to Bell subscribers in 1927. It was also in 1927 that commercial telephone service by radio between New York and London was opened for the first time, and made available through wire connection to all Bell and Bell-connected telephones in the United States, Canada, and Cuba. The cost from New York was a stiff forty-five dollars for the first three minutes, and the voices from London were often barely intelligible because of distortion and static; nevertheless, now at last, after centuries of ship-borne letters and almost a century of telegrams by cable, the old world and the new could talk to each other for a few rasping, fading sentences.[10]

And meanwhile AT&T for the second time in a decade was being led by its own technical inventiveness and the enterprise of certain of its executives into the temptation to get into the business of entertainment.

In 1925 a group of Bell Labs engineers, led by H. M. Stoller and A. S. Pfannstiehl, produced a Rube Goldberg–like piece of machinery, standing as tall as a man and featuring motors and belts and wheels and a phonograph turntable, that could accomplish what no previous machine had been able to do—it could synchronize sound with motion pictures, which, in their silent form, were at that time taking the entertainment world by storm. Western Electric began manufacturing the machine, and entered into an agreement with a promoter named Walter J. Rich under which the Vitaphone Corporation, a subsidiary of Warner Brothers, would make sound motion pictures using Western Electric equipment. The first full-length film produced by Vitaphone with Western Electric equipment—*Don Juan,* starring John Barrymore, and featuring synchronized music but little speech—opened in August 1926; a little more than a year later, in October 1927, under the same auspices, came *The Jazz Singer,* with Al Jolson in the title role, which is correctly recognized as having been the first full-scale "talking picture."

The fact that AT&T subsequently became as deeply involved in the production and distribution of sound motion pictures as it had previously become involved in radio broadcasting is largely due to the energy and enthusiasm—perhaps overenthusiasm—of John E. Otterson of Western Electric. Otterson was outside the Bell System executive mold in two respects. For one thing, he was not a career Bell System man, having come to Western Electric for the first time, as general commercial manager, in 1924, after a varied career elsewhere. Equally untypically, that career had been chiefly as a naval officer; Otterson had graduated from the United States Naval Academy in 1904, taken an advanced degree in naval engineering at Massachusetts Institute of Technology in 1909, and remained in the Navy until 1915, becoming a "naval constructor" with the rank of lieutenant. After leaving the Navy, he had become an officer and eventually president of Winchester Repeating Arms Company, the gun-manufacturing firm. Now, as an independent-minded Western Electric official, he soon showed that he had a deep commitment to a business philosophy that was in direct conflict with Gifford's. In an inter-office communication of January 13, 1927—later famous within the company as the "Four Square Memorandum"—he made it clear that he looked upon AT&T's inventions and patents outside telephony as instruments of industrial warfare for getting control of other industries. Drawing on military imagery, Otterson described the area of patent and license disagreement between AT&T and other companies as a "no man's land" in which a ruthless battle for domination should be prosecuted. "On the whole," he wrote, "it seems to be essential to the accomplishment of the AT&T Company's primary purpose . . . that it shall maintain an active offensive in the 'no man's land' lying between it and potentially competitive interests."

This, of course, came just a few months after AT&T under Gifford's direction had taken the precisely opposite course by deciding to withdraw from "no man's land" in the matter of radio broadcasting. The company repudiated Otterson's memo as a statement of its policy; indeed, in an official statement some years later, AT&T went further and declared that the Four Square Memorandum "does not express a policy ever followed by [AT&T] or even a viewpoint held by any responsible official." However, whether or not Otterson was a responsible official—and it certainly appears that he was—Gifford, for reasons unexplained, gave him his head to a marked degree in the matter of attempts to gain control of the new talking-picture business. In December, 1926, Western Electric organized Electrical Research Products, Inc. (ERPI) as a subsidiary to exploit nontelephone inventions of Bell System research, and in particular, talking pictures; Otterson was general manager of the new subsidiary from the start, and became its president a year later. Meanwhile, under the radio license agreement of the previous year, competing companies were entitled to licenses to use AT&T patents in sound reproduction, and one company, Radio Corporation of America, had decided to compete vigorously in talking pictures. Otterson, in April 1927, expressed his views on how such competition should be dealt with in another of his unbuttoned memos, this one addressed to Edgar S. Bloom, president of Western Electric: "In the talking motion picture field, [RCA is] competing very actively with us at present. . . . This is an extensive and highly profitable field and it is quite worth our while to go a long way toward making it practically an exclusive field. I believe that we could justify, from a commercial standpoint, paying a large price for the liquidation of the Radio Corporation for this purpose alone."

Clearly, whether or not this predatory expansionist-monopolist view of the company's role was shared by Bloom, it was not shared by Gifford, the man to whom both were responsible. But Gifford stayed aloof, treating talking pictures as a matter to be handled by Western Electric. As a first step, Western Electric pressed the "Big Five" of motion-picture production—Paramount, Metro-Goldwyn, Universal, First National, and United Artists—for an immediate reply as to whether or not they proposed to obtain licenses to use Western's sound-reproduction equipment. The producers, nervous about making the transition from then-booming silent pictures to untried sound pictures, stalled for time; in February 1927, the Big Five executed among themselves a "standstill agreement" by which they mutually agreed to postpone for one year all negotiations for licenses from any manufacturer of sound equipment. When the year had passed—and *The Jazz Singer* had become a hit—the producers decided to go ahead. They delegated a technical expert to choose between ERPI and RCA equipment; the expert chose ERPI, and by the summer of 1928, not only all of the Big Five but several lesser studios had license contracts with ERPI and were proceeding to make sound films with ERPI equipment.

Western Electric through ERPI, then, had an initial hold on the production of talking pictures, and the company soon took strong steps to strengthen it. For example, ERPI in its license contracts required that the licensees' films be played only on sound equipment that ERPI considered to be of quality equal to that of ERPI's own reproducing apparatus. Otterson justified the requirement on the basis of analogy with AT&T's refusal to allow attachment of its wires to equipment not owned by the company; it appeared, though, that at least part of ERPI's motive was to prevent or make difficult the showing of ERPI-licensed sound films at any but ERPI-equipped movie theaters. After some skirmishing between ERPI and RCA, in August 1928 a test of RCA reproduction equipment was conducted at the Astor Theater in New York, as a result of which it was—in the absence of Otterson, who was abroad—formally pronounced to be up to Western's standards. Over Otterson's continued objections (not shared by his ERPI colleagues), and in the face of threatened legal action by RCA, ERPI finally agreed, in December 1928, to amend its license contracts so as to make the studios themselves the judges of sound-reproduction quality in theaters.

The delay, though, had given ERPI a chance to get a big head start in equipping theaters with sound apparatus, as shown by the fact that as of the start of 1929, there were more than a thousand theaters with Western Electric sound equipment to less than one hundred with non-Western. (The proportion would change radically during 1929 in favor of non-Western-equipped theaters.) During that year, AT&T strengthened its grip on the new industry in another way—by investing, through stock and loans, in studios and theater chains, and even by financing the establishment of an entirely new company, Audio-Cinema, Inc., in Astoria, Long Island, to make educational and industrial sound films. All in all, at the end of the decade AT&T could—and in its 1929 Annual Report, did—boast that Western Electric's sound equipment was used in the making of 90 percent of then-current talking pictures; and in 1932 Otterson could boast to his superior, Bloom, that "we are the second largest financial interest in the motion picture industry. Our stake is next to that of the Chase Bank."

So AT&T was deep in show business for the second time in a decade; it was actively running a small studio, and because of its investments it was worrying about the plot, cast, direction, and distribution of entertainments with titles like *Crime Without Passion* and *Moonlight and Pretzels*. Eventually, after many court and industry battles, it would withdraw almost entirely from the motion-picture business in the middle 1930s. As for Otterson, he would remain as president of ERPI until its demise in 1935, and then would become, briefly, president of Paramount Pictures. But how could Gifford—the Gifford who in 1925 had taken the company out of radio broadcasting because "the objective of a broadcasting station was quite different from that of a telephone system," and at Dallas in 1927 had pledged it to the single-minded objective of providing the best possible telephone service at the lowest possible cost—have allowed such whoring after false gods to go on within his command? One possible explanation, of course, is that Gifford in 1926 and 1927 had for some reason considered the motion-picture business an exception to his policy against nontelephone investments. Another explanation, more favored by his old associates, is that Gifford was simply not much interested in motion pictures and delegated the whole matter to others. (Testifying before the Federal Communications Commission in 1936, Gifford said, "I can remember . . . a few discussions with Mr. Bloom and I think probably Mr. Otterson as to the possibility of disposing of ERPI, but I ran up against a blind alley [sic] and stopped. . . . As I recall it, the final stumbling block was the fact that ERPI had long-time contracts with producers and under those contracts ERPI was responsible for equipment put in and responsible for damage suits . . . and it seemed, unless we could get the producers' approval . . . practically impossible to transfer those contracts.") Either way—even though ERPI was moderately profitable, bringing between 1927 and 1935 net returns of about $12.5 million—the episode must, from the standpoint of consistent and enlightened policy, be counted among Gifford's failures.[11]

7

One last accomplishment—long distance television transmission —rounded out Bell Laboratories' list of technical innovations in the 1920s. The man responsible for the project was Herbert E. Ives, a baldish scientist whose habit of wearing rimless spectacles and a little goatee made him look every inch the learned German professor. In fact, he was a deep-dyed Yankee, a cousin of the celebrated and quintessentially Yankee composer Charles Ives, and the son of a Yankee inventor, Frederic Eugene Ives, who in 1878 had produced the first practical process for making halftone printing plates. Born in 1882, Herbert Ives as a young man studied light, color, and vision, often using natural materials such as phosphorescence and the glow of the firefly. In 1923, as a Bell scientist, he and several associates, by combining the photoelectric cell with the vacuum-tube repeater, produced the first commercial system for the rapid transmission of pictures over telephone wires, for use by the daily press. He then went to work on television, which he thought of as simply a speeded-up form of picture transmission. By May 1925, the project had advanced to the point where, in the laboratory on West Street, a face transmitted from a nearby room could be dimly distinguished at the receiving end. Refinements followed—notably a scanning beam devised by another Bell Labs man, Frank Gray—and in April 1927, television was ready for its first public demonstration in the United States. (It was not the first in the world; a Scottish inventor, John Logie Baird, had turned that trick between two rooms in London the previous year.) Now Secretary of Commerce Herbert Hoover sat in Washington talking into a telephone, and was not only heard but seen on a screen in New York by a group of guests that included AT&T President Gifford. To lighten the proceedings, a few amateur vaudeville turns were then telecast to the same rapt audience—prototype for so many millions in years to come—from a Bell Labs installation at Whippany, New Jersey. In June 1929, the Labs crowned the achievement by successfully staging the first American public demonstration of television in color.

The coming of commercial television would, of course, be long delayed as a result first of the Depression and then of World War II. Even so, perhaps especially so, the demonstration of color television in the euphoric summer of 1929 may be taken as the climax of AT&T's role as the largest of all corporations in the greatest, up to then, of all corporate booms.

When the stock market began to drop that autumn, AT&T shares at first resisted the trend. Through the great era of speculation, AT&T had been regarded as among the least speculative of stocks; the fixed dividend and the company's announced policy of "no melons" had discouraged speculators and made AT&T come to be regarded as the first-choice investment for widows and orphans. Nevertheless, during the early part of 1929, when investors coast to coast had all but taken leave of their senses, AT&T stock had been a beneficiary of the madness along with practically all others. From a price of under two hundred dollars a share at the start of the year it had—unaided by any unusually favorable news about company operations, and in the face of an actual company promise not to raise the dividend—soared to a high on September 3 of 304.

On September 5—the day the first premonitory lightning warned of the approaching storm—"Telephone," as Wall Street called it, dropped 6 points, much less than the *Times* index of industrial stocks, which lost 10. Even on Wednesday, October 23— the day before the one that the world knows as Black Thursday, and a day, incidentally, when the absence of telephone service between New York and the Midwest because of a sleet storm contributed to stock-market panic—Telephone lost only 15 points while General Electric was losing 20, Westinghouse 25, and J. I. Case 46. On Black Thursday itself, the worst day in modern stock-market history up to then, it was to U.S. Steel shares, not to Telephone, that a consortium of leading bankers turned when they sought maximum impact for an effort to turn the market around. AT&T, because of its very wide ownership, because it was owned by people who intended to keep it, and because it was so little owned by in-an-out speculators who had bought it with borrowed money, was simply too hard to move off center, upward or downward. It was, perhaps, depression-proof.

Or was it? On October 28—the day the *Times* industrial average went down 49 points—Telephone lost 34; by early November it stood at around 230, or almost 25 percent below its price of two months earlier. The widows and orphans themselves had caught the panic and were beginning to sell; and they would sell much more over the next three years, finally driving the price in mid-1933 down to 70.[12] Not the stock-market decline, however, but national economic conditions, would completely alter the aspect and prospects of AT&T over the next decade.

# CHAPTER 8

# Hard Times

The Great Depression that began in 1930 was comparatively slow to strike the telephone industry, for reasons that are not without their irony. The stock-market crash that both heralded and served to begin it had the perverse effect of bringing about millions of telephone calls, local and long-distance, between worried or desperate stockholders and their brokers. Beyond that, the disruptions of family, social, and business life attendant upon suddenly lost jobs and suddenly reduced incomes, or even bankruptcies, undoubtedly gave rise to further millions of calls. For a brief time, the nation's telephone business prospered just because its citizens were talking to each other about the consequences of national economic disaster.

At the end of 1930, Bell telephones in service were at an all-time record high of 15,193,000, having achieved a gain of 268,000 for the year. The average number of daily telephone conversations was running a million a day higher than in 1929. AT&T's record number of stockholders—567,000, up almost 98,000 from the previous year—were presumably made happy by the company's solid earnings performance of $10.44, enough to cover the nine-dollar dividend and substantially fatten up the corporate surplus. The Bell System's total revenues were at a record $1.1 billion, and even though the employee count was down by 60,000 from the previous year, the total annual payroll was another record. So expansive was AT&T's mood in 1930 that that October it purchased the Teletype Corporation, whose business of transmitting typed messages over leased wires was clearly telephone-related, and the following year inaugurated the teletypewriter exchange system, TWX, that became an important AT&T service.

This adventitiously rosy state of affairs could not last. A time had to come when many of the citizens who were keeping the telephone lines humming as they dealt with or discussed their money problems could no longer afford to have telephones at all. It came soon enough. In 1931 the total of Bell telephones in service declined by 292,000, marking the first such annual decline in history. AT&T's net earnings for the year, $9.05, barely covered the dividend. But it was in 1932 that the pinch really began to be felt. Bell telephones in service were down during that year by 1,650,000, or more than 10 percent; since there was a comparable reduction of independent telephone subscribers, this meant that border to border and coast to coast, one telephone in ten was disconnected in a twelve-month period. The resulting loss of revenue from the operating companies was the major factor in reducing AT&T's annual earning to $5.96 per share, the lowest for any year in the twentieth century up to then. But the particular disaster area of the Bell System was Western Electric. Geared to a constant and usually rapid increase in demand for telephone service, it suddenly found itself, in the face of a rapid decline in demand, with little to do. With the Bell System making virtually no additions to its plant, Western Electric in 1932 sustained a net loss of $12.6 million, and of course, paid no dividend to its owner, AT&T; in 1933, an even worse year, it lost $13.8 million as sales fell to $70 million—hardly more than one-sixth of its 1929 sales of $411 million. At the lowest point, Western Electric had laid off almost 80 percent of its work force; Gifford said later that but for the continuing job of converting telephones from manual to dial operation, the figure would have been nearer to 98 percent.[1]

The decline in demand for telephone service, coupled with the concurrent drastic decline in the prices of almost all goods and services, brought about a curiously anomalous situation for the state regulatory bodies. Regulation had from the first been geared to holding prices at their current levels, in order to prevent them from being raised in the absence of competition; now the situation was turned on its head, and the regulators found themselves in the position of involuntarily tending to hold prices at levels that, in a completely free market, would have gone lower rather than higher. The regulatory commissions had become *de facto* price supporters. The pioneer in bringing the regulatory process into line with the new situation was the Wisconsin Public Service Commission. In early 1931—when David E. Lilienthal, soon to ·become nationally known as chairman of the Tennessee Valley Authority and later of the United States Atomic Energy Commission, assumed office as head of the Wisconsin commission—the prices of most commodities and services were drastically down as a result of deflationary pressures, but those of public utilities were not, because the utilities operated under regulation and the regulators had not ordered any reductions. (Bell companies had made some voluntary reductions here and there.) They had not done so because the traditional procedure for changing utility rates involved holding hearings that often took several years. Lilienthal, realizing that such a delay in reducing utility rates would not only be onerous to consumers but might also have a strongly adverse effect on local recovery from depression, decided on emergency action; he hired Edward W. Morehouse, a Northwestern University economist, as the commission's chief economist, whereupon he and Morehouse set out on a nationwide tour to consult such renowned academic economic authorities as Jacob Viner, James Bonbright, and E. R. A. Seligman. Out of these discussions, which constituted a sort of preview of the functioning of the President's Council of Economic Advisers in the postwar years, came testimony that led to an unprecedentedly quick decision by the commission to order reduced utility rates, including telephone rates, in Wisconsin. The courts held up execution of the order for a time, but a new precedent was established. Other state regulatory bodies abandoned their traditional slow-moving procedures to meet the emergency, with the result that in 1933, general rate reductions were ordered in states with 5 percent of all Bell telephones in service. That was only a start, and later in the decade virtually all telephone rates, Bell and independent, would be drastically reduced as the gap between fast-acting competitive pressure in other industries and slow-acting regulatory pressure in the naturally monopolistic utilities was gradually closed. The Wisconsin innovation served to hasten the closing of that gap.

Meanwhile AT&T directors and top executives were facing their most crucial and controversial decision of the Depression years—whether or not to continue to pay the nine-dollar-a-share annual dividend in years when earnings were not sufficient to cover it and it would therefore have to be paid out of surplus. The first such year was 1932, when net earnings amounted to $5.96; the nine-dollar dividend was held, $3.04 of it coming from previously earned surplus. The second was 1933, when earnings were down to $5.38; the nine-dollar dividend was paid again, at a cost of $3.62 per share to surplus. The third was 1934; net earnings $5.96 per share, dividend again nine dollars. In 1935, earnings edged up to $7.11; the dividend held at nine dollars. By this time, the surplus had been dangerously reduced: $141 million was gone from the $234 million that had been in the till at the end of 1931, and it would take only about five more such years to leave it bare. Such a disastrous state of affairs was not to come about, since in 1936 the dividend was again earned, and in every succeeding year it was earned or nearly earned; but the crisis had not been surmounted without a good deal of hair-raising suspense, and the annual nine-dollar-a-share payment, which AT&T regarded as a moral obligation to maintain, had not been maintained without furious controversy.

Precisely how this interesting and far-reaching decision was reached remains somewhat cloudy. Responsibility for the determination of what dividend to pay rested then, as of course it still rests, squarely on the board of directors. The minutes of directors' meetings held during the years 1932–35, during which there was not a single quarter year in which the Bell System profits met the requirements to pay the nine-dollar dividend, reveal no discussion of so much as the possibility of temporarily reducing the dividend. However, we may reasonably suppose—perhaps even assume—that such discussions took place, either in the directors' meetings or among the staff members who sat on the board. We may also suppose that the decision to hold the dividend was essentially made in 1932 and 1933, the first years when AT&T's traditional policy of paying out in dividends less than it took in as profits was abruptly reversed; thereafter, it may be guessed, the matter was regarded as decided, the moral obligation to be met down to the last dollar of retained surplus.

By 1932 the custom was already firmly established that the board of directors took guidance on important matters from the company's hired managers. The managers who sat on the board in 1932 and 1933 were President Gifford, Vice-President Cooper, and

Vice-President Page—a large-minded generalist, a tough and experienced operating-company man, and a former publisher with strong humanistic proclivities. Ultimately those three were almost surely responsible for the decision, certainly with the approval of Charles A. Heiss, the company's respected old Vail-appointed controller. How, then, did they make it, and why? Gifford gave a clue to the "why" in 1936 when he told the FCC that, quite apart from the company's feeling of moral obligation to stockholders, "Had we been forced to reduce the dividend I think it very likely we would have equally been forced to do something on the rate of pay of labor." In other words, Gifford felt that the drop in the price of AT&T stock that would result from the shock of a reduced dividend would have so greatly impaired the company's financial position as to necessitate reduced wages. As to the "how," some former AT&T executives suggest, on a purely impressional basis, that it was Gifford's habit generally to devote himself to broad philosophical matters and to leave specific policy decisions largely to Cooper, and that accordingly the key man in the dividend decision was probably Cooper. The fact remains, of course, that Gifford as president bore responsibility for the decision—responsibility that he never showed any inclination to slough off.

And it was a heavy responsibility. The policy was as unpopular with labor as it was popular with stockholders. AT&T had held its dividend level while reducing its payroll by some 20 per cent; to labor representatives and their sympathizers, that meant on its face that the company had continued to let the entire brunt of the Depression fall on labor and none on capital. Critics pointed out that a reduction of one dollar in the AT&T dividend would have saved the company about $18,662,000 a year—enough to have paid about eighteen thousand of the employees who had been laid off.[2]

There was something to the argument. To the 95 percent of stockholders who owned less than one hundred shares each, the dividend reduction would have meant only an insubstantial decrease in income, while to the eighteen thousand laid-off employees who might have been retained, the difference was between a job and no job. However, the answers to the argument, if cold, are persuasive. What with drastically reduced demand for telephone service—with long-distance calls in 1933 running at thirty million a year instead of the fifty million of 1930—those eighteen thousand employees (most of whom had been switchboard operators) were simply not needed; to have cut the dividend in order to retain them would have been to set up a sort of free-enterprise leaf-raking program. In a larger sense, the maintained dividend prepared the way for the future. By keeping faith with its stockholders in bad times, AT&T assured their loyalty in better times to come, and that loyalty, in the form of new investment, would translate into more and better telephone service.

A dilemma of the mixed economy, then, had been resolved in the manner that, given the traditions of American social thought and in particular of AT&T management thought, was what might have been expected. It was also a manner—whatever else might be said about it—that led directly to the rise in the total of AT&T stockholders, in the years after World War II, to the previously unthinkable figure of three million.

2

Dividend policy was only the beginning of labor's objection to AT&T's conduct of its affairs. In the 1930s, the great age of organized labor in America was on its way; the idea was in the air that labor deserved and could get a bigger slice of the industrial pie. AT&T's payroll reductions in the years 1930 through 1935 provided just the bread-and-butter issue that labor organizers needed, and the company's continuing policy of sponsoring company unions added an ideological dimension to the difference. The situation at Southern New England Telephone in 1932 is a vivid paradigm of the state of affairs nationally. That company's paternalistic attitude dated back to the 1890s, when it had encouraged formation of a Telephone Employees' Mutual Benefit Society, a company union, and over the succeeding decades it had sponsored a union-run thrift plan, a health course, first-aid classes, an accident-prevention program, an employee life-insurance program, and a system of regular conferences between employees and management. Now, in 1932, the crunch was on; more than thirty thousand Southern New England telephones went out of service that year, the company was running at a deficit, and although no regular employees were laid off, wages had been effectively cut by reducing the work week from six to five days. In the face of these crisis conditions, the company tried to convince the employees that they were partners with it in adversity rather than victims of its cutbacks. President Harry C. Knight spoke to the company union leaders in Churchillian cadences: "There is no excuse for not keeping our heads up unless we have the view that everything is going to smash . . . management will continue to take the entire employee body into its confidence . . . and it will not abandon its policy of guarding the interests of its personnel as well as the interests of its stockholders and of the public." As their part in the partnership, employees were asked to spend their evenings and weekends, voluntarily and without pay, canvassing for new subscribers—a demanding job that quite obviously could not be carried out on the telephone. Evidence of the success of Knight's paternalistic approach is to be found in the fact that many of them did as they were asked.

Elsewhere as in New England, the Bell System got through the worst of the Depression without serious labor troubles, on the strength of past goodwill and vigorous promotion of local company unions. But there were rumblings of greater militancy to come, and they focused on the question of work-force reductions made possible by conversion from manually operated telephones to dial. This process, not by accident, was going on at an accelerated pace; in 1929 just 26 percent of all Bell System instruments had been dial-operated, and by the end of 1935 the figure was up to 48 percent. By the end of the decade it would reach 56 percent. Since one dial-switchboard operator could do the work of six manual-switchboard operators, the job-displacement situation was such as to suggest grounds for a Luddite revolt. (In 1811–16, in the industrial centers of England, workmen systematically wrecked newly introduced machinery, to which they attributed unemployment and low wages. They were called Luddites, after Ned Ludd, who thirty years earlier had destroyed knitting machines for the same reason.) No such revolt developed, apparently for two reasons. For one thing, the job of telephone operator had always been one in which there had been a high rate of turnover, chiefly because operators (all of them women at that time) were prone to leave their jobs to marry or to bear children; consequently the Bell System's elimination of some seventy thousand traffic-department jobs between 1929 and 1935 was accomplished with a minimum of hardship. Operators were seldom fired; they were simply not replaced when they left. Secondly, the Bell System must be credited with having managed the transition to dial service with efficiency and tact—an accomplishment acknowledged by the secretary of labor in the Roosevelt administration,

Frances Perkins, who called it "an almost perfect example of technological change made with a minimum of disaster."

Even so smoothly managed, the employment reductions attendant on dial service gave organized labor something to attack; and in the field of communications, as in so many other fields, organized labor in the 1930s was in a state of ferment. Section 7A of the National Industrial Recovery Act, signed into law by President Roosevelt on June 16, 1933, contained the historic words: "Employees shall have the right to organize and bargain collectively through representatives of their own choosing." This theoretically gave Bell System employees the right, if they chose to exercise it, to eschew the local company unions and join independent national unions without being subject to losing their jobs. In practice, though, Section 7A was never effectively enforced, and it was, indeed, a key factor in the Supreme Court's decision in 1935 invalidating the entire act as unconstitutional. That same year, however, saw passage of a new law with such teeth that it has been called the Magna Charta of labor—the National Labor Relations Act, or Wagner Act, which restated the basic rights-of-labor clause as "unions of their own choosing," categorically defined unfair labor practices on the employer's part, and implemented these provisions by creating a new National Labor Relations Board to supervise union elections in corporations, to certify the union duly chosen in such elections, and to issue cease-and-desist orders to employers who indulged in unfair labor practices.

The Wagner Act quickly brought about a drastic change in the climate of labor-management relations in almost all industries, served as the virtual death knell for company unions, and gave rise to the formation of the great nationwide combination of industrial unions, the Congress of Industrial Organizations. Its implications were not lost on the management of AT&T; clearly enough, it set the stage for the invasion of the Bell System by unions unsympathetic to management, and directed by men who were not Bell employees but professional organizers. Shortly after the Wagner Act's passage, there was a conference in New York City of top lawyers representing leading corporations, out of which came a consensus that the new law was unconstitutional and a resolution that those present should recommend to their various corporations that they ignore it. As is well known, some leading corporations, among them some of the automobile and steel manufacturers, did ignore or defy it, with resulting tragically violent confrontations in 1936 and 1937.

At AT&T, the decision on whether or not to defy the Wagner Act was a close call. Charles M. Bracelen, the company's general counsel, had attended the meeting with his counterparts from other companies, and he reported its conclusion with approval. An intrastaff debate followed, with the company's lawyers for the most part espousing defiance of the new law. The contingent for compliance with it was led, curiously enough, not by a man at the top but rather by a middle-management former working stiff with little formal education, who must stand as one of the minor heroes of this narrative. He was Oscar M. Taylor, manager of plant personnel; a former lineman with only a grade-school education, Taylor thought the anticompliance lawyers were wrong, and stated his case so strongly and eloquently that he carried the day and Gifford gave orders that the Wagner Act was to be complied with. In March 1937, the Supreme Court affirmed the Wagner Act and thus the legal basis for defying it was removed.

Taking advantage of the act, and hoping to succeed where the Electrical Workers union had previously failed, a new national union, the National Federation of Telephone Workers, was formed in June 1939, with some 92,000 members, most of them Bell employees. In 1941, after a series of congenial meetings between NFTW leaders and President Gifford, Gifford refused to grant the union formal System-wide recognition, on grounds that he "did not want to reduce the presidents of the operating companies to the role of Charlie McCarthys." (For the benefit of younger readers, Charlie McCarthy was the puppet of the well-known radio ventriloquist Edgar Bergen.) Nevertheless, NFTW's membership total would rise from 92,000 in 1939 to 217,500 in 1946, and its successor organization, the Communications Workers of America, would in the postwar years become the powerful principal union dealing with the Bell System.

As for Oscar Taylor and AT&T's decision to conform to the Wagner Act, there is good circumstantial evidence that the decision averted violence in the telephone industry in the late 1930s, and even that—what with generally hostile federal authorities waiting in the wings for signs of disorder in the status quo—it may have saved the Bell System as a private enterprise.[3]

3

The year 1933 saw a turnaround in the telephone business. Having lost 715,000 telephones in service during the first eight months of the year, AT&T gained back 85,000 in the last four months, and in 1934 and 1935 gained back an additional 298,000 and 466,500, respectively. By the end of 1937, Bell phones in service stood at 15,332,000, just above the record set in 1930, and thus at an all-time high. Except for a small temporary profit decrease in the recession and hurricane year of 1938, the Depression was over for AT&T. But its consequences were not. Bitterness remained in liberal and labor quarters about such matters as the maintained dividend during a period of labor-force reductions and the monopolistic implications of AT&T's ownership of its supplier, Western Electric, and this critical attitude was reflected in large-scale government action. The Communications Act of 1934, an early New Deal measure, had created a new Federal Communications Commission to replace the Interstate Commerce Commission as the federal agency with jurisdiction over telephones. Far from being a mere bureaucratic reshuffling, the change had the substantive effect of replacing a relatively somnolent old regulatory body more interested in railroads than in telephones with a new one more interested in telephones than anything else; indeed, it marked the beginning of serious federal regulation and supervision in the communications field. The new FCC, like most New Deal agencies, was largely staffed with reformers eager to expose and correct the misdeeds of corporate institutions and executives. The chairman of its telephone division, Paul Atlee Walker, was an Oklahoma lawyer of Quaker ancestry, in his fifties, who had previously been a high school principal in Shawnee, an instructor at the University of Oklahoma, and a special counsel to the State of Oklahoma in the matter, crucial to that agricultural state, of freight rates. Walker had a Quaker single-mindedness and idealism, and he was to be the greatest federal thorn in AT&T's side since Postmaster Burleson.

In November 1934, as virtually its first action, the FCC began an investigation of all telephone companies. The following March, Congress through a joint resolution zeroed in on AT&T, ordering the FCC to conduct a specific and full-scale investigation of it, and appropriating an initial $750,000 for the project. Gifford said in the 1935 AT&T Annual Report, "Every effort is being made to facilitate the progress of the present investigation in order that it may be completed as promptly as possible." In a public statement he said, "We welcome the investigation; there are no skeletons in our closet."

And indeed—whether because of AT&T's cooperation or because the FCC had subpoena power and no reluctance to exercise it—nothing was hidden. The investigation, which continued until 1938, employed the services of over three hundred staff researchers, and ultimately cost the government nearly $2 million and AT&T $1.5 million, resulted in what was later described by one of the key investigators as "probably the most complete [record of] factual information on the operations of an important American business enterprise in existence." It went back to the beginnings of the telephone business in 1876, and ranged laterally across the Bell System's operations through corporate structure, research and technology, inventions and patents, management policies, financial figures, labor policies, relations with independent telephone companies, ventures outside telephony, and public relations.

AT&T cooperated uncomplainingly with the investigation in the matter of turning over documents from its files. Its criticism of the investigation—which began in 1936, and became increasingly strident thereafter—centered on the fact that the FCC declined to allow the company to bring its own witnesses or to cross-examine the witnesses called by the FCC. Gifford, along with dozens of his fellow executives, testified at length; the transcript of his testimony at intervals during 1935 and 1936 comes to 273 pages, and ranges over AT&T's structure and financing, its relationship with Western Electric, its pay scale, its license contract with operating companies, the maintenance of its dividend, its nontelephone ventures, its promotion of its own stock through Bell Telephone Securities Company (which was finally dissolved in September 1936), and many other topics. The questioning by FCC counsel had an unmistakably badgering tone, and included what appeared to be a few deliberate traps to catch the witness; but Gifford—who arrived to testify with what was described as an Alice in Wonderland look—kept his temper and answered all questions with equanimity, if not good humor. "So far, the investigation has been one-sided," he permitted himself to comment in the 1936 Annual Report.

The investigation dragged on through the following year.

Finally, on April 1, 1938, Commissioner Walker made public a "Proposed Report." This document—the conclusions of which were largely Walker's work, and were not subscribed to by other members of the FCC—was a free-swinging and broad-based attack on AT&T's ways of conducting its business, with particular emphasis on the operations of Western Electric. In spite of the agreed-upon fact that Western Electric had been able to show that the prices it charged Bell operating companies were generally well below those charged by independent manufacturers, Walker contended that Western, through overcharges of various sorts, had been inflating the rate base from which telephone rates were derived, thereby bringing about unwarranted extra costs to telephone subscribers of about $51 million per year. He further contended that Western could cut its prices by about 37 percent and still earn 6 percent on its investment. As solutions, Walker proposed direct regulation of Western Electric's prices, and legislation that would require AT&T to buy equipment through competitive bidding between Western and other manufacturers. That fall, AT&T replied with a "Brief on the Proposed Report" of the FCC, in which it attempted to refute Walker point by point, and stated—as Gifford summarized it in the 1938 Annual Report—"that the *ex parte* proceedings held under the investigation were unfair and incapable of producing reliable conclusions, and that the 'Proposed Report' was incorrect, incomplete, and contained unsound recommendations." On the matter of Western Electric's rates, the brief contended that "the arrangements with Western Electric have enabled the Bell companies to obtain standardized apparatus of high quality at reasonable prices and have worked to the public advantage," and that insistence on competitive bidding for equipment was—given the nature of the Bell System—"to dodge the realities."

The fuss over the Walker Report had a serious, though not catastrophic, effect on the price of AT&T stock. The stockholders' resulting paper losses were considerable. The irony—a characteristic irony of a mixed economy—was a subtle one: by the very act of declaring that greater government participation in the telephone business would result in better service to the public, the government seemed to be creating market conditions that might render private enterprise less able to continue doing the job that it had been accused of not doing. The government case—even if unsound to begin with, as AT&T contended—might prove to be a self-fulfilling prophecy. However, after publication of the Walker

Report, AT&T stock recovered, and the company's financing capacity was restored. As for the FCC, that body met *en banc* in June 1939 and approved a substitute for the Walker Report—a "Report on the Investigation of the Telephone Industry in the United States" which, while retaining most of the factual data from the "Proposed Report," was much milder in tone and comment and, in particular, drastically softened Walker's recommendations as to future regulation of Western Electric.

The final FCC report, issued two and a half months before the outbreak of World War II, was largely ignored in the press of more dramatic events. But the investigation had had its impact, not to be forgotten. As Vice-President Page wrote in 1941, "The investigation did tend to emphasize some questions concerning the success of regulation of the telephone industry and the scope and direction of regulatory activity in the future." More than that, it drew clearly the new, post-Kingsbury lines in the continuing battle over AT&T as a monopoly: the battle between ideology and practice. In the postwar years the battle would be joined again.[4]

On September 21, 1938, the Bell System—recently challenged by human forces in government—was challenged again, this time by natural forces in the form of a devastating hurricane that swept over New Jersey, Long Island, and the southern New England states. The winds, waves, floods, and fires attendant on the storm caused the greatest loss of service in the history of the telephone. All over the storm area, trees, their roots saturated by five consecutive days of rain preceding the hurricane, went down like tenpins; New Haven, known from time immemorial as the Elm City, became virtually the former Elm City when seven thousand of the majestic trees went down in a single hour. Twenty-two thousand telephone poles fell in New Haven and elsewhere, but most of the damage was caused by the breaking of lines by falling trees. As the storm raged, telephone operators stuck to their posts, getting through such emergency messages as they could, until the switchboards went dead; in some cases the operators were finally evacuated by firemen in rowboats. No operators' lives were lost, but when the storm finally abated that evening, in the area where it had passed 494 persons were dead, 708 were injured, 18,000 buildings were destroyed, 515,000 telephones were out of service, and 240 communities were isolated by total service failures. In southern New England, 31 percent of all telephones were out.

The Bell System tackled the situation with the speed and resolution that few deny it usually musters in times of technical disaster. First, streets were cleared of fallen trees, poles, and wires, and temporary lines were strung for emergency service. Then, over the subsequent days and weeks, a battalion of men and equipment was rallied from almost all corners of the Bell System. Western Electric shipped supplies into the stricken area, and other Bell companies sent men, trucks, and surplus equipment. In all, the aid sent into New England alone totaled 2,338 men and 621 fully equipped motor trucks—some from as far away as Virginia, Arkansas, and Nebraska. Their arrival created a traffic-routing and billeting problem similar to that faced by a military expeditionary force, but the work went forward; the first damaged exchange to be repaired in Connecticut was restored to service within four days, the last disabled telephone in that state was reconnected on October 13, and the whole storm-struck area had functioning telephones before the end of November. The financial result of the catastrophe was that Southern New England Bell was forced to reduce its dividend for the last quarter of 1938, but the effect on AT&T's earning for the year was minor.

In a way, the hurricane was providental for AT&T. Coming as it did at a time when the company was under concerted government attack for its structure and policies, and when the attack was beginning to bring about a public view of it as ruthless and self-serving, the hurricane gave the Bell System a chance to do what it does very well—in fact, to assume the role of hero. The public acclaim thus gained may have been a factor in the mitigation of criticism in the final FCC report on the investigation; certainly it enabled AT&T to enter the World War II years with a good measure of public approval. Such are the capricious tides in the affairs of men, governments, and great corporations.[5]

4

The British novelist Norman Douglas said, "We can hardly realize now the blissful quietude of the pre-telephone epoch." His fellow countryman and fellow writer H. G. Wells wrote in an autobiographical essay, "I require a pleasant well-lit writing room in good air . . . a secretary . . . and, within reach, an abundant library and the rest of the world all hung accessibly on to that secretary's telephone. But it would be a one-way telephone, so that when we wanted news we could ask for it, and when we were not in a state to receive and digest news, we should not have it forced upon us." The American humorist Robert Benchley wrote, more positively, "There is something about saying 'OK' and hanging up the receiver with a bang that kids a man into feeling that he has just pulled off a big deal, even if he has only called up Central to find out the correct time." These statements, all of them made in the 1930s, suggest that in that decade the old transatlantic distinction in attitudes toward the telephone still persisted: the Englishman still seemed to miss the point—Douglas yearning for an irrecoverable past of quiet and privacy, Wells apparently failing to perceive the functional difference between a telephone and a radio—while the American, Benchley, was thinking of the instrument romantically as a means of fulfilling his fantasies. (Indeed, British telephone use continued in the 1930s to lag far behind American, and it does to this day. In 1973 there were more than sixty telephones in use per one hundred population in the United States, and in Britain only thirty—fewer per person than in Sweden, Switzerland, Canada, New Zealand, Denmark, Australia, Norway, and Japan. France, however, stood far below even Great Britain, with about twenty per hundred population. Worldwide, about one person in ten had a phone in 1973.) In 1931, a sociological study based on a survey of 1,000 telephone conversations conducted in New York City that year showed that of the 80,000 words spoken, only 2,240 different words were used, and the ones most frequently used were "I" and "me." This unsurprising finding was perhaps less significant than the fact that the survey had been conducted at all—a hint that the uniquely American love affair with the telephone went on in bad times as it had in good.

"TELEVISION KILLS TELEPHONY IN BROTHERS BROIL," goes an imaginary newspaper headline in *Finnegans Wake,* James Joyce's famous novel, published in 1939; the sentiment was, of course, bad prophecy—the coming of television would actually be accompanied by huge increases in telephone use—but it showed that the telephone and its effect on society was still a preoccupation of the Irish master writer. Toward the end of the 1930s, telephone users, chiefly in the United States, began to discover more radical uses of it in the fulfillment of larger fantasies than the one Benchley had described. Such uses had not become aggressive and hostile, as they would later; the obscene or threatening crank call was rare until after World War II, possibly because the persistence of party lines everywhere except in large cities militated against telephone privacy. Rather, they took the form of calls by ordinary citizens to famous and powerful persons to whom they wished to state their ideas. The doyen of this movement was probably Abe Pickens, of Cleveland, Ohio, who at various times placed, and more or less completed, long-distance calls to Hitler, Franco, Mussolini, Neville Chamberlain, Emperor Hirohito, and other world leaders at a total cost to him that he said was ten thousand dollars. In the case of Hitler, whom he called early in 1939, he was connected with the German Führer and said, "Hello, A. Hitler, this is A. Pickens of Cleveland, Ohio, U.S.A." Hitler, unable to speak or understand English, switched Pickens to an aide, to whom Pickens suggested that there should be a general election in Spain. Pickens had not communicated directly with Hitler, but clearly he had found an unusual satisfaction in the use of the telephone, and one that is not to be entirely dismissed as a joke: it had enabled him to feel a little less powerless before the apparently inexorable march of events toward world disaster.[6]

Technical advance, despite financial stringency, was substantial during the Depression. Improvements in overseas radiotelephony made possible rate reductions and many extensions of service; in 1930, the rate for a New York–London call was reduced from forty-five to thirty dollars for the first three minutes, with proportionate reductions for calls from other points in the United States, and in 1932 alone, South Africa, Thailand, Egypt, Peru, Portugal, the Bahamas, Venezuela, and Colombia were added to the countries that could be reached from any telephone in the United States. Less immediately visible, but certainly more important in the long run, were the effects of new advances in telecommunications made at Bell Labs. In 1930, Harold S. Black's negative-feedback amplifier opened up the field of high-fidelity sound reproduction, and would later be adapted to practically all types of communications circuits. In 1931, research on wave-guide transmission was begun at the Labs' then-tiny radio laboratory at Holmdel, New Jersey. In 1934, coaxial cable—"a radically new form of transmission cable," as it was described in that year's Annual Report, and a form eventually to become a staple and necessity of modern telephone and television, because of its low attenuation and high capacity—had reached the stage of trial installations; in 1936, the first Bell coaxial cables were put in service in New York City, and in 1940, such a cable was used to make it possible for the Republican National Convention in Philadelphia, at which Wendell Willkie was nominated, to be televised by NBC in New York. In 1937, Dr. Clinton J. Davisson became the first Bell Labs man to win the Nobel Prize, for an abstruse but scientifically crucial discovery as to the wave nature of the electron. And in 1938, the first "crossbar" central switching office—third of the four steps leading from the primitive manual switchboard to the electronic switching office— went into regular service in Brooklyn.

Something bigger than any of these advances was brewing at Bell Labs at the end of the decade. In 1936, Mervin J. Kelly, then director of research at the Labs and later their president, told William Shockley, a young physicist working in the vacuum-tube department, of his belief that telephone exchanges would work better and faster if they were electronic. With that bee in his bonnet, Shockley began tinkering with the notion of adapting electronic techniques to switching, and presently he began exchanging ideas with Walter Brattain, another young Bell physicist, whose special interest was copper-oxide rectifiers. The problem was that the use of electronics in switching would require an amplifier better than the vacuum tube, which required too much power and generated too much heat. The fruit of their conversations, in December 1939, was what Shockley called "in principle a sound concept of a semiconductor amplifier"—what was to become known as a transistor. Shockley and Brattain conducted experiments for the next two months; but the early results were not encouraging, and early in 1940 the two scientists' energies were diverted into war work. The coming of war thus postponed the coming of the basis of postwar electronic technology.[7]

Yet another thing—invisible to stockholders or telephone users or even government investigators, yet crucial to the company's future—was happening within AT&T through the Depression years. It was gradually and slightly, but significantly, changing its management style.

The key staff members appointed by Vail or brought up in the tradition of Vail—for the most part, as we have seen, men of a conceptual turn of mind, with reputations reaching far beyond the boundaries of their own corporation, strong on long-range planning and on putting company problems into national perspective, but generally without knowledge or experience in the running of telephone operating companies—were reaching retirement age, one by one. The vacancies thus created were by and large filled by men of a different stripe, comparatively weak on conceptual ability and strong on operating experience. Undoubtedly a large factor in this trend was the influence upon Gifford of Charles P. Cooper—himself, of course, a former long-time operating man with New York Telephone and Ohio Bell Telephone. It was with operating men rather than thinkers that Cooper felt most at home, and it was to Cooper that Gifford turned in the matter of staff appointments. "Cooper was the tough guy who made the tough decisions as to staff," an AT&T officer of the time says.

Accordingly, the new vice-presidents, and future powers in the affairs of AT&T, who were appointed during the 1930s were all men with operating backgrounds. Keith S. McHugh, appointed in 1937, served as general commercial engineer of the Chesapeake and Potomac Telephone Company from 1921 to 1925, and in the same capacity with the New York Telephone Company from 1925 to 1929. Brooklyn-born William Henry Harrison, appointed to be a vice-president and chief engineer in 1938, had studied part-time at Pratt Institute; begun working as wireman and repairman with New York Telephone in 1909, at the age of seventeen; spent the years 1914–18 with Western Electric; and then served, successively, as building and plant engineer for AT&T and engineering vice-president of Pennsylvania Bell. Cleo F. Craig, upon whom the vice-presidential mantle fell in 1940, had started his career with the AT&T Long Lines Department in St. Louis in 1913, and thereafter served continuously with Long Lines right up to 1940, except for a brief hiatus at the end of the 1920s and beginning of the 1930s, when he had been at AT&T headquarters charged with making transactions with power companies. These three vice-presidents—solid operating men all—were the new wave of talent coming up at AT&T in the years just before World War II, and in the postwar years they would constitute three corners of a four-cornered struggle for the presidency—the first such struggle in AT&T history.

On the other hand, at least one Bell System man very much in the Vail style was rather conspicuously being left in an operating job rather than being called to a key staff job at AT&T. He was Chester I. Barnard, a Massachusetts-born former Harvard student (and nongraduate because of a technicality), who had spent his entire working career in the Bell System, starting in 1909 in the statistical department of AT&T and becoming in 1922 assistant vice-president and assistant general manager of Pennsylvania Bell, a couple of years later vice-president and general manager of that company, and in 1927 president of New Jersey Bell, a job he would hold until 1948. Despite his impeccable record as a career telephone operating man, Barnard was far from typical of that breed. It was he who in the 1920s instituted the program, highly unorthodox at the time, to send Pennsylvania Bell executives to the University of Pennsylvania to broaden their scope by studying the liberal arts. During World War II, he would serve for three years as national president of the celebrated aid-to-servicemen group the United Service Organizations; later, in the postwar years, he would be a consultant to the United Nations Atomic Energy Commission, the author of two pioneering and widely read books on corporate management, president of the Rockefeller Foundation, a member of the American Philosophical Society, and almost certainly the only telephone company president or ex-president who, seated at a piano, could from memory play selections from virtually any classical composer someone else might name.[8]

All in all, Barnard became, in his time, the living symbol of a rare and valuable type, the top business executive imbued with culture and humanistic vision; but AT&T never chose to call him, as Vail would surely have done, to a key staff job where his influence could be felt throughout the Bell System. (Barnard himself told associates that he fully expected to be Gifford's successor.) It is possible, of course, that Gifford, Cooper, and their colleagues preferred to leave Barnard at New Jersey Bell because they felt he was indispensable there. The fact remains that by 1940 all the key staff positions at 195 Broadway were held by down-to-earth operating men rather than abstract thinkers, and that the Vail style of management, for better or worse, was in decline.

5

In 1939 the Bell System had assets of about $5 billion—by far the largest aggregation of capital ever controlled by a single company in the history of private enterprise. It controlled 83 percent of all telephones in service in the United States, 91 percent of all telephone plant, 98 percent of all long-distance wires, and 100 percent of all transoceanic radio telephony. Its subsidiary Western Electric manufactured 90 percent of all telephone equipment. There were 16.5 million Bell telephones in service. The company collected 90 percent of all U.S. telephone revenues, and had deposits in one-third of all active U.S. banks. AT&T's approximately 18 million common shares were distributed among 637,000 holders, making the average holding less than thirty shares; this prodigiously wide dispersion of ownership worked to the company's advantage not only by predisposing 637,000 citizens and their families to a favorable view of it, but also by making it all but impossible for any stockholder or group of stockholders to interfere in the management of the company. In practice, because of the inability of the stockholders to exercise the control that was formally vested in them, the president of AT&T had virtually absolute control over company policy. By a paradox of free enterprise, the democratization of ownership at AT&T, from the days of the Yankee capitalists through the era of Morgan to 1939, had served not to disperse decision-making power but to centralize it. In the postwar era, the biggest and most widely owned of all companies would be responsive in its style and character, not to the changing moods of its stockholders, but to the style and character of the particular man who occupied the position of chief executive.

All in all, AT&T and the Bell System in 1939 had come through the Depression sitting pretty. Its maintenance of the nine-dollar dividend through hard times had elevated AT&T to something like hero status among its stockholders and in the investment community at large. Public hostility based on its monopoly position and labor policies, which had found a focus in the FCC investigation, was now pretty well spent. The dividend was again being earned, and the business was again expanding. The future looked bright, apart from the darkening shadow that was falling not just over the telephone business but over all peoples and their affairs.

As Joseph Alsop and Robert Kintner told it:

At twenty minutes to three on the morning of September 1, 1939, a buzzer sounded at the White House telephone switchboard. The sleepy night operator plugged in her line. A voice came, "Paris calling," and then another voice, strangely sharp and harsh, "May I speak to the President?". . . The operator sounded the bell in the President's bedroom, and the President roused himself quickly and picked up the telephone by his bed.

"Who is it?"

"This is Bill Bullitt, Mr. President."

"Yes, Bill."

"Tony Biddle has just got through from Warsaw, Mr. President. Several German divisions are deep in Polish territory, and fighting is heavy. Tony said there were reports of bombers over the city. Then he was cut off. He'd tried to get you for half an hour before he called me."

"Well, Bill, it's come at last. God help us all."

Telephony had brought the President of the United States first word of a war in which it and its allied arts would play a major role—and which, by converting technical innovation from a luxury to a life-and-death necessity, would give rise to such advances as would revolutionize the art. The immediate effect on the Bell System was to bring about an unprecedented demand for service. Record numbers of new Bell phones were installed in 1940 and 1941—950,000 and 1,360,000, respectively—bringing the total in service to almost 19 million; by the end of the war in 1945 it would be 22 million. By 1941, when the nation was deeply engaged in a great debate as to whether or not to intervene in the war in Europe, the Bell System was anticipating a victory for the interventionists—or alternatively, the necessity for defending the nation against an invader—by engaging in war-related research and development, and by making unprecedented additions to plant. Over one million miles of domestic long-distance circuits were added during the year, including sixty new transcontinental circuits that increased the transcontinental telephone capacity by one-third. As a security measure, special identification began to be required for employees and others entering telephone buildings. In the area of technical innovation, as the 1941 Annual Report explained, "Extensive communications systems required in defense against enemy air attack were developed and installed during the year. These air defense arrangements are largely based on experience in Great Britain. . . ." The "arrangements" referred to were, of course, radar, which along with the courage and skill of Royal Air Force pilots had saved Britain from invasion the previous year, and the very name of which was still so secret in the United States that mention of it was considered a security breach.[9]

That December 7, the Japanese air attack on Pearl Harbor made the intervention-nonintervention debate academic, and telecommunications was thrust, along with modern life itself, into a new era.

CHAPTER 9

# Trial by Combat

World War II hit the Bell System like a thousand bombers coming in two waves. First, telecommunications, and especially their related services, were by the 1940s so crucial to the conduct of war that with Pearl Harbor the Bell research, development, and manufacturing arms instantly became among the most vital of national resources, ranking with the huge automobile assembly plants that were converted to the production of military aircraft. Beginning in 1942 and continuing until 1945, Bell Laboratories and Western Electric devoted themselves largely or almost entirely to military work. The domestic telephone network—the Bell System's real business—accordingly had to be slighted as to plant modernization and even maintenance. Yet at the same time, war brought on that network itself enormously increased demands. Servicemen calling home from distant bases within the United States, businessmen conferring with government or military authorities about contracts and deliveries, military units at home communicating with each other—all these meant telephone calls, many of them long-distance, so many as to make the demand for service not just unprecedented but previously unimagined. The very news of Pearl Harbor gave a preview of what was to come by causing an immediate increase of up to 400 percent in long-distance telephoning. During 1942 there were 114 million domestic long-distance calls—almost twice the 66.75 million of 1941, which had itself constituted a record. The Bell System, then, used to relying on close coordination between its right hand, telephone

operations, and its left hand, research, development, and manufacturing, was being asked to do much more than ever before with
its right hand with little help from its left, which was now busy
doing something else.

There was not even talk this time of a government takeover
of telephone and telegraph. The experience of the previous war
was remembered; moreover, military authorities were quick to
realize that in the Bell System they had a finely turned mechanism
ready to serve their needs just as it was, and that any drastic administrative change would, in the short run, only damage the
mechanism. Nor, in World War II, was there any systematic organization, as in World War I, of Bell signal units to build and operate American telephone networks overseas. That method had
worked brilliantly in the limited battle area of eastern France and
Belgium in 1917–18; it was not so well adapted to a worldwide war
in a time when well-developed telephone systems already existed
in most parts of the world. The Bell personnel contribution in this
war was to be in individual rather than collective terms: in all,
67,700 former Bell employees in the military services, 1,230 killed
in action. The largest and most important Bell construction undertaking outside the continental United States during World War II
was to be the establishment, by Western Electric and the Army in
1943, of telephone communications between the domestic network
and Alaska along the rocky Alaska Highway.

Most Bell System contributions to the war effort this time
were to be of other sorts, in the delicate and esoteric realm of technical innovation and production. Gifford wrote in his 1942 Annual
Report: "Emergencies are not new to the Bell System. They have
been met many times in past years through accidents of fires,
floods, earthquakes, and hurricanes. The System was prepared to
meet this trial of war." It would meet it and come out transformed,
projected willy-nilly into a new, futuristic era.


2


"The science underlying electrical communications is at the very
heart of modern war." Thus Gifford wrote to AT&T's stockholders
soon after Pearl Harbor. Already in 1942, Western Electric was
converted about 54 percent to war work; the figure would reach a

peak of 85 percent in 1944, and for the entire war, Western would fulfill about 1,600 separate government contracts, 20,000 purchase orders, and 10,000 modification orders. Its employee roll would skyrocket to almost 100,000, of whom in 1944 54 percent were women, compared to about 20 percent in 1941. Western Electric became to all intents and purposes a war plant rather than a telephone plant.

The military devices that it manufactured came, of course, off the drawing boards of Bell Labs. The Labs had fortuitously increased their physical capacity in 1941, when the Murray Hill facility, later to become headquarters of the whole far-flung Labs operation, had been opened; another northern New Jersey site, Whippany, originally acquired in 1926 for tests of high-powered radio transmitters, was destined to become the center of World War II military work. Beginning in 1942, virtually all of the Labs' six thousand people were engaged in such work, and Labs scientists were exempt from the draft because of the importance of their work, almost all of which was secret. "When the need for secrecy no longer exists and the facts can all be told, the contributions of [Bell Labs] to victory will be a source of pride to all concerned," Gifford wrote in the 1943 Annual Report. Midway through the war, the Labs established a School for War Training to instruct military men in the use and maintenance of the new devices; thousands of officers and men were thus trained in the application of science to war.

The need for secrecy is, of course, now long past, and the contributions of Bell Labs to victory can be detailed. The greatest of them was in the field of radar—a means of "seeing" distant or cloud-shrouded objects such as ships or planes on a cathode ray tube, in the form of the reflection such objects cause of bursts of radio energy sent out by a directional antenna from the radar station. Bell Labs did not invent radar. That accomplishment is generally credited to Sir Robert Watson-Watt, a Scottish physicist, in 1934–35. The invention was providential for Great Britain, which, under the pressure of threatened invasion, brought the application of radar in air warfare to a remarkable degree of sophistication in a remarkably short time. By 1940, when wave after wave of German bombers swarmed across the English Channel and the great three-month Battle of Britain ensued, the British had ground radar stations capable of spotting approaching enemy planes and identi-

36. 195 Broadway, AT&T's headquarters in downtown Manhattan, not far from Wall Street.

37. The Board Room, at the east side of the top floor. The directors meet here on the third Wednesday of every month. Portrait of Vail is on left.

38. Desk set (1930).

39. Six-button key set (1940).

40. Trimline twelve-button Touch-Tone (1968).

41. Walter S. Gifford, president of AT&T longer than any other man (1925–1948).

42. Cleo F. Craig, president of AT&T (1951–1956), whose tenure witnessed two "firsts": the use of the transistor and the transatlantic cable.

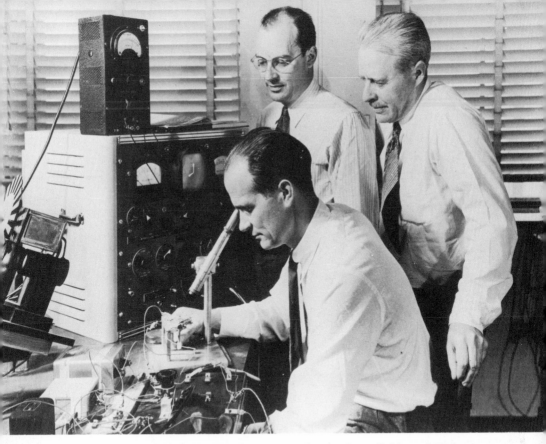

43. Inventors William Shockley (seated), John Bardeen (left), and Walter H. Brattain at Bell Labs in 1948. They were awarded the Nobel Prize in physics in 1956 for their invention of the transistor.

44. Early transistor. It replaced certain types of vacuum tubes in amplifiers and revolutionized modern electronics.

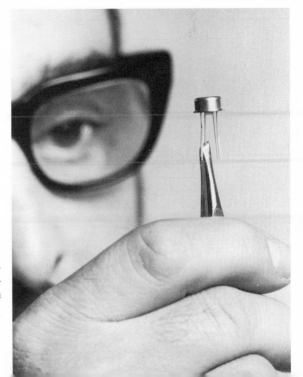

45. Transatlantic cable. The actual laying of the transatlantic cable began on June 22, 1955, in the hold of the cable ship *Monarch*. This cable covered two thousand nautical miles across the floor of the Atlantic—from Clarenville, Newfoundland, to Oban, Scotland.

46. On the rocky shores of Newfoundland, the western end of the cable dips
into the ocean. On its first day of commercial service, September 26, 1956,
close to six hundred U.S.–U.K. calls passed over it.

47. Missile Watchdog. Power radar detection antennas, larger than a football field turned on its side, are located at the Ballistic Missile Early Warning Station in Greenland. Western Electric provides the communications network for BMEWS.

48. Artist's version of Telstar. The world's first international communications satellite rocketed into orbit on July 10, 1962. This venture involved the collaboration of NASA and the Bell System.

49. Electronic Switching System (ESS) in Trenton, N.J. The first commercial ESS went into service in 1965.

50. Top left: 1890. This earliest booth, with dome roof and swing doors, featured fancy cabinet work, a writing desk, carpeting, and silk curtains. An attendant collected the charges.

51. Lower left: 1920. The "up-ended coffin," in wood.

52. Lower right: 1970. Coin-box walk-up, the "acoustical shelf" booth.

fying their position and approximate altitude, day or night and in all weathers; ground stations capable of distinguishing friendly from enemy planes, and enabling an officer on the ground to direct the friendly planes to intercept the enemy raiders; and airborne equipment so precise that it sometimes enabled British night fighter planes to identify, zero in on, and shoot down enemy planes without ever seeing them. Between August and October 1940, the Germans lost some 2,300 aircraft to less than a thousand for the British; and radar, more than any other technical factor, made possible that accomplishment.

The leaders in radar development in the United States were Bell Labs and the Massachusetts Institute of Technology's Radiation Laboratory, both of which started with the British discoveries and built upon them pioneering contributions of their own. Western Electric signed its first, highly secret radar manufacturing contract in June 1940, and began production that fall; before the war was over it had produced, from Bell Labs designs, 57,000 radar units of seventy different types for airborne, ground, and naval use, constituting about half of all U.S. radar manufactured. In October 1941, the first twelve field engineers were assigned to fighting units to train military personnel in the use of Western Electric radar; eventually this field force would grow to more than six hundred, deployed in all theaters of operations. In May 1943, it was Oliver E. Buckley, president of Bell Labs, who, in a radio talk on the Bell System's *Telephone Hour*, first introduced the American public to the word "radar." But Buckley spoke only in general terms, and what he unveiled was nothing but a word; through the rest of the war, in utmost secrecy, with the all but miraculous British achievements as a basis, Bell Labs, Western Electric, and others went on giving the military its crucial supernatural eyes. An interesting side effect of wartime radar work is that by concentrating the Labs' attention on microwave research, it paved the way for the development of microwave radio relay, which in the postwar world would become the principal means of transmission of television signals and long-distance telephone conversations in the United States.

Among other wartime Labs projects, probably the most important was the development of the M-9 gun director, precursor of guidance systems developed for antiaircraft and missile use in the postwar years. This project too began in 1940, when the

Army called on the Labs to develop an improved system for control of antiaircraft fire, substituting electrical for mechanical means. The solution—making use of electronic tubes and circuits originally developed for communication purposes, and constituting the first practical antaircraft system that was essentially automatically controlled—came off the Labs' drawing boards early in 1943. By that November, Western Electric's Hawthorne plant was producing one hundred and twenty-five M-9s per month. They were soon put in use—first in January through April 1944, at the Anzio beachhead in Italy, where a small force of Americans staved off repeated German air and land assaults; then that June at the Normandy landing sites of the Allied invasion force, and later the same year in England to shoot down 76 percent of all V-1 robot bombs fired from across the Channel and passing over areas patrolled by M-9 installations.

Finally, this surge of creativity that necessity forced on the scientists and technicians at Bell Labs resulted in various advances related only indirectly, or not at all, to the art of war. Among these was the synthetic polymer microgel, useful as a rubber substitute in either peace or war; and another that provided a curious link with the Bell System's past. Conceived by R. K. Patten of the Labs, it was called Visible Speech, and it shared not only its name but its purpose—helping teach the deaf to speak—with the invention made almost a century earlier by Alexander Graham Bell's father, Melville Bell. The difference was that the new Visible Speech, an outgrowth of a secret Army project, used not a list of symbols to indicate the position of teeth, tongue, and larynx in uttering various sounds, but rather the latest electric-electronic processes to project vocal sound patterns on a screen. So the Labs, in a sense, came full circle.[1]

The telephone business at home was roaring along almost out of control. In 1942 there were three-quarters of a billion more telephone conversations than in any previous year; in 1943 long-distance conversations were up 31 percent over the previous year's record to almost 150 million, some 50 million above the peacetime expectation and almost triple the number for 1938; in 1944 the total was up another 18 percent to 176 million. Strained to the breaking point, and lacking personnel and materials for maintenance or expansion, the network became less efficient, and in 1942 the average time required to make a long-distance connection went up from 1.6 minutes to 2.3 minutes. By 1944, AT&T was pleading with the public to give it less business—in particular, asking all civilians to refrain from calls to busy war centers, to limit all calls to five minutes, and to keep the lines as clear as possible from 7 to 10 P.M.

Concurrently, demand for new telephone installations rose to record highs. The demand could not be met; for the first time since the days when the little Charles Williams shop had been its sole supplier, the Bell System could not supply telephones to all who wanted them. Early in 1942, the War Production Board issued its first order restricting the installation of new telephones to situations that it considered essential. That October, it prohibited the *manufacture* of new telephone sets after mid-November except for military use. By the end of 1943—a year marked by the obviously war-vital extension of overseas radiotelephone service to the United States' ally, the Soviet Union—there were 650,-000 applications to the Bell System for telephone service unfilled and pending; this figure would increase steadily through the rest of the war, and would finally peak in September 1945, at 2,170,-000. This meant that for every ten persons who had telephones, there was one waiting to get one, and that for the only time in modern telephone history in the United States, getting one's own new telephone had become a function of special necessity or privilege rather than a right limited only by ability to pay the bill.

The wartime excess of demand for service did not, however, work in favor of AT&T's profits or the soundness of its plant or its financial condition. In 1942 the inflation of profit brought about by the forced deferment of maintenance activities was overbalanced by a huge increase in federal taxes, and the year's net after taxes came to $8.79, as against $10.26 the previous year. Again, as in the Depression years, the nine-dollar dividend had to be paid partly out of surplus. Over the remaining wartime years, the net hovered around the dividend figure—$9.50 for 1943, $8.89 for 1944, $8.93 for 1945. Meanwhile, despite a national rate of inflation previously matched only during the Civil War and the previous World War, the Bell System was unable to raise its rates at all. In October 1942, Congress passed a law authorizing the president to stabilize all prices. Obviously, the subsequent efforts of the Office of Price Administration to achieve this goal were not always successful, but in the telephone industry, subject as it was to close and universal regulation, they were; after the passage of the Stabilization Act, the Bell System, bowing to practical reality, simply forgot about rate increases for the duration, and indeed—under pressure from the FCC—made substantial reductions in long-distance rates in 1943 and 1944.

The result of all this was that the Bell System came out of the war in 1945 as much of the rest of the nation did—understandably proud of its accomplishment, but much the worse for wear. Its plant, so long overloaded, was near the breaking point; its war-restrained rates were unrealistically low; its appeal to investors was so low as to make its prospects for new capital to finance recovery precarious.[2]


3


The first postwar surprise was that the advent of peace brought not less demand for telephone service but more. Long-distance calls for the year—the last four months of which were the first months of the postwar period—were up to 11.6 percent over 1944. The logical explanation seemed to be that reconversion in its early stages called for even more communicating than fighting a war had, and that the new upsurge was therefore temporary. But when the increase carried over, with a vengeance, into the following year—seven billion more telephone calls of all kinds in the United States in 1946 than in 1945—it became clear that some other explanation was needed. Rising population, increasing general affluence, the habit of telephoning acquired in wartime, the sudden availability of new telephones, all combined, doubtless with other factors more metaphysical and less identifiable, to create a whole new situation: it became evident that in the postwar world, telephone use was going to go on increasing indefinitely, with the sky—literally, with the coming of communication satellites—the limit.

Reconverting to telephony on a crash basis, Western Electric delivered six hundred thousand telephones to the Bell operating companies in the last quarter of 1945. In 1946 it delivered over four million more; its sales, which two years earlier had been 85 percent to the military, were now 85 percent to the Bell System. The increase in Bell telephones in service during 1946 was 3,264,000, more than twice the increase recorded in any previous year; new phones were installed at a rate of over twenty-five a minute every working day, bringing the total to above twenty-five million. By the end of the year, over 80 percent of the more than two million people who had been waiting for service in 1945 had their telephones, and were, so it seemed, using them with the enthusiasm reserved for new toys.

In the nick of time, new projects at Bell Labs, some of them coming as by-products of secret war work, began to produce important advances in telephone technology. The Labs were a huge organization now; forced to become so by the pressures of national defense, they found themselves almost equally pressed in peacetime to keep pace with increased demand for domestic communication. The first commercial mobile telephone service, linking moving vehicles to the telephone network by radio, was put in service in St. Louis in June 1946. Coaxial cable, first widely used in military radio and radar during the war, now found a huge peacetime demand because of its unique ability to carry television signals from a point of origin, which by itself could broadcast only to points within line of sight from its antenna, to far more remote places. The first New York–Washington television transmission by coaxial cable came in February 1946. Thereafter—as television itself, its expansion long delayed by the war, gradually began to gain a fierce hold on the national imagination —for places too far from any television broadcasting station to be within line of sight of it, coaxial cable came to be the sole means by which the new wonder could be experienced: a life line to the urban experience of the time, and a latter-day counterpart of the first rural telephone lines strung by farmers out of home instruction books, back at the turn of the century.

It was in 1947 that microwave radio, later to become the dominant carrier for long-distance telephony in the United States, was first used experimentally for that purpose. This was a direct outgrowth of war work—in particular, that of Harold T. Friis of Bell Laboratories and his associates at Holmdel, New Jersey. Friis had originally joined the Bell System as a young immigrant from Denmark back in 1920, before Bell Labs existed; Western Electric sent him to work on radio research in a shack in Elberon, New Jersey, equipped with a desk consisting of a board laid over two packing cases. After the organization of the Labs, Friis became the moving spirit of Holmdel—the "old" Holmdel, consisting not of a huge ultramodern building such as stands at Holmdel now, but of a couple of farmhouses on the Jersey plain at a spot chosen for favorable radio conditions, where a handful of scientists did research. Before World War II, Friis and an associate, A. C. Beck, had created the horn-reflector antenna now used everywhere on microwave relay towers; he and his group had also put together the basic elements of a microwave radio-telephone system that could handle 2,400 conversations over five working channels. This system, primitive by later standards but obviously remarkable in its capacity, became one of the most closely guarded of Bell Labs' wartime secrets, and was used in combat in the European and Pacific theaters; the secrecy was finally lifted through a demonstration of it between the West Street lab and Neshanic, New Jersey, in October 1945. Two years later, the first experimental circuits for domestic telephone use were installed. Today Bell microwave radio facilities provide some 380 million miles of long-distance telephone circuits, and more than any other, the man behind that network is Harold Friis, of whom one of his colleagues said that his notes alone told more about the conduct of research than all the books on the subject ever printed. Bell Labs had been forged by war into probably the greatest invention factory in any field of science that the world had ever seen.[3]

4

And it was in the early postwar years that AT&T for the first time in its long history faced the common fate of large American business enterprises, serious labor troubles.

In 1943, at the height of the war, the fast-growing National Federation of Telephone Workers acquired a dynamic new president in Joseph Anthony Beirne, a handsome, outspoken young Irishman of thirty-two with a liking for broad-brimmed Stetson hats. Born in Jersey City in 1911 to two immigrants from county Roscommon—his father was a locomotive engineer and a loyal member of the Brotherhood of Locomotive Engineers who had allegedly been "broken" as an oiler because he had respected a picket line—Beirne went to parochial school in Jersey City and then quit high school after two years to work as an office boy for F. W. Woolworth and then as a utility man in the inspection department of the local Western Electric plant. Meanwhile he returned to high school at night and then studied at night at St. Peter's College of Jersey City. In 1937, still with Western Electric but now in sales, he became involved in union activities; he attended the NFTW organizing convention in Chicago in 1938, and rose in five years to its full-time paid presidency—a position he would hold until shortly before his death in 1974.

Beirne as a union leader was a subtle combination of firebrand and careful administrator. A labor colleague, Jack Barbash, said of him, "Beirne is not the kind of person who can readily evoke sentiments of 'do or die for good old Joe.' . . . He has an orderly mind with a capacity to absorb and digest detail. He has a sense of efficient organizational administration, and unlike the rough-and-tumble labor leader—which he gives the impression of being, but isn't—he doesn't play the job by ear." Rough-and-tumble or not, Beirne brought the NFTW a new militancy in sharp contrast to the posture generated by his predecessor, Paul Griffith, under whose leadership the union had been generally known as belonging in the "loyal employee" category. One of his first actions was to press for union representation on the War Labor Board, which had all but dictatorial power over labor matters in wartime; a compromise was agreed to in December 1944, under which the board did not grant a seat to labor but agreed to establish a national telephone panel with labor members. Meanwhile NFTW pressure on the National Labor Relations Board impelled it to disestablish various surviving Bell unions that were found to be company-dominated. In November 1944 came the first large uprising of telephone workers since the Wagner Act had given them the leverage they needed—an operators' strike over wages in Dayton, Ohio, that lasted eight days, involved walkouts by some 10,000 telephone workers in Ohio, Detroit, and Washington, D.C., and ended in arbitration of the dispute. Then in October 1945, shortly after V-J Day, 15,500 workers at Western Electric's Kearny plant walked out for four hours in a jurisdictional dispute and some 250,000 NFTW telephone workers joined them in an impressive—or, to AT&T management, ominous—showing of solidarity. The following month, an NFTW affiliate in Illinois and Indiana struck for a six-dollar weekly wage increase—and, after six days on the picket lines, got it.

It was a heady time for the American labor movement, with strikes in the air everywhere, the greatest of them being the 1946 walkout of 400,000 bituminous coal workers, which resulted in President Truman's seizing the mines and ended with the United Mine Workers' president, John L. Lewis, being held in contempt of court and the union fined $3,500,000 (a sum subsequently reduced to $700,000). Wartime restraints were over, nationwide union membership had increased vastly (about fourteen million members in 1946 against less than nine million in 1940), and the unions were flexing their muscles. Between V-J Day and March 1946, more than four million workers were out on strike at one time or another. In such an atmosphere, and with such a leader as Beirne, it was in the cards that the NFTW should resort to a large-scale strike sooner or later. In fact, it did so soon enough. In January 1946, the NFTW-affiliated Western Electric Employees' Association struck again at Kearny, this time demanding a 30 percent wage increase for all production workers. When the strike was two days old, there ensued a pitched battle that A. H. Raskin of *The New York Times* described as follows: "Using fists and clubs to compensate for their comparative lack of members, 42 pickets succeeded . . . in denying entrance to 1000 non-striking executives, supervisors, and maintenance employees who made a mass dash to get into the huge plant." The president of the union charged that the rush on the picket line was "a well-organized plot by management to incite a riot." No one was seriously hurt by the fists or clubs, and the strike was a failure, but the telephone industry had had the first violent labor confrontation in its history. A week later, three thousand telephone operators in Washington, D.C., began a walkout over working conditions that lasted eight days and caused substantial service problems.

The man in charge of labor relations for AT&T in 1946 was the vice-president for personnel, Cleo F. Craig, whom the reader has already caught a glimpse of as one of the new, operations-oriented vice-presidents appointed in the years just before the war. Craig in 1946 was fifty-three years old, redheaded, and, in a quiet way, combative—a worthy antagonist for Joe Beirne. An old colleague and friend tells of Craig's competitiveness as a golfer: once when Craig was about to play a match that was important to him, his colleague said teasingly, "Your opponent has my moral support"; Craig lost, and glowered at his colleague for two days thereafter. On another occasion, at an AT&T Christmas party, Craig tried so hard to balance a feather on his chin while walking a course that he ended up on a stretcher with a wrenched back.

But dealing with Beirne was not balancing a feather. On the contrary, the new militancy of the union seems to have caught the company off balance. In February 1946, the bargaining at Kearny was getting nowhere, and other NFTW unions, representing about 150,000 Bell System workers, had filed strike notices as required under the Wagner Act. On February 18, these unions, by a margin of 121,997 for to 30,761 opposed, voted for a nationwide strike on March 7. Out of forty-two NFTW unions whose employees worked for AT&T or its operating companies, seventeen committed themselves to strike and thirty-three indicated that they would respect picket lines, while only two declined to support a strike. As the days until the strike deadline ran out, negotiations of a sort went on in New York between Beirne and his aides for the NFTW, and Craig and his aides for AT&T. The formal union demands were for a ten-dollar-a-week increase for a forty-hour week, and a minimum hourly wage of sixty-five cents; but there was another and perhaps more important issue. Beirne was seeking to force AT&T to negotiate for the whole Bell System, thereby setting up a pattern of nationwide bargaining similar to the pattern that the unions had achieved with the huge automobile and steel companies; Craig, on behalf of AT&T, was continuing to insist that the operating companies were independent and negotiated separately for themselves, while AT&T did so only for Long Lines.

The struggle went down to the wire. Beirne and Craig knew each other well by now, and had developed a good degree of mutual respect; indeed, they had first negotiated with each other as early as 1940, when, in a curious initial exchange, Beirne had suggested arbitration of all union wage disputes with AT&T, Craig had asked, "Do you really want that?" and Beirne—then a raw recruit to union leadership—had admitted that on consideration he didn't. But now, six years later, Beirne and the NFTW were in no such accommodating mood. In the early-morning hours of March 7, while operators were already leaving their switchboards in Cleveland, Detroit, Washington, Philadelphia, and other large cities, and the negotiations in New York had been in session for twenty consecutive hours, agreement was reached. At 5:30 A.M.—half an hour before the strike deadline—Beirne and Craig initialed a memorandum committing AT&T to a settlement of the Long Lines wage dispute on terms acceptable to the union, and to using the Long Lines settlement as a pattern for settlements with the operating companies; and committing Beirne to call off the strike immediately. This Beirne did, and there was no strike in 1946.

Clearly, it was a victory for Beirne and his union. As a union sympathizer pointed out, "the negotiation of a memorandum of agreement between a vice-president of AT&T and the president of a national union binding on their respective affiliates was, from the point of view of the company, a rash act . . . entered into under the impression that it could not afford a nationwide strike. . . . Otherwise, why would a management which had successfully kept unions out for a generation have committed an act which ran counter to every public statement issued by the company? The Beirne-Craig agreement was an act of desperation." Craig, talking to the author many years later, agreed only in part. He said, "I suppose you could say that the paper Beirne and I initialed committed the whole Bell System. The operating companies could have reneged on it, but they never did, and I would have been disappointed if they had done so. To a degree, Beirne did force us to negotiate nationally."

It was a round for Beirne, then, but there was another round coming. The Beirne-Craig memorandum in effect committed the company to nationwide bargaining for 1946, but not for the future, and the following year, that and other issues were wide open again. Early in 1947 the NFTW formulated a new package of wage, working conditions, and fringe-benefit demands, and gave a policy committee representing all its affiliates the authority to call a national strike if agreement were not reached by April 7. This time, AT&T was ready for anything—including, if necessary, a nationwide strike. As Sanford B. Cousins, who was Craig's chief assistant at the time, has said, "In 1946, both sides in the negotiations were babes in the wood. We learned a hell of a lot very quickly." Cousins says that early in 1947, for seven straight weeks he worked one hundred or more hours a week on the negotiations, sleeping regularly at 195 Broadway. As the deadline approached, it became clear that a major issue in the dispute was local versus nationwide bargaining. But this time there was no last-minute agreement, and at 6 A.M. on April 7, more than three hundred thousand telephone workers in thirty-nine states walked out, beginning the first nationwide strike in telephone history.

The strike was traumatic for all concerned. Long-distance service was immediately cut to about 20 percent of normal; local service was near normal on the 16.5 million Bell dial phones, but was entirely stopped for about 6 million of the 9 million that had not yet been converted to dial. Some 60,000 Western Electric workers immediately joined the walkout, and there was mass picketing at the Kearny plant. As the strike continued, public indignation, directed mainly at the union, mounted, and legislation against public-utility strikers began to be rushed through Congress and the state legislatures. AT&T, realizing that its advantage grew as public opinion turned against the strikers, began offering settlements to NFTW locals on condition that they break away from the national union. On May 8, Long Lines settled for a $4.40 weekly wage increase—slightly more than one-third of the original $12 demand; similar settlements followed quickly; by May 20 all major disputes were over, and by the first week in June the strike belonged to history.

Considering its magnitude, it had been remarkably non-violent: some pickets were jailed and fined, some cables were slashed, and one union man was slightly injured by a police gunshot wound, but no one was killed or badly hurt. It seems safe to say that both the NFTW (which later in 1947 changed its name to the Communications Workers of America) and AT&T were left feeling chastened by it. Beirne commented later, "A strike against the Bell System is like throwing pebbles at the *Queen Mary* while it steams down New York Harbor." He would never mount another nationwide strike against it. As for AT&T—the nominal winner this time, both on wages and on the matter of nationwide bargaining—it was left with doubts about the continuing feasibility of holding out for local bargaining, and a new respect for Beirne. Cousins said much later, "We were kidding ourselves that the operating companies did their own bargaining.

As for Joe Beirne, he never went back on his word that I know of."
Craig, a magnanimous winner, says, "Beirne showed statesmanship. Joe dealt fairly. He never doublecrossed me. When he was
mad, you could always tell because he'd be wearing his white
Texas hat. Measured against other union leaders, he was a very
good man, and we were fortunate in having him rather than
someone else as an antagonist."[4]

## 5

The transistor, key to modern electronics, was invented at Bell
Labs' Murray Hill facility in December 1947. As is so seldom
the case in scientific innovation—and was, of course, not the case
with the invention of the telephone itself—there was no simultaneity or near-simultaneity among various researchers working
along parallel lines. There are no rival claimants to the invention
of the transistor—the event is clear-cut and pure.

As we have seen, in the years just before World War II a
Labs team had been working, without success, on the development of a semiconductor amplifier to replace and improve upon
the vacuum tube, for specific application in the development of
a system of electronic switching of telephone calls. The underlying principle involved was not new even then. Certain semiconductor phenomena, such as the cat-whisker detector familiar
on the old radio "crystal set," had been used since the turn of the
century—but not understood. Nor were they understood by William Shockley and Walter Brattain in 1936–39. Interrupted by war
work, the semiconductor project was resumed late in 1945 as one
of the Labs' first postwar undertakings. Shockley came back to
Bell Labs from wartime service at the Pentagon. There he and
Brattain were soon joined in the project by John Bardeen, a theoretical physicist in his middle thirties who had previously been
a geophysicist, an assistant professor at the University of Minnesota, and a researcher for the Naval Ordnance Laboratory in
Washington. The addition of Bardeen to the team seemed to provide a spark that had been missing. It was, however, a spark that
was slow to ignite. For almost two years—using silicon and germanium, the two best-understood semiconductors of electricity,
and introducing into their researches a new element, Bardeen's

special interest in "surface states"—the three made attempts to observe the "field effect" of semiconductors and its potential use for amplification. The efforts failed, but produced a better understanding of the properties of semiconductors; as Shockley said later, "This failure became a stepping stone to creativity."

On November 17, 1947, began the last phase of discovery, a period that Shockley refers to in an almost mystical way as "the magic month." That day, following the suggestion of their colleague Robert B. Gibney, Shockley, Brattain, and Bardeen tried generating a strong electric field perpendicular to the semiconductor. The germanium crystal that they had set up in contact with two wires two-thousandths of an inch apart began amplifying forty times. The "transistor effect" was discovered. Thereafter, the team was inspired by what Shockley calls "the will to think"; working with a kind of supernatural feverishness, perhaps comparable to Bell's and Watson's in the spring of 1876, it thereafter achieved a new breakthrough every three days or so. By mid-December the results were ready to be shown. On December 23, Shockley sent a casual note to a few of his Murray Hill colleagues inviting them to his laboratory to see a demonstration of "some effects." "I hope you can break away and come," Shockley said. What he, Brattain, and Bardeen showed them was a clumsy-looking little device several inches high, wide, and deep, consisting of gold contacts pressed into a bit of germanium supported by a piece of insulating material. What they demonstrated was the transistor effect, and the device was the first point-contact transistor.

There were more troubles ahead; exquisitely tiny amounts of internal impurities cause transistors to perform poorly or fail, and such failures came soon. Shockley says, "I recall a most trying week somewhere in late December or early January when for some reason no transistors worked." But what Shockley calls "creative-failure methodology" prevailed; the failures led the team to important new discoveries. On July 1, 1948, Bell Labs was ready, at its original headquarters on West Street in New York City, to demonstrate what, in a press release, it described as "a device called the transistor, which has several applications in radio where a vacuum tube is ordinarily employed."

The phrasing showed how little even the inventors or their corporate sponsors realized what they had accomplished. The device with "several applications in radio" would make possible integrated circuits with multiple applications containing thousands of transistors, capacitors, and resistors all concentrated on a silicon chip the size of a match head; it would bring deaf people inconspicuous hearing aids, doctors new instruments for diagnosis, naturalists a new means of tracking the migration of wildlife; it would accomplish what it was first intended for, the electronic switching of telephone calls, and have a host of other uses in communications. Without it, the modern world and modern history would be radically different; there would, for example, be no computer industry on the current scale, no communications satellites; and there would have been no trips by man to the moon.[5]

In 1956 Bardeen, Brattain, and Shockley were awarded the Nobel Prize for their work. Bardeen had left Bell Labs in 1951 to become a professor of physics at the University of Illinois, a post he still holds. Brattain stayed there until his retirement time in 1967. Shockley, who left the Labs in 1958 to form the Shockley Transistor Corporation, and later to become a university professor, but remained for some years a consultant to the Labs, went on to conceive and promulgate bizarre and highly controversial ideas in genetics, a scientific field far from his area of special competence. And the invention of the transistor remains, and is likely to remain, Bell Labs' single greatest accomplishment.

Human perception of the telephone and its role in life changed in the postwar years as its technology became more complex and its effects ever more pervasive. Gian-Carlo Menotti's *The Telephone* (1947), except for the fact that it marks the first important appearance of the telephone in opera, looks back to an old telephone joke: it is about Ben, who, trying to propose to Lucy, is continually interrupted because of Lucy's passion for telephone conversations; in desperation he rushes out to a phone booth, telephones his proposal, and is accepted. But other literary works and human events of the period suggest a new mood of frustration bordering on panic, a kind of surrealistic view of the telephone as a convenience that has grown into an uncontrollable monster. AT&T at the time refused to put turn-off switches on all the extensions of a single number; thus at least one telephone in a home had to be in ringing order, making the ring all but inescapable—and few subscribers protested this incursion on their right to silence and isolation. Some, reacting to the new mood, thought (incorrectly) that the nature of the ring itself had been charged to increase its urgency. A writer for *The New Yorker* imagined an AT&T Vice President in Charge of Ringing saying to his colleagues, "Alexander Graham Bell was all right in his day, but he didn't know beans about motivational psychology. It took my Anxious Ring to put his little gadget on its feet."

In 1947, a story by Robert M. Coates in the same magazine described, cleverly and wittily, a situation in which about thirty people are in a chain of frustration in which no one can get through to anyone else. The telephone has become an instrument that *prevents* people from communicating with each other. In 1948, Lucille Fletcher produced the play *Sorry, Wrong Number,* a hair-raising evocation of the telephone's ability to accentuate paranoia and terror, in which a woman gradually learns, through a series of telephone conversations, about a plot to murder her, and then is powerless to prevent the murder.

Apart from Menotti's, none of these fantasies would have been appropriate, or perhaps possible, in the prewar world. But now reality was to outrun fantasy in strangeness. In 1949 a psychotic veteran in Camden, New Jersey, went on a rampage and killed thirteen people; later, barricaded in his room, he took time out from holding off the police in a gun battle to answer the telephone. The avant-garde philosopher Marshall McLuhan's comment on this incident was that it showed the telephone's "cooling participational character."

In the uneasy postwar world, people seemed to be coming to associate the telephone with their frustrations, their fears, and their sense of powerlessness against technology.[6]

# 6

The corporate picture at AT&T in 1948 was a mixed one. Bell telephones in service passed the thirty million mark that year, a gain of about forty percent since the end of the war; use of them was still setting new records every year; service was generally good; and gross revenue was running at record highs. In spite of continuing serious shortages of steel, zinc, lead, and copper, Western Electric was turning out equipment at such a rate that its 1948 sales topped one billion dollars for the first time, 90 percent of those sales being to the Bell System. In terms of the volume of its business, then, AT&T seemed to have achieved the nirvana of industry, a never-ending growth curve.

But in fact it was a financial bind. Net annual earnings per share were in an ominous downtrend. In 1947 the dividend was not earned, just as in Depression days, and the company's return on total capital fell below 5 percent for the first time since those days. Large amounts of new capital were needed every year for new facilities to meet the ever-increasing demand for more telephone service. Somewhat more than half of this was generated internally, that is, by plowing back current revenues and depreciation into expansion; but the remainder—$2.75 billion between the end of the war and the end of 1948—had been produced by tapping the capital markets through the issue of new securities. Because of the uninspired performance of AT&T common stock, most of this new money from outside was necessarily being obtained through debt rather than equity securities—bonds and debentures rather than stock; as a result, by the end of 1948 AT&T's ratio of debt to equity in its capital structure had risen from the old, conservative figure of 33⅓ percent to above 50 percent. In simpler language, AT&T was finding it hard to induce new investors to share in the ownership of the business and therefore was forced repeatedly to meet its capital needs by borrowing money. And like any habitual borrower, it was headed for serious financial trouble.

Largely because of the failure of earnings to rise, the stock was out of favor in Wall Street. In the wild days of 1929 it had sold for a short time above 300; as late as mid-1946 it had been about 200; but during 1948—when AT&T's gross annual revenues were running at $2.6 billion, as against $1 billion for 1929—it was hovering around 150, and in 1949 would sink to around 140. In 1901, the year after AT&T had become the Bell System's parent company, its stock price range had been 151 to 182. An investor who had held it over the whole period of almost half a century had, of course, benefited from a liberal and uninterrupted flow of dividends, and from frequent preemptive rights to buy new stock at below the market price. Apart from those benefits, though, his investment could scarcely be said to have done well. Over a period during which inflation, as measured by the government's wholesale commodity price index, had reduced the value of a 1901 dollar to about thirty-six cents, the market price of his shares had actually dropped slightly. In terms of buying power, they were now worth roughly one-third of what they had been worth in 1901—hardly a record to make new investors come running.

The problem, of course, was telephone rates, which in the years since the price freeze of 1942—years of rapidly rising costs—had hardly been increased at all. AT&T, while business boomed along as never before, was caught in a closed chain of adverse financial events. Fixed rates with rising costs meant a profit squeeze; the profit squeeze meant a low stock price; the low stock price meant that new capital had to be raised by borrowing rather than selling stock; repeated borrowing meant a rising debt ratio in the capital structure; and the rising debt ratio, if extended indefinitely, would mean a spiral of higher interest rates, lower stock prices, and more forced borrowing leading eventually to financial ruin. In sum, the source of the problem was too-low telephone rates. The regulatory process, insufficiently countervailed by pressure from the regulated, was in the process of strangling its charge and ward.

As we have seen, with the Price Stabilization Act of October 1942, the Bell System had forgotten about rate increases for the duration, and had, in fact, reduced long-distance rates in 1943 and 1944. Nor were there any increases during the first postwar months at the end of 1945. In 1946 Bell operating companies obtained increased rates for local service in eight states amounting overall to increased revenues of $12.6 million, and at the end of that year, applications to regulatory commissions were pending in sixteen other states. By the end of 1948, rate increases granted since 1946 totaled $178 million annually, and applications were pending for increases that would come to $260 million more. But, as the AT&T financial situation made abundantly clear, it was not enough. The company, in Gifford's last years as its president, seemed to be heading for the financial shoals because of lack of energy, or skill, or both in the unlovable but necessary art of persuading regulators to allow it to charge more for telephone service.

Gifford had never had any particular talent for the taxing political battles involved in rate-getting—nor, during most of his long presidency, had he needed it. Apart from that, Gifford, in truth, had probably served as president too long. He had reached his peak as a business statesman early in his presidential term, with his Dallas speech in 1927; he had kept his head and his temper through the bad times and the FCC investigation of the 1930s; and he had guided the company well through the wartime years with their difficulties, one of which, for Gifford, had been the death in combat of his son, Walter Gifford, Jr. Now in the postwar years, as his term in office approached the quarter-century mark, he showed signs of relaxing and turning over more and more authority to his deputy, Vice-President Cooper. "In the early postwar years, we got our sailing orders from Proctor Cooper," an associate of Gifford's in the AT&T executive hierarchy has said; another puts the matter more flatly, saying, "I think Cooper was running the company in those years." Still another eloquently describes the office attitude toward Gifford by saying, "We were all acutely aware of what he had done in the past."

But Gifford had one more decision to make, and one of his most important ever. In keeping with long-established company tradition, a retiring president of AT&T had the ultimate responsibility—after consultation with his colleagues, and of course subject to ratification by the board of directors—of choosing his successor. As we have seen, the loss of owner control that went with the extraordinarily wide dispersion of AT&T stock thrust more and more power into the hands of the president—so much, indeed, that by 1948 the AT&T presidency was, at least potentially, surely the most powerful position in American business. The president was a kind of king. To choose the man to fill that position, at a time when the company faced bad problems, was a heavy responsibility indeed.

And the choice was not easy. The otherwise logical successor, Cooper, was ineligible because he was a few months older than Gifford and therefore would face mandatory retirement at age sixty-five a few months before Gifford would. The previous transitions—from Forbes to Hudson, from Fish to Vail, from Vail to Thayer, from Thayer to Gifford—had been logical to the point of being obvious, and had been accomplished with a minimum of internal tension and subsequent bad feeling. But now there were no fewer than four staff vice-presidents who had good claims on the presidency. Accordingly, when Gifford let it be known in 1947 that he intended to retire as president early in 1948, soon after his sixty-third birthday, for the first time in its history AT&T faced a serious contest for its presidency, with attendant infighting, and perhaps resulting disruption of the organization.

There was Keith McHugh, fifty-two, a sound and experienced operating man with an engineering background, who, having been a vice-president since 1937, had the edge over the other candidates in seniority in office.

There was also Cleo Craig, fifty-four, a vice-president since 1940—Craig, who preferred operating jobs to staff jobs, and hated New York; who had shown his skill and nerve as a labor negotiator in 1946 and 1947; whose personal competitiveness was so strong as to be almost an office joke; and who, nevertheless, was the gentlest of the candidates.

There was William Henry Harrison, fifty-five, appointed a vice-president in 1938, who in World War II had become a major general in the Army Signal Corps—and who, despite an entire career with the Bell System except the years 1943–4–5, nevertheless listed his occupation in the 1948 edition of *Who's Who in America* as "army officer," and wanted to be addressed as "General." Considered brilliant but undependable, Harrison was given to florid, melodramatic touches in his business dealings. Once, seeking to convince a group of operating company vice-presidents that gas in manholes was dangerous to telephone crews, he had called them together for a demonstration in which he had subjected some guinea pigs to manhole gas, knocked them out cold—and then, to satisfy humanitarians, revived them with oxygen. A few months after the great Midwest floods of 1937, he had gone to Pittsburgh to give a pep talk to discouraged telephone men there. After dinner, Harrison got up and motioned to the door, whereupon six pallbearers entered bearing a casket. Harrison took out of the casket a panoramic view of Pittsburgh in the flood, displayed it, said, "Gentlemen, let's bury the goddamn flood"—and sat down.

And there was one other candidate. He was Leroy A. Wilson, youngest of the four by several years: born in Terre Haute, Indiana, in 1901; graduate in civil engineering of Rose Polytechnic Institute, Terre Haute, in 1922; a beginner at Indiana Bell as a traffic clerk that same year. After seven years with Indiana Bell and ten with AT&T at 195 Broadway, including one spent in charge of telephone directories, he had found his calling—that of being a rate-getter through negotiations with regulatory agencies. In 1940 he was made "rate engineer," and in 1944, vice-president in charge of revenue needs.

Within the company, Wilson was known as a driving nonstop worker with a strong strain of abrasiveness and ruthlessness. Slick-haired, and handsome in a forceful way, he was widely known to lead a chaotic life, to be particularly fond of gambling, and to take his losses in life or at the tables in good part. All in all, hardly the image of an AT&T president. But Wilson was the one man in the company who knew the most about the political problems of negotiating with regulators, and who had the most personal force to apply to such negotiations; perhaps, in view of the financial situation, a time had come to have a totally different kind of president, a hard-driving and hard-driven salesman rather than a business statesman. It is clear that Gifford weighed the matter of his successor long and carefully, particularly as between Wilson and Craig—a man far more like himself than Wilson was. On one occasion, Gifford privately discussed the presidency with Craig, without actually offering it to him; Craig, even though he was eight years Wilson's senior, replied that he felt he wasn't yet ready for the job. Tense weeks passed, with office politicking at 195 Broadway going on at a pitch more often associated with small, struggling companies than with an imperial giant like AT&T. Then, in February 1948, "the word waved," as a senior staff man put it later—and Leroy Wilson was named president. Gifford moved up to the chiefly advisory post of chairman of the board. (In 1950 he would begin a three-year term as U.S. ambassador to Great Britain, during which he would enjoy good relations with Winston Churchill's government.) Craig took Wilson's place as financial man and revenue-getter; a new vice-president, William C. Bolenius, replaced Craig in personnel; while McHugh and Harrison remained where they had been.

The repercussions were quick in coming. Harrison, bitterly disappointed not to have been chosen, said so in strong language at the following Monday morning's Cabinet meeting, maintaining that he had been unfairly treated; shortly thereafter, he left to become president of International Telephone & Telegraph, not yet a conglomerate; he would hold that post until his death in

1956. McHugh, also disappointed but less acutely so, left 195 Broadway to become president of the New York Telephone Company.

So Wilson assumed office facing not only a labyrinthine financial problem but also a situation almost entirely new to AT&T —a staff that had been seriously disrupted by competition for office. His presidency would be brief and stormy, and the scars from it would last a long time. Moreover, always having been a staff man, he came to the office drastically short of experience in running an organization; as revenue vice-president, for example, he had been directly in charge of only seven people. But he had been chosen essentially to do one job—to take off the gloves in the battle for higher rates—and that was the job he would do. There is a maxim in AT&T staff circles that "God takes care of the Bell System," miraculously thrusting to the top the right man at the right time. But in this case, on consideration, the credit should probably go not to God but to Gifford.[7]

# CHAPTER 10

# Tiger and Thoroughbred

"Higher earnings are needed," Wilson wrote, with characteristic bluntness, in his first Annual Report to AT&T stockholders, covering the year 1951. A curious point for a president to urge on stockholders, who, out of their pure economic function, presumably want nothing else? Not in a regulated company in which higher earnings depended largely on the consent of regulatory agencies—and, behind them, the public—to the charging of higher rates, and in which the stockholders, numbering more than a million, themselves constituted a significant and influential segment of that public. Bluntly, abrasively, sometimes ruthlessly, Wilson went about getting higher earnings by getting telephone rates raised.

The change from Gifford to Wilson provided the first evidence of to what an extent the character of the largest corporation in the world could now be changed almost overnight in reflection of the character of its chief executive. The change was, interestingly enough, invisible to AT&T stockholders, who continued to receive the same dividend and the same stream of demure and solid-seeming company publications, their tone only subtly changed. But to Bell System executives and telephone regulatory bodies, it was neither invisible nor obscure. What had been a gentlemanly, slow-moving, tradition-conscious, seniority-worshiping concern—a "genial old monopoly," as the writer Geoffrey T. Hellman had called it, to the rage of some of its officials—became a driving, aggressive one full of people in fear for their

232

jobs. Intolerant of staidness and time-serving, Wilson emphasized accountability; on staff or line, executives were required to perform or get out. Heads rolled—particularly in operating companies that, as Wilson judged the matter, dragged their feet about undertaking the unpleasant and politically risky task of tackling their regulatory agencies for rate increases. The whole System's predilection for seniority, and its concomitant skeptical attitude toward youth, was turned around: Wilson was looking for the person who could perform, regardless of age or seniority. Largely as a result of these policies, he was to be remembered as the most hated president in AT&T history.

However, even those who hated Wilson had to give him credit. His ruthlessness was, in the context of what had to be done, an unpleasant necessity. He had Vail's ability to quickly identify a problem and then quickly redeploy a vast and unwieldy organization to handle it. Moreover, his bluntness sometimes was for its victim's benefit. Ed ("Boom Boom") Clarke, a loud-talking, brilliant, somewhat bumptious and carelessly dressed executive of Pennsylvania Bell, was passed over for the presidency of that company during Wilson's term, and came to Wilson to complain. Wilson unhesitatingly replied that the trouble was that Clarke looked and acted too much like a tramp to be a Bell company president. Clarke modulated his voice and bought six new suits and an opera subscription and went on to become president of Southwestern Bell, and a first-rate one.

One man who worked on Wilson's New York staff and disliked him heartily nevertheless said later that, in a long Bell System career, his years under Wilson were the most satisfying of all.

Wilson had been in office less than a year when, on January 14, 1949, the Justice Department filed suit in the U.S. District Court of Newark, New Jersey, under the Sherman Antitrust Act, charging that "the absence of effective competition has tended to defeat effective public regulation of rates charged subscribers for telephone service, since the higher the price charged by Western Electric for telephone apparatus and equipment, the higher the plant investment on which the operating companies are entitled to earn a reasonable return"; and asking, among other things, nothing less than that Western, by court decree, be divorced entirely from AT&T and split into three separate companies that would then compete with other manufacturers for Bell System business.

The suit had been a long time coming; in fact, it had arisen directly out of the FCC investigation of the 1930s. Holmes Baldridge, an astute Oklahoma lawyer who had served as Commissioner Walker's principal attorney in that investigation, had gone on to join the Justice Department's antitrust division as chief of its general litigation section. In that job he had continued to maintain the position, held by Walker and a minority of his colleagues in 1939, that the public would be better served if AT&T and Western Electric were legally split apart. In 1947 and 1948—years, ironically enough, when Bell companies' rate-getting activities were so ineffectual as to be instrumental in bringing about a System-wide financial crisis—regulatory authorities from two states, Tennessee and Minnesota, came to Baldridge to complain that their rate-setting powers were hobbled by their inability to determine whether Western's equipment charges were fair. On the basis of these complaints, Baldridge decided that the time had come to strike. It was chiefly on his initiative that Attorney General Tom Clark was persuaded to take the far-reaching and historic step of suing to break up the Bell System.

AT&T's response was to ask for a postponement of prosecution of the antitrust suit—first an indefinite postponement, and then, when that was refused, one of two years, or at least eighteen months. Despite the Justice Department's refusals, a de facto postponement ensued. It was not until August 1951 that the government got around to asking AT&T to produce documents on subjects covered in the suit's allegations; then, after another year, came the 1952 presidential campaign and the prospect of a change of administration in Washington. Apart from continuing government study of the mountains of paper that AT&T had submitted, the case remained at a standstill through the 1952 campaign, the election of Dwight D. Eisenhower as president, and the interregnum period before the new Republican administration assumed power the following March.

Thus a Republican government inherited a suit that had been initiated by Democrats holding a different philosophy of government as regards many matters, including the enforcement of the antitrust laws. But, as will appear presently, AT&T had by no means heard the last of the matter.[1]

Meanwhile—inadvertently, it would appear—the Democratic government had given AT&T a hostage. In September 1945, the month after the atomic bombing of Hiroshima and Nagasaki, General Leslie R. Groves, head of the nation's atomic program, had ordered the construction at Sandia Base, an airfield near Albuquerque, New Mexico, of a laboratory for the design and production of a national atomic bomb stockpile. The new facility was to be a branch of the Los Alamos Scientific Laboratory, some sixty miles to the north, where the first atomic bombs had been developed; like Los Alamos, Sandia was to be operated by the University of California. In 1946 scientists and technicians from Los Alamos began moving into Sandia Laboratory, and by 1948 its activities were far enough advanced so that its payroll amounted to one thousand persons, tanks and war dogs had been brought in for protection of its security, and, as Sandia's historian would write later, "the amount of design work . . . was prodigious."

However, in other respects progress at Sandia was less than satisfactory. For one reason or another—according to some accounts, a major reason was backbiting and competition among the scientists who staffed the project—very few bombs were being turned out, and this, in a time when the cold war was becoming a fact of life, was looked upon by military authorities in Washington as downright dangerous. Then on December 31, 1948, the University of California informed the Atomic Energy Commission, which had taken over control of all U.S. atomic activities in 1947, that it wished to divest itself of the Sandia operation by July 1, 1949, on grounds that production and stockpiling of weapons were inappropriate activities for a university. To Sandia's other problems was to be added that of being leaderless.

There followed an urgent search by the Atomic Energy Commission for a new contractor to take over Sandia—urgent because, as AEC Chairman David E. Lilienthal wrote later, on assuming office the previous year he had found to his "shock" that "the substantial stockpile of atom bombs that we and the top military assumed was there, in readiness, did not exist." Lilienthal—formerly of the Tennessee Valley Authority and, as we have seen, the Wisconsin Public Service Commission—now had what he called a "hunch" that the organization with the capabilities in research, industrial techniques, and operation to take over Sandia already existed, and that that organization was the Bell System. Accordingly, in the spring of 1949 the Washington authorities got in touch with Dr. Buckley, president of Bell Labs. Buckley replied flatly that the Labs could not consider taking over Sandia because internal policy restricted the Labs' commitment of their resources to defense work to 15 percent of total budget. The AEC persisted, and—at the suggestion of Dr. Mervin J. Kelly, then executive vice-president of Bell Labs and later president—a compromise proposal was worked out: could the Bell System consider taking over merely the *management* of Sandia, leaving the Los Alamos laboratory to continue doing the technical and scientific work? Under such a scheme, Sandia would have the benefit of the Bell System's skill at industrial production to straighten out Sandia's organizational problems, and at the same time, since the Bell financial commitment would be small, the 15 percent problem would be avoided.

In the subsequent negotiations, government and corporation played a game of cat and mouse. Wilson for AT&T insistently linked a Sandia commitment to the pending antitrust case. On May 13, President Truman, acting on the advice of Lilienthal, wrote Wilson formally asking the Bell System to take over the direction of Sandia and thereby "render an exceptional service in the national interest." Wilson replied four days later asking for time to consider the matter. On May 30—Memorial Day— Lilienthal met with Wilson. Wilson, as Lilienthal recalled later, said that while his company "did not relish another great load such as this," nevertheless the Bell System would accept the assignment "as in the national interest." But Wilson said more. In Lilienthal's paraphrase: "I must tell you, he said, that a few months ago the government . . . filed a suit under the Sherman Antitrust Act to sever Western Electric from the Bell System, as well as to split up Western Electric into several parts. What the government asks in this lawsuit, Mr. Wilson indicated, is that the courts break up and dissolve the very organizational unity and size you say this vital security job requires." As if that were not clear enough, Wilson write Lilienthal on July 1, in formally accepting the Sandia assignment on behalf of Western Electric and Bell Labs: "We are concerned by the fact that the antitrust suit . . . seeks to terminate the very same Western Electric—Bell Laboratories—Bell System relationship which gives our organization the unique qualifications to which you refer. If Western Electric should enter into a contract to operate the Sandia Laboratory, that company and the Bell Laboratories would indeed work as one . . . and the effectiveness of their work would depend . . . upon their close connection as units." By clear implication, if the government suit against Bell should succeed, the effectiveness of the Bell project for the government would be impaired. Lilienthal's answer to Wilson, by including no mention of Wilson's comments on the antitrust suit, implied, in turn, that the government—or at least the Atomic Energy Commission—accepted the point.

The Sandia Corporation was formed in September 1949 as a fully-owned subsidiary of Western Electric, "to engage in any kind of research and development, and any kind of manufacturing production and procurement to the extent that may lawfully be done." Since the basis was to be cost and no fee, AT&T would profit not at all. On November 1—by which time news of the first successful Russian atom-bomb test had given the project added urgency—Sandia Corporation took over operation of Sandia Laboratory. The effect of the new management, consisting of about fifty Bell System people detached from their regular jobs, was astonishingly quick to be seen. On November 17 an AEC field director told the Associated Press that "Sandia Laboratories are no longer experimenting with atomic weapons, they are producing them." The emphasis on production continued through 1950 and 1951, during which an unannounced number of bombs were turned out, including some of new design. As Sandia's historian writes, "One new weapon was started into design in 1948, two more in 1949, and three in 1950. The floodgates opened in 1951, when many designs for guided missiles were introduced." By 1952 the state of the stockpiles was such that the emphasis was shifted back from production to design; meanwhile the employee count at Sandia had grown from 1,740 in November 1949 to 5,200. Western Electric's original five-year contract was renewed in 1954 and again in 1959; by 1963 Sandia was, in its historian's words, "a corporate entity . . . with nuclear hardware responsibilities unmatched in the Free World. . . . Its special devices are widely employed along the guarded frontier between East and West." As of the mid 1970s, Western Electric was still operating Sandia for the AEC, with a management cadre reduced from the original fifty to about twenty, and with a changed mission that embraces "the whole range of nuclear weapon system conception, design, and development, excluding only the nuclear explosive package."[2]

Some questions remained, and still remain. Self-evidently, the Bell System has made no profit on Sandia and was reluctant to take it on. Did the System, then, assume the heavy responsibility truly in the national interest, or as a lever in the antitrust suit? It may reasonably be assumed that both motives were factors. A more delicate and perhaps more important question is, What was a telecommunications company, any more than a university, doing running a bomb factory? That AT&T is sensitive on the subject is suggested by the fact that it makes little of the operation in its public utterances and releases. In a time of widespread antiwar militancy, and in view of AT&T's prior commitment to stick to communications, this attitude is not hard to understand. The AEC-AT&T association typifies the much-hated "military-industrial complex" working, nevertheless, at a high degree of harmony and efficiency to what few Americans can doubt was, at least in the early cold war days, a necessary end.

2

Because of normal delays in the operation of the regulatory process, Wilson's nationwide rate-getting campaign was slow in taking effect. But when it did take effect, it did so with a vengeance. By the end of 1949, telephone rate increases granted since World War II amounted to an additional $360 million in annual revenues, and increases granted plus requests for increases pending amounted to a 20 percent increase. As a result, the financial picture began to improve sharply. Return on capital jumped from 4.9 percent in 1949 to 6.07 percent in 1950. AT&T net profit for 1949 was down slightly to $9.70, but for 1950 it topped the ten-dollar mark. In response, the stock price began to rise (from 150 to near 165 early in 1950) and the new desirability of the stock made it possible to raise much new capital on favorable terms through convertible debentures (bonds that would eventually be converted in whole or in part into stock), thereby reducing the company's ratio of debt to equity. That figure, after peaking out at a dangerously high 52 percent at the end of 1949—almost high enough to deprive AT&T of its top rating in the bond market—was down to 48 percent by the end of 1950. Nevertheless, as Wilson said, "This general level of debt is much too high." The corner had been turned, and the straightaway lay ahead.

Labor troubles cropped up again in 1950, and Wilson showed himself to be as formidable an opponent to the union as he was to the regulatory agencies. Beirne and his Communication Workers of America had been through a spell of organizational troubles that had reduced their militancy for a couple of years. In 1947 Philip Murray's Congress of Industrial Organizations, the great nationwide amalgamation, had moved into the telephone industry by forming a Telephone Workers Organizing Committee in rivalry to the CWA. In 1949, after a long and painful internal debate, the CWA affiliated with the CIO and joined forces with the new TWOC. Virtually all Bell companies dealing with CWA unions reacted by withdrawing recognition of those unions, and launched proceedings with the National Labor Relations Board, charging that the CIO affiliation cast doubt on CWA's right to speak for the majority of Bell-employee members. The NLRB dismissed these proceedings, but the union felt intimidated nonetheless; in September 1949 a group of CWA leaders decided that "a successful strike in 1949–50 is just ·not in the cards" because CWA's affiliation with CIO had made AT&T officials "furious" and they would attempt to "embarrass and show up" the union. That was in 1949; by the following year, Beirne and his men had reorganized their forces for a new attack.

Wilson's deputy in labor matters was Craig's successor as vice-president for personnel—William C. Bolenius, a square-jawed, hard-nosed Dutch Presbyterian from upstate New York who had spent most of his career (an all–Bell System career, as usual) with New York Telephone. Early in 1950, negotiations began between Beirne, Bolenius, and their aides at the University Club in New York (of which, incidentally, Bolenius was a member and Beirne was not). Apart from wages and benefits, the basic issue was the same as in 1946 and 1947: Beirne wanted to force AT&T into openly negotiating for the entire Bell System, and Bolenius wanted to maintain the appearance of local bargaining while he actually bargained nationally. Bolenius now says, "We negotiated what amounted to a national contract," although it was announced as being a series of local contracts. The bargain was arrived at in the melodramatic circumstances so often characteristic of such settlements. After all-night talks in the last hours before the union's strike deadline, Beirne announced that the strike was on, and began to walk out of the room—but paused with his hand on the doorknob. Bolenius said, "Come on back, Joe." (Bolenius always addressed Beirne as "Joe" while Beirne, at his own preference, called his adversary "Mr. Bolenius" or just "you.") Beirne came back, and after twenty more minutes, they averted a strike by arriving at an accommodation in which, as Bolenius has since said with grim satisfaction, "We gave them almost nothing."

The settlement gave rise, later in 1950, to Senate Labor Committee hearings on Bell negotiating methods and telephone wages. A committee investigator came up with statistics to show that, among 123 industry groups, telephone workers in 1939 had been twenty-second in weekly earnings and sixteenth in hourly earnings, while by 1949 they had fallen to eighty-sixth and seventy-fifth, respectively. The implication was that AT&T had been retarding wage progress by engaging in unfair labor practices. Beirne testified that "there is no bottom to the bag of tricks which the Bell System uses to slow up and delay negotiations" and spoke roundly of AT&T's "insane desire to render unions impotent." Bolenius, his tongue firmly planted in his cheek, affirmed that in labor matters AT&T merely gave "advice and suggestions" to the associated companies, which the companies were not obliged to accept. He also, by his own account, negotiated behind the scenes with Beirne as to Beirne's testimony, pressing the union leader not to divulge the fact that earlier in the year Bolenius had for all practical purposes negotiated for the whole Bell System. "Joe," Bolenius says he said, "if you tell that, you'll never walk into my office again." Beirne, defying the threat, replied that he intended to testify to just that—and he did so. After the hearings—which ended inconclusively, and did not lead to new legislation—Beirne, Bolenius, and their aides decided to get together for drinks, in the friendly-enemies tradition. Bolenius characteristically reports that the telephone executives drank the union leaders under the table.

That November there was a ten-day strike of Western Electric installers and Michigan operators, which ended in compromise wage settlements. In the years since then, there have been occasional local telephone strikes, some of them prolonged, but never another national one calculated to stop most or all telephone service; and of course, as in all other industries, there have been frequent and substantial raises in telephone workers' wages. The CWA finally won its point on national bargaining, presumably once and for all, in 1974, the year of Beirne's death.

Bolenius is less charitable than Craig on the subject of Beirne. "Joe would lie," he says, "but not unless it was awful important. He was forced to do it by expediency—there was heavy pressure on him from within his own union. After the Washington hearings, he came repeatedly to my office—I forgot about the threat to keep him out, and anyhow, I left the personnel job in mid-1951—and asked us to help bail him out of his intra-union troubles. We could have cut him off at the pockets, but we didn't. He became a more responsible labor leader later, when he got out of his internal fight for survival." (Obviously, and regrettably, missing here is Beirne's opinion of Bolenius. Beirne died while the present author was waiting for an interview with him.) AT&T's relations with CWA and the many other unions it deals with were relatively placid over the next quarter century. The short era of confrontation ended in 1950.[3]

Midway through that year, a quite different kind of crisis arose. Wilson's doctors diagnosed leukemia and told him that he had a year to live. Thus, for the first time in its long history, AT&T faced a terrible problem well known to many other companies, not to mention national governments—that of continuing to move forward with a dying chief executive at the helm. The problem was complicated by another familiar circumstance: the executive was unwilling or constitutionally unable to yield any degree of power. For six months, Wilson continued to function normally. Things were going well; profits were improving and record issues of convertible debentures were going on the market at intervals, to be gobbled up by investors. Only Craig and Bolenius, as Wilson's most trusted staff men, knew of his condition, and they kept the knowledge to themselves. But early in 1951 Wilson's condition worsened; he began coming to his office no more than one day a week or less, and running the company the rest of the time from his home in Short Hills, New Jersey.

Dying kings clinging to power have wrought prodigies of

mischief in their last days, and it is to Wilson's credit that he did no more mischief than he did. Craig, on whom chiefly fell the burden of such decision-making as Wilson would or was forced to relinquish, characterizes the last six months of the Wilson regime as "a nightmare." Weakened in body, but as strong as ever in will, Wilson went on driving day and night for rate increases, improved profits, and equity financing. He and Craig had sharp policy differences; there was a high-level office story (which Craig denies) that after one such difference the two men were for a brief time not on speaking terms. Over his doctors' warning that it might shorten his life to do so, Wilson left his sickbed to conduct the 1951 AT&T annual meeting, held, as was usual in those days, in the third-floor auditorium of 195 Broadway in mid-April. He gave the one thousand stockholders present a ten-minute address—shorter than usual, but so forcefully delivered that few present suspected he was ill.

Up to his last week, Wilson kept saying to his closest colleagues, "I'm going to beat the doctors." During that last week, he had a final difference with Craig about the pricing of a new issue of debentures. Wilson called from a hospital bed to ask that the price be raised. Craig said no, and Wilson didn't argue. On June 27, 1951, Craig was named "acting president" during Wilson's illness, which was thus officially acknowledged by AT&T for the first time. On June 28, Wilson died. The following week, Craig—who, despite all, had been Wilson's choice as his successor—was formally elected president by the board of directors.

In July the board passed the following resolution on Wilson: "In the short period of his presidency he met the most serious problems in Bell System history with distinguished success. There are few instances in the management of great enterprises when one man has done so much in so little time."[4]

3

For the System as a whole, the coming of Craig was like a clearing after a storm. It was evident from the first that, in contrast to Wilson, he would hold an easy rein. First to feel the easing were the operating companies, some of whose top executives had been driven by Wilson's autocratic handling to the point of open revolt. At his first presidents' meeting as AT&T president, Craig summed up his management philosophy in a sentence: 195 Broadway should never have to issue a direct order to any operating-company president, because "I don't want to have to live with my bad decisions."

Craig was a delegator who liked to give people their heads. Somewhat introverted, a master of figures, something of an intellectual as business executives go, he was diplomatic in dealing with business associates, and enthusiastically extended Wilson's policy of bringing younger people along. And yet, perhaps paradoxically, he was incapable of dealing easily with politicians or government appointees. In further contrast to Wilson, he hated politics and the political wrangling involved in rate-getting. If Wilson had been a politician outside the company and anything but a politician inside it, Craig was the opposite. Craig always said that the primary influence on him as an executive had been Arthur Page, the outright intellectual from the publishing business who had been brought to AT&T by Gifford. It is interesting to note, in looking back over the company's history, how often the presidents seem to have alternated between hard-driving, highly specialized businessmen and milder-mannered men with broader interests—especially interesting, perhaps, in view of the fact that each president for practical purposes chose his successor. In any case, Craig's arrival was perfectly timed; his predecessor had pressed the System right up to the breaking point.

Plainly enough, however, without the accomplishments of Wilson's regime the liberalism of Craig's would not have been possible. Wilson's driving made room for the luxury of Craig's permissiveness. For indeed, business was booming by the time Craig came in. More than two million new Bell telephones were installed in 1951, setting a new annual record; the following year, the company was able to report that more new phones had been installed since the war than had been in service before it. The regulatory log jam having been broken under Wilson, new rate rises now continued to be allowed in spite of Craig's distaste for political battles. In 1952, intrastate rates were raised in thirty-seven states, bringing the increase since 1940 to about 30 percent —slightly more than one-third of the national cost-of-living increase over the same period; and Craig was able to tell the stockholders, "There is evidence of better understanding by regulatory authorities that good earnings and a sound financial structure are essential to providing the best telephone service." AT&T earnings remained between eleven and twelve dollars in 1951 through 1954—a good, sound range, high enough to make new stock attractive to investors, low enough to provide evidence that revenues were not excessive and telephone rates not extortionate. The regulated-monopoly system was working the way it is supposed to work; and in 1951 AT&T became the world's first private corporation to have over one million stockholders (of whom one-fourth were Bell System employees).

Gradually the Bell coaxial-cable network for the transmission of television signals extended its tentacles, bringing the benefits, if such they were, of network TV to even more remote corners of the nation. By the end of 1953, this network linked 260 stations in 161 cities, and consisted of 50,000 miles of cable bringing network programs within the range of about 100,000,000 people. The role of coaxial cable in telephone transmission was greatly enhanced in 1953 when a new system, the L-3, was placed in commercial service, making it possible for one pair of cables to carry 1,800 telephone channels, triple the capacity of earlier cables. Microwave relay, soon to become the dominant method of transmission for domestic long-distance telephony, was coming into its own. Its towers with their horn-like antennas were sprouting on hilltops everywhere, and as early as August 1951, the two coasts were linked by microwave. By 1953, more than 80 percent of Bell telephones had been converted to dial. And a dramatic innovation, direct dialing of long-distance calls, came about during Craig's tenure. In 1951 about 38 percent of domestic long-distance calls were being dialed by an operator in one city to an operator in another, rather than being handled by voice; that November, it became possible for the first time for subscribers in Englewood, New Jersey, to dial calls to twelve other cities just as if they were making a local call. By 1956, the new direct-dialing service had been extended to the point that 11 million customers could dial directly to nearby cities, 2.7 million could reach by direct dialing 20 million other telephones throughout the country, and 89 percent of all Bell telephones were dial-operated at least for local service. The local operator as a message center, answering service, and information spreader was a vanishing American. More to the point, direct-distance dialing, or DDD, was the precursor of a whole array of developments that would make possible repeated reductions of long distance rates; as such, it was the most important development directly affecting service of the postwar period.

Even so, the most spectacular technical advance of the Craig regime was the successful installation of a transatlantic telephone cable—an accomplishment no more striking in itself than in the fact that it had been so long delayed. Transatlantic telegraph cables had been in reliable operation since the 1850s; why, then, had a century—and the most scientifically innovative century in the history of the world—gone by without the accomplishment of the logical and seemingly simple step of the adaptation of submarine cables to telephone use? The answer is that the step was not simple; rather, it proved to be one of the most delicate and complex problems in the whole technical history of telephony. The heart of the problem was that the use of submarine cables to carry voice over great distances requires enormously greater amplification than is needed to transmit telegraph signals. The capacity for such amplification was simply unavailable before the invention of the vacuum tube and its application in telephone repeaters. With the overland repeater in hand, Bell engineers early in this century set about developing one for undersea use. But many problems remained, and above all, that of maintenance. Repairing a repeater strung between telephone poles or buried shallowly in the earth was one thing; raising one from two or three miles under the sea to replace a part was another. The engineers calculated that the process of locating a single defective repeater, raising it from the ocean floor, repairing it, and putting it back in place would impair service for a long period and cost about $250,000.

The urgency of developing a submarine cable was lessened by the coming of transatlantic telephone service by radio in 1927, and then further set back by the Depression and World War II. But overseas radio telephony by pre-satellite long-wave transmission was intrinsically noisy and unreliable, and in the late 1940s, Bell Labs undertook the task of developing what came to be called "the perfect product"—a submarine repeater that could be counted on to perform without repair for twenty years and would thereby make a submarine telephone cable economically feasible. The design for such a product came off the Bell Labs drawing boards in the early 1950s. It would be a torpedo-shaped object about three feet long and eighteen inches in diameter, weighing five hundred pounds, containing five thousand miniature parts, and costing about one hundred thousand dollars; connected into submarine cables at intervals of ten to forty miles, it would, presumably, carry voices over any distance. As early as 1950, a prototype repeater-assisted submarine cable was put into trial service over the ninety miles between Miami and Havana, Cuba. In the 1953 Annual Report, before the perfect product was in production, Craig felt enough confidence in it to announce plans for the transatlantic cable system: it was, he said, to be jointly owned by AT&T, the British Post Office, and the Canadian Overseas Telecommunication Corporation; it was to consist of two cables, each carrying messages in a single direction over the two thousand nautical miles between Newfoundland and Scotland, at depths up to three miles; it would cost thirty-five million dollars and take three years to complete, and when finished it would be able to carry thirty-six separate conversations at a time.

The Hillside, New Jersey, shops of Western Electric began shipping the first completed submarine repeaters in January, 1955. That June 22, the cable ship *Monarch* left Clarenville, Newfoundland, to lay the cable. It was a bizarre and romantic operation. As the *Monarch* steamed along toward Scotland, paying out two-inch-diameter cable and much larger repeaters from huge reels on her stern, like a spider spinning a web, men on shipboard talked constantly to shore over the evolving cable, to be sure that no breaks had occurred and all was well so far. Craig himself was aboard the *Monarch*, in fog-shrouded waters off Newfoundland, when the first repeater was lowered. Although it was past midnight, everyone on board was up and watching, in an atmosphere of high tension. The repeater safely on bottom, the cable was tested out to shore; it worked, loud and clear. All but those on duty went to bed, and the *Monarch* steamed on.

On September 26, the *Monarch* and its now-empty reels reached Oban, Scotland. The one-way amplified cable worked, and the job was half done. There remained the return journey to complete the circuit. It was made in the summer of 1956, and completed on August 14, when the *Monarch* arrived at Clarenville and the last section was spliced to shore-end cable. There followed a little more than a month of adjusting and testing;

then, on September 25—six days after Craig had resigned as president—the transatlantic cable was opened to commercial service by a three-way call between Craig, and FCC Chairman George C. McConnaughey in New York, British Postmaster General Charles Hill in London, and Canadian Transport Minister George C. Marler in Ottawa.

On September 26, the first full day of commercial service, 588 completed calls passed over the cable—75 percent more than the average traffic by radio over the ten previous days. By December, traffic over it was averaging 870 completed calls a day, and it had become an accepted part of the Atlantic community's life. Its final cost had been $42 million, a 20 percent overrun of Craig's estimate. As to the perfect product, it has lived up to its billing; twenty years later, no submarine repeater has ever had to be raised for repair.[5]

4

Truly, the Craig years, especially the later ones, were palmy days for AT&T. As earnings went up in reflection of better rates and the unprecedented prosperity of the whole nation—to an all-time record $13.10 per share in 1955, and another record $13.16 in 1956—the stock price rose to around 185, and thereby huge amounts of equity financing were made possible. The man Craig assigned the financial vice-presidency was Bolenius, the former operating man who as personnel chief had been such a stubborn labor negotiator. Bolenius came to the job with no real experience in finance, but with firm convictions derived from his grandfather, who had believed that one's money should be invested "the Dutch way": one-third stocks, one-third bonds, one-third real estate. That formula scarcely could be applied to a corporation whose voracious need for new capital for plant construction made it a constant seller rather than a buyer of securities. Still, it served as a starting point; moreover, during nine earlier years with New York Telephone in Albany, Bolenius had become fascinated with the securities markets and had made a weekend hobby of studying them. Under the direction of this enthusiastic amateur of finance, aided by favorable market conditions, AT&T in the middle 1950s developed a uniform pattern of financing that worked like a well-regulated watch. At regular intervals, the rights to buy huge issues of convertible debentures would be offered to existing stockholders—not through underwriters but by AT&T's own securities organization—in amounts proportionate to existing holdings. The debentures, since they carried a market-competitive rate of interest, were sound investments simply as bonds; and the fact that they could be converted into stock at a fixed price gave them the additional value of amounting to options to buy more AT&T stock below market value. Alternatively, if stockholders didn't want to buy the convertible debentures, they could sell their rights and thus have a sort of extra dividend. The usual experience was that 30 to 40 percent of each new issue was immediately taken up by stockholders, most of whom would later convert their bonds to stock; the rest would go—as a result of stockholders' selling their rights— into the hands of professional speculators and arbitragers, who, so long as the AT&T stock price was rising, would also eventually exercise their conversion privilege.

The net effect of this process—bewildering to a layman, but crystalline in its purity and elegance to a financial man—was that large amounts of new stock were added to the AT&T capital structure, and comparatively little new debt; thus the crucial debt-to-equity ratio progressively came down to safer levels. From 48 percent at the end of 1950, it went to 40 percent in 1952; it rose temporarily to 41 percent at the end of 1953, because a huge issue of convertibles had recently been issued and, since they had not yet been converted to equity, were listed as debt; but then it sank in 1954 to 37 percent, in 1956 to 33 percent—just where it had been in prewar years, and a figure that would surely have pleased Bolenius' grandfather.

It can be argued—and would later be argued by federal regulators—that by pursuing such a conservative financial policy of reducing its debt and constantly increasing the number of shares of stock outstanding, AT&T was artificially holding down its earnings per share and thus averting pressure to lower telephone rates—in other words, that the company's rocklike financial position of the late 1950s was achieved at the expense of the subscribers. But Craig—always financially conservative, and increasingly so as time went on—saw things a quite different way. When net earnings reached about thirteen dollars per share in 1955, he became defensive about them. In the Annual Report for that year, he argued that the figure was only barely adequate because, with six million new shares issued that year, and all of those new shares requiring dividend payments and treasury surplus to back them up, 85 percent of the year's earnings had been used in paying dividends and holding the company's retained surplus per share at a constant level. But this rather tortured argument could easily be turned on its head. Another way of putting the matter would have been to say that, even though the number of outstanding shares had increased by six million, or more than 12 percent, the net earnings *per share* had nevertheless increased by $1.18, or almost 10 percent—hardly an unimpressive showing or one suggestive of stringency.[6]

Conservative as he was in financial matters, Craig was an unmistakable liberal in the social policies of the corporation. Institutions—national governments and corporations alike—are inclined to treat human and cultural values as a luxury, to be afforded in economically good times but not in bad. The Craig regime was AT&T's Age of the Renaissance. A garden of programs was suddenly made to blossom that had no lesser aim than to reverse the company's management trend of twenty years' standing toward narrow technicians, by attempting to change its managers into philosophers of sorts. The chief gardener was one of the more extraordinary figures in the history of AT&T management—Robert K. Greenleaf, a long-faced Indianan with an owlishly humorous manner that lightly masked a fundamental seriousness. Born in Terre Haute and graduated in 1926 from Carleton College in Minnesota, Greenleaf had spent three years with Ohio Bell before coming to AT&T in 1929—the end of an earlier golden age—as a specialist in management research. Early in Craig's term as president, he appointed Greenleaf to the position of director of management development, a job not high in the management hierarchy but one with a sort of roving commission, and with a special privilege of reporting directly to the chief executive rather than going through channels like everybody else. Personally, too, Craig and Greenleaf had a special relationship, mutually wary and respectful. Craig liked to speak of Greenleaf— a Quaker who was radical not in politics but in management philosophy—as his "kept revolutionary."

Craig's first manager-broadening move was, with the cooperation of Wilfred D. Gillen, president of Pennsylvania Bell, to revive and enhance Chester Barnard's earlier program for sending managers to the University of Pennsylvania to study the humanities. Such programs had been out of favor at AT&T in the early postwar years, when executives were pressed to stick to business, and sometimes were actively discouraged from vigorous participation in the affairs of their communities. Now they were taken off the line, twenty-five per year, and sent with their families to Pennsylvania for a ten-month course not in management or telephony but in such subjects as English literature, European history, and Greek classics—all the while drawing their regular Bell System salaries.

Under the umbrella of the Pennsylvania program, Greenleaf was given a mandate to inaugurate others. "We've got to get off our high horse," Craig said to him. "You aren't spending enough money." Greenleaf responded by starting shorter humanities programs for Bell executives at Swarthmore, Northwestern, Williams, and Dartmouth, as well as a four-week training course at Asbury Park, New Jersey, involving case studies and lectures rather than humanities courses, through which all nine hundred Bell System department heads eventually would pass. At their peak, Craig-and-Greenleaf-instituted management training or mind-broadening courses were taking the entire Bell System management cadre off operations an average of one week per man per year, and were costing the company many millions per year.

Although Craig clearly cared deeply about the human side of business, he sometimes warned Greenleaf, "Remember we're running a business, not a social service agency." At least one Greenleaf program took somewhat chilling account of this injunction. It was a series of evaluation sessions for newly hired management employees, most of them fresh out of college, that was modeled categorically on a program used by the Office of Strategic Services during World War II for the evaluation of potential espionage agents. In the AT&T version, a group of seventy or eighty college graduates newly hired by one of the operating companies would be sent for three and a half days to some remote spot—say, a camp in northern Michigan—and there subjected by a staff of six graduate psychologists to a series of tests of character as well as intellect that included competitive business games, interviews designed to measure the subjects' reaction to conflict, and parties to test their handling of liquor. This program, under the general direction of Douglas W. Bray, a Yale-trained psychologist, was instituted in the summer of 1956 and continued through that of 1960. The limits of Craig's, Greenleaf's, and AT&T's liberal humanism are delineated by the fact that they were willing to screen future managers by a process modeled on one designed to screen future spies.

The management-broadening programs were beginning to run out of steam before the end of Craig's tenure. Some within the company objected to their cost; others found them unsuccessful in their own terms. An AT&T study of the Pennsylvania program concluded that it was a failure because highly placed managers were refusing to send their best subordinates on grounds that they couldn't spare them, and because some of those who did go became so humanized that they lost a degree of interest in corporate management (a conclusion with which Pennsylvania Bell officials disagreed, and still disagree). Swarthmore soon dropped out of the program because of the strain it caused on local facilities. Taken all in all, though, the programs improved Bell management morale, served to point the company's leadership in a more public-spirited direction that would be a life-saver in the next decade, and provided a classic example of an economic polity responding to good times by assuming a new benignity.[7]

5

In the matter of the government antitrust suit, which sought to dismember it, AT&T could neither afford a new benignity nor did it care to assume one. Rather, it was fortunate enough to find a new benignity in its adversary.

Herbert Brownell, the Republican attorney general who assumed office in 1953, soon after his appointment expressed general displeasure with the various antitrust cases his office had inherited from the Democrats, and promised a thorough review of them. That April, Hal S. Dumas, AT&T's executive vice-president, seizing the advantage to AT&T that seemed to be implied in those statements, sought out Brownell through an intermediary for a personal talk. In the meeting, which took place at the Statler

Hotel in Washington, Dumas urged that the suit against AT&T be dismissed; Brownell, according to Dumas, "listened politely" but was "uncommunicative." He was more communicative in another meeting, this one with T. Brooke Price, AT&T's vice-president and general counsel, that took place on July 27, 1953, at a judicial conference at the Greenbrier Hotel in White Sulphur Springs, West Virginia. At the Greenbrier affair, Price, who had met Brownell briefly before, asked him for a private interview, and Brownell responded by inviting Price to his cottage. Sitting with the attorney general on the cottage's porch, Price, as he later described it, "made a number of statements about the injury the case threatened to our efficiency and progress as a communications company and to our contribution to the national defense" and said that "we were hopeful that he would see his way clear to have the case dropped." Brownell "reflected a moment and said in substance that a way ought to be found to get rid of the case" through a compromise that would involve "practices that we might agree to have enjoined with no real injury to our business." Price characterized the meeting by saying that it was his impression that Brownell had been giving him "a little friendly tip as to how we might approach them to get something started in the way of negotiation."

It was later widely believed that the process that led to the consent decree that eventually ended the suit was set in motion at this private, casual, and—from the point of view of supporters of the antitrust suit—questionable meeting. "After White Sulphur Springs . . . the final result was never seriously in doubt," concluded the majority report of the Antitrust Subcommittee of the House Judiciary Committee in 1959. (Some AT&T officials close to the case held and still hold a different view, insisting that all the meeting amounted to was "Brownell suggesting negotiations on a consent decree" and that Price—for reasons that are hard to imagine—"romanticized the story" in recounting it.) At all events, there can be no doubt that Price's reference to AT&T's "contribution to the national defense" was a telling point, because by 1953 —as the cold war began building up toward its frightening climax, the Cuban missile crisis of 1962—the company in its integrated form was a leading national-defense asset. The Sandia management commitment was only the beginning. In 1950, the U.S. Army had chosen Western Electric as prime contractor for the Nike Ajax guided antiaircraft missile, with entire responsibility for production; early in 1953, the first finished Nike Ajax missiles began coming off the production line. Later the same year, the company took on production of a more advanced weapon, the Nike Hercules, equipped with a nuclear warhead that the Pentagon said would make it capable of "destroying entire fleets of incoming aircraft." In 1954, Western Electric and Bell Laboratories, in association with the Lincoln Laboratories of Massachusetts Institute of Technology, began working on an extension of the Distant Early Warning air-defense radar system—originally installed in northern Alaska in 1953—eastward across the entire top of the continent; this mammoth installation would be in place at around the end of the decade. AT&T's sales to the government on defense projects set new peacetime records almost every year in the middle and late 1950s. The Army would ultimately pay over $1.5 billion to Western Electric on the Nike project alone (of which much would go to the subcontractors, such as Douglas Aircraft), and Western Electric would make a profit of $112.5 million.

Clearly enough, then, the branches of the government concerned with national defense had reason to be cool to the antitrust suit against AT&T. Indeed, the Department of Defense became AT&T's categorical ally in the matter. On July 10, 1953—a fortnight before the Greenbrier meeting—Secretary of Defense Charles Wilson wrote to Attorney General Brownell, "The Department of Defense wishes to express its serious concern regarding the further prosecution of the antitrust case now pending against Western Electric Co. and the AT&T Co." and going on to argue against the case in language that, with minor differences, had been supplied to the Defense Department a few days earlier by none other than Dr. Kelly of Bell Labs. However, the Justice Department had its pride and its independence; as Victor H. Kramer, a militant young Justice Department prosecutor, put it, "The antitrust division . . . was rather cynical about letters from Defense Secretaries seeking postponement or settlement of cases," and as late as May 1954, the attorney general was still pressing formally for divestiture of Western Electric.[8]

Negotiations dragged on unfruitfully into 1955, and in January of that year there took place another private meeting that would later be adduced as evidence of behind-the-scenes collusion between suer and sued. This time the participants were Price—

shortly to retire as AT&T's general counsel—and Edward A. Foote, a new man at Justice who had been assigned a few months earlier to take charge of the AT&T negotiations. Seeking to get, in Price's words, "a more informal down-to-earth contact with the case" than was possible in formal meetings, Foote was so indiscreet as to invite Price to his Washington house. Price said later that they had a "nice dinner" and afterward "talked about this case and really gossiped about it"; and that in the course of the gossip, Foote expressed the view "that this complaint was a monstrosity, it was badly drawn and full of perfect absurdities and you just could not go to trial on that kind of complaint."

Pretty clearly, then—although Justice was divided within its own councils, Victor Kramer still being strongly for a trial seeking Western's separation from AT&T—the government had decided by this time to settle for a consent decree. The pace of negotiations picked up, and that summer AT&T, at Foote's request, prepared a memo setting forth the pros and cons of various settlement possibilities. In November 1955, after the Federal Communications Commission (also, like Justice, divided within) had expressed itself in favor of settlement rather than trial, Justice formally notified AT&T that it would negotiate on the basis of no divestiture of Western. Thereupon, a three-man AT&T team, with staff support, moved into Washington, setting up headquarters at the Statler. The team consisted of Horace P. Moulton, who in September had succeeded Price as AT&T general counsel; George Best, the company's vice-president in charge of relations with other utilities; and Frederick R. Kappel, president of Western Electric. For the government, the chief negotiators were Foote; Walter D. Murphy, a trial man; W. D. Kilgore, Jr., of the enforcement section; and Kramer, who remained the government's hardest-liner and, as Moulton later put it, "made the spitballs." Through December, negotiations went on several hours a day, sometimes including Sundays; Moulton recalls that one night the two sides knocked off for dinner together at a French restaurant, then went to the Metropolitan Club to play billiards—only to be stopped by a resident member who appeared in pajamas and night tuque and complained that they were disturbing his sleep.

The agreement, or consent decree, settling the case was wrapped up in Washington right after New Year's Day, 1956, and on January 12 (with Kramer dissenting) it was formally presented to and approved by Judge Thomas F. Meaney in the U.S. District Court in Newark. Its provisions were long, complicated, and technical, but the most important of them may be summarized briefly: First, Western Electric would not be separated from AT&T; second, Western Electric, except for its government defense work, agreed to confine itself to manufacturing equipment of types bought by the Bell System, rather than seeking other markets; third, the Bell System agreed not to engage in any business other than common-carrier communications and "incidental operations"; and fourth, the Bell System agreed to grant nonexclusive licenses and related technical information to any applicant on fair terms.

Who had won? Both sides claimed victory in styles that accorded with their interests: the Justice Department, which had spent seven years and millions in public money on the case, in a loud voice; the Bell System, which did not wish to appear to be crowing over the federal government, much more mutedly. Brownell spoke of the decree as a "major victory." AT&T noted with satisfaction that "the system setup has been legally confirmed as O.K. under the Sherman Act" and that, outside of the patent and technical information fields, the decree "made no change of any importance as regards Western." (In fact, AT&T had been substantially complying with the manufacturing, operations, and patent-licensing provisions of the decree for years.) Moulton says now, carefully, "Well, we kept Western, but at some cost patent-wise." Kappel, then Western's president, told a meeting of company officials shortly after the settlement, "We probably did as well as could be expected . . . the decree . . . generally makes legal an integrated Bell System . . . we preserved the really important thing." (The notes of an executive who was present indicate that he also said, in essence, "Use discretion in passing along. Don't brag about having won victory or getting everything we wanted.")[9]

Indeed, in historical perspective AT&T had hardly got everything it wanted. True, the decree had essentially put the stamp of the law on the Bell System as it was. But in a democratically governed country the stamp of the law is, for practical purposes, not indelible. Later revelations of the Republican administration's apathetic attitude toward the suit, and of the cozy private meetings preceding its settlement, would give rise to public murmurings against it, and staff men at the Justice Department would for a generation go on viewing it with dissatisfaction. As for the reaction of legislators, in 1959, after extensive hearings, the majority of the Antitrust Subcommittee of the House Judiciary Committee concluded that "the consent decree . . . stands revealed as devoid of merit and ineffective as an instrument to accomplish the purpose of the antitrust laws." The 1956 decree was the most important turning point in AT&T's relations with the government and the public since the Kingsbury Commitment of 1913. It would lead directly to a third and equally important turning point in the 1970s.

6

Perhaps the most quoted phrase in J. D. Salinger's *The Catcher in the Rye*, the 1951 best-selling novel that went on to be the object of a 1950s youth cult, concerns the telephone. "What really knocks me out," says the teen-age hero-narrator, Holden Caulfield, "is a book that, when you've done reading it, you wish the author that wrote it was a terrific friend of yours and you could call him up on the phone whenever you felt like it."

The telephone was becoming the American teen-ager's entertainment, friend, and perhaps psychological necessity. As a large-scale national phenomenon, this was something new in the 1950s. Previously, the economic stringencies of the Depression, and then the equipment stringencies of World War II, had made individual lines largely unavailable to children. Concurrently, the advancing fragmentation of the family may have increased children's need for communication with their peers. In a time when more and more students lived at distances from their schools that required transportation by bus, car, or train, the after-school gossip session in a drugstore or on a street corner came more and more to be replaced by the telephone conversation after getting home. Moreover, psychologists pointed out that the telephone has a functional advantage over face-to-face contact between teen-agers, particularly between boys and girls: they appreciate the invisibility and the possibility for immediate retreat that it affords. All in all, the telephone seemed to have been invented to serve the needs of this tense, educated, somewhat alienated first generation of the atomic and television age. Affluent parents differed bitterly over when or whether their children should have their "own" telephones. Telephone calls in the United States in the Eisenhower era ran at a rate of nearly half a billion a day; the percentage made between persons under twenty was uncounted and cannot be estimated, but impression suggests that it may have been startlingly high.

The same era also marked the rise of "services" in which the telephone is used as an on-demand broadcasting medium rather than for two-way communication. Time checks had first been provided to callers to a certain number—often ME 7-1212, or NERVOUS—in New Jersey in 1927. Weather broadcasts, based on information supplied by the Weather Bureau to the local telephone companies, began in Cleveland and Philadelphia in 1950. Next came religious messages. Around 1955, a number of churches—notably the Hitchcock Memorial Presbyterian Church in Scarsdale, New York—began broadcasting brief recorded prayers continuously by telephone; after the Hitchcock's service had been publicized in a local newspaper, there was such a backlog of calls that the Scarsdale telephone system became temporarily jammed. By 1956, so many Dial-a-Prayer services were being offered by churches around the nation that *Time* said they had become "almost a characteristic feature of U.S. religion," and one such service, that of the Fifth Avenue Presbyterian Church in Manhattan, was averaging eight hundred calls an hour. About that time, a Chicago restaurant began advertising itself by a telephonic service that seemed to offer not faith but love. Callers were greeted by a honey-dripping female voice saying, "Hello, darling. I'm so glad you called." There were 183,000 calls per month. Later, in the 1960s and 1970s, there would be many variations, most of them live rather than recorded: Dial A Shoulder, in New York, offering a sympathetic listener to any problem; Medicall, in Chicago, offering quick medical consultation for a small fee; Operation Venus, in Philadelphia, a free venereal-disease information service; Hot Line, in Los Angeles, offering advice on personal problems to teen-agers; and Dial-a-Joke, in New York, designed to brighten a caller's moment by making him laugh at a recorded routine by a professional comedian.

What the dial services represent in telephone history is, of course, the closing of another cycle—a return, or attempted return,

258 | T E L E P H O N E

to the days of the town or country operator who gladly dispersed to all callers the time, the weather, sympathy, solace, jokes, or the train schedule. It is a return with a difference, in that the new messages are either recorded or delivered by someone unknown to the caller. But the situation neatly exemplifies the tension, basic to an understanding of American life, between nostalgia and the desire for change.[10]

In 1956 Cleo Craig's work as president was, as he saw it, essentially done. Financially, the debt ratio in capital had been reduced from above 50 percent to a safe, perhaps even ultra-safe, 33 percent. Technically, the transatlantic cable had been laid and was about to go into service. Legally, the antitrust suit had been disposed of. Morally, the company as a whole had been raised a notch or two in appearance and, indeed, in reality. If Wilson before him had been a tiger, Craig had conducted himself like a thoroughbred race horse. At sixty-three, he decided to step down from the presidency—or rather, as was the custom for retiring presidents, to step up to chairman of the board, which was then a largely honorary position. Before doing so, he chose a successor utterly different from himself in temperament as well as personal and business philosophy. The man who assumed the presidency on September 19, 1956—and whom Craig had picked out, he said later, because "I knew he had iron up his backbone" —was Frederick R. Kappel.

# CHAPTER 11

# Putting Razzle-Dazzle in Ma Bell

Kappel, who would serve as AT&T's chief executive officer for a decade—first as president, then as chairman of the board—was to emerge as probably the most vivid executive figure in the company's modern history.

In 1961 the title "chairman of the board" came to be applied to the overall boss, while "president" came to describe his second in command. "Chairman of the executive committee" became the name of the pasture to which chief executives retired. At that time, Kappel became chairman of the board and Eugene J. McNeely president. The change was largely in name rather than substance, since Kappel and McNeely had previously been serving as No. 1 and No. 2 men. A heavy-set, muscular Minnesotan of German descent, with a square jaw, thick wrists, and heavy arms, Kappel had joined the Bell System in 1924, the year of his graduation from the University of Minnesota, as a ground man with Northwestern Bell, and had risen to become president of Western Electric in 1954, just in time to play a major role in concluding the negotiations with the government on the antitrust suit. He was proud of the fact that one of the Army generals he had dealt with in connection with the DEW line contract had called him "the toughest so-and-so I ever dealt with"—and of the fact that the product had subsequently been delivered and installed on budget and ahead of schedule. At the time he assumed the AT&T presidency in 1956 (as, indeed, at all other times), he was forthrightly and sometimes belligerently right of center in

259

politics, he unabashedly used the word "liberal" as a term of denigration, and he cheerfully described himself as "cantankerous." His idea of running a company was that when something needs to be done, often the only way it can get done is for the boss to get in there and push it through—a "philosophy" that he described as a "field" point of view as opposed to a "staff" one. Thus he represented an epitome of the trend in AT&T management style that had gradually and irregularly been evolving since Gifford's time.

Executives who worked with Kappel as chief executive all had their stores of Kappel anecdotes. "What do I care about history?" Kappel once demanded of an aide, upon finding a reference to Theodore Vail in the aide's draft of a speech for Kappel to deliver—but the reference stayed in. On another occasion, after the same aide had tried to explain the nuances of a problem, Kappel, color rising in his neck, stormed, "God damn it, I don't want to understand it, I just want to know what to do about it." Later the aide slyly put that very sentence—attributed to an unnamed business leader—into the draft of a speech Kappel was to deliver denouncing "anti-intellectualism in business," as a horrible example of the thing being denounced. Kappel made no comment, and the quote stayed in the speech through several versions, only to be excised by Kappel, again without comment, in the last.

Kappel's unaided prose style made up in forcefulness for what it lacked in literary quality. Once, angry about some shortcoming of the operating companies, he fired off to all their presidents a memo that he refused to let his staff see before he sent it. By all accounts, it was virtually illiterate from start to finish—but there was no mistaking what Kappel wanted done, or that he wanted it done quickly.

Kappel's bark was worse than his bite. While his shouting and storming alienated many in press, public, government, and stockholder ranks, almost all of those who worked closely with him within the company rather astonishingly held and continue to hold him in a high regard that verges on reverence. Robert K. Greenleaf, who sums him up as "kind of a ham, but with elements of greatness," feels that under Kappel's bluster there was serious self-questioning, as evidenced by the fact that once—after Kappel on a public platform had delivered ad-lib remarks of which Greenleaf, who was in the audience, strongly disapproved—Kappel asked him, "All right, what went wrong while you were staring at the floor?" Prescott C. Mabon, who served as Kappel's assistant and perhaps closest associate, says of him, "He was tough, but direct, honest, and able to take criticism. And if a critic turned out to be right, he was promoted." William G. Sharwell, who was personnel research supervisor in the early 1960s (and who went on to become executive vice-president of New York Telephone in critical times for that company), sums up Kappel: "If you roared back at him, he'd be reasonable; if you lay down, he'd walk all over you. Philosophically, we're at opposite poles, but I'd carry a cross for him."[1]

One of the first moves of Kappel's presidency was, from the point of view of AT&T stockholders, who now numbered more than a million and a half, among the most dramatic in the history of the company. It was to split the stock. The reader will recall that in the stockmarket boom of the 1920s, AT&T had been tempted to split its stock, but had resisted the temptation. In the latter-day boom of the middle 1950s, stock-splitting was an even more popular sport. Its effect, and indeed its purpose, was more psychological than substantive. A company's directors would simply declare that the company now had two, three, or four times as many common shares outstanding as previously, and that each old share now represented two, three, or four new shares. New certificates representing the new holdings would then be sent by mail to each old stockholder. The market price of the new shares would become the appropriate fraction of the old price. In theory—apart from the dividend rise that often accompanied a split—nothing economic had happened. Each stockholder's holding still had about the same dollar value as before, and the company had acquired no new capital; the practical justification for the split was merely that it brought the price of a share of stock down to a figure within reach of the millions of small new investors who were crowding into the Wall Street game, creating day by day the first truly mass stock market in the world's history. But the stock market is at least as much a psychological as an economic activity, and the popular view was that a stock split meant that a company was riding high and expected soon to be riding even higher. Mere rumors of a split to come caused the price of a stock to rise, and as often as not, the price of the new stock would rise after the split had been accomplished. In practice, splitting became a way for company managements to increase the popularity of their stock and the market value—as opposed to the paid-in amount—of their equity capital.

By 1956, virtually all the other giants of American industry—General Motors, Standard Oil of New Jersey, Gulf Oil, General Electric, and so on—had split their stock at least once during the decade, and there was talk among Wall Street analysts of an impending split by one of the last holdouts, AT&T. Indeed, at the time Craig had assumed the presidency in 1951 a report issued by Merrill Lynch, by far the largest of brokerage firms, had predicted that AT&T would announce a split by the end of that year. The report could not have been more wrong. In fact, Craig was philosophically opposed to a split in 1951 and would remain so for a long time thereafter. His reasoning, and that of many others within the company, was that the matter should be deferred until AT&T's financial house was in better order. On a more emotional level, there was also the matter of the dividend. A stock split would, of course, mean a lower dividend per share (even though perhaps a higher dividend per dollar invested, if the split was accompanied by a rise in the rate), and an end of the nine-dollar-per-share rate that had been maintained through thick and thin since 1921—surely the most celebrated single figure in the history of American investing, and long the symbol of AT&T's stability and unshakable sense of obligation to its shareholders. To change it by splitting the stock, the argument went, would appear to the uninitiated to be an abandonment of the sense of obligation.

Even during Craig's term, a minority of directors, led by the Boston banker Lloyd D. Brace, favored a split. Nevertheless, when Kappel assumed office in 1956, he found that the nine-dollar dividend was generally considered within the company to be holy writ; as he put the matter later, "it brought tears to people's eyes," and the notion of changing it was "not even allowable conversation." Kappel, however, was never wary of engaging in disallowable conversation. Bent on modernizing the company financially as well as in other ways, and obsessed with the idea that AT&T should operate insofar as possible like unregulated companies, he began a campaign for a stock split. Financial

Vice-President Bolenius and Treasurer John Scanlon got together what Kappel called "the numbers" on why a split would be a good idea (the main "number" being the current price of AT&T stock, which at almost 200 was thought to be deterring new investors of modest means). Kappel, supported by Bolenius, then visited every member of the board of directors to press the matter.

Kappel could be a powerful persuader, but it was slow going —in vintage Kappel language, "a real hair-puller." For one thing, even those who agreed in principle to a split differed as to its nature. Should it be two new shares for every old one, bringing the price of the new stock to around 100? Three for one, bringing it to around 67? Or four for one, bringing it to 50? For another thing, Craig—who was still a member of the board, and who carried the prestige of a retired president—was continuing to hold out on principle against *any* split. When the board met on December 17, 1958, to resolve the issue, it was still very much in doubt.

The formal minutes of that meeting are laconic, as minutes of corporate directors are apt to be, omitting any reference to differences of opinion. However, some of the participants have since described the proceedings in general terms. The hair-pulling stage of the debate being clearly in the past, Craig, as a compromise, proposed a split of two for one. Kappel held out for three for one. It quickly developed that Kappel had the majority on his side, and Craig, as a gesture of solidarity, made the motion that was adopted: "*Resolved,* that there be included in the proxy material for the annual meeting of stockholders to be held April 15, 1959, a proposal of this Board that the capital stock of the Company be split on a three-for-one basis . . ." and that a public announcement be made to the effect that the quarterly dividend on the split shares be $3.30 per share—meaning that holders of old shares would now get not $9 per year per old share, but $9.90. The company secretary, S. Whitney Landon, set in motion the dissemination of the news, and a short time later all hell broke loose in Wall Street.

Apart from a spectacular leap of thirteen points in the price of AT&T old stock over the next two days, several important things had happened. For once, the directors, however much pressured by the chief executive, had made a key decision on their own. Kappel had established his leadership by winning his first important internal battle. And AT&T, long thought of in the financial markets as a fuddy-duddy investment for the Aunt Janes, had transformed its investor image at a stroke into that of a modern "growth" company.[2]

In the strict financial sense that that term implies in Wall Street, it was such a company in those years. Net earnings on the new, split stock were $5.22 per share for 1959, $5.53 for 1960, $5.79 for 1962, and $6.06—equivalent to $18.18 on the old stock— for 1963. The dividend was raised progressively until by the end of 1965 it was running at a rate equivalent to $13.20 per share of the old stock. The stockholder family was becoming something more like a nation; the year 1964 saw a scarcely believable increase of 423,000 in the stockholder count, bringing the total within striking distance of three million—a figure that would be reached in 1966. In those halcyon days of the early 1960s, when the whole national economy seemed to have achieved a millennium of permanent growth without significant inflation, AT&T found it necessary to make comparatively few requests for rate increases, and was able to continue the long-established downward trend of long-distance rates; all-time-record profits could be racked up almost every year merely by improving the efficiency of production (Western Electric's prices in 1965 were actually 16 percent below those of 1950) and taking advantage of the huge increase in volume of business that went with the national boom. Naturally, the stock price rose—from about 90 after the split to highs of 108 in 1960 and 140 at the end of 1961. At that time, investors who had bought AT&T when the split had been proposed three years earlier had doubled their money. AT&T had come to be regarded by many Wall Street analysts as a "high-technology" company with prospects for future growth and stock appreciation comparable to those of unregulated companies. This entirely new attitude is vividly exemplified by the contrast between the roles of AT&T stock in the 1929 crash and in the temporary but frightening collapse of 1962. As we have seen, in 1929 AT&T was more or less on the sidelines, gratefully yielding market leadership to more glamorous issues like Steel and Radio. At 11:45 A.M. on Tuesday, May 29, 1962—the day after all stocks listed on the New York Stock Exchange had undergone a paper loss of $20.8 billion, more than twice as much as had been lost on Black Thursday in 1929—"Telephone" was being watched above all other stocks as the bellwether of the market, the single stock of which an upward turn might be expected to signal a similar turn of the whole market. Having dropped 11 points, or about 10 percent of its overall value, on the previous day, Telephone at 11:45 was being traded at about 99. Ten minutes later, there was a small transaction at 100, followed over the next hour by a large number of successive ones at higher prices up to 106. The rest of the market followed, to finish the day with a huge gain, and the fear of "another 1929" was ended. George M. L. La Branche, Jr., chief floor specialist in AT&T stock at the time, later paid a lyrical tribune to Telephone—the stock, not the company—as it appeared, in those days of its greatest puissance, to one with the intense yet limited vision of a man who devoted his days to trading it with his peers and indeed with the whole country. "Telephone is kind of like the sea," he said. "Generally, it is calm and kindly. Then all of a sudden a great wind comes and whips up a giant wave. The wave sweeps over and deluges everybody; then it sucks back again. You have to give with it. You can't fight it, any more than King Canute could."

Early in 1964, the stockholders voted on motion of the directors to split AT&T stock a second time, this time two shares for one. That July, the price of the new shares reached 75—the equivalent of 450 on the original pre-1959 shares. Good times do not last forever, and that price stands, twelve years later, as the all-time high.[3]

2

In other ways Kappel moved quickly to put more razzle-dazzle into Ma Bell. Indeed, he had made one such move prior to becoming president of AT&T. Up to the middle 1950s, the company's attitude as to color of equipment was much the same as Henry Ford's had been as to the Model T—that is, the customer could have a telephone in any color desired, so long as the color was black. White and even pastel telephones were available on an unadvertised, custom basis, but were actually seen chiefly in the never-never land of the movies. Kappel resolved to make color phones readily available to all subscribers—a change he described as "moving out of the Dark Ages"—and to do so, he proceeded in a characteristically forthright way. Knowing that there would be internal opposition to such an innovation, which might have almost a smack of depravity to some traditionalists within the company, he personally, and without telling anyone, arranged for an advertising agency to prepare four large advertisements of color telephones for leading magazines. Then, as a virtual *fait accompli*, he announced at a corporate conference that Western Electric proposed to put color phones in mass production and mass marketing. The coup succeeded in spite of the dim view taken of it by President Craig (who says now, with a trace of admiration, "The color phone was Fred Kappel's special baby"), and soon a touch of Hollywood began to blossom on Main Street and in Suburbia Hills.

With Kappel as boss of AT&T, a profusion of new customer equipment burst forth. In 1959 the Princess telephone—light and stylishly feminine in design, and white, beige, pink, blue, or turquoise in color—was introduced in selected areas. In 1963 came the first offering of Touch-Tone service, featuring telephones with push buttons instead of rotary dials; and in 1965 the Trimline, with the dial built into the handset, which proved to be an immediate hit. For business customers, there was Centrex, first introduced in 1961, enabling a large office to maintain its own automatic switching exchange and internal numbers to be dialed directly; and Data-Phone, making it possible for the new wonders of the business world, computers, to communicate with each other via telephone wires.

All these special services were offered for premium charges, and carried their weight on the balance sheet. Meanwhile existing services were being extended almost to their ultimate point. Dial service was available to 97 percent of Bell subscribers by 1960, and direct distance dialing to 80 percent three years later; by 1965, the Bell System could claim to be serving 85 percent of all households in the areas where it operated, as against only 50 percent in 1945. But Kappel was wary about offering new services that did not bring important new revenue. Like Wilson, he was obsessed with the need to improve profits; going beyond Wilson, he repeatedly argued for profits comparable to those of unregulated companies. In his first Annual Report as president he said, "In this rising economy, successful nonregulated industry earns two or three times as much on investment as the Bell companies. . . . The present disparity is certainly greater than it should be." In 1958, a year of record earnings, he hammered at the point again: "Ours is decidedly a growth business. . . . The gap between our earnings and those of unregulated companies continued to widen."

There was one other way to increase earnings besides asking for rate increases, and that was by economizing on service—a process that could be described as either "increasing efficiency" or "degrading service," depending on one's point of view. Some Bell officials maintain that during Kappel's term a conscious decision was made to take some of the desired new profits out of service costs. Some of them remember him saying flatly to a meeting of top Bell brass, shortly after he took office, "The System is giving too much service for the revenues received." An interesting example of how this policy was put into effect concerns a technical system called the line concentrator. One of the most dramatic service changes of the 1950s was the disappearance of the party line from American life; astonishing as it now seems, in 1950 three out of four residence telephones were on party lines, while by 1960 the figure had been reduced to 40 percent and by 1965 to 27 percent. This vast improvement in the efficiency and privacy of customer equipment was somewhat lessened by the widespread introduction in the early 1960s of the line concentrator, which made it possible for only one of a group of dial phones to be used at a time. Thus one of the undesirable features of party-line service was reinstated: although there was now no opportunity to listen in on other people's calls, when a "concentrated" line was in use, other subscribers on it simply couldn't get a dial tone.

In that and other ways, the Bell System in the early 1960s economized on service in the cause of financial "growth." William Sharwell of New York Telephone has put it this way: "It would not be far off the mark to say that a deliberate decision was made to improve earnings by reducing operating costs. I am sure that there was never any specific thought of debasing the service. Think of it in terms of an analogy. A car is supposed to be lubricated every two thousand miles. You say, 'Well, let's try twenty-five hundred.' It still runs, so you try three thousand. Then, on the hottest day of the summer, all of a sudden the oil burns up." Later in the decade, particularly in Sharwell's bailiwick, the oil would burn up, and AT&T as well as its customers would pay the price.[4]

3

The Bell System was getting to be big and complex beyond human imagining. Its annual operating revenues of over ten billion dollars boggled the mind; its stockholder total of three million seemed a fanciful figure; its technology, in the age of the integrated circuits and of such wonders as TASI, the device introduced in 1960 that could double the capacity of ocean cables by contriving to use idle time on one conversation to convey another, was coming to seem something out of science fiction. The public was beginning to react with the suspicion and hostility induced by things too big or complex for comprehension. Around 1954, the AT&T public-relations department mounted an effort to make the Bell System appear "little, local, and lovable." As Mabon, vice-president and assistant to the president, put it later, the campaign "never got off the ground." Realizing that it was up against a hard, unyielding fact, the department went back to its usual practice of seeking to make the Bell System appear fair, kindly, and flexible in *spite* of its bigness.

Public relations and its concomitant, advertising, had, of course, been important activities of AT&T for many years. As we have seen, the first telephone advertisement was printed in May 1877, barely more than a year after the first telephone conversation. Public relations was totally ignored until after the turn of the century, with deleterious results—specifically, until 1903, when AT&T's public image had sunk so low that it finally retained the services of the Boston-based Publicity Bureau, the nation's first public-relations firm. Vail, on his accession to the presidency in 1907, promptly dismissed the Publicity Bureau, ostensibly on grounds that it was claiming credit for work it hadn't done, but perhaps more substantively because Vail—a master of public relations in the broadest sense of that term—knew that he could do the job better himself. By the 1920s, all Bell operating companies maintained public-relations staffs that regularly engaged in persuasion of local newspaper writers and editors, apparently with sometimes striking goals and results; an official of Ohio Bell in that decade stated at a Bell System conference, "The closer we are to a newspaper, the better the chances [the editor] will edit the story and take out some of the sting," and a man from South-western Bell stated flatly that his company planned "to try rate cases in the newspapers" before they even reached the regulatory authorities. Gifford's hiring of Arthur Page in 1927 represented an effort, and a brilliantly successful one, to return Bell "public relations" to the broad standard, emphasizing candid disclosure rather than parochial propaganda, that Vail had established. Over the subsequent years, the objectives and methods of the company's PR and advertising varied from high to medium, depending on who was in charge and how tight a spot the company was in. One trend, though, was in a single direction. As the business grew, so did the advertising and public-relations budget. Overall annual Bell System advertising expenses in the late 1920s and through the Depression varied from about four million to seven million dollars. By the 1970s advertising and PR had become a large budget item, although a smaller percentage of revenues than in most American companies. Apart from the cost of maintaining PR and advertising staffs at AT&T, Western Electric, Bell Labs, and all the operating companies, the Bell System in 1972 spent about eighty million dollars on advertising via newspapers, magazines, radio, and television, the largest single item being the weekly *Bell System Family Theatre* on television.

The question arises, why should a regulated monopoly indulge in advertising and public relations at all? Since telephone rates are based on return on capital, and since return on capital is reduced by higher advertising-PR expenses as it is by any increase of business expenses, isn't the telephone subscriber in effect paying the company to blow its own horn and perhaps try to pull the wool over his eyes? The answer, of course, is the one that all advertising and PR people give at all times: that their activities, on balance, reduce costs by enlarging the market. Paul M. Lund, a former official of the J. Walter Thompson advertising agency who was AT&T's vice-president for public relations and employee information from 1972 until his death in 1975, justified the company's advertising-PR expenses on two bases: information and promotion. As to the former, Lund pointed to, among other things, a special informational campaign regarding the savings obtainable from a customer's using direct distance dialing that, he maintained, saved the Bell System sixty million dollars. As to the latter, he pointed to the fact that in the first eighteen years after 1954, when advertising to promote long-distance calling was begun on a national basis, such calling increased by 323 percent, far more than the increases in U.S. population, number of Bell customers, or disposable personal income, and thus contributed to a substantial reduction in long-distance rates; and that much Bell advertising, such as that urging customers to make calls at night or on weekends, is aimed at helping subscribers to save money rather than to spend it. Lund summed up, "Advertising pays off—for us and for the customer."

Certainly it makes sense, from the user's point of view, for a company offering as bewildering a variety of services at as bewildering a variety of rates as the Bell System did in the 1960s and does now to spend substantial sums in informing the public objectively of exactly what is available for how much. Nor is there any question that statistical studies can be produced to show that the larger markets obtained through promotional activities have resulted in reduced costs. The question is whether the Bell System, or any regulated utility, should be allowed to use company-image advertising, or rate advertising, as an authorized expense for rate-making purposes.[5]

A new program of Kappel's term that turned, unexpectedly, into a public-relations problem of the first order was the introduction of digit dialing—which AT&T preferred to call All Number Calling, or ANC. Since the 1930s, dial telephone numbers in the larger cities had uniformly consisted of two letters, standing for an exchange name, followed by five numerals. In the early postwar years, when dial phones were gradually coming to be almost universal, and when the situation was being complicated by the introduction of direct distance dialing and its three-number area codes, two letters and five numbers finally came to be used for all dial telephones, Bell and independent, so as to create a uniform system amenable to automation for all telephones in the country. But then, as population and telephone use went on increasing, a new problem arose. Mabon has said it was a matter of simple arithmetic: telephone numbers that began with the first two letters of a pronounceable exchange name, and that did not conflict with area-code numbers, were simply running out. Moreover, Bell Labs technicians, looking to the future, foresaw further problems in international direct dialing if letters were involved, resulting from differences in alphabets, dial arrangements, and letter shapes.

The logical solution was to do away with letters entirely and use all-numeral telephone numbers. After generations of using exchange names, it was a radical move, and AT&T approached it gingerly, by degrees. Early in the 1950s, directory listings in several cities began to appear only by letters rather than by the full exchange name—CR 1-2345 instead of CRestview 1-2345. In 1954, *Bell Telephone Magazine* reported "no adverse effect to date." The next step was to introduce new exchange letters that did not stand for a word—TN, say, or XS—and therefore had to be pronounced as letters rather than as a word. Again, little confusion and few protests resulted. At last came all-number telephone numbers, first, in the late 1950s, in a few small towns in both Bell and independent territory, and then, in March 1960, in a good-sized place—the 26,000-telephone Bell installation in Council Bluffs, Iowa.

Emboldened by the increased efficiency brought about by the changeover, and by the apparent absence of strong opposition to it, AT&T moved ahead by introducing ANC on a large scale in California. Beginning with rural areas, about half of all Pacific Telephone & Telegraph's telephones were converted by midsummer 1962, and plans called for the start of conversion in the San Francisco Bay area that fall. And then, quite abruptly, intense public opposition appeared. What had apparently been acceptable to smallish towns seemed to be a good deal less so to large cities. A free-lance public relations man named Carl May, a Quaker and sometime antiwar activist, formed the Anti Digit Dialing League in opposition to what he called the "cult of technology." His first classified advertisement in the San Francisco *Chronicle* brought more than 3,500 replies, and the League was off and running. Moreover, supporters were by no means entirely recruited from the ranks of the eccentrics and radicals who abounded in the Bay Area; they included solid citizens with a wide range of social and political beliefs, among them university professors, a conservative Republican investment counselor, and leading local lawyers. Obviously, May had touched a sensitive nerve; a survey conducted by the *Chronicle* showed that over 80 percent of those polled favored the old system. And as AT&T began introducing ANC in other large cities, the opposition movement spread. In Washington, D.C., there was formed an organization that optimistically called itself the Committee of Ten Million to Oppose All-Number Calling. In New York, although no indigenous organization sprang up, the strong opposition of many to ANC was discernible in letters to newspapers and in press comment. Just as San Francisco loved its KLondike, YUkon, and SUtter, exchange names redolent of the region's past, so New Yorkers cherished SPring, its first exchange name, dating from 1879; its BEekman and RHinelander, named for old local families; its MUrray Hill and CHelsea, named for familiar local neighborhoods; and its BUtterfield 8, describing the heart of the silk-stocking district, and used, as such, as the title of a famous novel by John O'Hara.

The astonishingly intense and bitter fight over ANC, which appears to have taken AT&T largely by surprise, ended in a kind of compromise. In California, which remained the heartland of the opposition, it reached the regulatory authorities; May's League petitioned for a restraining order against further ANC conversions, and in March 1963 the California Public Utilities Commission ruled in favor of Pacific T&T. Nevertheless, the revolt had its effect, and thereafter the Bell System moved more cautiously. By 1966, nearly three-fourths of all telephones in the United States and Canada had ANC numbers; but in some of the big cities where opposition had been strongest, the company had apparently retreated from its original plan to convert all numbers to ANC, and was following a policy of using all numbers for new exchanges while letting old ones continue to be designated by letters. San Francisco still had its KL, YU, and SU. In New York City, AT&T itself set an example by taking an ANC number for its own headquarters in 1961 (393-9800); but in the middle 1970s one still found SP, BE, MU, CH, and BU in the Manhattan Telephone Directory, and many, including some AT&T officials, continued to speak of those exchanges not just by their old initials but by their old names.

Mathematics notwithstanding, AT&T still has misgivings about the ANC conversion. "It may have been a mistake," wrote Kenneth P. Todd, Jr., a long-time Bell System public-relations and advertising man, in a company pamphlet published in 1972. What the company had clearly come to realize by that time was that it had misjudged the public temper and failed to understand the overtones of what it was doing. All Number Calling—it is clear in hindsight—stood in the minds of many for the age of the impersonal, when people live in huge apartment buildings, travel on eight-lane highways, and identify themselves in many places—bank, job, income tax return, credit agency—by numbers, and when computers talk to each other. The impulse against it, irrational but human, was similar to that of the students at Berkeley in 1964 who, in the first of the great campus revolts, carried signs reading "I Am a Person. Do not fold, spindle, or mutilate." Moreover, ANC provided a handy issue to be seized upon by those who already disliked the Bell System for other reasons. It galvanized the opposition. One result of the ANC storm, says Todd, was "a reassessing of the Bell System public relations department's role in the System." In this small but illuminating matter, however, AT&T's failure to grasp the symbolic meaning of what it did for unassailable technical reasons was more than a public-relations failure. It was a measure, perhaps, of the extent to which management, in its necessary and miraculously productive obsession with technology, had lost the larger vision so prized by Theodore Vail.[6]

4

That obsession with technology continued to suit the taste of the military authorities, and to play a large, although gradually decreasing, role in national defense. The main section of the Arctic DEW line radar defense system was completed in 1957, and two extensions—a western Aleutian section and an eastern stretch from Baffin Island all the way to Iceland—in 1959 and 1961, respectively. Kappel maintains that the completion of the DEW line marks the moment when the Bell System was able to turn its primary attention back to telephony; but many military and military-related projects spilled over into the 1960s or were inaugurated then. For example, in 1957, the Nike Hercules program being completed, it was succeeded by a more advanced project, the Nike Zeus, with Western Electric again as prime contractor; in a test made at Kwajalein Atoll in the Pacific in July 1962, a Nike Zeus scored the first successful interception of an intercontinental ballistic missile. In 1958, the first sector of a vast computer-assisted network of air-defense direction centers called SAGE was declared operational, with Western Electric in charge of its engineering. Also in 1958, Western took on the prime contract to build the rearward communications network of a Ballistic Missile Early Warning

System with far-flung stations in Alaska, Greenland, England, Colorado, and Nebraska. BMEWS, as it is called, was finished in 1963. In the Cuban missile crisis of 1962, the Bell System, in eight days of furious activity, added hundreds of new long-distance channels linking various military installations in Florida, flew twenty-one switchboards from Miami to the Florida Keys and put them in operation there, and chartered twenty-two planes to supplement trucks in carrying tons of equipment to the scene of possible action from eight Western Electric factory and warehouse locations. Later in the decade, Western Electric installed and turned over to the North American Air Defense Command a continent-wide military telephone network; built and installed a nine-thousand circuit coast-to-coast blast-resistant telephone cable, designed to withstand nuclear attacks short of direct hits; and, in 1967, topped off the various Nike projects by becoming prime contractor for the Sentinel antiballistic missile system, probably the largest and most complex military defense array ever envisioned.

Concurrently, the Bell System provided much of the communications and guidance systems for the entire United States space exploration program, from the first Explorer satellite in January 1958 to the moon landing in June 1969. In 1962, at the request of national space-program authorities, a new corporation along the lines of Sandia—Bellcomm, situated in Washington, D.C., and jointly owned by AT&T and Western Electric—was formed to provide systems-planning support for the manned space program.[7]

Another space program in which the Bell System was deeply involved both technically and politically, this one calculated to improve terrestrial communications, came almost literally out of science fiction. The idea of using earth satellites as relay stations for an international microwave radiotelephone system was first proposed in a British technical journal in 1945—more than a decade before the first successful earth satellite was launched—by Arthur C. Clarke, then a young scientist and officer of the Royal Air Force and later to become a leading science-fiction writer and coauthor of the celebrated motion picture *2001: A Space Odyssey*. AT&T, finding that rapidly increasing demand for telephone service across the North Atlantic would eventually exceed the capacity provided by cables and ordinary radio circuits, undertook to develop the idea. By the end of the 1950s, a Bell Labs team headed by John R. Pierce had built three prototype communications satellites; since the National Aeronautics and Space Administration had jurisdiction over U.S. space activities, their launching depended on satisfactory arrangements with the government. In December 1959, AT&T flatly asked NASA that it be given title to the entire satellite communications field, with the exclusive right to build and operate a system at its own expense, subject to NASA and FCC regulation. Other communications and aerospace companies howled their objections, and NASA turned the plan down.

With the political fat in the fire, technical progress went on. In August, 1960, NASA successfully launched Echo I, a "passive" communications satellite—that is, one designed to reflect but not actively retransmit signals—consisting of a balloon one hundred feet in diameter with a plastic skin one quarter the thickness of a human hair. AT&T participated in experiments in which messages, including one from President Eisenhower, were successfully sent across the United States and to England and France, thus demonstrating the feasibility of satellite communications. That November, John F. Kennedy was elected to succeed Eisenhower as president; and the following January 19—the very day the new president assumed office—AT&T was at last authorized to launch its satellite, named Telstar, an "active" or retransmitting satellite, for experimental purposes. But the coming of the new administration by no means ended AT&T's political troubles regarding satellite communication. All through that year and most of the next, a battle raged in Washington as to how the system would be organized and controlled. AT&T—its troops led by Kappel, General Counsel Moulton, and Executive Vice-President James E. Dingman—contended that a satellite communications system was only an extension of the existing telephone network—a microwave system in the sky—and that therefore it should be owned and operated entirely by private communications companies. But many senators and congressmen, not to mention many government authorities, maintained that it would be primarily a *space* program, that space was publicly owned, and that therefore a communications satellite system should be publicly owned. Senator Robert Kerr of Oklahoma introduced a bill that would have created a satellite organization favoring private interests, and the administration countered with one favoring public interests.

Kappel has since said that the debate "got to be ridiculous," that it "provides an example of how tough it is for private enterprise to serve the public," and that once, in his frustration, he locked a NASA man in a private office without a phone, to shut him up. At all events, on July 10, 1962, when the debate was at its height, AT&T's Telstar I, powered by a three-stage Delta rocket, was launched into orbit by NASA from Cape Canaveral, Florida. Weighing 170 pounds and containing 1,064 transistors and 1,464 diodes powered by 3,600 solar cells, it had cost $1 million and represented an AT&T research effort of about $50 million, while the launching costs, also borne by AT&T, came to $3 million. The first communications test, conducted on the sixth orbit, fifteen hours after launch, was between AT&T's principal ground station at Andover, Maine, and Washington, D.C. President Kennedy having refused to take part in it because of possible compromise to his political position on satellite control, Kappel at Andover was to talk to Vice-President and Space Coordinator Lyndon Johnson in Washington. The test was almost a disaster, for the homely reason that too many AT&T people (about twenty) were listening in on a terrestrial circuit necessary in preparing for the satellite test, and thereby overloading it. A Bell Labs man in Andover came on and said loudly and authoritatively, "Will everybody please get off this line?" Whereupon Kappel said, via satellite, "This is Fred Kappel talking, calling from the earth station, Andover, Maine." Vice-President Johnson heard him clearly and replied, and communication by earth satellite was a reality.

The Telstar launch and test hastened the debate and the passage of a law. A compromise Communications Satellite Act—creating a new corporation to be called Comsat, sponsored by the government and to be owned half by private communications companies and half by private investors—was put forward and debated fiercely, particularly in the Senate, where ten senators, convinced that the bill represented a giveaway of public resources to private interests, conducted a fourteen-day filibuster against it. This last-ditch effort having failed, the Communications Satellite Act, which had passed the House in May, sailed through the Senate by a vote of sixty-six to eleven on August 1, and was signed into law by President Kennedy on September 1.

The new company was formed that autumn, with its original headquarters at Tregaron, a twenty-two acre Washington estate rented from the heirs of the late Ambassador Joseph E. Davies. Comsat stock—the 50 percent of it designated for public ownership

—was offered for sale to the public for twenty dollars a share on June 2, 1964; although Comsat had no prospect of earnings or dividends for several years, the stock proved instantly popular with investors and particularly speculators, and by December 1962, its market price had soared above 70, three and one-half times the original price. Meanwhile AT&T had bought the 27.5 percent block of Comsat stock to which the act entitled it at the original price—2,895,750 shares for $57,915,000—and had appointed the three Comsat directors (out of a total of fifteen) to which it was entitled—Dingman, Moulton, and Harold M. Botkin, an assistant vice-president in Long Lines.

The history of Comsat since then has been one of almost uninterrupted success, and that of AT&T's relation to Comsat of evolution from part owner (and highly successful investor) to prime customer. In the winter of 1964–65, the Olympic Games in Tokyo were successfully telecast via a NASA satellite, Syncom III, to much of the rest of the world—the first of many athletic events to be thus broadcast live overseas. In April 1965, Comsat orbited its own first satellite—Early Bird, or in French-speaking countries, L'Oiseau Matinal. Commercial telephone service across the North Atlantic via Early Bird began that June 28, with the foreign telephone proprietors (in most cases governments) sharing the revenue with Comsat, just as was done with other international calls. By 1968 Comsat was profitable, and in December 1970 it paid its first quarterly dividend—twelve and a half cents. In 1972 the FCC, reversing its original position on AT&T's relation to Comsat, pressured AT&T to sell its stock and give up its three directorships. After some more wrangling, this was done. The stock sale, made in the spring of 1973, netted $104 million, for a neat profit of $46 million over the cost. Meanwhile Comsat circuits, for the use of which AT&T paid Comsat a fee, had come to be used for nearly half of all international calls. AT&T's transition from part owner to best customer was complete.

Kappel has said with some asperity that he considers the law upon which Comsat is based "about the most bobtailed piece of legislation I ever saw." By way of annotation, Mabon says, "I think Fred just assumed satellite communications would be part of the Bell System—a new technique for Long Lines. I think he was shocked it didn't come out that way." The result marks one more case—after domestic telephone and telegraph early in the century, and radio broadcasting and motion pictures in the 1920s—when the company or parts of it had made serious efforts to establish outright monopolies based on new technology, only to back off or compromise under government pressure.[8]

Of all the new 1960s wonders of telephone technology—satellites, ultramodern Traffic Service Positions for operators, the Picturephone, and so on—the one that gave Bell Labs the most trouble, and unexpectedly became the greatest development effort in Bell System's history, was the perfection of an electronic switching system, or ESS.

It may be recalled that such a system was the specific end in view when the project that had culminated in the invention of the transistor had been launched back in the 1930s. After successful accomplishment of that planned miracle in 1947–8, further delays were brought about by financial stringency and the need for further development of the transistor itself. In the early 1950s, a Labs team began serious work on electronic switching. As early as 1955, Western Electric become involved when five engineers from the Hawthorne works were assigned to collaborate with the Labs on the project. Kappel, in his first Annual Report as president, in the year 1956, wrote confidently, "At Bell Labs, development of the new electronic switching system is going full speed ahead. We are sure this will lead to many improvements in service and also to greater efficiency. The first service trial will start in Morris, Ill., in 1959." Shortly thereafter, Kappel said that the cost of the whole project would probably be $45 million.

But it gradually became apparent that the development of a commercially usable electronic switching system—in effect, a computerized telephone exchange—presented vastly greater technical problems than had been anticipated, and that, accordingly, Bell Labs had vastly underestimated both the time and the investment needed to do the job. The year 1959 passed without the promised first trial at Morris, Illinois; it was finally made in November 1960, and quickly showed how much more work remained to be done. As time dragged on and costs mounted, there was concern at AT&T, and something approaching panic at Bell Labs. But the project had to go forward; by this time the investment was too great to be sacrificed, and in any case, forward projections of increased demand for telephone service indicated that within a few years a time would come when, without the quantum leap in speed and flexibility that electronic switching would provide, the national network would be unable to meet the demand. In November 1963, an all-electronic switching system went into use at the Brown Engineering Company at Cocoa Beach, Florida. But this was a small installation, essentially another test installation, serving only a single company. Kappel's tone on the subject in the 1964 annual report was, for him, almost apologetic: "Electronic switching equipment must be manufactured in volume to unprecedented standards of reliability. . . . To turn out the equipment economically and with good speed, mass production methods must be developed; but, at the same time, there can be no loss of precision. . . ." Another year and millions of dollars later, on May 30, 1965, the first commercial electric central office was put into service at Succasunna, New Jersey.

Even at Succasunna, only 200 of the town's 4,300 subscribers initially had the benefit of electronic switching's added speed and additional services, such as provision for three-party conversations and automatic transfer of incoming calls. But after that, ESS was on its way. In January 1966, the second commercial installation, this one serving 2,900 telephones, went into service in Chase, Maryland. By the end of 1967 there were additional ESS offices in California, Connecticut, Minnesota, Georgia, New York, Michigan, Florida, and Pennsylvania; by the end of 1970 there were 120 offices serving 1.8 million customers; and by 1974 there were 475 offices serving 5.6 million customers. But the development program, when the final figures were added up, was found to have required a staggering four thousand man-years of work at Bell Labs and to have cost not $45 million but $500 million.

The British Post Office, AT&T's counterpart as the telephone authority in Great Britain, meant no compliment to Bell Labs when it commented publicly that the Labs' approach to ESS had been to "take the problem and trample it to death." Warren A. Tyrrell, the Labs' executive director for technical relations, has said that he considers the huge misestimate of the work and cost required to have been the Labs' greatest single mistake, and that living through the whole thing was "a traumatic experience." The lesson, perhaps, is that scientific problems do not always yield readily to being trampled to death. Would a more delicate approach, based more on inventiveness and less on the sheer weight of manpower and resources, have produced electronic switching faster and at a saving of millions or hundreds of millions of dollars to the Bell System and its customers? No one can say. Whatever the case, according to company statisticians the actual service demands of the middle 1970s could not have been met without ESS.[9]

5

As Kappel's term as chief executive wore on, his style remained unchanged. If anything, he became more unguardedly forthright. To the distraction and occasional despair of some of his colleagues, he went on always saying exactly what was in his mind. In particular, he provided an ideal antagonist, and foil, for the chairman-baiters among the "professional" stockholders who regularly attend and speak at the annual meetings of large corporations. After the 1964 annual meeting, the company sent out questionnaires to some four thousand stockholders who had attended, asking for their reactions. Some respondents expressed the opinion that Kappel had been "very impatient, almost rude, in his answers to shareholders' questions," or that he had been "rather aloof from the audience, at times rather sarcastic"; but others praised his dignity and self-control, and 75 percent thought the meeting had been "very or quite worthwhile." Emboldened by this result, Kappel began taking a much harder line with stockholders who asked silly or provocative questions. At the 1965 meeting, in Philadelphia, he allowed himself to remark rather abruptly, "This meeting is not being run by Robert's [Rules of Order], it's being run by me." The following year, in Detroit, after a wrangle with Mrs. Wilma Soss of the Federation of Women Shareholders, he silenced her by summarily having her floor microphone turned off.

Within the company, the catalogue of Kappel anecdotes was growing all the time. The point of them was usually that just under his habitual bluster lay a willingness to listen to reason, and even to defend ideas that he did not hold himself. Less than wholly sympathetic to Craig's and Greenleaf's liberal-education-for-executives programs, he encouraged their cutback until they were down to a single one—an eight-week summer course at Dartmouth, chiefly business-related as to subject matter and involving evaluation as well as training of its executive-students, which ran from 1959 until 1964. Far from denigrating this program, Kappel actively defended it against revolts within the company. Once Greenleaf, who was in immediate charge of it, picked up his phone and heard Kappel ask, without introduction, "What are all those preachers doing in our program?" Greenleaf, who had arranged to have several clergymen engage in discussions with the Dartmouth group, replied that the point was to expose the executive-students to various modern ethical viewpoints. "O.K., that's what I wanted to know," Kappel said, and abruptly hung up. On another occasion, when Robert Heilbroner, the radical economist, had been scheduled to lecture in the Dartmouth program, conservative elements within AT&T raised such a storm that eventually the matter was brought up by one of them in the Cabinet itself. Kappel cut off the discussion with the comment, "Now look, we're doing what we ought to do up there, and I don't want to hear any more about it."[10]

Suddenly, in the middle of the decade, when most things were going as smoothly for AT&T as they had ever gone in its history, there arose a new challenge to the company that gave ample occasion for Kappel fireworks. It concerned federal regulation of interstate and overseas telephone rates by the FCC. Such regulation, along with state regulation of intrastate rates, had been—and continues to be—a bone of contention. Critics maintained, with some evidence to support them, that regulatory commissionships, state and federal, too often went to politicians who had no particular qualifications for the job, and that once in office, such commissioners were too often prone to form "cozy relationships" with telephone-company officials, the result being that regulation lacked stringency or even substance. (A Ralph Nader task force report in 1973 went so far as to suggest that nominal telephone regulation exists solely to provide a rationale for granting the telephone industry antitrust exemption.) AT&T, on the other hand, often maintained that the problem was the exact opposite—that is, that commissioners too often took an anticompany stand on the basis of political considerations rather than the public interest. Both sides, at any rate, agreed that Vail's ideal of a "jury concept" of regulation had too seldom been realized.

In fact, from the time of the FCC's creation in 1934 until the middle 1960s, it had not actually set interstate telephone rates; indeed, it had not even suggested a percentage return on capital that AT&T should be allowed. The regulatory procedure was based on informal negotiations, and the informal limit for return on capital was about 8 percent. When AT&T's return approached that figure, FCC and AT&T men would sit down together and hammer out an agreement acceptable to both sides. Such agreements resulted in Long Lines rate reductions in 1963 and 1964, among many other years. In 1963 the FCC got a new chairman, who soon became convinced that the procedure should be changed. He was E. William Henry, a graduate of Yale University and Vanderbilt Law School, a friend of Robert Kennedy, a former campaign worker for John Kennedy, and at thirty-four, the youngest man ever to head the FCC. Following his first round of horse-trading with AT&T, Henry decided that such negotiation was no proper was to make a "reasoned judgment" about rates, and notified AT&T to that effect. AT&T objected, and in 1964 there was an informal, unpublicized two-day session between the two sides, out of which no substantial agreement emerged. During 1965, pressure from within the FCC and from political forces outside it began building for something the FCC had not undertaken since the days of Commissioner Walker—a full-scale, on-the-record investigation of interstate rates with a view to determining what constituted a fair return and precisely how the rate base should be calculated. Knowing in general what was in the wind, Kappel in mid-October went to Washington, where he met with Henry, as well as several other FCC commissioners. Kappel said that AT&T was poised for further growth, and that he did not want to see the prospect disturbed by the adverse publicity that would come with a public investigation. He asked Henry for more time for AT&T to collect and submit pertinent data. Henry replied that that sounded reasonable; however, the same afternoon, after Kappel had left to return to New York, Henry by his own account changed his mind, decided that an investigation must begin immediately, and so notified AT&T's Washington vice-president, Edward B. Crosland. Arriving back in New York, Kappel—before he could be reached by Crosland—learned that the investigation was to go forward, and concluded that he had been double-crossed.

Thus the great FCC rate inquiry—which is still in progress as this is written, more than a decade later—began in an atmosphere of rancor. On October 27, when the investigation was formally announced, Kappel promptly said that it was "totally unwar-

ranted and unnecessary," and went on, "The telephone-using public will be the loser. . . . There are no interstate problems confronting the FCC that could not be resolved faster and with far
less expense by means other than the sweeping action taken by the
Commission." The following day, AT&T stock dropped 1½ points
to just above 65—its lowest price since 1963. On November 2,
AT&T, calling the order for the investigation an "arbitrary repudi-
ation" of methods that had worked for thirty years, asked the FCC
to revoke it; just before Christmas the FCC, by a five-to-one vote,
turned down the request. Three days later, when Kappel was
asked by a reporter whether AT&T had formed a "battle group"
headed by Dingman to fight the investigation, he replied, "You
can call it anything you want." Commenting on AT&T's reaction to
the whole affair, an FCC spokesman said that AT&T people had
acted like "stuck pigs." Early in January 1966, Kappel and Henry
had a confrontation in New York, the details of which the two men
disagree about. In Kappel's version, when Henry came to his New
York office to explain the manner of the October announcement,
"He talked and said nothing. I said, 'A liar to me is a liar.' Then I
offered him a ride to the airport in my car, which he refused."
Henry says he had previously heard from a government colleague
in Washington that Kappel had called him a liar, that he had come
to New York for the purpose of straightening the matter out, and
that nothing of the sort was said in the New York meeting. Either
way, AT&T–FCC relations started the year 1966 at a new low.

The investigation, with which AT&T cooperated extensively
as to testimony and documents, moved forward. In the hearings,
and in its 1966 Annual Report, the company contended that its
return on capital should be at least in the range of 8 percent to
provide "excellent and continuously improving telephone service
at low cost" and "a capital structure appropriate to the risks of our
business." (Since AT&T's overall rate of return for that year was
7.91 percent, the request was in effect for a sanctioning of the
status quo.) In April 1967, the FCC completed hearings in Phase
IA of the inquiry, the phase concerned with rate of return. In July
of that year, it announced its interim decision calling for an interstate rate of return in the range of 7–7.5 percent and a concomitant
reduction of Bell interstate revenues of $120 million per year. In
September, following an AT&T appeal, the FCC backed off somewhat, asserting that its July decision did not place an "arbitrary

ceiling" on the Bell rate of return. In other words, it wasn't a binding order. That October, the FCC moved on to what is called Phase IB, concerned with AT&T's rate-making principles. As for Kappel, he stuck to his point of view, remarking much later, "That damn investigation has been a false alarm. It affected AT&T financing, lowered the level of our thinking, and diminished the total effectiveness of our management. I'd hate to know what it has cost our customers."[11]

## 6

Unlike most of the chief executives who had preceded him, Kappel remained in office until the last day he was eligible to do so under AT&T's mandatory retirement-at-sixty-five policy: January 31, 1967, when he was succeeded by H. I. Romnes, who came to the job, as Kappel had done, as a former president of Western Electric.

In Kappel's last year, it was clear that, through no particular fault of his, the financial good times that had prevailed for the company during his tenure were coming to an end. A whole complex of forces—a national money crunch with resulting high interest rates, a rapid rise of material and labor costs, and to a lesser extent the economic effects of the FCC's greater militancy—were combining to reduce AT&T's rate of annual earnings growth, which had totaled 35 percent over Kappel's last five years in office and would come to only 8 percent over the next five years.[12] There is evidence that in some respects Kappel had helped sow a wind that Romnes would reap as a whirlwind. But in his bull-like way Kappel had exuberantly dominated an exuberant period, and he went out of office as he had gone in, saying exactly what he thought—as Greenleaf said, kind of a ham, but with elements of greatness.

CHAPTER 12

# Days of Wrath

Haakon Ingolf ("Hi") Romnes, chief executive for only five years—1967–72—has an important place in AT&T history, and indeed in American social history, as the man who guided the company and its million employees through some of the most troubled of American times. In background and character, he presents a study in comparison and contrast to Kappel. Like Kappel, he was a thoroughgoing Midwesterner (born in Stoughton, Wisconsin, to parents of Norwegian ancestry) and an engineering graduate of his home state's university. Like Kappel, he started his Bell System career soon after his graduation in a low-level job with his local Bell company (he had previously worked as an assistant in his father's bakery business), and went on to become president of Western Electric, a position he held from 1959 until 1964. Quite unlike Kappel, however, he was relatively colorless in outward appearance—slow to anger, soft of speech, and gentle in demeanor.

Romnes was an engineer through and through, and yet an engineer acutely aware of the traditional humanistic deficiencies of followers of that calling, and anxious to correct them in his own case. As early as 1961, when president of Western Electric, he was insisting in public speeches that "increasingly, we are finding it necessary to take account of complex social, economic, even political factors which do not figure in the contents of the Engineers' Handbook," and urging all businessmen, engineers or not, to assume greater responsibility for meeting the social and economic problems of comunities. In 1963 he said, "Equal employment opportunity makes good business sense." (In 1960 the Bell System employee rolls, totaling 735,000, included only about 29,-000 nonwhites, or less than 4 percent, and comparatively little, certainly by later standards, was being done about either that low percentage or about community problems.) In 1970, in an address to the Telephone Pioneers of America, he spoke of "one final ingredient that will serve us well as we marshal our strength for the tasks ahead. Our children—unabashedly—call it Love. We who are inclined to be somewhat more reserved in the use of that term might choose to call it fellowship or mutual respect or concern for one another." It would be an interesting, if perhaps frustrating, exercise to search for the word "love" in public utterances of other top business executives, past or present. Romnes' use of it suggests the sort of engineer he had come to be by 1970. As to his high-minded utterances of earlier years, his years as chief executive would provide the test of whether they represented conviction or rhetoric.

An acute social problem involving telephones and their use —a harbinger of many others to come—began to be a serious matter in the middle 1960s. It was the use of the telephone for the purpose of conveying abusive, obscene, or threatening messages to strangers, usually women. Two factors, one technological and one sociological, seem to have contributed to this sinister effulgence. For one thing, the rapid changeover of party lines to private lines in the years around 1960 increased the caller's privacy and therefore decreased his risk of being caught and prosecuted. For the other, the disorganization of American society and the weakening of American social norms that took place in the years after the assassination of President Kennedy created conditions in which various forms of antisocial activity could flourish. The venom of the poisoned, the bad blood of society, was spread through the national blood vessels of the telephone network.

By 1965, the problem had reached such proportions that AT&T took notice of it in the Annual Report for that year, Kappel declaring, "We want it known that in every instance we are anxious to help and will do so to the limit of our ability. . . . We shall take every appropriate action." The problem, of course, was that the victim of an abusive call could seldom notify the police or the telephone company without first hanging up, and the process of tracing the call could not begin until after the connection had been broken. Beginning late in 1965, Bell companies began offering a device named "called-party holding," enabling the victim to push a button that simultaneously notifies the central office and locks the circuit, enabling the calling telephone to be traced even after the caller has hung up. This led to many arrests and convictions. However, in 1966 the Bell System received 375,000 complaints of obscene or abusive calls, in spite of an intensive advertising campaign advising subscribers how to deal with them, and many states still had no specific laws against such calls. Since then, legislation has been stiffened and telephone tracing devices have been improved, but the problem persists. A leading psychiatrist explained in a 1968 article that making obscene calls was a symptom of an emotional disorder closely related to exhibitionism. That, however, was cold comfort to victims, whose understanding of the psychodynamics could scarcely help them short of finding a way to get the abusive callers into the psychiatrist's care.[1]

Simultaneously, in the middle 1960s, beginning in particular with the riots in the Watts section of Los Angeles in 1965, race relations in the nation's large cities degenerated at an alarming rate. The telephone business by its nature being concentrated where people are concentrated, the urban crisis was inevitably very much AT&T's business. Leaving aside the matters of moral responsibility that Romnes had been addressing himself to, the company was physically right on the firing line. Attacks on Bell System equipment and even threats to telephone installers and repairmen working in black urban areas came to be commonplace. The company—traditionally white-oriented and comparatively complacent about racial matters—reacted slowly, but in the end forcefully. In 1967, Western Electric, whose installers and maintenance men were always at work in all cities, launched a variety of programs aimed directly at urban social and economic crises, including job-training programs for the unemployed, the majority of them black, in Newark, Los Angeles, Chicago, Phoenix, and other cities. That year's Annual Report was the first ever to discuss the problem directly. "Nearly three-quarters of our business is done in urban areas," it said. "The future of the Bell

System . . . depends largely on the sound development of urban life . . . Our greatest opportunity and responsibility, we believe, lie in the areas of education and unemployment. Training and jobs . . . We are also expanding employee training that aims to increase respect among people of different race." Early in 1968, Romnes in a speech publicly set forth the company's objectives in cities: an expanding effort to redesign existing jobs to make them more satisfying; encouragement of voluntary community services by employees; and "commitment to provide equal opportunity in employment and, beyond that, to hire, train, and develop men and women who are not qualified according to traditional or conventional employment standards."

At the end of the decade, the results of these commitments began to be seen. In 1968, the Bell companies took on about five thousand students classified as hard-core unemployed as temporary summer workers, committed themselves to a program to hire six thousand other persons so classified over a two-year period, and set up a new Western Electric assembly plant in a slum area of Newark specifically to employ hard-core jobless. By the end of 1970, minority employees in the Bell System at last amounted to about the same percentage as in the national population. However remarkable an achievement this turnaround in a few years represented, it was unsatisfactory to federal authorities. In December 1970, the Equal Employment Opportunity Commission, created by legislation in 1965, intervened with the FCC, asking it to deny AT&T's pending request for interstate rate increases until the company ended its alleged discrimination in employment practices against both racial minorities and women. Romnes called the charges "outrageous" and insisted that "in the field of equal employment we have been leaders, not followers." But the ironical fact was that AT&T, in the very moment when for the first time in its history it had achieved anything approaching such leadership, was for the first time in its history formally accused of being a laggard.[2]

2

Romnes was scarcely settled in office when the Bell System faced its worst operational crisis since the two-phone era at the beginning of the century: the service failures of 1969–70.

In New York City, one of the most acute and by far the most visible of the problem areas, the trouble was triggered by an unprecedented and unanticipated rise in demand for service, brought about partly by a favorable national economic situation and partly by local factors. One of the latter was an astonishing and unpredicted rise in trading volume on the New York Stock Exchange, with 20-million-share days, previously unknown, suddenly becoming common by late 1968. Since each trade almost certainly involved at least one telephone call and some involved many, the effect on demand for service in the Wall Street district was enormous. Another factor was a decision of the local welfare authorities in 1968 that the cost of local telephone service could be included in welfare payments, leading to a sudden huge increase in requests for new telephone installations. A third, less measurable factor—cited by, among others, John D. deButts, then AT&T's vice-chairman of the board—may have been the pervasive fear of crime that was gripping New York City citizens at that time, leading, presumably, to more telephone calls at night in lieu of visits. At all events, from whatever cause, 191,400 new phones were installed in New York City in 1968, almost 50,000 more than in 1967. New York Telephone at the time was under strong pressure from AT&T to improve its earnings and concomitantly reluctant to make drastic increases in its construction and maintenance budget; accordingly, about half of these new connections were made by improvising on existing facilities rather than by installing new circuits.

The first actual service difficulties, becoming serious around the beginning of 1969, resulted from no fault of the telephone company. They were caused by an appalling increase in thievery and vandalism of public pay telephones—an effect, it seems safe to conclude, of the mood of violent revolt, particularly among the young, that characterized that time and place. By February 1969, an average 35,000 of New York City's 100,000 pay phones were being wrecked each month, at least 25 percent of them were out of order at any given time, and the company was losing at a rate of $5 million a year in repairs and stolen coins. But then the ill effects of overloaded circuits began to be felt. Callers began to have to wait for dial tone, sometimes as much as two or three minutes. Calls began to fail to get through; after dialing, the caller would get a false busy signal, or else just a dead line (a condition described in telephone circles as "high and dry").

Cross talk, false rings, and incorrect bills became common. The situation came to a dramatic climax in July 1969, with the almost total failure of PLaza 8, a key exchange in the heart of the city's commercial district. All of the 10,400 phones on that exchange were entirely out of service for the major part of the business day for several weeks. On July 14, Benton & Bowles, the advertising agency, took a full-page ad in *The New York Times* over the names of the firm's 801 employees, saying, "These are the people you haven't been able to reach at PLaza 8-6200." New York Telephone, and the Bell System, were publicly chagrined.

The man in overall charge of New York Telephone's affairs was Cornelius W. Owens, a one-time Boston College football star who had been president of the company since 1965 and was known as the apple of Kappel's eye. But the man most constantly and intricately involved in the service crisis—the man, so to speak, at the eye of the hurricane—was William G. Sharwell, who had assumed the key position of vice-president for operations on November 1, 1968, just as the failures were beginning. Sharwell was that comparative anomaly among operating-company executives, an intellectual; he had once been a professor at Seton Hall University and, within the Bell System, was a staff-trained man strong on what Greenleaf liked to call "conceptual" ability, who had, in fact, been a Greenleaf protégé when he had served in management research at AT&T in the late 1950s. When the service overload began developing, Sharwell's first decision—which he now describes as a bad mistake—was to install the demanded new telephones first and worry about switching-center overloads second. "If I had it to do again," Sharwell says, "I'd say to those requesting new phones, 'I'm sorry, I'm going to take care of my present customers first.' " As things were, the problem that arose out of the new installations was essentially one of hardware— simply not enough switching capacity. But it was also one of personnel. Partly as a result of cost-saving programs of the preceding years, New York Telephone was caught with a salary scale somewhat below the market at the craft level: $95 a week to start as a repairman, with a potential of $184 a week after six years. As a result of this and other factors, the rate of turnover was high to the point of absurdity: 50 percent of repairmen in New York were leaving within two years, while the average time required to become expert in their work was three years. As to operators, more than half of all of them in New York City were quitting their jobs each year, with the result that new replacements, many of them primarily Spanish-speaking, were too inexperienced to cope with the city's geography, its bewildering variety of speech accents, or other intricacies of their jobs. The price of cost-cutting was being paid by everybody.

Ironically, the PLaza 8 exchange that failed so spectacularly was not an old panel or crossbar, but one of the pioneer experimental installations of the lightning-fast electronic switching system. The problem was lack of technical experience. No ESS had ever been subjected to overload; it now turned out that, unlike a panel or crossbar office, which was known to overload gradually, giving warning signals all along the way, an overloaded ESS went out virtually all at once. Sharwell, following the failure and the advertisement, went personally to apologize to the chairman of Benton & Bowles. "It was a pretty traumatic experience," he has since said. "What can you tell a man in those circumstances? That you're sorry you caused him trouble? There was no valid explanation." Two weeks later, New York Telephone announced that it was bringing in fifteen hundred out-of-town workmen from other operating companies to help out until service was back to normal, and putting local workers on heavy overtime schedules. The local workers resented the coming of the outsiders, the company had to spend one million dollars per month for food and hotel expenses for the emergency help, and its payroll costs jumped about 30 percent; but the work went forward. In an unprecedented maintenance operation, the entire main frame of the PLaza 8 exchange was replaced, and within a few weeks it was operating nearly normally.

But the New York service crisis was not over; in the later months of 1969 and the early ones of 1970, it struck many parts of the city that had previously been unaffected. A kind of surrealistic telephone chaos reigned, all too suggestive of a world run mad. People would pick up their telephones and hear several strangers talking among themselves—first shouting, "Get off my line!" and finally, in despair, laughing and engaging in get-acquainted conversations. Subscribers who had made only local calls would find on their monthly bills that they had been charged for calls to San Francisco or Honolulu. (In such cases, New York Telephone not only admitted its error on the long-distance charges, but often remitted that month's basic charge for local service.) Jokes about telephone snarls became sure laugh-getters in Broadway and cabaret skits. But the matter was not funny to many telephone subscribers, and certainly not to New York Telephone or the Bell System, which were losing day by day a reputation built up over almost a century. Some company officials went into a state of shocked disbelief that such a thing could be happening. Henry M. Boettinger, head of AT&T's Management Sciences Division, explained to a reporter, "You have to understand the heroic ego. There is an unwillingness to admit that there's anything we can't do." "At this writing, not all our service difficulties have been eliminated," Romnes wrote grimly in the 1969 Annual Report. "But we are making good progress. The job will get done." At New York Telephone there was some wavering as to how to handle the all but insurmountable public-relations problem—whether to put a good face on things or admit how bad they were. In December 1969, President Owens denied that the situation was a "breakdown," insisting that it was an "episode" amounting to "pockets of trouble in some critical areas." But the following month Vice-President Sharwell said flatly in a *New York Times* interview what everyone knew to be true—that service in New York City was "lousy." As a result, he maintains, some within the company refused to speak to him for a long time thereafter.

In 1970, as the New York City crisis gradually abated, troubles cropped up in other areas, again set off by unprecedented and unpredicted demands for service. The various operating companies, alerted by the New York situation, had scrambled to head off similar troubles in their own areas, with some success. But the deluge of calls was too great, and over the next two years there were service snarls in Boston, where the troubles were almost as serious as in New York, and lasted longer; Denver, where the repair and reconstruction methods developed in New York were not applicable, because most of the exchanges were of the old step-by-step type rather than more advanced models; and Houston, where the problems were similar to Denver's but complicated by a high water table that resulted in wet cables.

What, apart from unexpected service demands, caused it all, and could it have been prevented? In general, Bell System people answer to the first question, "Many things," and to the second, "Just possibly." The most obvious culprit—bad forecasting of service demands—is generally dismissed as a primary cause. New York Telephone's forecasts of demand for new telephones proved to be 14 percent too high for 1966, 19 percent too high for 1967, and 20 percent too low for 1968—certainly not a consistent pattern of underestimates. Neither the rise in Stock Exchange trading nor the change in welfare rules could have been anticipated. Sharwell says that the New York City network, being unique in many ways, did not fit the Bell System statistical models; as a result, "If you look at the prior statistics now, in hindsight you get a message of problems coming. The trouble is that at the time, you read the statistics subjectively." The referee in a subsequent stockholder-derivative suit against AT&T in connection with the service crisis concluded that "New York Telephone's forecasting procedures were reasonable and . . . would have been correct but for an extraordinary upsurge in telephone demands."

The suggestion has been made, and concurred in to some extent by some Bell Labs men, that the Labs, as the visionary dreamer as well as the technical innovator of AT&T, should have seen what was coming and set its vast creative resources to the task of preventing disaster. The Labs' most recent historian, Prescott Mabon, has suggested that in the middle 1960s the Labs were so preoccupied with the new high technology that they may have given insufficient attention to mundane problems involving current telephone-operating equipment. The point is, obviously, debatable. Somewhat more measurable is the conclusion, put forward by many within the Bell System, that the service crisis can in part be traced back to a policy pursued in the Kappel years of seeking to take increased profits out of service costs rather than out of increased rates. In a lecture-demonstration presented at an AT&T Presidents' Conference in April 1973, Jack A. Baird, AT&T vice-president for engineering, and James E. Olson, then president of Indiana Bell, concluded that "the common denominator [of all the service failures] was a degraded switching network" and that "unrealistic replacement programs had encouraged reduced maintenance effort." Thus—if we are to accept the conclusions of two key Bell system officials who had made a close study of the subject—the Bell System had faced a hard dilemma and made an honorable but losing gamble. Needing higher earnings to maintain its financial stability, it had rejected the course of seeking higher rates and chosen that of taking the earnings in part out of service costs. To some extent, that decision had contributed to the service failures of 1967–70. (By no means all top Bell System officials share the conclusions implicit in the Baird-Olson report. Kenneth G. McKay, a key vice-president of Bell Labs from 1962 to 1966, vice-president for engineering of AT&T from 1966 to 1973, and thereafter executive vice-president of the Labs, insists that all through the 1960s the Bell System never wavered from its traditional commitment to service first; that the attribution of the service failures in any part to maintenance cost-cutting is "too simplistic"; and that the Baird-Olson paper must be read as an internal propaganda document designed to warn against any skimping on service expenditures by the operating companies in the future.)

To whatever extent the Bell System's policies share the blame for causing the crisis, its performance in ending it was magnificent. In New York, Western Electric set up a "war room" to expedite orders for new equipment and negotiate to have quantities of it diverted to New York Telephone from other companies—a huge operation on the style and scale of what would be done in case of a national disaster. Bell Labs sent an expert team from its Network Planning division at Holmdel, headed by Network Planning Director Irwin Dorros, to New York to live and work directly with New York Telephone for about a year, applying their technical expertise to assessing the problems and designing near-term solutions under conditions that Dorros described as "fighting a war." Where new circuitry was called for, the problem was flashed back to Holmdel, and sometimes a new circuit was designed there, under emergency conditions, over a weekend. Sharwell, at New York Telephone, found AT&T willing and ready to commit unlimited resources to the quick and permanent solution of the problems. He says, "We needed a cornucopia and we got one. Their attitude was simply, 'How much do you need?'" Baird and Olson estimated that additional expenses incurred as a result of service problems in downstate New York over the years 1969–72 amounted to more than $110 million; over those years, the physical plant in New York City was virtually rebuilt. In the other trouble-spot cities, comparable mobilizations of resources were made, and the methods developed in New York were applied insofar as possible.

Gradually, adequate service was restored everywhere. Romnes could write in the 1971 AT&T Annual Report, "Service difficulties that derive from insufficient capacity have for the most part been eliminated or will be soon," although problems reflecting an inexperienced work force remained. In the 1972 report he could discuss service as being back to normal. Sharwell, perhaps summing up the sentiments of many others who found themselves on the firing line, says now, "Those were back-breaking years. I wouldn't give up the experience, but I don't think I could go through it again."

Some Bell System people, Sharwell among them, fear that the lessons of the service crisis have been insufficiently learned within the Bell System. It does seem safe to say that the corporate trauma caused by the crisis has served to foreclose the option of "taking increased earnings out of service" for a long time to come. One area where the lessons appear to have been learned is at Bell Labs. The great invention factory, the most complex and crucial of whose products had suffered a partial breakdown of previously unimaginable proportions, reacted by making a distinct turn away from wild-blue-yonder long-range research and toward day-to-day mingling in the work of operating companies. Soon after the crisis, the Labs began putting new emphasis on keeping Labs task forces constantly at work in each of the operating companies; and to symbolize the change in attitude, an old administrative protocol under which Bell Labs men talked to the operating companies only in the presence of someone from AT&T was abolished to allow direct contact. Would such close coordination between thinkers and doers, so long delayed in coming about, prevent what had happened from ever happening again? Bell Labs men, at least, believed that it would.[3]

3

As the new decade began, along with service troubles AT&T faced social problems stemming from those that afflicted the nation at large. In the spring of 1970—that crucial year of ferment, particularly as regards continuing American military involvement in Vietnam—Romnes found himself conducting the annual stockholders' meeting in Cleveland while more than two thousand young people marched outside, shouting their opposition to the war and AT&T's alleged complicity in it. In the meeting, Romnes responded to them with forthrightness. The Bell System's work for the military, he said, was almost exclusively in the field of communications, and accounted for only four cents of that year's net earnings of four dollars per share. Nor did the Bell System seek out military work: "We never are pounding on the doors in Washington looking for work in this area." Why, then, did the Bell System undertake any at all? "Because—and simply because —it is a responsibility we owe the country." The protesters were not placated. A month later, when United States troops undertook the instantly unpopular invasion of Cambodia, both Bell System employees and outside citizens, most of the latter students, began besieging Romnes with requests that he, as head of the largest American corporation, take an explicit stand against further American participation in the war. He tried to answer every letter from outside, and as to Bell employees, he had what he later described as an "earnest and extended discussion" with a delegation consisting of eight of their representatives. "I am afraid," Romnes said later, "that in neither instance were my answers fully satisfactory. I can only repeat what I told them— that whatever I might say about the war would be inevitably construed as the views of the business I head, and that—on matters that are beyond our competence as a corporation—I do not believe I have the right to make such a commitment." To make one, Romnes felt, would be not only unfair to those within the Bell System who held opposing views, but also a misuse of AT&T's great economic power. The point, of course, is an arguable one philosophically; but no one can question, or did question, Romnes' sincerity or candor in facing the issue.[4]

Apart from the problem of defining the corporation's role as a public citizen, as the 1970s began, the dovetailing problems of financing and regulation were becoming more acute. Having asked in 1966 for a rate of return of 8 percent on total capital and been granted up to 7.5 percent in the FCC interim decision of 1967, AT&T soon came to feel that, what with changed conditions, it had to raise its demands. By 1968, with enormously increased costs of material and labor and skyrocketing demands for telephone service, the Bell System was finding that it needed to raise $1.5 billion a year in the financial markets, and since the price of the stock was now lagging so badly as to making equity financing all but impossible, that sum had to be raised by borrowing, the average interest cost of which in 1968 was 6.61 percent and by 1970 would reach 8.7 percent. Early in 1969, Romnes announced that "under these circumstances past views of what constitutes a proper rate of return on telephone investment are no longer appropriate" and that AT&T was now asking the regulatory authorities for at least 8.5 percent. The FCC's immediate response was to concede that factors other than cost— that is, market conditions and competitive prospects—might properly be taken into account in establishing rate levels for interstate service. This evidence of greater regulatory flexibility was followed in 1970—a year when AT&T carried out its largest construction program in history, and paid, at the maximum, an unprecedented 9.43 percent for the money to finance it—by the granting of FCC permission for interim rate adjustments that would produce some $250 million per year in net earnings before taxes. At the same time, public service commissions in many states allowed local rate increases—in almost all cases, the first in a decade or more.

But from AT&T's point of view, earnings were still far from adequate because they did not make possible financing by the sale of stock. The failure of the 1970 warrants issue to raise a significant amount of new equity capital was an eloquent demonstration of this fact. Earnings, after years of rising briskly for years, had become "flat"—$4 per share for 1969, $3.99 for 1970, $3.99 for 1971—and under such conditions, investors became increasingly reluctant to buy AT&T stock, whose price, which had reached 75 in 1964, sank in the 1970 bear market to a low of 40⅜. The resulting constant recourse to debt financing meant a steady rise in the proportion of debt in AT&T's total capital—from about 35 percent in 1967 to over 47 percent in 1972. This trend was strongly encouraged by the regulators, because it automatically contributed to an increased rate of return on equity capital (although not on total capital), but was viewed more uneasily by the company because it entailed a shift from a safe "sleep well" financial stance to a riskier "eat well" posture.

To some extent, the problems of Leroy Wilson's time had returned—and Romnes was no ruthless rate-getter like Wilson. In fact, under the influence of better business conditions and the enforced "eat well" financial policy, AT&T's net earnings would rise again fairly briskly in the years 1972 through 1974. But investors would continue to keep AT&T stock at arm's length, and its price would stubbornly remain at around 50 or lower. As a result, continued massive debt financing would be necessary, the ratio of debt in capital would rise in 1975 to above 50 percent for the first time since 1949, and in July 1975 would come the stimulating, but by implication ominous, innovation of the sale of a $100 million AT&T note issue to the government of a foreign power, Saudi Arabia. The implication, of course, was that the domestic supply of funds to pay for the American telephone system was diminishing. Where money would come from in the future, and at what cost, was very much a question.[5]

Meanwhile a new problem was coming up fast—or, rather, an old one was making a reappearance. The Kingsbury Commitment of 1913 and the Communications Act of 1934 had established, presumably once and for all, the principle that the telephone industry operated best in the public interest under a system of regulated monopoly rather than one of competition. The federal antitrust suit of 1949–56 had been a huge and explicit attempt to reestablish competition in the supply of telephone equipment; but it had failed. Following that failure, the FCC, in a gradual reversal of previous policy, began encouraging competition in various areas of the telephone business—specifically, at first, as to the right of subscribers to attach non-Bell equipment to Bell lines.

Prior to 1968, attachment of almost all such equipment was for practical purposes illegal. Bell System "tariffs"—regulations as to the cost and conditions of its service, approved by the state and federal regulators—provided flatly that the telephone company had the right to deny service to any subscriber found to have attached foreign equipment to his line, on grounds that such attachment might damage the delicate mechanism of the whole network. Thus the Bell System and the independent companies had a firm monopoly on customer equipment. In 1955, the FCC decided regarding the Hush-a-Phone—a silencer fitted onto a telephone mouthpiece, designed to permit a caller to speak normally into the mouthpiece without being overheard by others in the room—that since the Hush-a-Phone was a purely acoustic device not attached electrically to the telephone network, AT&T could no longer outlaw its use on Bell telephones. The decision was set aside by the Court of Appeals in Washington, D.C., in 1956. Nevertheless, the Hush-a-Phone case tended to establish the subscriber's right to attach his own nondetrimental equipment to Bell lines, and thus served as an interim wedge for the introduction of competition in terminal equipment.

During the late 1950s and early 1960s, a sizable bootleg business sprang up in customer telephone equipment, mainly antique or colored phones, that was sold directly to telephone subscribers and then attached illegally to their lines. The Bell companies, when they found such attachments, would disconnect them and in some cases exercise their right to terminate the offending customer's service. But in many cases they did not find them. An antique-phone dealer on Sixth Avenue in New York reported openly and happily in 1962 that he was selling four hundred instruments a month. Many customers began to feel that they had a right to own their own telephones, and the Bell System became increasingly concerned about the technical integrity of its network—and looking further ahead, its revenues. The issue came to a head in the case of the Carterfone, a device manufactured by Carter Electronics Corporation of Dallas, Texas, to interconnect private two-way radios with the telephone system via a base station. The Carterfone, although basically acoustical like the Hush-a-Phone, also involved some electrical connection, and thus went to the heart of the issue. In June 1968, the FCC in deciding that the Carterfone could be connected to Bell lines without rendering the user subject to disconnection, struck down existing interstate tariffs prohibiting attachment to the public telephone system of customer-owned equipment. Such attachment was now permitted, provided only that the telephone company be allowed to install protective equipment between the line and the alien device.

General Counsel Moulton, chief of the AT&T legal team that argued against the Carterfone decision, says of it, "That's one I'd rather forget," and adds that it is "a fair question" whether AT&T could have headed off the far-reaching decision by amending its tariff in advance. Such a move, he concedes, would have required a revolution in thinking inside AT&T, which believed— and indeed had long been encouraged to believe—that the public consensus favored treating the telephone business in all its aspects as a regulated monopoly. At all events, the floodgates were now opening to competition in supply of customer equipment, and what had seemed a comparatively trivial problem in the 1960s became a great one in the 1970s. A small but flourishing new industry, the so-called "interconnect industry," arose to supply customer-owned telephone equipment to be connected to the existing Bell and independent networks. By the end of 1970, competitors' equipment was being used in almost 1 percent of private office telephone exchanges in the Bell companies' territory. Romnes summed up AT&T's attitude as expressed to the FCC: "If you find it in the public interest to open up these sectors of telecommunications to competition, then it's all right with us so long as you make the ground rules the same for all parties, including us."

In other words, AT&T, although it had argued as vigorously as possible against the Carterfone decision, now felt able to live with it. But the FCC pushed on further. In May 1970, in another reversal of previous policy, it decided that the public interest would be served by allowing independent companies—called "specialized common carriers"—to set up intercity microwave relay systems for private leased-line telephone use by businesses, in direct competition with similar Bell System facilities, and by requiring the Bell System to furnish these new carriers with connection to Bell System customers. Not long after that, the commission, going well beyond Carterfone in the matter of non-Bell terminal equipment, began considering the establishment of a system of "certification" that would permit telephone subscribers to install alien terminal equipment without even the intervention of protective devices, provided the alien equipment was certified by technical experts representing the government.

For the first time since the Kingsbury Commitment, substantial competition now existed in American telephony. True enough, it existed in only two specific areas—terminal equipment and intercity leased lines—but in those areas it was expanding rapidly. By 1973, sales of the competing interconnect industry were up to about two hundred million dollars and rising fast, while advertisements aggressively promising savings to businesses that bought their own office telephone equipment from Bell competitors were becoming commonplace on television and radio. The leading leased-line competitor, MCI Communications, Inc., had annual revenues of fifteen million dollars.

At this point AT&T decided to dig in its heels. In September 1973, Chairman John deButts, who had succeeded Romnes in February 1972, made a fighting speech on the subject to the National Association of Regulatory Commissions in Seattle. DeButts came out swinging against the new FCC policies on two basic grounds: first, that both new forms of competition would force AT&T to replace revenues lost as a result of them by raising the cost of ordinary service to the average subscriber; and secondly, that continued interconnection of alien equipment, even with "certification," might compromise the integrity of the whole system, causing cross talk, wrong numbers, line noise, and billing errors—almost all the horrors of the well-remembered service crisis. As to intercity leased private lines, deButts maintained that the FCC was being unfair by encouraging competitors to try to grab the cream of the business, the profitable high-volume traffic such as that between New York and Chicago, while requiring AT&T not only to maintain, but to put at the disposal of its competitors, the lower-volume, higher-cost and often unprofitable links between lesser cities. The effect, deButts said, would be to force the Bell System to abandon its long-time policy of nationwide rate averaging—using revenues from high-volume circuits to partially subsidize low-volume ones—and thus to penalize the users of low-volume circuits by forcing them to pay higher rates.

DeButts' speech was only the initial salvo. Early in 1974 the infantry and artillery were moved into place; the whole panoply of AT&T public-relations power was applied to an attempt to win the public to the company's point of view rather than the FCC's, including an elaborate slide-and-film presentation, to be delivered around the country to whoever would listen, that featured the statement, "The telecommunications industry is fast approaching what may be a significant crossroads in its history."

Was it really? The interconnect and specialized-common-carrier industries' few hundred million dollars a year were a drop in the bucket compared with the Bell System's annual revenues of over $25 billion. Even looking ahead a couple of years, the Bell System in 1974 projected a 1976 revenue loss due to competition with specialized common carriers of only $220 million. At the time AT&T began its all-out campaign, it looked as if an elephant were trampling a mouse—a fact that AT&T realized well enough; an internal company report in 1974 warned that, as regards the principle of free competition, "our argument asks the public to accept the antithesis of what they have been encultured to believe." But deButts believed that much more than money was involved, and that the risk of public obloquy was worth taking. To him the issue was clear: "No system of certification we can envision, and no interface equipment, can provide a fully adequate alternative to the unequivocal and undivided responsibility for service that the common-carrier principle imposes." His assistant, Alvin von Auw, put the matter more broadly: "The fundamental basis of our business is under attack on a broad scale." The basic and permanent philosophical dilemma of AT&T—that its effective low-cost operation as a monopoly defies the deep-seated American belief that the consumer is served best by free competition—was brought sharply into focus. That deButts was right, at least from AT&T's point of view, to take a strong and unpopular stand when he did is suggested by the fact that hardly more than a year later the matter of telephone competition would move from the FCC to the courts in the largest federal antitrust suit ever filed.[6]

4

Romnes retired as chairman and chief executive officer in March 1972, the month he turned sixty-five and only a year and eight months before his death. All but unnoticed amid the storms and turmoils of his term in office had been steady progress in network growth and technical innovation. In 1967 the first dialed calls from New York to London and Paris were made; in 1968 Data-Phone 50, a new high-speed switched service for transmitting computer data and facsimile, went into service; in 1970 a new transatlantic cable, the fifth, was put in service, and Picturephone service was first offered commercially, and in 1971 Data Under Voice, a new technological development of great importance permitting data signals to hitchhike on existing microwave radio systems, was announced, and Bell System telephones in service passed the one hundred million mark. The year 1972 saw an all-time record telephone-in-service increase of just over five million, 10 percent more long-distance calls than in any previous year, and three times as much overseas traffic as five years earlier. Demand for telephone service was still soaring at rates that confounded the Bell Labs planners, and whatever else might be said about AT&T, those demands were being met.

In perspective, it was a technological miracle, a prodigy. Romnes, the engineer with humanist leanings, had quietly seen that the engineering job had got done while publicly displaying the humanist leanings. A chastened Bell System was devoting itself more single-mindedly to telephony than at any time since its early days. Bell Labs, "traumatized" by the service crisis, had shifted its emphasis away from the direction of high-technology projects more or less vaguely related to telecommunications, and into the direction of "trampling to death" the basic problem of providing the best possible telephone service now and in the future. Western Electric, transferring the Labs' designs from blueprint to production line, had reduced its military commitments to the lowest percentage of total effort since the start of the cold war, and was now largely sticking to making telephone equipment. The operating companies, having awakened from the nightmare of 1969–70, were bending to the task of ensuring that the nightmare not be repeated. Superficially it seemed that under deButts the company was heading into a period of calm and orderly expansion comparable to Kappel's.

That impression was drastically wrong. Expansion would take place, and earnings would increase; but nothing would be calm and orderly. In 1974, two years after assuming office, deButts would say to a visitor, almost wistfully, "You know, wasn't Fred Kappel lucky, in that good quiet period with all that clear sailing he had?"

# Scandal and a Lawsuit

Accelerated progress in minority hiring and training did not induce the government to relent in its criticism of AT&T policies after 1970. Rather, such criticism intensified. As the nation's biggest corporation and one with a long and well-known tradition of hiring comparatively few members of racial minorities, and of relegating its vast force of women employees to certain kinds of jobs, AT&T was a huge target for the new and militant Equal Employment Opportunity Commission, despite remarkable and unprecedented reforms in its hiring policies since 1965. It was a target not to be resisted.

Negotiations on the 1970 EEOC complaint—the last large responsibility of Horace Moulton, whose term as general counsel had begun with the 1956 antitrust settlement, had spanned the 1960s, and now continued to the end of 1972—were laborious and frustrating. The EEOC was required by the FCC to desist from its effort to tie the matter of minority rights to the matter of telephone rates. With those issues separated, the tugging and pulling went on. In August 1972, AT&T filed a memorandum replying in detail to the EEOC charges of discrimination against the company. The memorandum pointed out that under the National Alliance of Businessmen program set up in 1968, in consultation with the government, to provide jobs for the disadvantaged, the Bell companies had pledged themselves to hire 15,167 of the hard-core unemployed within a three-year period—more than were pledged by any other employer in the nation—and that commitment had actually been exceeded by more than 2,000. As to women, in the memo AT&T characterized the EEOC charge that "the Bell Monolith is, without doubt, the largest oppressor of women workers in the United States" as "hyperbole of monstrous proportions." (That charge, anomalous on its face in view of the fact that the Bell System was and had been for almost a century the nation's largest employer of women, was directed, of course, to the relatively low number of women in craft and management jobs.)

In January 1973, after more than a year of public hearings, the EEOC, the Department of Labor, and AT&T signed a comprehensive agreement, in the form of a consent decree entered in the U.S. District Court in Philadelphia. The thirty-one-page document included, among other things, commitments by AT&T to facilitate the movement of qualified women and minority-group members into better jobs; to institute a new promotion pay policy for employees transferred into higher-rated jobs; to introduce a special program to assess the interests and qualifications of female college graduates hired into management; and to make compensatory one-time payments totaling about fifteen million dollars to some fifteen thousand present employees.

From the AT&T point of view, the agreement was supererogatory—a formal promise to do what the company maintained it intended to do anyway. The Bell position throughout the negotiations had been to insist that the company had changed and was now simply the wrong target. "What should be plain is that we have no male jobs, no female jobs, no black jobs and no white jobs," declared the 1972 Annual Report, issued shortly after the agreement had been signed. To substantiate this boast, the Bell System could claim that minority members now constituted 13 percent of total employment and 4 percent of management employment, while women held 28 percent of management posts. By the end of 1974, deButts was able to report that women held one-third of all management posts, while the number of women in craft jobs traditionally held by men—repairmen, installers, and the like—stood at about 14,400, compared to 2,100 at the end of 1970. Meanwhile, by way of avoiding reverse discrimination, the Bell System by that time could point to 8,000 male telephone operators—5.8 percent of all operators coast to coast.

It was all not enough for the EEOC. A second consent decree, entered into on May 30, 1974, provided for a new promotion pay policy for Bell management employees and for additional back pay awards of seven million dollars to about seven thousand employees, of whom about 60 percent were women or minority members. In May 1975, still another agreement was signed by AT&T and the federal agencies; in this one, the government conceded that the Bell System's equal-employment performance in 1973 and 1974 had been a "substantial accomplishment," while AT&T, for its part, conceded that it had not complied fully with the 1973 agreement and agreed to pay an estimated $2.5 million more in compensation and penalties.

The extent to which government may or should determine a private corporation's hiring policies, promotion policies, and pay scale—a matter entirely unexplored in the past history of free enterprise—remains to be settled in the future. What a fair-minded observer almost had to concede in the middle 1970s was that in a couple of decades the Bell System, whether chiefly on its own initiative or chiefly because of outside pressure, had transformed itself from a company as backward as American society itself regarding equal employment and promotion into— if not quite a shining example for others—a responsible corporate citizen.[1]

2

Along with the pressing and continuing problems of present and future financing, federal encouragement of competition, and federal criticism of employment practices, the Bell System, as it headed into its and the telephone's centennial year of 1976, faced a cluster of more or less serious, more or less unexpected troubles.

The most local and transient, but not the least dramatic, of these was a fire of unknown origin that swept through a switching center at Second Avenue and Thirteenth Street in lower Manhattan on February 27, 1975, causing the worst single service disaster ever suffered by any single Bell operating company. Starting around midnight in the cable vault under the eleven-story building's basement, the fire spread rapidly upward. Alert work by New York City firemen confined it to the lower floors and saved the building itself from destruction, but dense smoke from burn-

53. Annual Meeting, Chicago, 1973. AT&T has some three million stock-holders, all of whom are invited to attend this event and air their opinions.

54. Twister wire, a component of memory devices in ESS, is barely one-quarter the thickness of sewing thread.

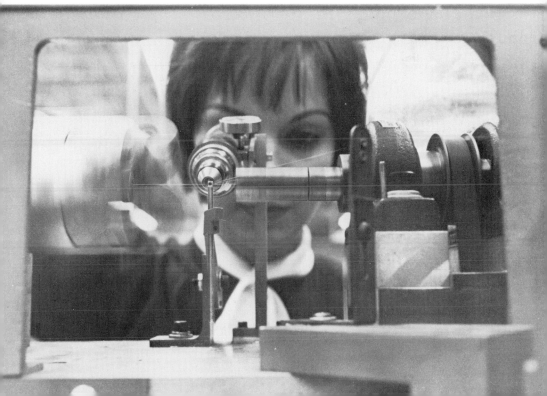

55. Circuit packs. Containing transistors, diodes and other miniature electronic devices, circuit packs accept information from one of the memory units, interpret it, and execute an order every few millionths of a second.

56. Scientist working in a Bell Lab.

57. H. I. ("Hi") Romnes, chief executive offi-cer (1967–1972). He saw the Bell System through a time of social turmoil.

58. Frederick R. Kappel, AT&T's top man, 1956–1967. He made the first telephone call via satellite.

59. On February 27, 1975, an unprecedented fire blazed out of control for seventeen hours in this New York City telephone switching center at Thirteenth Street and Second Avenue. Some 170,000 telephones were knocked out.

60. A 4,000-man Bell System task force worked around the clock for weeks to restore service in the 300-square-block area.

61. This diagnostic center at Napierville, Illinois, provides expert help 24 hours a day to any ESS central office that runs into trouble.

62. John D. deButts, present Chairman of the Board and chief executive officer.

63. On the boards, full cycle. First male operators since the boy operators of the early years handle toll calls in the Wichita Falls office, April 1972.

64. Picturephone Meeting Service, available in Chicago, Washington, D.C., New York City and San Francisco. Such a service was used in a civil claims court case hearing by a three-judge panel in Washington with counsels for the plaintiff and defendant in New York City, October 1975.

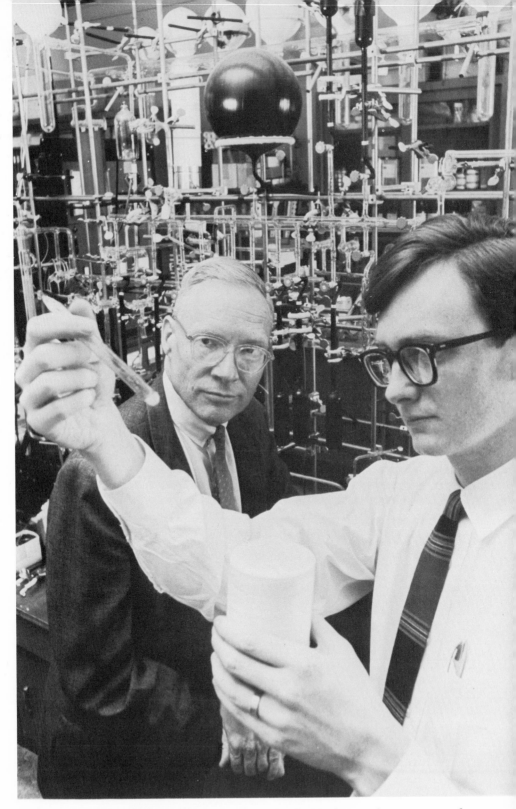

65. Dr. William O. Baker, president of Bell Telephone Laboratories, watches a photochemistry experiment.

ing cable insulation suffused the unburned parts of the building, and virtually all the equipment in it was put out of service. By afternoon, when the fire was finally declared under control—with no loss of life to either firemen or telephone people—twelve Manhattan telephone exchanges, embracing three hundred city blocks and 104,000 subscriber lines serving 170,000 telephones, were out of service, and among the institutions bereft of working telephones were six hospitals and medical centers, eleven firehouses, three post offices, one police precinct, nine public schools, and three higher-education institutions, including New York University.

Before firemen had given telephone repairmen the O.K. to enter the building, the Bell System had begun one of the typical crisis mobilizations of which it is justly proud—indeed, the largest such mobilization ever. New York Telephone, AT&T Long Lines, Western Electric, and Bell Labs contingents converged on the area, and a crisis headquarters—inevitably called a war room —was established in a rented storefront on Fourteenth Street, under the immediate direction of Lee Oberst, New York City area vice-president of New York Telephone. (Oberst, the type-cast hero for such an operation, was a South Bronx–born man of fifty-six who had started his Bell System career in 1946 as a twenty-eight-dollar-a-week switchman.) Within twenty-four hours, emergency telephone service had been restored to the medical, police, and fire facilities affected, and in hardly more time the Bell task force assessing damage and beginning to restore service had reached its peak strength of four thousand, working around the clock in twelve-hour shifts of two thousand each. Western Electric officials were ordered to commandeer or quickly manufacture huge quantities of replacement equipment; shipments by air began the day after the fire, and eventually the amount of new equipment shipped in amounted to three thousand tons. The work to be done in the damaged building varied all the way from installing new ESS equipment and writing computer programs for it to cleaning smoke-damaged relays with toothbrushes and Q-tips. A couple of happy circumstances speeded the work along. One of these was the fact that the third floor of the burned building happened to be standing vacant at the time, thus providing space for the rapid installation of an entirely new main frame for handling trunk calls, which was shipped by cargo jet on February 28 from Western Electric's Hawthorne works. Another was the convenient availability for emergency use of excess switching capacity, from the ESS installations at Seventh Avenue and Eighteenth Street and at New York Telephone headquarters at Sixth and Forty-second. Such capacity could temporarily accommodate 28,000 of the 104,000 severed lines.

"The miracle on Fourteenth Street," Oberst kept calling it—a bit melodramatically, and, it appeared for a time, overoptimistically. On March 11, New York Telephone announced plans to restore service to all ordinary telephone subscribers on March 16. As that date approached, it developed that water used in the fire-fighting operation had damaged many of the cables entering the building, and that the miracle would be postponed. Except for a few stray problem lines, service was restored just before midnight on March 21—twenty-two days after the disaster, instead of the year or more that would have been required under normal conditions. The restoration was ceremoniously marked by a call from William Ellinghaus, New York Telephone's president, to Mayor Beame of New York at the mayoral residence, Gracie Mansion. The cost of the job, still not precisely calculated six months later, had been about ninety million dollars, of which almost all was covered by insurance, so the disaster cost no increased rates to subscribers or lost profits to stockholders. It remains a fair question whether New York Telephone had been prudent, in the most telephone-dependent area in the country, to house twelve exchanges and five toll switching machines in a single building.[2]

Almost simultaneously with this physical, if not exactly natural, disaster came accusations of a sort that the Bell System, considering its size, diffuseness, and availability as a political target, had been remarkably free of over the course of its history. They were accusations of outright scandal in two Bell operating companies. There had, as we have seen, been the charges of company bribery of civil authorities in San Francisco back in the two-phone era, which had led to the trial and conviction of a Bell official. Over the almost three-quarters of a century from then until 1974, an occasional senator or congressman had accused AT&T of using illegal or unethical methods to gain its ends; such charges had fallen of their own weight, or been quietly allowed to drop, or—if the interpretation of reformers may be credited—

been crushed by the economic and political power of the corporate monolith. By almost anyone's standard, however, the Bell System, whatever its other merits and demerits, had earned a reputation beyond cavil as a law-abiding corporate citizen. Now came accusations of wrongdoing, not from outside but from former Bell employees, that threatened the system's internal morale and external image as much as anything since the all-but-forgotten San Francisco affair.

The story began like a thriller novel. On October 17, 1974, T. O. Gravitt, fifty-one-year-old vice-president of Southwestern Bell Telephone Company, with responsibility for all operations in Texas—a swashbuckling, private-plane-piloting executive who, at the time, was under investigation by Southwestern Bell on suspicion of having misappropriated company funds for his private use—committed suicide by inhaling automobile exhaust fumes in the garage of his home in Dallas. He left a suicide note and various memoranda accusing the company of a litany of misdeeds, among them the making of political payoffs from a slush fund maintained for that purpose, the illegal tapping of telephone wires, the misuse of company funds, and—most serious of all from the public point of view—the securing of high telephone rates in Texas by providing regulators with false or misleading information. The suicide note ended, "Watergate is a gnat compared to the Bell System."

Southwestern Bell immediately denied all the charges, a spokesman describing them as "hogwash" concocted by a man seeking to cover his own misdeeds; and eight days after Gravitt's suicide, James M. Ashley, a Southwestern Bell rate negotiator who had been one of Gravitt's closest associates, who was similarly suspect by the company of improper conduct, and who now confirmed and enlarged upon the suicide-note charges, was summarily dismissed. Nevertheless, on its face the matter was serious. Southwestern Bell was no run-of-the-mill Bell operating company. Based in St. Louis and serving Missouri, Kansas, Arkansas, Oklahoma, and Texas, it is the third largest Bell company, and its dividends for 1974 amounted to over 12 percent of all AT&T dividend income; as to its Texas operation, rate of return on investment in that state had run consistently higher than the Bell company average for more than two decades, and in eleven recent years (although not in the past five) had been the highest in any state served by AT&T—a dazzling performance record that may or may not have been related to the fact that Texas was the only state of the Union that regulated telephone rates at the municipal rather than the state level, and that had long been known for its skeptical attitude toward business regulation of *any* kind. At all events, that dazzling record now came under suspicion of being tainted by tampering with such regulatory authority as did exist. The situation was further complicated when, on November 18, Ashley and members of Gravitt's family filed a $29 million damage suit against Southwestern Bell charging that Gravitt's death had resulted from a company conspiracy against him to keep him quiet.

From the first, the position taken at 195 Broadway was that whatever the truth of the Texas situation, it was an isolated and transient case. But in January 1975, John J. Ryan, a former vice-president for Southern Bell Telephone Company in charge of service for North Carolina, who had been forced to retire in June 1973 on grounds of "unsatisfactory performance," said in a series of local newspaper interviews that over a period of years he had made political contributions to candidates who were expected to be favorable to the interests of Southern Bell, deriving the funds from salary kickbacks extorted from leading Southern Bell executives that had been concealed by the use of false vouchers. On January 22nd, L. Edmund Rast, president of Southern Bell, issued a statement in which he conceded that he had learned of the preparation of bogus vouchers in June 1973—just before Ryan was forcibly retired—that the proceeds of the vouchers "may have been diverted to political contributions," and that all such activity had been promptly and permanently stopped.

With the suggestion of widespread rather than localized wrongdoing, the situation obviously became even more serious. At 195 Broadway, deButts, after long consideration and a wrestle with his conscience, decided that the proper and prudent course was to grasp the nettle and deal directly with the charges rather than to try to deprecate or minimize them. In a talk to a Bell System conference at Port St. Lucie, Florida, in January 1975, he said, "A great deal of damage has been done. The integrity with which we conduct this business has been called into question. . . . Compromise of the integrity of this business casts a shadow over everything we do and impairs our ability to reach every goal we strive for." In a supplement dated January 20, 1975, to a prospectus for AT&T's Share Owner Dividend Reinvestment and Stock Purchase Plan—prepared like all stock prospectuses under the surveillance of the SEC, which had intervened in the Southwestern Bell case a few days earlier—the company took official note of both that and the North Carolina situation by including a brief but candid description of them. By February—by which time not only the SEC but the Department of Justice, the Federal Wiretap Commission, the FCC, and the Texas attorney general were all involved in the cases in one way or another— AT&T itself was, understandably enough, deep in its own investigation of them. The company's Annual Report for 1974, issued in March 1975, pointedly alluded to the Texas and North Carolina allegations and commented—conspicuously without denying them —that "it would be regrettable were . . . conclusions drawn reflecting on Bell System management as a whole and the integrity with which it conducts its business . . . the Bell System has not undertaken systematically to subvert the regulatory process through clandestine political contributions, however derived." (Not surprisingly, in view of the standards of business morality of AT&T and of the nation prior to 1910, there had been no mention of the San Francisco affair in the company's annual reports of the time.) It was at the 1975 annual stockholders' meeting, held at Anaheim, California, on April 16 with about five thousand present, that deButts took his fullest public stand. Turning, in his remarks to stockholders, from reports on operations to what he called "a less agreeable matter" that he had "pondered long and hard before deciding to include in these remarks," he said that "there is no blinking the fact that these allegations [in Texas and North Carolina] have called into question the integrity with which this business is conducted." Then deButts laid out AT&T policy with respect to political activities: first, "Bell System policy does not countenance—or the laws allow—any use of corporate funds for political purposes. That is just plain wrong"; second, any pressure that infringes the right of any employee to make his or her own voluntary political contributions is equally contrary to policy; and finally, "should the investigations now under way prove that any Bell System manager at whatever level broke the law or breached the standards of conduct that are his responsibility to maintain, appropriate action will be taken—up to and including dismissal. . . . I have made it plain to the presidents of the Bell companies and to their comptrollers that we are determined to assure that nowhere in our business today is there any trace of the irregularities in the conduct of our public affairs and regulatory activities that have been attributed to us and, if there is, that it will be rooted out unequivocally and forever."

"Perhaps," deButts said in concluding the subject, "I have overreacted in this matter." It would not appear that he had. Six months after deButts spoke—by which time none of the various investigations of the Texas and North Carolina situations were concluded, and the only substantive action taken had been the belated creation in June of a state regulatory commission in Texas (to become functional in 1976), bringing that state at last into line with all other states in the matter—it still seemed pretty clear that some dirty Bell linen had been exposed. Besides threatening AT&T's treasured reputation for integrity, the charge, if true, implied a failure of management. While no suggestion of the crucial element of a true Bell System "Watergate"—complicity or a cover-up at 195 Broadway—had been so much as raised, the question arose as to just how well AT&T could control the activities of its operating companies. In constantly, and necessarily, pressing them to produce higher earnings—and systematically rewarding them for success and penalizing them for failure—did the parent company sometimes inadvertently convey a message that was not intended, a message that said not "Get higher earnings by any fair means," but rather, "Get higher earnings by fair means or foul"? Before the matter could be laid to rest, deButts' bold words to the stockholders—words of a sort seldom uttered in public by chief executives of great corporations—would have to be implemented in such a way as to ensure that headquarters' pressure for results never in the future, anywhere in the far-flung organization, be taken as a license to get the results by means that are not fair and legal.


3


The thunderclap in whose aftermath the first century of AT&T and the telephone would end came on November 20, 1974. It was the federal government's second antitrust suit to break up the Bell System, and it marked—after the Kingsbury Commitment of 1913, the FCC investigation of 1935–39, and the previous antitrust cast of 1949–56—the fourth historic confrontation between AT&T and the United States government. Rightly or wrongly, the Bell System would approach its centennial on trial for its life.

Like the 1949 suit, this one had been a long time coming. Immediately after the 1956 consent decree had ended the earlier government case, certain career staff men in the Justice Department, as well as various senators and congressmen, had begun expressing their disapproval of it. The criticism continued, and the threat of new antitrust action continued to hang over AT&T; there are those at AT&T who maintain that when Robert F. Kennedy was attorney general in the early 1960s, he categorically mentioned the possibility of a new antitrust suit in the course of negotiations with AT&T on the communications satellite bill. But that issue was compromised, and the threat (if in fact there had been one) lifted. The matter went on simmering for another decade.

It was in the fall of 1973 that Mark Garlinghouse, AT&T's vice-president and general counsel since the retirement of Moulton the previous December, first learned that Justice was seriously considering mounting a new case. Garlinghouse, a dryly humorous, iron-gray Kansan of fifty-nine, who in his youth, while attending college and law school, had been a police reporter in Topeka in the gaudy days of John Dillinger and Pretty Boy Floyd, had become acquainted earlier in the year, in connection with other matters, with the Justice Department's antitrust staff, headed by Assistant Attorney General Thomas E. Kauper. Now the Justice lawyers served AT&T with an investigative demand for documents regarding intercity carriers and related matters. AT&T responded by supplying the documents—some eighty thousand pages. Then, in August 1974, came events that resulted in Garlinghouse's realization for the first time that the matter was, as he put it, "damn serious." Summoned to Washington, he was informed by the Justice people that although they had not yet decided to proceed with action, they had decided on the basis of their investigation that the government had a case—based on Section 2 of the Sherman Act of 1890, which prohibits monopolies or attempts or conspiracies to create monopolies—to break up the Bell into a group of separate entities.

There followed a silence of three months. The manner in which the antitrust suit was finally brought, in November, involved misunderstandings strikingly reminiscent of those attending the start of the FCC rate investigation in 1965. In the middle of the month, William Saxbe, the attorney general, called John Fox, AT&T's Washington lawyer, asking for a meeting with him and Garlinghouse on the morning of November 20. Both Fox and Garlinghouse happened to have previous appointments for that day; however, informed that the matter was urgent, they canceled their plans and agreed to the meeting. At the same time, Kauper assured the AT&T men that the meeting's purpose was not to announce a new antitrust suit. At the November 20 meeting, Saxbe—to the apparent surprise of Kauper, who later apologized to Garlinghouse for having misled him—stated that the government had decided to file suit at once. Garlinghouse and Fox pleaded for more time, on grounds of the adverse effect that such abrupt action at that particular moment might have on AT&T's current financing plans, which included a six-hundred-million-dollar bond offering scheduled for closing the following week. Saxbe, after leaving the meeting to caucus with his colleagues, returned to say that he would "think it over and let you know." At one forty-five that afternoon, Garlinghouse got a call from Kauper's assistant informing him that suit against AT&T would be filed that afternoon, and at four o'clock, the largest antitrust suit in the nation's history was filed in the U.S. District Court for the District of Columbia.

By all accounts, the Justice staff had had the complaint prepared and ready to file for months or longer; the question was why it was filed when it was. Justice gave no explanation of its timing—nor of the apparent absence of coordination within its own ranks—but certain logical reasons suggest themselves. For one thing, the department had been receiving complaints of monopolistic activities by AT&T from its new competitors in the terminal-equipment and specialized-common-carrier businesses; indeed, representatives of both those businesses had their own antitrust suits against AT&T already pending. For another thing, recent court decisions on related matters had encouraged Justice to believe that the prevailing judicial climate was now such that, in a new effort to break up AT&T, it had a good chance of winning. Finally, the post-Watergate environment in Washington was unmistakably making it more difficult for the politically appointed heads of departments and agencies to overrule their staffs—and key members of the Justice staff unmistakably were, and for a long time had been, in favor of a new legal joust with AT&T. At all events, the new 1974 antitrust suit was far more comprehensive than the old 1949–56 one. Not content to ask that AT&T be made to divest itself of all its stock in Western Electric, and that Western Electric itself then be divided into at least two companies, it went on to pray the court that AT&T be forced to "separate some or all of the Long Lines Department of AT&T from some or all of the Bell Operating Companies," and that Bell Laboratories be ordered "to appear and answer the allegations contained in this Complaint, and to abide and perform such orders and decrees as the Court may make"—which, of course, might include separation of the Labs themselves into a separate company. AT&T, Western Electric, and Bell Laboratories were named as defendants in the action, while all the Bell operating companies were named as coconspirators.

In sum, the suit provided for the possibility at most of total dismemberment of the Bell System. And the nature of the violations alleged in the complaint made plain what the burden of the government's argument would be. The most specific of these charges concerned alleged attempts by AT&T to obstruct interconnection of competing terminal equipment and specialized-common-carrier equipment, all of which was technologically new since 1956. The government was going to argue that new technology and new FCC policies since that date had made the old consent decree obsolete. "Our case is based entirely on [AT&Ts] post-Decree conduct," a government lawyer would declare in a later court proceeding; and while not all his government colleagues strictly agreed with him on that point, the fact seemed to be that—although, strangely enough, the FCC had not even been notified of the suit before it was filed—the new case was based solidly on the argument that the recent FCC decisions opening up specific areas of telecommunications to competition had created new conditions that made the continued existence of an integrated Bell System no longer legal or in the public interest.

AT&T's first reaction was one of shock and intransigence. DeButts, the deceptively mild-mannered North Carolinian who had previously dug in his heels on FCC competition policies, now dug them in again on legal action arising out of those policies. In a statement made immediately after the filing, he pronounced himself "astonished" at the government's action, and went on to say that the divestitures being sought "could lead to fragmentation of responsibility for the nation's telephone network" and "destroy a unique national resource," with the result that "telephone service would deteriorate and cost much, much more." The following day, at a crowded press conference at 195 Broadway, he enlarged on those sentiments, cited AT&T's record of keeping the increase in telephone rates well below that of the consumer price index of all goods and services, and Western Electric's of selling equipment at prices substantially below those of other manufacturers. He then declared that it was AT&T's intention to fight the suit to the end this time around, rather than seek a consent decree. In a letter to stockholders sent four days later, he said, "Let me assure you without equivocation that we are confident that we are not in violation of the antitrust laws." As for the Justice Department, a spokesman for it conceded at the outset, "I don't believe we can promise that winning this suit is going to lower rates"—but insisted the law was the law and must be enforced.

With the battle lines thus drawn, the long but necessary legal gavotte leading to a trial began. On February 4, 1975, AT&T filed its answer to the government complaint, challenging the validity of the entire action on grounds that the legislative history of the telecommunications industry—the Graham-Willis Act of 1921 and the Communications Act of 1934—indicated the intent of Congress to maintain the integrated structure of the telephone industry, and that, moreover, that intent had already been judicially confirmed by the consent decree of 1956. Meanwhile the two sides were engaged in initiating what is known legally as a discovery process—the exchange of pertinent documents and the establishment of ground rules concerning their handling and retention. That process brought its problems. AT&T offered to allow the Justice Department to search its files, an offer that Justice declined for understandable reasons: the files contain between nineteen and twenty billion pieces of paper, of which the scope of the government inquiry covered some seven billion; to search these would cost perhaps three hundred million dollars. Instead

AT&T was asked to produce specific papers on demand. On February 18 and 20, there were arguments before the presiding judge—Joseph C. Waddy of the U.S. District Court in Washington—on this matter and on the question of the retention of AT&T documents germane to the case that were held by government agencies other than the Justice Department. On February 27, Judge Waddy on his own motion ordered that prior to the start of a trial the two sides must give their answers on three matters of a sort known, in elegant legal parlance, as "threshold questions": first, should the Washington court, rather than the New Jersey court that had heard the 1949–56 case, have jurisdiction over this one? second, did the 1956 consent decree bar the new action in whole or in part? and third, was the suit barred in whole or in part by reason of the extensive regulation to which the Bell System was subject?

Threshold or not, these questions were crucial; affirmative answers to either the second or the third would lead logically to dismissal of all or part of the suit. After both sides had filed detailed memoranda on them, the threshold questions were argued orally in Washington on July 23, 1975, in the first dramatic confrontation of the case—a legal proceeding attended chiefly, apart from the litigants themselves, by interested legal professionals, with no general reporters present and with no subsequent newspaper or wire-service coverage; and yet a landmark argument in modern telecommunications history and, in a sense, in American social history.

The scene was Judge Waddy's courtroom on the second floor of the federal courthouse on Constitution Avenue, across the hall from the room where Judge John Sirica had conducted the Watergate cases. Behind the bench at the far end sat Judge Waddy, a man of about sixty, a little gray, with an amiable manner but also a distinct air of command; a 1938 cum laude graduate of the law school of Howard University, in Washington; a practicing Washington lawyer from 1939 until 1962; a Kennedy appointee that year to the post of associate judge in domestic relations in the Washington Municipal Court; a judge of the U.S. District Court there since 1967, and a judge now hearing only the second antitrust case of his career. On the left side, as one faced the judge, sat the lawyers for the defense: Garlinghouse, as AT&T general counsel; Harold Levy, head of a team of twenty-two AT&T law-

years working full-time on the antitrust cases under Garling-house's direction; George Saunders, antitrust expert for the Chicago law firm of Sidley and Austin, who would do the actual arguing for AT&T; and another "outside" counselor, Leonard Joseph of the New York firm of Dewey, Ballantine, Bushby, Palmer and Wood. On the right side were the lawyers for the government, two young people of conservative mien, entirely without hallmarks of the youth culture: Philip L. Verveer, in his earlier thirties, shy, slight, clean-shaven, with an air of high seriousness; and Barbara Reeves, not yet thirty, pleasant-looking, skirt above her knees but not flamboyantly so, who had been chosen for the case because she had helped write the government briefs in two recent Supreme Court cases that were believed by AT&T to be relevant to this one, and who, not without apparent and understandable awe, was about to make the first oral argument of her life for the Department of Justice. In the audience in front were perhaps one hundred spectators, many of them recognizable to the AT&T lawyers as their opponents in the other pending antitrust cases brought against AT&T by the interconnect companies and specialized common carriers. Evidently they were here now to keep abreast of AT&T's larger antitrust challenge—and perhaps, too, to witness the social drama of the biggest antitrust case in history, between the most powerful government and the largest corporation in the world, being heard by a lone judge who happened to be black.

Each side was permitted two hours for argument, and each side used its full time, with the judge interrupting their arguments frequently with questions that reflected close and detailed study of the case and its complex issues. As to the jurisdiction of the Washington court rather than that of New Jersey or some other district, neither side objected to Washington, and the matter was quickly dropped. Saunders then launched into the argument for the defense. Speaking, as lawyers seldom do under such circumstances, entirely without notes—he had previously written out several versions of his presentation, more or less memorized them, and then thrown the papers away—he laid heavy stress on the doctrine of *res judicata*, "a matter already decided." The main plea of the government complaint was that AT&T and Western Electric be separated; the association between the two companies dated from 1882; the government had previously sued for their separation in the 1949–56 case and had failed to achieve it; therefore, Saunders insisted, *res judicata* barred the new action insofar as it referred to acts of AT&T before the consent decree of 1956—and those acts, of course, included its acquisition of ownership of Western Electric. Indeed, Saunders insisted, under the provisions of the Communications Act of 1934, "if this Court entered an order breaking up the Bell System, the [Federal Communications] Commission could put it back together tomorrow . . . and immunize it expressly from the antitrust laws."

But of course, the complaint specified actions of AT&T long since 1956, alleging that it had obstructed competition in fields recently opened up by technical advance and by decisions of the FCC. Saunders argued that since AT&T's actions in those matters are subject to "pervasive regulation" by the FCC and the state regulatory commissions, those regulatory bodies have "exclusive jurisdiction" over such actions of AT&T, and court jurisdiction was accordingly barred. Antitrust laws, so Saunders contended, simply cannot be applied to activities in a regulated industry where to do so would subject companies within that industry to conflicting standards—in this case, the public-interest standard of the FCC versus the free-competition standard behind the antitrust laws. To buttress this part of his case, Saunders had the advantage of two judicial windfalls. Only a month earlier, the Supreme Court had decided two important cases in a way that seemed to make his very point. In *Gordon* v. *New York Stock Exchange*, it had found that inasmuch as the Exchange is closely regulated by the Securities and Exchange Commission, "implied repeal of the antitrust laws is, in fact, necessary to make the Exchange Act work as it was intended." In a similar case, *U.S.* v. *National Association of Securities Dealers*, the Court had ruled, in almost the same language: "Here implied repeal of the antitrust laws is necessary to make the [regulatory system] work."

The issue, perhaps as complex and intellectually interesting as any in American jurisprudence—and as old as regulation of business and antitrust laws themselves—was the extent to which those two methods of controlling the power and rapacity of free enterprise are mutually exclusive, and the first confers immunity against the second. In broad language, the Supreme Court had said the antitrust laws must be inapplicable where pervasive regulation exists—as Saunders insisted it did in the case of AT&T. Needless to say, the Justice lawyers took a different view. Verveer —brushing aside the *res judicata* argument by saying that the government case was based entirely on actions of AT&T since the consent decree of 1956, and therefore could not be "a matter decided" in that decree—put his emphasis on the question of jurisdiction between the antitrust laws and the FCC. It was his contention that the illegal acts alleged against AT&T were simply not controllable by the FCC under its mandate. But on this point Judge Waddy intervened with some hard questions. "I will tell you quite frankly, I am having difficulty finding out exactly what you are complaining about," the judge said. In reply, Verveer listed the specifications in the complaint: that AT&T had withheld interconnection rights to specialized common carriers, that it had resisted interconnection of competing terminal equipment, and so on. In each case, Waddy asked whether the matter was a subject of inquiry by the FCC, and in each case Verveer had to concede, with certain qualifications, that it was.

So the arguments went. In the afternoon, as the government's allotted time was running out, Miss Reeves came forward to speak on her area of special knowledge, the two recent Supreme Court cases. ("Is that Miss Reid?" Judge Waddy asked. "Reeves, may it please the Court," replied Miss Reeves, in a firm voice.) In the NASD case, she pointed out, the Court had made a finding not quoted by Saunders, which "implied antitrust immunity is not favored and can be justified only by a convincing show of clear repugnancy between antitrust laws and the regulatory system." So the argument, in its last stages, came down to the meaning of the word "repugnancy." (In logic, the word "repugnancy," derived from the Latin *repugnans* by way of Old French and Middle English, means "inconsistency" or "contradiction.") Was there or wasn't there, in the field of telecommunications, a clear repugnancy between antitrust laws and the regulatory system? Verveer and Miss Reeves thought not; Saunders and his colleagues thought so. When the arguments were over, Judge Waddy said, "I will take this matter under advisement. You are not to take any heart on either side as to the questions I've asked. They indicate no point of view."

The court was adjourned, the lawyers shook hands, and everyone went home. Two weeks later, Judge Waddy requested that the FCC, which so clearly had a large role in the case, submit comments in a "friend of the court" brief. So the matter stands as this is written. The prospect late in 1975 was that getting the case ready for trial would take two or three years, and that the trial itself would take three or four years more, and subsequent appeals a year or more after that.

Thus the earth may very likely be well into the 1980s before the government's second suit to break up the Bell System is finally concluded. New events now unimaginable will have taken place; a political climate now unimaginable will prevail. If the government finally loses, the Bell System's structure will continue as it is now. If, on the other hand, the government succeeds in achieving its principal purpose, that of separating Western Electric from AT&T—and the FCC or Congress itself does not then reverse the action, as suggested by Saunders in his argument—what will be the consequences for telephone users, for the Bell System, and for AT&T stockholders?

As to telephone service, we have seen that AT&T is firmly, even passionately convinced that the fragmentation of supply services and possibly operating units would result in less efficient service, while the increase in supply costs brought about by free-market supply conditions would result in higher rates; and the Justice Department itself does not promise better service or lower rates should it prevail in the case. As to the Bell System, in its altered form it would go on. Telephone service would not come to a stop. However useless toward achieving any valid social purpose, the change would be no major disaster for American telephony. DeButts, in a television interview four days after the filing of the suit, conceded that with Western Electric divestiture, although the System would work less efficiently, "it's possible for it to work," probably with the intervention of some form of national coordinating body to replace the coordination made possible by unified ownership and management. Nor would the Bell System be a thing of the past. Even without Western Electric—indeed, even without Western Electric and Long Lines—it would still be the dominant element in American telephony and one of the largest of American corporations. Finally, how would AT&T stockholders fare? Presumably, after the divestiture they would find themselves stockholders not in one company but in several; in addition to their shares in AT&T, they would have shares in each of the various companies into which Western Electric was split. It seems logical to some (though not all) financial analysts to assume that Western Electric, freed of the price constraints imposed by the regulatory process, and able to take competitive advantage of its skill and efficiency, would be a highly successful company or group of companies, and that the value of its stock would rise, perhaps sharply. But at the same time, it may logically be supposed that the Bell operating companies, deprived of their integrated supply arm and forced to pay more for equipment, would become less successful. Present stockholders might lose as much or more on their new AT&T stock as they gained on their Western Electric stock.

Some shrewd and impartial observers believe that even though Western Electric divestiture may result in less efficient service at higher prices, it is inevitably coming sooner or later anyhow, because of the American public's deep-seated hatred of the idea of monopoly and love of the idea of free competition. In any case, such observers argue, divestiture, while harmful to the System, would be far from disastrous to it, and might actually represent a lesser concession to popular and political pressure—and a lesser abandonment of monopoly power—than did the Kingsbury Commitment of 1913. Accordingly, the argument goes, AT&T ought to agree voluntarily to sell its stock in Western Electric, as a measure of expediency at the expense of principle, a sacrifice of the ideal of the best service at the least cost on the altar of public approbation and political peace. Clearly enough, as the Bell System approached its centennial that view was not shared by AT&T's hound-dog-tenacious chief executive officer, John D. deButts.[4]

CHAPTER 14

# Toward a New Century

Early in 1974, seeking to get the look, feel, and smell of the Bell System in action—as one would wish to get to know well a person whose biography one had for some time been in the process of writing—I spent several weeks visiting a sampling of its installations, including a leading Western Electric plant and a couple of other Western facilities, the two principal Bell Laboratories installations, Long Lines headquarters, and various parts of a fairly typical operating company. In some cases I was accompanied on my visits by a Bell public-relations officer; in other cases I was not. In all cases, I sought to look at what I was seeing with an eye as detached as if I were a visitor, if not from another planet, at least from a foreign country—and a visitor, like myself, with an intense interest in society and its institutions, but without technical background.

My first visit was to one of Western Electric's longest-established plants, the Kearny Works at Kearny, New Jersey. Dating back to 1925—which makes it the second-oldest Western installation, after Hawthorne—the Kearny Works is situated on a bleak, all-industrial, man-made peninsula, built on concrete piles over what was originally salt marsh at the confluence of the Hackensack and Passaic Rivers, within sight of the Manhattan skyscrapers. Its 13,000 employees include many members of various ethnic groups—blacks and Puerto Ricans from Newark, Polish from Bayonne, and so on—and in keeping with the age of the plant, they are unusually old for industrial workers, with an

323

average age of forty-six. It is an old-fashioned multistory factory rather than a modern one-story one. Its products are as varied as those of any Western Electric plant—65,000 separate items, ranging from cable to electronic switchboards, power equipment to printed circuits and submarine repeaters; the last-named, crucial to the effectiveness of submarine cables, are made at no other Western plant. Kearny's director of operations—the man in direct charge of all its manufacturing operations—was Tom Arthur, a wiry, intense, white-haired man in his fifties who in 1974 had been thirty-two years with Western in various capacities and in various locations. Arthur spoke of the plant, its products, and its people in a personal, possessive way. "I make submarine repeaters," he would say, as if he were running a two-man enterprise in a garage. He took me on a tour of the cable-making operation, where copper wire is first coated with insulating pulp (itself made in the same room in great vats); then dried in ovens; then twisted into pairs by machines so noisy that their operators must wear ear pads; then combined into units, of many pairs, which are drawn into cable and wrapped with insulating paper. The cable—1,800 pairs of wire in the one I saw being made—is encased in aluminum and steel, soldered, coated with plastic, and fed onto huge reels; the ends are checked by women who sit sorting out the varicolored pairs as if they were sorting strands of yarn, and testing them with a beeper device. At last the finished cable is charged with gas to keep out moisture, capped, and shipped out by truck or rail. There is a truck depot and a railhead right outside the building. Almost all the cable-making equipment is old, some of it dating back to the plant's establishment in 1925, and Arthur spoke of cable-making as being a personal thing calling for more than mere skill. "You have to have a feel for cables," he said. "There's a lot of art in cable-making."

Next he showed me Kearny's new waste plant, designed to neutralize the factory's effluent. "We don't pollute," he said, but had to add that the advantage to the community was small, since sewage and industrial waste from other sources have made the Passaic one of the most polluted rivers in the United States. We moved on to what everybody at Kearny calls the "Ford Building," because it was owned by the Ford Motor Company, and used for building subchasers in World War I, before Western Electric bought it; now it houses the Kearny Works' relatively high-technology operations, chiefly in miniaturization. Among these is what Arthur described to me as Kearny's own "industrial break-through": a way for making small printed circuits, some four by six inches and used in switching equipment in business offices, by a silk-screen printing process.

On the fourth floor of the "Ford Building," the tiny components of printed circuits were being mounted in their places—resistors and capacitors by machine, relays by hand. There were many handworkers here, and signs about union meetings, recreational activities, and the like posted in the corridors; some of the signs were in Polish. On a woman's desk I noticed a mimeographed paper that read, "Our union is a real sellout"; but in Arthur's opinion the Kearny union—Local 1470 of the International Brotherhood of Electrical Workers—is a strong and responsible one. (Not long after my visit, as if to bear Arthur out, it staged a month-long strike.)

At lunch with Arthur and several of his colleagues in Kearny management, I found them emphasizing the cost-reduction program, which they said has been saving some five million dollars a year in recent years, and their plant's competitiveness, both with other Western installations and with outside manufacturers. "I can manufacture with anybody," Arthur said. It was striking, and illuminating, to find such an intense competitive spirit in a manager running a plant that operates in a monopoly situation. I found myself ready to believe that in Kearny's old-fashioned, no-nonsense way, Arthur could.

Just outside Princeton, New Jersey, Western Electric maintains an Engineering Research Center, where several hundred scientists and technicians, 40 percent of them Ph.D.'s, work on developing, improving, and reducing the cost of telephone manufacturing *processes* (as distinguished from Bell Laboratories' mission of designing new *products*). The center was established in 1958, when it became clear that the transistor and other innovations of the electronic age were going to have a major effect upon manufacturing methods in telecommunications, and that a major research effort was in order, to meet the challenge. With an atmosphere of quiet and almost academic calm in its offices and laboratories, the Engineering Research Center is a different world from noisy, clanking Kearny. Taken on a tour by Fred Wallitsch, director of research and development, I found in one lab a researcher working on ways of drawing down a string of molten fiber to a diameter of 3/1000 of an inch, the thickness of a human hair; such fibers are capable of carrying telephone conversations in the form of laser beams, and are expected in the future to make possible the use of cables much smaller, lighter, and cheaper than present ones. In another lab, work was going forward on improving the production of postage-stamp-sized integrated circuits used in electronic-switching offices; when the new processes are perfected, they will immediately be put into practice in the high-technology production lines at Allentown and Merrimac Valley. In a third lab, the subject of research was how to get a better splice in a broken wire by means of the heat caused by a small detonation. A researcher demonstrated the process, and the bonding explosion made a small pop like that of a toy balloon being punctured. The researcher said that the new method was just being put into use at the Atlanta works. In yet another lab the subject was worker safety; a machine was being devised to measure precisely the air's content of vinyl chloride, a grimly dangerous chemical of which a small amount is released in the decomposition of the polyvinyl chloride used in cable covering.

Next door to the Engineering Research center is the Corporate Education Center, Western Electric's "university." Complete with its own dormitories, eating facilities, computer and metallurgy labs, a film studio for making training films, and classrooms equipped with instant TV playback facilities so that students may look with satisfaction or distress at their own performances, the center gives courses in engineering, computer technology, and business administration to some 4,500 students per year, almost all of them Western Electric employees and the rest from elsewhere in the Bell System. The teachers are Bell System men borrowed from their regular duties for two- or three-year stretches, supplemented by some two hundred visiting professors a year who come for short periods from colleges or universities. Most of the courses take twelve weeks, divided into two six-week stretches, but there is a special high-powered course for high-potential young managers that runs six months. The director of the center, J. L. Thiesmeyer—an unlikely "university president" who in his time has pumped gas and worked for an ice-cream store, besides working thirty years for Western—declared that graduation from this special course is equivalent to a degree from Harvard Business

School, except that the knowledge gained at Princeton pertains specifically only to the Bell System rather than to business in general.

The center's students live in a motel-like residence hall, are not allowed to bring their families with them, patronize a bar that is open for forty-five minutes twice a day, are required to wear jackets and ties or dresses at dinner, and behave themselves. "We had no campus riots in 1968 or 1969," said Thiesmeyer, with a certain thin-lipped satisfaction.

Bell Labs—that paragon of inventiveness, that outwardly cumbersome but inwardly rigidly disciplined corporate Edison of our times—has its headquarters at Murray Hill, New Jersey. The Murray Hill facility, high on a hilltop in the heart of upper-income New York City suburbia, was opened in 1941; prior to then all the Labs' activities except a stray few were conducted at the West Street site in New York City. Murray Hill was the nation's first totally "modular" laboratory, that is, the first in which all the interior walls are movable; in fact, each one is moved on an average of every seven years, and the lab where the transistor was invented cannot now be found, simply because it has long since been unceremoniously dismantled. Walking the corridors of Murray Hill, where about 3,700 Bell Labs people now work, one finds laboratories in close proximity to executive offices; on bulletin boards one finds notes and posters that suggest the scientists' and technicians' relatively esoteric tastes in recreation—notices of meetings of chess clubs and chamber-music groups. In the cafeteria one finds French-speaking and Italian-speaking tables. In one of the offices, its walls lined with books by Bell Labs scientists, one finds William O. Baker, since 1973 president of Bell Labs.

Baker, like most top executives of Bell Labs, came up through the scientific ranks. Born in Chestertown, Maryland, in 1915, graduated from Washington College in 1935 and awarded a Ph.D. in physical chemistry by Princeton in 1938, he joined Bell Labs in 1939, concentrating in research in polymer molecules; his chief discovery was of a new synthetic polymer molecule called microgel, which turned out to be of great value in the World War II rubber crises. Eventually his greatest talent proved to be not in scientific research but in administration; as an administrator, his research background is useful in giving him (as such a background has given all past Bell Labs presidents) the respect of the scientists and technicians under his direction. Baker is a fair-haired man given to conceptual thinking, histrionic gestures, and dramatic statements that sometimes seem to be overstatements. Certainly he is the antithesis of the stereotyped researcher, the introverted, uncommunicative laboratory gnome. On my visit to him, he inveighed in an unrestrained way against federal government interference that, he said, threatened if successful to leave Bell Labs and indeed all of the Bell System "a pile of rubble." I found myself wondering whether such unbuttoned language, expressive of an extreme partisan point of view, was consistent with the cool scientific spirit presumably required in one running a huge industrial laboratory. I decided that perhaps in the long run it was. Perhaps inspiring leadership was called for more than scientific detachment; perhaps what Bell Labs needed at the top was a brilliant cheerleader made persuasive by his scientific credentials.

Down a labyrinth of hallways from Baker's office, Dean Gillette, formally entitled executive director for systems research and informally called the house philosopher, talked to me about Bell Labs' relations with the operating companies. "People in the companies out West tend to think we have dirty toenails and spend our time sitting around writing papers," he said. "It's our job to live down that reputation by showing them we can help them give better telephone service." Down another labyrinth, Warren A. Tyrrell, executive director for technical relations with foreign telephone companies (virtually all of which are government-owned and operated), gave me a sample of Bell Labs' overview of the role of the telephone in the modern world. Even today, he pointed out, in many countries the telephone simply isn't generally accepted or taken for granted. Frenchmen, for example, continue to feel uncomfortable doing business by phone, and only recently has the government put on pressure for better service; in Soviet Russia, the usefulness of telephones is deliberately restricted by a government policy of making directories all but impossible to come by; and China apparently doesn't even want to have a telephone in every home, preferring to install them on street corners for communal use. Some highly developed countries have very low counts of telephone per population, calling into question the notion—generally unquestioned in this country—that a highly developed communications network is essential to economic growth. The United States, with 40 percent of the world's telephones and the highest ratio of telephones to population (considerably more than one for every resident of Washington, D.C., for example), stands out as a telephone-mad nation; and this, Tyrrell finds, is a phenomenon that does not yield to rational explanation.

Such philosophizing about communications is an important part of the Labs' work as its leaders conceive it; but technical innovations come from nothing but actual laboratory work. With a group of visiting high-school students and their science teachers, I visited a few laboratories. In the first, a young black scientist wearing an Afro haircut and a bright sports shirt was working on solidification—"the way things freeze," as he put it. He showed microscopic photographs, which looked like abstract art, of various materials being frozen, and explained that although solidification is important in the making of various key materials in telephony, his research is basically theoretical. "We aim," he said, "to learn as much as we can—and, perhaps, to come up with applications."

A second lab, in the field of development as opposed to research, was devoted to making bipolar integrated circuits—tiny affairs, with many uses in telephony, in which an entire complex circuit is included on an almost microscopic chip of silicon, with gold used as the electrical conductor. The researcher, in this case a young woman, explained that a single particle of dust introduced during the assembly can destroy such a circuit; therefore the lab must be "superclean"—less than one hundred particles of dust with a diameter of more than one-half micron per cubic foot of air. To preserve this standard, everyone in the lab, including us visitors, wore plastic caps, coats, and gloves, giving the project an air of surgery. Unlike most surgery, the work was done entirely under microscopes.

In yet another development lab a young scientist was working on improving the efficiency of optical fiber wave guides, the new transmission method—one of the hottest processes currently under development in telephony—that I had seen being brought nearer to actual production at Western Electric's Engineering Research Center. Already, the scientist said, such wave guides have been shown to be capable of transmitting voice and data with less line loss than either a twisted pair of wires or coaxial cable. Their commercial use in the future now seems assured; when it comes, it will be a development not without irony, inasmuch as the transmission of sound by converting it into light was tried a century ago, not very successfully, by Alexander Graham Bell.

Other Bell Labs basic research projects are more exotic. A handful of researchers were working on DNA, the substance that transmits human genetic traits—a project that would seem to belong to biology rather than telephony, but that, as President Baker explained to me, is actually an obvious Bell Labs undertaking because DNA is "the most beautiful, elegant form of communication, and, moreover, basically electric." Who knows, Baker asked rhetorically, but that better understanding of DNA may lead by analogy to telephone systems now beyond imagining? Again, since about 1955 there has been in progress a behavioral project, designed to discover more about the relationship between communication and the rest of human behavior. At first, academic social scientists were repelled by Bell Labs' statistical approach, its attempt to put behavior in an engineering context; but Bell Labs persisted, and has been rewarded by coming up with some provocative findings, among them that telephone numbers would be easier to remember if the exchange letters or numbers came last instead of first. (All agree that it's too late to make the change now.)

On another afternoon, I visited Holmdel, largest of all Bell Labs installations, with a staff of more than four thousand. It is situated on the New Jersey coastal plain, an hour's drive southeast from Murray Hill. When first opened in the late 1930s, it was a tiny facility occupying a couple of farmhouses chosen for radio research because their location enjoyed an unusual degree of radio quiet; in contrast, the present main building, opened in 1962, is a huge and eye-catching affair designed by the celebrated architect Eero Saarinen, with glass walls and offices and labs with balcony corridors arranged around interior garden courts under huge ceiling skylights. While the atmosphere of Murray Hill is businesslike and everyday, that of Holmdel is echoing and futuristic. Yet the work done there is mostly eminently practical; it includes systems research and engineering and development of switching, transmission, and customer equipment, and Holmdel is the nerve center of a crucial Bell Labs activity called network planning. Network planning's job is to look at the telephone system from the customer's viewpoint, and to decide how best to serve his needs, present and future, by determining such things as how to allocate maintenance dollars and where to install computers. At Holmdel I talked to Irwin Dorros, executive director of network planning, a youngish, Brooklyn-born executive whose background is in electrical engineering. Dorros recounted some of the wonders of a new small-computer system that the Bell System was in the process of deploying; using it, a telephone-company employee can simply dial a number that is having service trouble and instantly see displayed on a cathode-ray screen everything pertinent about that particular line—its current status and its past record of service failures. Dorros also spoke with pride of a new system, the product of the work of about ten people stretching over nearly five years, that he said "aggregates the need for new plant in Long Lines over a thirty-year period, allowing for new technology," and is called the "Mod I Optimizer." (In 1972 the Bell System issued a booklet containing more than 750 acronyms and abbreviations in use at Bell Labs from "AA" [Administrative Assistant] to "YIG" [Yttrium Iron Garnet].) I asked to see the Mod I Optimizer, and Dorros told me, with a smile, that I couldn't because, being a computer program rather than a piece of hardware, it has no bodily existence.

Bell Labs people spoke to me candidly about the fact that they have made their share of mistakes. Apart from whatever responsibility the labs bore for the great service crisis, there was, for example, the gaily colored Princess phone, introduced in 1959, which was quickly found to be so light that it often fell off a table when the user was dialing, and had to be redesigned. The "ready-access terminal," a Bell Labs innovation designed to save time and money in the making of line repairs, proved to be a technical success but a behavioral failure: repairmen found it infuriating to work with. There was also, of course, the huge underestimate, previously described, of the cost of developing a workable electronic switching system.

But whatever Bell Labs' shortcomings, most certainly, to date at least, it has accomplished its mission to supply the technology necessary to meet the demands for telephone service. Without its innovations in telephony alone, for current service demands to be met everyone in the United States would have to be a telephone operator. Speaking of the telephonic future to be brought into being by innovations still to come, President Baker waxes visionary, and uses phrases like "anti-entropy"—scientific minimizing of human energy waste. He goes on to say that by the year 2000, telephony and its related arts will "civilize the citizens of the nation," and in the process will "minimize collectivism" and "offer access by telephone to the wisdom and processes of the society." Others may fear that the very innovations Baker rhapsodizes about may work to destroy privacy, foster uniformity, and make possible centralized thought control. The difference is a matter of faith.

The headquarters and nerve center of the Long Lines Department of AT&T has for many years been an old brick building at 32 Sixth Avenue, in the run-down commercial district of Manhattan Island between Greenwich Village and Wall Street. (The headquarters will be moved in 1977 to Bedminster, New Jersey; but the operating functions at Sixth Avenue will remain.) Here the whole complex network of Long Lines, domestic and international, is centrally controlled, and through the facilities here passes every network television program that originates in New York, en route from the studios by Long Lines transmission systems to local stations around the country. A visit to the network management room, on the twenty-fourth floor, gives one the heady feeling of having a finger on the telephonic pulse of the country and much of the world. Two huge status boards dominate the walls, one covering the domestic network and the other the international; the boards are dotted with orange and red indicator lights—orange to show that automatic call-switching equipment is working, red to indicate that human intervention is required to complete a circuit. (It is Long Lines' boast that 1.5 percent of attempted long-distance calls result in the message "no circuits available.") Also in the room is a commercial television set, kept playing to monitor certain network programs that give rise to huge numbers of long-distance calls; and an equipment status map, marked in crayon in the appropriate places with such messages as: "Cable failed 2-9-74. Repair ship 'Northern' dispatched 2-10-74. ETA unknown. Search prevented by ice conditions."

So automated is the network that only a dozen or so persons are on duty at any given time in the network management center. They are youngish men with drooping mustaches and crisp young women, black and white; their earnings are in the area of eighteen to twenty thousand dollars a year; and they handle their apparently awesome responsibilities with cool aplomb, engaging in terse conversations with trouble spots here and there around the network as casually as they might order groceries. On certain special occasions that generate millions of calls, such as Mother's Day, the status board lights up like Broadway at night and the network controllers become tense and harassed; but even then, when the part of the center devoted to Operations wants to talk to the part devoted to Facilities, they are inclined to forget about telephones and just shout across the room.

Relatively few overseas calls are yet handled by direct distance dialing, and therefore, in the overseas operating rooms at 32 Sixth Avenue, there are rows of operators sitting at ordinary switchboards, each one marked "London," "Paris," "Tokyo," "Rio de Janeiro," or whatnot. The atmosphere is prosaic, but the overseas boards are sought after by operators for the opportunity they offer for a life of vicarious travel.

Now at last—to round out this flying view of the parts of the colossus of talk—a look at the entity that directly serves and directly deals with the telephone user, the regional operating company. To see an operating company in action, I spent several days in Philadelphia visiting the Bell Telephone Company of Pennsylvania.

I chose Pennsylvania Bell because it is among the oldest of the operating companies, dating back to 1879, two years after commercial telephone service began; because it is of medium size (sixth largest out of twenty-two, with 6.8 million telephones in service in 1974); because it is technologically among the most advanced of the Bell companies; and because its prime operating area is Philadelphia, a huge, densely populated city containing large minority groups—the sort of area where relations with customers and the public are the most demanding and abrasive. I went first to a Pennsylvania Bell business office. The office, in rented space on Chestnut Street, serves 7,000 business customers as well as 91,000 residence customers, three-quarters of whom are

black. To do so, it maintains a staff of seventy service representatives, most of them white women, and eight supervisors presided
over by a manager, a calm and equable young man. "Service
representative" is the highest nonmanagement job in a Bell operating company; each such representative, sitting at a desk beside
a large file drawer of customer records, handles seventy to eighty
customer calls a day, discussing bills, new installations, service
complaints, and so on. A large status board on the room's wall
enables representatives to promise a customer a certain installation
date, and reference material kept at hand supplies the answers to
95 percent of the questions usually asked. But there remains the
other 5 percent, and each representative is given wide latitude
in dealing with unexpected problems: he or she may adjust a bill
up to twenty-five dollars without consulting a superior, or may
decide (within guidelines) whether to disconnect a customer for
nonpayment or extend further credit, or may speak sharply to a
rude or abusive customer, or may speak in endearments to a
troubled one. The stated task of the service representative is to
dispose of or contain the problem—above all, to prevent the
customer from appealing to the president of the company (who,
however, personally answers all such appeals, whether by mail
or telephone) or to the Pennsylvania Utility Commission. It is a
difficult and responsible job, in effect amounting to taking the
blame for mistakes made by others, and from what I saw the
service representatives clearly enjoyed their work. On the other
hand, it is a job subject to surveillance and constraints that must
sometimes be maddening: service representatives' conversations
with customers may be monitored at any time by a supervisor
equipped with a stopwatch, and the rules exactingly require
them, when they have to go searching for records, to answer the
customer within seventy-seven seconds.

From the business office, I went far out Chestnut Street to
the west to see a Plant Department office, charged with responsibility for installing, testing, and repairing phones for some 140,000
customers in West Philadelphia. When a new-installation order
arrives here from a business office, the first Plant Department job
is to figure out which underground cable serves the address of
the new customer; the second is to locate a free pair of wires in the
cable that can be used for the new installation. Then a dispatcher
—one of a group of technicians called "deskmen," who sit in a
big room at boards covered with pushbuttons—sends out an in-

staller to make the hookup, and tests it with the installer by both voice and electrical test equipment. The busy time at this particular office, I was told, comes every June and September, when some six thousand students at nearby Drexel Institute and the University of Pennsylvania suddenly want to have telephones installed or disconnected. I listened in on the conversations of a deskman who was dealing with a service problem. He called the customer, and a woman's voice informed him that her trouble was that although she could receive calls, she couldn't dial them. After some checking and testing, the deskman told me that he had found the trouble: the phone was a Touch-Tone, and the wires were reversed, which is fatal for Touch-Tone dialing. He called "Frame"—the main frame in the switching office to which the customer's telephone was connected—and asked for a reversal. The customer still couldn't dial. The deskman called "Frame" again and asked, "What pair did you put my reversing shoe on?" A further adjustment was evidently made, because this time, when he asked the customer to try to dial him, she got him immediately and happily reported that everything was fine now.

Then I stopped in, a few blocks away on Hanson Avenue, at a Pennsylvania Bell garage, where fifty-five installation and maintenance trucks are housed; the installers—all men, 65 percent white and 35 percent black at this particular location—get their orders from the business office and set out to do the work. The garage foreman, a forceful young man named Robert ("Dutch") Wurzbach, told me that they operated in a tough area—what the company calls a "red area"—and that vandalism of trucks and safety of installers had been a constant problem until recently, when the situation had been saved, and the local image of the telephone company reversed, by a series of small goodwill gestures by the company. Wurzbach proudly showed me a sheet listing such acts, among them the following:

> Financed a bus trip to Smithsonian Institute . . . for 150 people.
> Provided 2 basketball backboards and 3 basketballs for the Youth Conservations Corps.
> Made a contribution of $75 to Mrs. White for a play area.
> Donated a small couch to the Third Christian Church.

As a result, Wurzbach said, "In this district now, you're safer in a telephone company truck than in your own car."

Next, having seen the anatomy of telephone installation in

Philadelphia from start to finish, I visited three call-handling centers—an automatic switching center with one of the oldest types of Bell System equipment; an automatic switching center with the *newest* type of equipment; and a traffic center offering the up-to-date forms of operator assistance. The old center was the EVergreen exchange, handling some twenty thousand telephones. The equipment consisted of a roomful of ceiling-high frames, weathered-looking but clicking away as they automatically switched dialed calls. Even though this type of switching equipment, called "panel," dates from the 1920s and is now considered obsolete, it is so automated that about twenty technicians keep the whole thing running.

The ultramodern equipment, Philadelphia's Electronic Switching System Control Center, was one of the first operating applications of the fruit of Bell Labs' huge, $500-million undertaking of the 1960s. Philadelphia in 1974 had eighteen ESS centers in operation, more than any other U.S. city. The control center for all of them is at Ninth and Race Streets, on the edge of Chinatown; in front of the building is a phone booth with a pagoda-style roof. Essentially—as Robert de Haven, head of the ESS Control Center, explained to me—the difference between conventional switching and electronic switching is the difference between "hardware" and what computer men call "software"; in the former case, maintenance is done on the spot, with screwdriver and pliers, while in the case of electronic switching, it can be done remotely, by computer, from a central point, making it possible to have only one or two technicians on duty at a time at each switching center. In Philadelphia, the central ESS maintenance point is de Haven's domain. He showed me a room where a huge computer was gathering data as the various switching centers electronically reported their own defects, and "repairmen," sitting in front of cathode-ray tubes, were "talking" by computer-connected typewriters to the particular ESS machines that were malfunctioning. It seemed unreal, dumfounding; yet I knew that across Philadelphia the talk went on, the telephones worked. What, indeed, had God wrought?

But automation has, of course, not eliminated the operator; she—or, more and more frequently in the last few years, he—is still needed to handle collect calls, person-to-person calls, credit-card calls, calls billed to a third party, and so on. I visited a

Pennsylvania Bell "traffic center" at 1835 Arch Street, where 122,000 calls a day, made by people who for one reason or another have dialed "O" for "Operator," are handled by operators using the new Traffic Service Position System equipment. TSPS, as it is called, replaces the long-familiar "cord board" at which operators sit in rows, shoulder to shoulder, plugging cords into the jacks in switchboards in front of them. (There is only one cord board left in the Philadelphia telephone system; it handles a few stray functions such as calls from mobile telephones and conference calls.) A TSPS operator has a separate console of her (or his) own, with a punchboard of buttons, a television-style screen on which such pertinent information as the toll for the call being completed is automatically displayed, and a memory unit in which billing information is automatically recorded. By eliminating the need for making out call slips and otherwise speeding the operator's work, TSPS makes possible the saving of several million dollars a year in Philadelphia alone. I sat for a while with a male TSPS operator, listening to his conversations on a monitor phone. Some of the callers were people who had been unable to complete calls and wanted help in doing so; most of the rest were from people who claimed that they had inserted dimes in pay phones, failed to get through, and not got their dimes back. In such cases, I was somewhat surprised to learn, if the customer will give his name and address the company will generally mail him a check for ten cents on no evidence except his word.

What is it like being an operator in the age of automation? To try to find out, I had lunch at the traffic center's cafeteria with four TSPS operators: a woman with twenty years' experience, two younger women with considerable experience, and one man, an ex-Marine, who was in his first year as an operator. The consensus of the women, all of whom had once worked on cord boards, is that the march of progress has made the operator's job less exciting because less personal and responsible. Long ago, in pre-dial days, the operator—particularly the rural operator—had a chance to achieve a kind of heroism: seeking out the doctor for a midnight medical emergency, rounding up the volunteers to save a house from fire. As we have seen, in the early years of this century the telephone operator was a folk-hero in popular American fiction. But even at an urban cord board only a few years ago, the operator was often called upon to "build up" calls to distant points by choosing the best routes; now, with TSPS, that is all done automatically. The experienced operators I talked to all agreed that working in TSPS is "less romantic" and gives less sense of accomplishment. They felt, too, that the elimination of the old cord-board closeness with other operators makes it a "more lonesome" job. Part of the operator's function has been usurped by the use of "Automatic Intercept"—the recorded voice that irritatingly cuts in to say, for example, that the number being called is no longer in service. But on the other hand, operators' pay and job security is better now than ever before. The change in the operators' situation seemed to be a paradigm of the equivocal and ironical change that has affected so many people in mass society: greater security, comfort, and efficiency paid for in the coin of boredom and loneliness.

The young ex-Marine described a separate but perhaps related problem. From the earliest days of telephony up to the latter 1960s, telephone operators were all women; then, as we have seen, pressed by the newly formed federal Equal Employment Opportunity Commission, the companies began hiring male operators. Even so, male operators are by no means fully accepted by the public; the ex-Marine told me that his chief complaint about the job was that telephone users were so often unwilling to believe that he was an operator, and would interrupt his efforts to help them by telling him to get off the line.

I ended up my visit to Pennsylvania Bell by stopping in at company headquarters, a shining ten-year-old building at 1 Parkway, in downtown Philadelphia, with a reflecting pool in front. There I talked with a representative of the engineering department, who pointed out that planning to meet future telephone needs in a great urban center like Philadelphia involves, above all, an understanding of social trends—what areas will be developed next, which ones will tend to be abandoned. Errors in anticipating such trends may lead to service crises, and indeed, such errors unquestionably played a role in the 1969–70 service crisis (although they did not in Pennsylvania Bell, which escaped trouble at that time). Surprisingly, Pennsylvania Bell employs no professional sociologists, leaving future planning to its engineers.

The exact nature of the relationship, usually good but occasionally strained, between an operating company like Pennsylvania Bell and the parent company, AT&T, was the subject of my last conversation at 1 Parkway—with William S. Cashel, Jr., who at the time of my visit had been president of Pennsylvania Bell for about four years. A 1941 Dartmouth College graduate, a World War II Marine, and a lifetime Bell System career man, Cashel, with a crew haircut, a trim build, and a forthright manner, had the aspect of a Marine Corps officer. He said:

"Pennsylvania Bell has been fortunate, during my term as president, in not having serious problems. Our service has been good and our operating results satisfactory. Our problems have been of a pedestrian kind. This situation has permitted our relationship with the parent company to be quite pleasant. On the other hand, I have heard from some of my colleagues—other Bell operating company presidents—that when there *is* serious trouble they are apt to get a kind of supervision that I, personally, wouldn't care for, a kind that makes managing not as much fun as it ought to be.

"As for us, we are pretty much left to our own devices. Sometimes weeks go by during which I have no contact with AT&T by either mail or telephone. There are various formal contacts, in the natural course of things, and also various informal ones. Of course, there are the monthly (or almost monthly) Presidents' Conferences, attended by the top AT&T officers and almost always all the operating company presidents. In addition, once a year I go with my principal operating officer to 195 Broadway for a formal discussion of hoped-for earnings and other plans for the coming year, with the AT&T president, vice-chairman, and their associates. Less formally, I have conversations with AT&T officers on particular topics perhaps half a dozen times a year, and my various officers—operating, finance, and so on—have similar conversations with their AT&T counterparts from time to time. Once a week or so, I get a letter from one AT&T vice-president or another about some specific matter—energy saving or whatnot. Then, there are the handwritten notes that I get from John deButts in response to our monthly reports on service quality. They're brief and to the point. One month the note will say, 'Bill—great, J. deB.' But another month, when something has gone wrong, it may be, 'Bill—oops! J. deB.'

"Here's an example of how we do our own thing. In the late 1950s and early 1960s, Pennsylvania Bell gradually, over a period of five or six years, changed its structure to a more decentralized organization. Gene McNeely, who was president of AT&T from 1961 to 1964, didn't like it. He said you couldn't develop departmental skills under the system we were introducing. We said, in effect, 'That's a bunch of baloney, Mr. McNeely.' It was a daring move on our part. There were fears that heads might roll. But they didn't, and we were allowed to go forward with the reorganization, which was later imitated to some extent in other Bell operating companies.

"The fact is that there are several areas in which tensions are likely to develop between AT&T and an operating company. One is in labor relations; the companies have different agreements with the unions, and standardization won't always work. Another is in management salaries, which are not uniform among the companies. Still another is in operating procedures. AT&T may want telephone service centers to be run exactly the same in all companies; some companies may resist, and want to do it their own way. Then there is the matter of direct orders. AT&T, since it owns every share of our stock, is obviously in a position to issue us direct orders, but we are sensitive about getting them—and they are tactful about not issuing them. In fact, just the other day we got the first direct order of my years as president of Pennsylvania Bell. It came from Bob Lilley, and it went not just to us but to all Bell operating companies. It had to do with compliance with the Equal Employment Opportunity Act, which we are sure we were already complying with. A thing like that is so unusual that it causes raised eyebrows around the system, and makes us think that there must be some special explanation for it that we don't know about.

"In the end, a lot flows back to the earnings: if your earnings are good, AT&T is very permissive; if not, it isn't. There is pressure from AT&T to improve your earnings—sometimes great, sometimes less great, depending on circumstances. But that pressure never, never takes the form of directly suggesting that you degrade service to improve earnings. Just for one thing, once you get into a poor-service mode, it's very expensive to get out, and it also results in bad relations with the regulators, so poor service ends up not paying. However, such suggestions do occasionally come from the operating companies to AT&T. An operating company may say to deButts, 'I can deliver so many dollars in additional earnings if you will let me reduce the service index from 98 percent to 92 percent. The customers will never notice the difference.' I know at first hand that such a suggestion has been made. It was rejected.

"One aspect of AT&T control is certain: I was appointed to this position by 195 Broadway, and so are all the other operating-company presidents. Election by our own boards of directors is just a formality. Our board gives advice, but seldom initiates action. An operating-company president is in the Bell System corporate hierarchy as much as if the whole system were one integrated company. The reasons it isn't an integrated company are mainly political and psychological, having to do with community and government relations; but if it were, Pennsylvania Bell's relationship with 195 Broadway would be exactly the same as it is now."

2

As much as the structural future of AT&T, the future of telephony itself is cloudy. New developments now in process, which have already been shown to be feasible theoretically, may never come to be because of nontechnical problems such as uneconomically high cost or lack of customer demand. On the other hand, the unpredictable scientific breakthroughs of the future—the Nobel Prize–winning accomplishments of 1980 or 1990—may bring with them telephonic innovations not yet even conceived.

Bell Labs men, carefully explaining that they are not necessarily offering a preview of the future, provide a list of new devices and processes that *may* come into use in the early years of the telephone's second century. One is a pocket-sized cordless telephone that would make it possible for calls to any number in the world to be made by anyone anywhere—a pedestrian waiting for a bus, a stranded mountain climber in need of rescue, a construction worker who, with both hands occupied, could talk to his boss in an office, or to a cousin in Rangoon, through his hat, in which a cordless telephone would be installed. Another is a watchman telephone that, activated by a fire, flood, or burglary, would automatically give notification by calling the appropriate number. Others are medical retrieval of visual information, whereby a doctor could "dial" X ray pictures stored in another city; a service enabling merchants and banks to handle such functions as check verification and check-cashing authorization by telephone; and a service making it possible for daily newspapers and other printed material from afar to be shown on a home wall screen—the screen itself, according to the suggestion of a leading Bell Labs man, to be made decorative when not in use by being made to show, perhaps, a seashore scene equipped electronically with moving waves and the sound of surf. Students of telecommunications outside Bell Labs have suggested one other innovation—already possible technically—that might have important political implications: a home voting terminal, with buttons marked "Yes" and "No" and an attached cable connected to a telephone jack, that would make it possible for a national plebiscite on a current question to be conducted in about ten minutes.

Such visions of the future will be greeted with mixed feelings by those who, like George Orwell in his *1984*, fear that the additional human convenience brought by future technology will be paid for in lost human privacy, individuality, autonomy, taste, and decency. The matter is an enigma. In any case, the likely telephone innovations of the next quarter century of a sort visible to the telephone user are of minor importance when set beside those that have already taken place. They pale, for example, beside the introduction of local telephone service itself; of first limited and then ever-expanding long-distance service; of dial telephones; of overseas service; of direct distance dialing; of transmission of computer data; of television transmission by coaxial cable and earth satellite. So far as the imagination of 1976 can conceive, the world telephone and television network is largely in place.

AT&T's great technical task of the immediate future appears to be the application of new technology toward two objectives: first, meeting the continuing growth of telephone traffic, which, if projections of present trends may be trusted, will call for five to ten times the present capacity by 1990; and second, supplying that capacity at reduced rates to the customer. The last such application of the telephone's first century—the No. 4 ESS, first put into service in Chicago early in 1976—dramatically furthers the attainment of both objectives. It is capable of processing

350,000 toll calls per hour, three times as many as the fastest non-electronic switching system, while requiring only one-fourth the space and one-third the maintenance cost; moreover, present estimates are that by 1985 expense savings of the Bell System attributable to No. 4 ESS installations may approach one billion dollars per year. Beyond that, the plan at Bell Labs is to meet increased demand and reduce costs by a vast expansion of the now-still-emergent revolution in telecommunications technology brought about since 1950 by the transistor and the computer. New transmission, switching, and information-storage devices now under development—with names like "magnetic bubble," "light-emitting diode," "charge-coupled device," and "millimeter waveguide," and functions not capable of being quickly grasped by a layman—will probably come into play. And so, most likely, will the fulfillment of Alexander Graham Bell's dream of the transmission of speech by light beams—through hair-fine flexible fibers of glass that may eventually connect homes and offices to the nationwide communications network (which may itself consist of such fibers). Because glass fiber is plentiful and cheap, such technology offers further potential of cheaper as well as better telephone service.

Like the future of the world, then, one's view of the character of the future of telecommunications balances on the hairline of individual temperament: optimists think of greater efficiency and convenience at less cost, pessimists of a progressive mechanization of man and concomitant loss of his humanity.[1]

Some curious ironies attend the Bell System's centennial year. The objectives of Vail—one system, one policy, universal service—have largely been achieved; yet in the course of their achievement Vail's large-spirited and forward-looking style of management has often been lost. Moreover, the issues in contention in Vail's time, apparently settled once and for all in his time and in the years after his death, are very much in contention again. The structure of the telephone business in the United States may be at as great a turning point as it was in 1913. What would seem to be needed, perhaps as much as new ESS machines or optical fiber transmission, is a resurgence of the spirit and style of Vail in AT&T management. There are signs that the company is reacting with a conscious effort to recapture that spirit and style. That deButts had been closely studying Vail and his work was shown in a talk he gave in 1973 to the Commercial Club of Boston, which consisted entirely of an appreciation of Vail and a discussion of how his principles apply to modern Bell System problems.[2] Vail would seem to have come, belatedly, to be accepted within the company as its prophet. Whether deButts and his successors over the coming years will truly learn and apply the prophet's wisdom, or will merely take from it what is useful to their purposes, remains to be seen.

What, meanwhile, are we to make of it all? Is the Bell System in its present form—vertically integrated, erratically regulated, increasingly pressed for new capital, anomalously permitted the economic heresy of essential monopoly—good, bad, or morally neutral? Serious social observers, over the years, have shown a tendency to lose their objectivity in contemplating the Bell System, to react not so much in terms of its characteristics as in terms of their own predilections. Free-enterprise advocates, citing the generally accepted superiority of Bell telephone service to that supplied by government-run companies in other countries, have used it as a classic example of the superiority of free enterprise to state socialism; advocates of state socialism have pointed out the contrary situation as regards ownership and service in railroads, and insisted that the Bell System would give even better service at lower rates as a state monopoly. Those whose philosophical bent is toward bigness and integration in industry credit the Bell System's success to those attributes; the advocates of competition and diversity—from the New Deal FCC through the Justice Department in 1949 and again in 1974, down to Ralph Nader's organization in the 1970s—have insisted over the years that the integrated Bell System tends to exploit its monopoly and that a fragmented telephone system would tend to serve the public better. One is tempted to conclude that the Bell System, through age, tradition, complexity, and sheer size, has taken on a modern industrial equivalent of the meaning of ancient monuments like Stonehenge and the Sphinxes—that is, that it ends up meaning to the observer not what he sees but what he is.

This is called inscrutability. The present observer, like those before him, has looked at the Bell System as hard and as objectively as he could, and, like them, has come up with what may be tentatively advanced as a theory. The essence of the theory is that in assessing the Bell System, the important thing to look at is not its morality—which, after all, can scarcely differ radically from the prevailing morality of its times and of its million employees—but its vitality. Compared with other American corporations of exceptional age, size, and power, AT&T has weathered the years strikingly well—has, indeed, come through a century with a remarkable vitality intact. Experience has shown that great size and power in corporations generally leads sooner or later to case-hardening, to a deterioration of imagination, to a blind following of old forms that results in decline and decay. Railroading, the first great American industry, has degenerated into bankruptcies and passenger service that is appalling or nonexistent; automobile manufacture, the industrial miracle of a half century ago, has become increasingly unresponsive to public needs. Yet telephony, scarcely younger than railroading and considerably older than the automobile, presses on with ever more rapid technical innovation as if it were in the bloom of youth.

Why? Perhaps the answer lies in the fact that the telephone business by its nature enforces constant, daily contact with the customer, not just through his representatives in Washington but face to face and voice to voice, through talk with the local service representative or through installation and repair of equipment by the man on the truck from the local equipment garage. The railroads have escaped the public by concentrating on shipping freight rather than moving passengers; the automobile makers have interposed between themselves and the public a vast network of dealers. But telephony has no users except people, and no middleman dealers. Talking to customers tends to counteract the most self-destructive habit of great corporations, that of talking to themselves. The century-old telephone business—Bell and independent—may have been saved from hardening of the arteries by the necessary discipline of direct, everyday contact with the millions of people it serves.

# Notes

CHAPTER 1. The Colossus of Talk

1. Author's interview with Warren A. Tyrrell, Bell Telephone Laboratories.

2. M. D. Fagen, ed., "Impact: a Compilation of Bell System Innovations in Science and Engineering" (Bell Laboratories, 1971); H. W. Bode, "Synergy: Technical Integration and Technical Innovation in the Bell System" (Bell Laboratories, 1971).

3. "Where Is Interconnection Taking Us?" *Telephony*, January 7, 1974.

4. *Harvard Business Review*, January 1974.

5. "An Introduction to the Bell System," pamphlet, 1968.

6. *New York Times*, May 14, May 15, May 16, August 21, 1975.

7. N. R. Danielian, *AT&T, the Story of Industrial Conquest* (New York, 1939), p. 409.

Other facts in this chapter are derived from unpublished Bell System sources and from interviews with Bell System executives.


CHAPTER 2. Beginnings

1. William C. Langdon, "Myths in Telephone History," *Bell Quarterly*, April 1933.

2. Frederick Leland Rhodes, *Beginnings of Telephony* (New York, 1929), pp. 54–6, 225 ff.; J. E. Kingsbury, *The Telephone and Telephone Exchanges* (New York, 1915), pp. 4, 10–11; Alvin F. Harlow, *Old Wires and New Waves* (New York, 1936), pp. 8–9, 341 ff.; *The Bell Telephone*: the Deposition of Alexander Graham Bell in the Suit Brought by the United States to Annul the Bell Patents (Boston, 1908), pp. 211–2.

3. Rhodes, Chapter 1; Robert V. Bruce, *Bell: Alexander Graham Bell*

*and the Conquest of Solitude* (Boston, 1973), Chaps. 1, 4; *The Bell Telephone*, pp. 7, 208.

4. Rhodes, p. 2; Bruce, pp. 37, 50; Kenneth P. Todd, Jr., "A Capsule History of the Bell System," pamphlet (American Telephone and Telegraph Company, 1972), pp. 6–7.

5. Bruce, pp. 51–2, 65–9.

6. Bruce, pp. 94–6, 100; Rhodes, pp. 4 ff.

7. Rhodes, pp. 4–5, 13–14; Bruce, p. 121.

8. *The Bell Telephone*, pp. 88–9; Thomas A. Watson, *Exploring Life* (New York, 1926), pp. 57–9.

9. Watson, p. 61; Bruce, pp. 131, 140.

10. *The Bell Telephone*, pp. 57–9; Bruce, pp. 143–7; Rhodes, pp. 22–5; Watson, pp. 66–72; Kingsbury, pp. 37–8.

11. Bruce, pp. 148–54.

12. Bruce, pp. 156, 163, 168; Watson, p. 75; Harlow, pp. 356–7.

13. *The Bell Telephone*, pp. 86–7, 194–5; Harlow, pp. 357–62; Bernard S. Finn, "Alexander Graham Bell's Experiments with the Variable-Resistance Transmitter," *Smithsonian Journal of History*, Winter 1966.

14. Watson, pp. 77 ff; Bruce, pp. 178 ff.

15. Bruce, pp. 184–6; Finn, "Bell's Experiments . . ."

16. Bruce, pp. 190–5; Watson, p. 85.

17. Bruce, pp. 201–2, 215, 229; Watson, pp. 85–6, 93–4, 99–103.

18. Watson, *Exploring Life*, pp. 115–18; Watson, "The Birth and Babyhood of the Telephone," pamphlet (AT&T, 1971); Bruce, p. 224; *The Bell Telephone*, pp. 152, 196–7.

19. Bruce, pp. 227–35, 282; Watson, p. 123.

20. Bruce, pp. 252, 281, 283, 399–400, 457–8.

21. Watson, pp. 177, 306, *passim;* Bruce, pp. 494–5.

CHAPTER 3.   Through the Valley

1. From the files of the American Telephone and Telegraph Company; reprinted in "The Early Corporate Development of the Telephone," pamphlet (AT&T, 1964).

2. J. Leigh Walsh, *Connecticut Pioneers in Telephony* (New Haven, 1950), pp. 29, 48, 81–2; Bruce, pp. 265–8.

3. Matthew Josephson, *The Robber Barons* (New York, 1934); Josephson, *Edison* (New York, 1959).

4. Bruce, pp. 220–1.

5. Walsh, pp. 69, 93; Angus Hibbard, *Hello—Goodbye* (Chicago, 1913), p. 202; Herbert Laws Webb, *The Development of the Telephone in Europe* (London, 1910).

6. Walsh, pp. 41–2, 50–4; Hibbard, pp. 7–17; "Events in Telephone History," pamphlet (AT&T, 1971); Herbert Casson, *The History of the Telephone* (Chicago, 1913), pp. 153–4; Hibbard, p. 25; Marion May Dilts, *The Telephone in a Changing World* (New York, 1941).

7. Danielian, pp. 40–1; Albert Bigelow Paine, *Theodore N. Vail: A Biography* (New York, 1921).

8. Kingsbury, pp. 119–24; Rhodes, p. 79; Bruce, p. 262.

9. Walsh, p. 85; Bruce, p. 270; Todd, p. 21; Watson, p. 170.

10. Watson, p. 181; Paine, p. 142; Charles Neider, ed., *Complete Humorous Sketches and Tales of Mark Twain* (New York, 1961); American Bell Annual Report, 1880.

CHAPTER 4.  God's Electric Clerk

1. "Events in **Tele**phone History."

2. Arthur S. **Pier**, *Forbes—Telephone Pioneer* (New York, 1953).

3. Rhodes, pp. 208, 209; Casson, p. 96; Bruce, p. 278.

4. Harlow, p. 387; Rhodes, pp. 56 ff.; Casson, p. 97.

5. Rhodes, pp. 61 ff.; Bruce, pp. 278–9.

6. Rhodes, pp. 64 ff.; Harlow, pp. 388 ff.; American Bell Annual Report, 1887; Joseph C. Goulden, *Monopoly* (New York, 1968).

7. U.S. Government Historical Almanac, 1800–1910; Coon, pp. 72–3; J. Warren Stehman, *The Financial History of The American Telephone and Telegraph Company* (Boston, 1925); American Bell Annual Reports, 1880–90.

8. "Western Electric Company 1869–1944," booklet (Western Electric Company, 1944); Paine, p. 181; Goulden, pp. 52–4; Danielian, pp. 100 ff.; American Bell Annual Report, 1887.

9. Casson, pp. 121, 126, 132; Walsh, p. 153; Hibbard, p. 28.

10. Pier, *Forbes;* Bruce, pp. 275–6; Rhodes, p. 71; Allan Nevins, *Grover Cleveland: A Study in Courage* (New York, 1932), pp. 294–5.

11. Rhodes, pp. 94–5; "Events in Telephone History"; "The Early Corporate Development of the Telephone," pamphlet (AT&T, 1964); Pier, *Forbes.*

12. Webb; Harry B. MacMeal, *The Story of Independent Telephony* (Chicago, 1934), p. 90; Casson, pp. 247–57; Kingsbury, pp. 193, 203–5; Hibbard, pp. 236–7; Dilts, p. 42.

13. *The Annals of Iowa,* Vol. XXIII (1941–42); Dilts, pp. 29–30; Hibbard, p. 81; Daniel J. Boorstin, *The Americans: The Democratic Experience* (New York, 1973), pp. 87, 399; J. C. Furnas, *The Americans* (New York, 1969), p. 807.

14. Kingsbury, pp. 306–34; Walsh, pp. 170 ff.; Hibbard, pp. 107 ff.

15. Hibbard, p. 140; Coon, p. 74; "Events in Telephone History"; Todd, p. 31; MacMeal, p. 271; Kingsbury, pp. 394, 410.

CHAPTER 5.  "Both Phones"

1. James B. Hoge, "Independent Telephone Development," *Journal of the Franklin Institute*, 1907; Danielian, p. 96; Walsh, pp. 201–2; MacMeal, p. 85; AT&T Annual Report, 1900 .

2. Stehman, pp. 94–5; MacMeal, pp. 31, 36, 68, 80, 81; Coon, pp. 80, 83; Goulden, p. 64; Walsh, pp. 213, 225–6.

3. MacMeal, p. 106; Danielian, p. 46, 58; Coon, pp. 86–7.

4. Coon, pp. 88–90; *The Annals of Iowa,* Vol. XXIII, pp. 287–308.

5. *Telephones: 1907*, Special Report, Department of Commerce and Labor, Bureau of the Census (Washington, D.C., 1910), pp. 76, 116; Mac-Meal, pp. 148, 158.

6. AT&T Annual Report, 1901; Goulden, pp. 61–3; MacMeal, pp. 138–48.

7. MacMeal, p. 159; Hoge; Goulden, p. 64.

8. Casson, pp. 204–6; *Telephones: 1907*, pp. 19, 20; *Scientific American*, Vol. 94 (June 16, 1906) and Vol. 104 (February 18, 1911); MacMeal, p. 170.

9. "The Telephone's New Uses in Farm Life," *The World's Work*, April 1905; "Outrages of the Telephone," *Lippincott's Monthly*, July 1909.

10. Coon, pp. 84–5; "Events in Telephone History"; Kingsbury, pp. 436 ff.; Rhodes, pp. 137 ff.; Harlow, p. 400; Casson, pp. 138–9.

11. Todd, p. 35; Danielian, pp. 57–69, 75.

12. Paine, pp. 175 ff., 186 ff., 220, 227, 229–30; Danielian, pp. 70–1.

CHAPTER 6.   A Big Man

1. Paine, pp. 231–2; Danielian, pp. 72, 102; Rhodes, *John J. Carty* (New York: privately printed, 1932), p. 66.

2. Paine, p. 234; AT&T Annual Report, 1907.

3. Todd, p. 37; Danielian, pp. 74–6.

4. AT&T Annual Report, 1910; Danielian, pp. 76–7; Coon, p. 113; MacMeal, pp. 204–10.

5. "Events in Telephone History"; Rhodes, *Carty*, pp. 70, 79, 85; Prescott C. Mabon, *Mission—Communications* (New York, 1975), pp. 21–2; Danielian, p. 105; Todd, pp. 40–1.

6. "Events in Telephone History"; Rhodes, *Beginnings of Telephony*, pp. 189–94; Danielian, pp. 103–5; Rhodes, *Carty*, pp. 90–6.

7. Carl Sandburg, *Chicago Poems* (1916); Danielian, pp. 335, 369; Stehman, pp. 125–6. Vail's 1915 San Francisco speech is reprinted in a pamphlet in the AT&T files.

8. Paine, pp. 235, 290, 292, 300, 304; author's interview with Katherine Vail Marsters.

9. MacMeal, 204; Danielian, 243–50, 369–70; Coon, 136–54; Paine, 320–4; AT&T Annual Reports, 1911–18.

10. Paine, 326–47.

CHAPTER 7.   Happy Days and Happiness Boys

1. A. Lincoln Lavine, *Circuits of Victory* (New York, 1921), pp. 122, 237 ff., 389, 416, 489; Danielian, pp. 254–70; Coon, pp. 145–54.

2. Arthur W. Page, *The Bell Telephone System* (New York, 1941), p. 2; "The Ring of Success: 75 Years of the Independent Telephone Movement," pamphlet (U.S. Independent Telephone Association, 1969).

3. William Peck Banning, *Commercial Broadcasting Pioneer: The WEAF Experiment 1922–1926* (Cambridge, Mass., 1946).

4. Danielian, pp. 122–6; Banning.

5. AT&T Annual Reports, 1920–25; Danielian, p. 183; Jack Barbash, *Unions and Telephones: The Story of the Communications Workers of America* (New York, 1952), Chap. 1; speech by Howard W. Johnson at the Western Electric Symposium Commemorating the 50th Anniversary of the Hawthorne Studios, Chicago, November 12, 1974.

6. "Events in Telephone History."

7. Jack Alexander, "Chief Operator," *The New Yorker*, June 5, June 12, June 19, 1937; Page, p. 134; Anthony Sampson, *The Sovereign State of ITT* (New York, 1973), p. 23; "Events in Telephone History"; Danielian, pp. 127–30; Banning, pp. 289–90.

8. Page, pp. 197–9; "A Statement of Policy of the American Telephone and Telegraph Company," an address by Walter S. Gifford before the convention of the National Association of Railroad and Utilities Commissioners, Dallas, Texas, October 20, 1927; author's interview with Robert K. Greenleaf.

9. Noël Coward, *Collected Sketches and Lyrics* (New York, 1932); John Gassner, ed., *Twenty-Five Best Plays of the Modern American Theatre*, including *The Front Page* (New York, 1949); Virginia Shortridge, ed., *Songs of Science*, including "The Telephone" (New York, 1930); *The Viking Portable Dorothy Parker*, including "A Telephone Call" (New York, 1944); Jean Cocteau, *The Human Voice*, English trans. by Carl Wildman (New York, 1930).

10. Coon, pp. 182–3; Page, pp. 18–27, 54, 202; "Events in Telephone History."

11. Danielian, pp. 113–16, 138–65; Todd, p. 52.

12. Mabon, pp. 113–14; "Events in Telephone History"; J. K. Galbraith, *The Great Crash* (Boston, 1954); John Brooks, *Once in Golconda* (New York, 1969).

CHAPTER 8. Hard Times

1. AT&T Annual Reports, 1930–33; Danielian, pp. 203–4; Walter S. Gifford, "Testimony Before Congressional Committees," Vol. II (AT&T, 1937).

2. AT&T Annual Reports, 1932–36; author's interview with David E. Lilienthal; Gifford, "Testimony," p. 100; Danielian, pp. 202, 216–17.

3. Walsh, pp. 280–1; Danielian, p. 212; Alexander, "Chief Operator"; Barbash, pp. 20–30; author's interview with Greenleaf.

4. *Who Was Who in America*, Vol. IV (1961–68); AT&T Annual Reports, 1935–38; Coon, pp. 11–14; Danielian, Preface; Gifford, "Testimony"; *Proposed Report—Telephone Investigation*, Federal Communications Commission, 1938; *Brief on the Proposed Report*, AT&T, 1938; Page, pp. 174–5.

5. AT&T Annual Report, 1938; Page, pp. 148 ff.; Dilts, pp. 77, 123–4; Walsh, pp. 291–6.

6. Rudolf Flesch, *The Book of Unusual Quotations* (New York, 1937); H. G. Wells, *Experiment in Autobiography* (New York, 1934); "The

World's Telephones," pamphlet (AT&T, 1973); "The Frequency of Words Used Over the Telephone," *Science*, August 14, 1931, quoted by Sidney H. Aronson, "The Sociology of the Telephone," *International Journal of Comparative Sociology*, Toronto, September 1971; "The Talk of the Town," *The New Yorker*, December 23, 1939.

7. "Events in Telephone History"; Mabon, *passim;* W. Shockley, "The Invention of the Transistor—an Example of Creative-Failure Methodology" (lecture, July 1973, Bell Telephone Laboratories).

8. *Who Was Who in America*, Vols. III (1951–60), IV (1961–68); *Year Book of the American Philosophical Society*, 1961.

9. Joseph Alsop and Robert Kintner, *American White Paper* (New York, 1940); AT&T Annual Report, 1941.

CHAPTER 9.   Trial by Combat

1. Todd, pp. 55–7; "Events in Telephone History"; Mabon, pp. 27, 57, 142–5.

2. AT&T Annual Reports, 1942–45.

3. AT&T Annual Reports, 1945–47; "Events in Telephone History"; Mabon, pp. 57–67.

4. Barbash, pp. 33–5, 40–2, 54–5, 60–2, 67–75, 212–15; *Historical Statistics of the United States, Colonial Times to 1957* (Washington, D.C., 1961); *New York Times*, January 6, 1946, April 6–9, 1947, September 3, 1974; author's interviews with Cleo F. Craig and Sanford B. Cousins.

5. Shockley, "The Invention of the Transistor"; "The Magic Crystal: How the Transistor Revolutionized Electronics," pamphlet (AT&T, 1972); *Telephony*, December 18, 1972.

6. Robert M. Coates, *The Hour After Westerly and Other Stories* (New York, 1957); Arthur Hoppe, "If a Man Answers, He's Crazy," *The New Yorker*, November 26, 1960; Marshall McLuhan, *Understanding Media* (New York, 1964), p. 273.

7. AT&T Annual Reports, 1945–48; author's interviews with Craig, Greenleaf, William C. Bolenius, and Cousins.

CHAPTER 10.   Tiger and Thoroughbred

1. *Report of the Antitrust Subcommittee of the Committee on the Judiciary, House of Representatives, Eighty-Sixth Congress, First Session, Pursuant to H. Res. 27 . . . on Consent Decree Program of the Department of Justice* (Washington, D.C., 1959), pp. 35, 45 ff.; Goulden, pp. 80–3; author's interviews with Greenleaf, Craig, Bolenius, and Horace P. Moulton.

2. Frederick C. Alexander, Jr., "History of Sandia Corporation Through Fiscal Year 1963," pamphlet (Sandia Corporation, 1963); David E. Lilienthal, *Big Business: A New Era* (New York, 1953), pp. 100–5; *New York Times*, November 19, 1949; letters: Truman to Wilson, May 13, 1949; Wilson to Truman, May 17, 1949; Lilienthal to Wilson, June 24, 1949; Wilson to Lilienthal, July 1, 1949; Lilienthal to Wilson, July 6, 1949.

3. AT&T Annual Reports, 1950–52; Barbash, pp. 121–5, 143, 145–7; *New York Times*, January 24, January 31, August 12, August 31, 1950; author's interview with Bolenius.

4. Author's interviews with Bolenius, Craig, and Greenleaf; *New York Times*, April 19, June 29, July 8, 1951; AT&T Annual Report, 1951.

5. "Events in Telephone History"; AT&T Annual Reports, 1951–56; *The New Yorker*, December 1, 1956; Mabon, p. 175.

6. AT&T Annual Reports, 1954–56; author's interviews with Bolenius, Craig, Mabon, and John J. Scanlon; *Bell System Statistical Manual*, p. 902.

7. Douglas W. Bray, Richard J. Campbell, and Donald L. Grant, *Formative Years in Business* (New York, 1974); author's interviews with Craig and Greenleaf.

8. *Report of Antitrust Subcommittee*, pp. 52 ff., 56, 319; Goulden, pp. 82–87; AT&T Annual Reports, 1954–56; author's interview with Moulton.

9. *Report of Antitrust Subcommittee*, pp. 35, 73–5, 84, 96–8, 108–9, 290; author's interview with Moulton.

10. Aronson, "The Sociology of the Telephone"; Boorstin, *The Americans; New York Times*, May 20, 1956; *Newsweek*, July 4, 1955; *Time*, December 10, 1956; *Newsweek*, August 28, 1972; *Seventeen*, April 1972; *Newsweek*, April 7, 1969; *Saturday Review*, September 30, 1972.

CHAPTER 11.  Putting Razzle-Dazzle in Ma Bell

1. Frederick R. Kappel, *Vitality in a Business Enterprise* (New York, 1960); author's interviews with Bolenius, Craig, Greenleaf, Kappel, Mabon, and William G. Sharwell.

2. Minutes of AT&T board of directors meeting, December 17, 1958; author's interviews with Bolenius, Craig, Kappel, Mabon, and Scanlon.

3. AT&T Annual Reports, 1959–65; John Brooks, *Business Adventures* (New York, 1969), pp. 16–18.

4. "Events in Telephone History"; AT&T Annual Reports, 1958–65; author's interviews with Craig, Greenleaf, Kappel, Sharwell, and C. L. Stong.

5. Scott M. Cutlip, "The Nation's First Public Relations Firm," *Journalism Review*, Summer 1966; Goulden, p. 189; Danielian, pp. 271–313, 314–17; Mabon, "A Personal Perspective on Bell System Public Relations," pamphlet (AT&T, 1972); *Bell Telephone Magazine*, September–October, 1972.

6. Todd, pp. 59–60; Goulden, pp. 224–42; "Events in Telephone History"; *The New Yorker*, October 27, 1962; author's interview with Mabon.

7. AT&T Annual Reports, 1961–65; Western Electric internal historical documents.

8. "Events in Telephone History"; Goulden, pp. 98, 99, 102, 103, 126; John Brooks, "Comsat," *The New Yorker*, January 30, 1965; author's interviews with James E. Dingman, Kappel, Mabon, and Moulton.

9. AT&T Annual Reports, 1956, 1960, 1966, 1967; Mabon, pp. 77–84; author's interviews with William O. Baker and Tyrrell.

10. AT&T, "Study of Share Owner Reaction to the 1964 AT&T Annual Meeting," 1964; Brooks, *Business Adventures,* pp. 257–63; author's interview with Greenleaf.

11. "Events in Telephone History"; Goulden, pp. 279, 313 ff.; *New York Times,* October 28, October 29, December 24, December 26, December 27, 1965; AT&T Annual Reports, 1965, 1966; *The Monopoly Makers: Ralph Nader's Study Group Report on Regulation and Competition,* ed. Mark J. Green (New York, 1973); author's interviews with Kappel, Moulton, Scanlon, and E. William Henry.

12. AT&T Annual Reports, 1961–71; *Bell System Statistical Manual.*

CHAPTER 12.    Days of Wrath

1. H. I. Romnes, "A Decade of Change: Selected Talks 1961–71," five pamphlets (AT&T, 1972); author's interview with Alvin von Auw; AT&T Annual Reports, 1965, 1966; *Time,* April 8, 1966; *Newsweek,* May 30, 1966; Raoul Nadler, "Approach to Psychodynamics of Obscene Telephone Calls," *New York State Journal of Medicine,* February 15, 1968.

2. AT&T Annual Reports, 1967, 1970; Romnes, "A Decade of Change"; *U.S. News & World Report,* November 11, 1968, pp. 90–4.

3. *Newsweek,* July 7, 1969; *Business Week,* August 2, 1969; *Time,* February 28, 1969, March 23, 1970, May 4, 1970; *Life,* December 5, 1969; address by J. A. Baird and J. E. Olson, AT&T Presidents' Conference, April 30, 1973, Hot Springs, West Virginia (FCC Docket No. 19129, Phase II); author's interviews with Sharwell, John D. deButts, Kenneth G. McKay, Irwin Dorros, and Mabon.

4. Romnes, "A Decade of Change," Vols. II, V; author's interview with von Auw.

5. AT&T Annual Reports, 1968–72; *Bell System Statistical Manual.*

6. AT&T Annual Reports, 1968–74; Goulden, pp. 155–6; address by John D. deButts, National Association of Regulatory Commissions, September 1973; *Forbes,* February 15, 1974; *New York Times,* June 6, 1974; Albin R. Meier, "Where Is Interconnection Taking Us?" *Telephony,* January 7, 1974; AT&T documents: "Let the Public Decide: Phase II, External Speech A" (1974), "Questions and Answers on Competition" (1974); author's interviews with Moulton, deButts, and von Auw.

CHAPTER 13.    Scandal and a Lawsuit

1. "Events in Telephone History"; AT&T Annual Reports, 1972–75; "Before the Federal Communications Commission, in the matter of petitions filed by the Equal Employment Opportunity Commission, *et al.,* Memorandum Accompanying the Aug. 1, 1972 Submission of the Bell Companies"; "Memorandum of Agreement, AT&T, E.E.O.C., and U.S. Department of Labor, Jan. 18, 1973"; *New York Times,* May 13, 1975; author's interview with Moulton.

2. *New York Times,* February 28, March 13, March 24, March 30, 1975; AT&T Share Owners Newsletter, First Quarter 1975.

3. *New York Times*, November 18, November 30, 1974, February 9, February 11, 1975; *Business Week*, June 23, 1975; Supplement dated January 20, 1975 to Prospectus dated March 20, 1974, for Share Owner Dividend Reinvestment and Stock Purchase Plan, AT&T; *AT&T Management Report*, January 23, April 17, 1975; AT&T Annual Report, 1975.

4. U.S. District Court for the District of Columbia, United States of America, Plaintiff, vs. American Telephone & Telegraph Company, Western Electric Company, and Bell Telephone Laboratories, Defendants; Civil Action No. 74–1698, filed November 20, 1974; *New York Times*, November 21, November 22, 1974; U.S. District Court for the District of Columbia, Civil Action No. 74–1698, Transcript of Proceeding (Hearing on Jurisdictional Issues), July 23, 1975; *Telecommunications Reports*, July 28, 1975; author's interviews with Mark Garlinghouse, Paul M. Lund, Harold Levy, and Robert K. Greenleaf.

CHAPTER 14. Toward a New Century

1. "Telephone and the Future," slide presentation, Bell Laboratories, 1975; Dean Gillette, "Telecommunications Futures" (mimeographed; Bell Laboratories, 1975); *Bell Laboratories Record*, January 1975; *New York Times*, Nov. 3, 1974; "Copy Platform for No. 4 ESS," AT&T release, Sept. 23, 1975.

2. J. D. deButts, talk to the Commercial Club of Boston, Boston, Mass., April 10, 1973.

# Index

357